James Riley Weaver's Civil War

CIVIL WAR SOLDIERS AND STRATEGIES
Brian S. Wills, Series Editor

James Riley Weaver's Civil War

The Diary of a Union Cavalry Officer and Prisoner of War, 1863–1865

Edited by John T. Schlotterbeck, Wesley W. Wilson,
Midori Kawaue, and Harold A. Klingensmith

The Kent State University Press

Kent, Ohio

© 2019 by The Kent State University Press, Kent, Ohio 44242
All rights reserved
Library of Congress Catalog Number 2018038358
ISBN 978-1-60635-368-4
Manufactured in the United States of America

Library of Congress Cataloging-in-Publication Data

Names: Weaver, James Riley, 1839-1920, author. | Schlotterbeck, John T., editor. | Wilson,
Wesley (Wesley W.), editor. | Kawaue, Midori, editor. | Klingensmith, Harold A. (Tony),
editor.

Title: James Riley Weaver's Civil War : the diary of a Union cavalry officer and prisoner of
war, 1863-1865 / edited by John T. Schlotterbeck, Wesley W. Wilson, Midori Kawaue,
and Harold A. Klingensmith.

Description: Kent, Ohio : The Kent State University Press, [2019] | Includes bibliographical
references and index.

Identifiers: LCCN 2018038358 | ISBN 9781606353684 (cloth)

Subjects: LCSH: Weaver, James Riley, 1839-1920--Diaries. | United States. Army. Pennsylvania
Cavalry Regiment, 18th (1862-1865) | United States. Army. Cavalry--Officers--Diaries. |
Soldiers--Pennsylvania--Diaries. | Pennsylvania--History--Civil War, 1861-1865--Personal
narratives. | United States--History--Civil War, 1861-1865--Personal narratives. |
Pennsylvania--History--Civil War, 1861-1865--Regimental histories. | United States--
History--Civil War, 1861-1865--Regimental histories. | Prisoners of war--United States--
Diaries. | United States--History--Civil War, 1861-1865--Prisoners and prisons.

Classification: LCC E527.6 18th W43 2019 | DDC 973.7/81--dc23

LC record available at https://lccn.loc.gov/2018038358

23 22 21 20 19   5 4 3 2 1

John Schlotterbeck: For my students at DePauw University and my family—
Barbara, Jesse, Marian, Ava, and Alina

Wesley W. Wilson: For Elena

Midori Kawaue: For Tomiko Hattori

Anthony Klingensmith: For Pam

Contents

Illustrations

Acknowledgments

Editing James Riley Weaver's diary has been a collaborative enterprise, and I especially thank my coeditors' shared enthusiasm and individual talents for making this project possible. In January 2015, Tony Klingensmith, an independent scholar, sent Wes Wilson, the DePauw University archivist, a transcription of the text from the digitized diary pages Wes had posted on Flickr. The draft's surprise arrival encouraged us to dream of publishing the seven-hundred-page diary. That summer, Wes, Midori Kawaue, an undergraduate history major, and I received a student-faculty summer research grant from DePauw University to continue the editorial work. Midori corrected Tony's draft against the original and added our suggestions. Together we developed editorial guidelines. Midori continued revising the text in fall 2015, and she and I read scholarship on Civil War prisons and writings by prisoners. Her annotated bibliographies provided insights on each reading's themes, reliability, and usefulness that were invaluable in writing the introductory material. Midori's meticulous work and her great cheer and spirit are an inspiration.

Wes's immense knowledge about the history of DePauw University and the United Methodist Church and his personal connections, through Elena S. Wilson, to the Weaver family have been vital in understanding Weaver's life. He collected additional Weaver material from individuals and archivists and selected and secured permissions for the illustrations. Tony's research on the 18th Pennsylvania Cavalry was indispensable in understanding military events and in identifying individuals Weaver mentioned in the diary. The two outside readers made many suggestions for revisions that significantly improved the final manuscript. The enthusiasm and professionalism of the staff at Kent State University Press made bringing Weaver's diary to publication a pleasure. Colleagues at DePauw have been uniformly supportive of the project and several have contributed in special ways. My wife, Barbara Steinson, provided steadfast encouragement and careful comments on the introduction, prologue, epilogue, and chapter introductions that improved the prose and clarified themes. John Dittmer read the entire manuscript and offered a valuable perspective from someone whose expertise is outside the Civil War era. Yung-chen Chiang helped explain Weaver's contributions as a teacher. Beth Wilkerson prepared the maps and patiently responded to our numerous revisions. Finally, we are grateful to the Faculty Development

Committee and to Anne Harris, vice president of academic affairs, DePauw University, for their material support.

JOHN T. SCHLOTTERBECK

Many thanks to David H. Howard and Joanne Howard Kouris for their donation of the diary and supporting family material to the Archives and to John Schlotterbeck for taking an archival transcription project and bringing it to publication. Thanks also to Mary Graff Dove for her donations of Weaver family items and information about James Riley Weaver's daughters and son-in-law. Fellow archivists provided invaluable research assistance, including Suzanne Williams at the Merrick Archives at Allegheny College and Frances Lyons at the General Commission on Archives and History, United Methodist Church. The staff at the Sandusky (Ohio) Public Library provided further assistance in locating Matern family information. Help in locating photographs was provided by Michael Kraus, curator of collections and historian, Soldiers and Sailors Memorial Hall and Museum; Marlea D. Leljedal, operations clerk, US Army Heritage and Education Center; and Jessica Eichlin, photographs manager, West Virginia, and Regional History Center, West Virginia University. Special thanks go to my wife, Elena S. Wilson (who is also James Riley Weaver's cousin) for her valuable research assistance and discoveries, helpful insights, and enthusiastic support throughout the project.

WESLEY W. WILSON

As a Japanese international student, I would never have imagined being able to take part in such a large transcription project. I thank the Grew Bancroft Foundation, Hirotsugu "Chuck" Iikubo (DePauw '57), and the Rector Scholarship Program for providing me the opportunity to do firsthand research on the American Civil War. Their steadfast belief in "investment in humanity" made it possible for me to participate in this project. I am also grateful for the training from members of the DePauw History Department. I have been fortunate to have several mentors like Hope Sutherlin, John Schlotterbeck, David Gellman, and Nahyan Fancy. I am also overwhelmed by the kind support that my family has provided me. In 2015, I spent an unforgettable summer with Mindy and Jeff Peters, my host parents, who kindly opened their home for me to stay while I was editing the diary. This immersion in American family life has been a valuable experience for me to comprehend American life back in the nineteenth century. Yoshiki and Michiko Kawaue, my father and mother, have been lifelong supporters of my history work. My preoccupation with American history started with a historical novel that was gifted by them. I dedicate this book to them.

MIDORI KAWAUE

My participation in this project was only made possible by the willingness of De-Pauw University to share the Weaver diary online, with the goal of transcribing the original pages into legible text. DePauw University archivist Wesley Wilson was instrumental in posting the entire diary online and graciously accepted transcriptions for every page. I would also like to thank John Schlotterbeck, Wesley Wilson, and Midori Kawaue for their willingness to include me in the project, and for their individual contributions to complete the transcription and to organize it for publication. Each of the four editors brought a different skill set to the undertaking, which enabled us to provide the best manuscript for publication.

HAROLD A. KLINGENSMITH

Introduction

In July 2011, DePauw University president Brian Casey received James Riley Weaver's Civil War diary from his descendants with the stipulation that it be transcribed and made available to the public. Weaver, a Pennsylvania farmer's son, devout Methodist, schoolteacher, and Allegheny College student, enlisted as a private in the 18th Pennsylvania Cavalry in October 1862 on his twenty-third birthday. He was subsequently promoted to sergeant major, second lieutenant, and first lieutenant. At the end of each day, from June 1, 1863, to April 1, 1865, Weaver filled a four-by-six-inch page or more of his leather-bound diary in neat handwriting with comments on activities, individuals, wartime events, and the state of his morale. His diary provides a remarkable, unbroken 666-day record of military engagements as a Union cavalry officer, experiences as a prisoner of war in seven Confederate officers' prisons, and his return to civilian life. The depth of detail, variety of topics, clear prose, emotional restraint, and dissection of human nature under duress yields an unparalleled eyewitness account of one man's Civil War.[1]

Scholars of Civil War prisons have long acknowledged the challenges of analyzing prisoners' narratives. Whether written during the war or decades later, most published accounts served polemical purposes, including accusations of intentional mistreatment by callous Confederate officials, perpetuation of political advantage through atrocity stories, or claims that prisoners' sufferings equaled combat soldiers' sacrifices.[2] Unlike Weaver's entries, survivors' accounts based on wartime diaries and letters emphasized dramatic episodes, colorful personalities and anecdotes, and philosophical ruminations rather than a careful chronology and record of daily events.[3] Relatively few prisoners' narratives, unlike Weaver's, encompassed both soldiering and imprisonment or spanned the diverse range of Confederate prisons and outdoor camps.

Surprisingly, many themes first developed in prisoners' accounts persist in the extensive secondary literature on Civil War prisons. To be sure, few modern writers charge government officials with war crimes against prisoners because of deliberate physical abuse and denial of adequate housing, clothing, food, and medical care. Debates continue, however, over whether this callousness originated from policy decisions by Abraham Lincoln and Jefferson Davis, who prioritized military and political considerations over their own prisoners' continued suffering, or from growing partisan hatreds arising from prolonged war, or from prison officials' poor planning, inadequate resources, and limited medical knowledge.[4] Recent surveys of Civil War prisons provide a wealth of detail on the physical, emotional, and psychological traumas prisoners experienced, as do numerous studies of individual prisons. The extremely harsh conditions and unusually high mortality at the prison in Andersonville, Georgia, in fact, has come to represent the experiences of all Civil War prisoners, even though the Union prison in Elmira, New York, was equally horrific.[5] Other recent studies continue prisoners' emphasis on dramatic events, especially prison escapes.[6]

Weaver's diary not only details the harsh physical and emotional experiences of combat and imprisonment but also provides a fresh perspective by one of the 85 percent of Union prisoners who survived their incarceration. Unlike prisoners' letters, which could be limited to a single page or to censorship by authorities, and with no plans to publish his diary, Weaver freely expressed his thoughts and emotions in entries that are frank, analytical, and unusually even-tempered in assessing daily life as a cavalry officer and as an inmate in different Confederate prisons. His diary connects soldiering, imprisonment, and personal experiences with awareness of events beyond prison walls. Weaver, moreover, was typical of many Union volunteers in the war's first years: young, unmarried, American native, rural residence, and literate. His religious faith, unwavering commitment to the Union, and belief in blacks' natural inferiority were shared by many other Northern soldiers. Like them, personal contact with African American prisoners, though limited, gradually tempered Weaver's racial beliefs.[7]

Weaver shunned romanticized descriptions of daring cavalry raids for the mundane details of drilling, marching, and foraging and the dangers of scouting, picketing, and fatigue duties that exposed cavalrymen to the elements and to the enemy. Even the 18th Pennsylvania's fearless charge against the extreme Confederate right on the third day of the Battle of Gettysburg received less attention in his diary than the continual skirmishes, raids, and casualties during the preceding and following weeks. While stationed in northern Virginia or marching through border-state Maryland and Union Pennsylvania, Weaver observed war's impact on soldiers' morals and morale and on white and black civilians' shifting loyalties. Weaver's introspective nature emphasized the emotional experience of warfare and how rumors revealed soldiers' anxieties about combat. Cavalrymen faced sudden threats as they probed the contested ground between two rival armies. Caught between two cavalry units of the Army of Northern Virginia at Brandy Station, Culpeper County, Virginia, and unable to break through to Union lines, several officers and men of Weaver's company were captured on October 11, 1863. He and thirty-one other comrades marched under guard to Richmond, the Confederate capital, where they shared the lot of the one in eleven Union soldiers who spent time in Southern prisons.

Weaver's arrival at Libby Prison occurred after the collapse of the July 1862 exchange cartel, which had emptied Richmond's holding pens as prisoners were rapidly paroled. Now, the city's prisons were overflowing again. Although officers received privileges denied privates—better accommodations, letters, care packages, books, money to purchase food, special exchanges, and, occasionally, local paroles—they shared the physical, mental, and psychological traumas of prolonged confinement. Weaver's lengthy, unbroken record of war news, exchange rumors, civilian visitors, physical conditions, escape plots (which he eschewed with one exception), prison guards' behavior, health and sickness, mock elections, and social amusements are affirmed in other officers' narratives.

Libby, however, was but the first and the longest (October 1863–May 1864) of Weaver's nearly seventeen months of incarceration that included Danville (May 1864); Macon, Georgia (May–July 1864); Charleston, South Carolina (July–October 1864); and Columbia, South Carolina (October 1864–February 1865). His observations of the "little world" inside each prison and outdoor camp with men drawn from "every class of society, high and low, rich and poor, and from every country and clime" encompass the variety and changing nature of imprisonment over place and time.[8] Prison walls were surprisingly permeable, as visitors, guards, new arrivals or "fresh fish," recaptured escapees, and Southern newspapers allowed Weaver to glean keen, if fleeting, insights into life inside the Confederacy. Glimpses through prison windows, camp enclosures, and railcars also revealed the outside world. Diary-keeping provided an outlet for expressing suppressed emotions, ruminating on a seemingly endless confinement, testing patriotism and will to survive, and affirming a nonincarcerated self. Significantly, Weaver's diary entries became longer as his imprisonment continued, and he reflected more often on the war's purpose and its impact on Southern civilians. Reading literature and copying satiric verse sustained his spirits, yet even the stoic Weaver succumbed to occasional bouts of deep depression. The diary ends with his parole in March 1865, homecoming, and gradual transition from soldier to civilian.

Like many other men of his generation, Weaver's wartime experiences framed the rest of his life. His successful career as a diplomat in Europe and as an educator at DePauw University drew upon his military experiences and his Methodist connections. Weaver survived prolonged imprisonment physically and mentally intact; he was 80 years old when he died, but he only wrote about his prison experiences once in an essay, "A Phi Psi's Christmas in Libby," published in 1899.[9] Weaver expanded his brief diary entry for December 25, 1863, to capture the sounds, sights, and smells of prison life and the feverish preparations for that occasion, which strengthened bonds of solidarity and compassion among the prisoners while intensifying their emotions over their loss of freedom. Weaver's eye for revealing detail, precise prose, and even temper had not diminished over the decades. Like his diary entries, Weaver drew on the mundane of everyday life to make keen observations about the human condition under adversity. This veteran proudly wore the appellation "colonel," a reminder of his Civil War service that was an important turning point of a long and remarkable life.[10]

Abbreviations

Adjutant	Adjt.
Admiral	Adm.
Artillery	Art.
Assistant	Asst.
Battery	Batt.
Brigadier	Brig.
Captain	Capt.
Cavalry	Cav.
Colonel	Col.
Commander	Cdr.
Company	Co.
County	Cty.
Department	Dept.
Division	Div.
General	Gen.
Infantry	Inf.
Lieutenant	Lt.
Major	Maj.
Private	Priv.
Quartermaster	QM
Regiment	Regt.
Sergeant	Sgt.
Squadron	Squad.
Township	Twp.
USN	US Navy
Volunteer	Vol.

Editorial Method

James Weaver's readable penmanship facilitated the editors' goal of producing a transcript that is as close to the original text as possible. We kept Weaver's spellings, capitalizations, underlined words, and abbreviations. Additional information, noted with square brackets, clarifies original spellings or ambiguous words, adds missing words for readability, notes illegible words, or marks blank spaces. A question mark inside the brackets denotes uncertain readings. To aid readers we created the chapter divisions; standardized the dates of the entries; punctuated clauses, sentences, and quotations; and added paragraph breaks for a few long entries.

Like many Civil War diarists, Weaver referenced numerous individuals, places, and events. Personal names, when known, are identified the first time they appear in each chapter. Other annotations add clarifying information by briefly explaining events, military campaigns, unfamiliar terms, and cultural productions. Maps trace the movements of the 18th Pennsylvania Cavalry up to Weaver's capture and the locations of his imprisonment. The illustrations and a timeline provide a visual record and a chronology, respectively, of Weaver's life. The prologue and epilogue trace Weaver's life before and after the war, and each chapter begins with a short introduction to a section of the diary. Finally, we include Weaver's only published essay about his wartime experiences.

James Riley Weaver's Civil War

Fig. 1. James Riley Weaver, age 23, after his promotion to second lieutenant in June 1862. (Theophilus F. Rodenbough, Henry C. Potter, and William P. Seal, *History of the 18th Regiment of Cavalry, Pennsylvania Volunteers,* 1909)

Instilling the "Ideal of Christian Manhood,"

1839–1863

On October 21, 1862, his twenty-third birthday, James Riley Weaver enlisted as a private in Company B, 18th Pennsylvania Volunteer Cavalry, for three years. Enrollment at Allegheny College, Meadville, Pennsylvania, in fall 1860 likely had delayed his entering military service, but when John W. Phillips and James W. Smith, both Allegheny College alumni, and David T. McKay, a classmate, barnstormed Crawford County in September and October 1862, recruiting volunteers, Weaver and fellow student Thomas J. Grier signed up. All five men were members of Phi Kappa Psi, a social fraternity at Allegheny College, and local newspapers appropriately dubbed this company the "College Cavalry." An ambitious young man from a modest farm family, Weaver likely was familiar with horses (Union recruits had to pass a test in basic horsemanship), and the cavalry promised flashier uniforms, more prestige, and greater opportunities for advancement and adventure than the infantry. Volunteers, in addition, received a twenty-five-dollar government bounty and avoided the stigma of being drafted. Although his college education set Weaver apart from most of the other recruits in Company B and, undoubtedly, led to early promotion, he shared with them his youth, native origins, rural background, and single status.[1]

Weaver rarely mentioned his modest origins in his diary, but his parents instilled in their second-oldest son a strong faith in education, the Methodist Church, hard work, patriotism, and personal ambition. John and Eliza Weaver's fourth child was born August 21, 1839, in Youngstown, Westmoreland County, in southwestern Pennsylvania. The Weavers were descendants of a prolific pioneer family whose patriarch, John William Weber, Weaver's great-grandfather, was a prominent Reformed minister who had moved into the area following the American Revolution. Young James grew up near many members of an extended family clan. In 1860

1

he lived in his parents' household on a rented farm in Unity Township outside Youngstown along with his four brothers and five sisters. Despite the township's mostly hilly terrain, it was one of the county's more prosperous sections with limestone soil on fertile bottomlands, upland meadows, extensive timber stands, and proximity to the Philadelphia-Pittsburgh Turnpike. Weaver's childhood encompassed rapid economic change, and he likely witnessed the arrival of the first train in November 1852, which marked the Pennsylvania Railroad's extension through the county. Monopolists soon developed extensive lumber and coal mining operations in the 1850s, and after the Civil War coke ovens supplied the burgeoning Allegheny Valley steel mills. Youngstown, Unity Township's old commercial hub on the turnpike, declined as Latrobe, located on the rail line, became the county's commercial and professional hub.[2]

Weaver's parents inculcated in their son a lifelong devotion to the Methodist Episcopal Church, a minority faith in a county dominated by the Presbyterian, Reformed, and Lutheran Churches, and to the importance of education. Indeed, religion and education were intertwined in the mid-nineteenth century, as prayers, Bible readings, and catechism were part of the school curriculum. All the Weaver children attended local schools, and James continued his education at private academies and at the Lancaster County Institute. In 1856, he passed the school superintendent's exam and began teaching in district schools, a common pattern for many young men of his generation until they found their life's calling. By 1860, he was living in rural Sunville, Venango County, near the oil boomtown of Titusville, likely teaching school.[3]

Weaver's education was proficient enough to secure enrollment in fall 1860 as a junior at Allegheny College in nearby Meadville. Founded in 1815, the liberal arts college came under Methodist patronage in 1833 and, like other antebellum liberal arts colleges, offered a classical curriculum in a heavily sectarian atmosphere. Every faculty member was a Methodist clergyman and most students came from Methodist homes. The campus's intimacy, with five instructors and about a hundred collegiate and preparatory students, forged strong personal ties. In addition to Latin and Greek (Weaver was particularly close to the Rev. Alexander Martin, his Greek instructor), his coursework included mathematics, rhetoric, science, and theology. Instruction emphasized lectures, class recitations, senior orations delivered at commencement exercises held in July and November, and a capstone course on moral philosophy taught by the college president that sought to instill the "ideal of Christian manhood." A smallpox epidemic canceled the 1862 commencement, and Weaver completed the remaining course work by examination before his company officers and received the AB degree in March 1863.[4] The personal connections, social skills, religious atmosphere, and intellectual broadening Weaver experienced during his two years at Allegheny fa-

Fig. 2. Bentley Hall, Allegheny College, Meadville, PA, ca. 1870. Originally constructed in 1829, Weaver attended classes here from 1860 to 1862, and received his degree by examination after his enlistment. (Allegheny College Archives, Wayne and Sally Merrick Historic Archival Center, Pelletier Library, Allegheny College, Meadville, PA)

cilitated military promotions, sustained his morale during a long imprisonment, and opened career opportunities after the Civil War.

Company B was not the first military unit from Allegheny College. Students had debated the slavery question in the 1850s' heightened partisan atmosphere, and *rage militaire* swept the school after Fort Sumter's fall. On April 20, 1861, students raised the Union flag over Bentley Hall and demanded the immediate departure of Southerners who had cheered the fort's capture. Some eighty students joined the Allegheny College Volunteers that spring and were later mustered into service as Company I, 39th Regiment of Pennsylvania Volunteers. As they left for Camp Wilkins in Pittsburgh in June 1861, Weaver likely heard the patriotic speeches by faculty members, band music, citizens' cheers, and a presentation of New Testaments and a hand-sewn company flag from the town's women. Other students joined the Meadville Volunteers, later Company F, 9th Regiment, Pennsylvania Reserve Corps, but Weaver continued his studies at Allegheny until the war's second year.[5]

On November 15, 1862, Company B mustered into service at Camp Simmons near Harrisburg, along with nine other companies of mostly western Pennsylva-

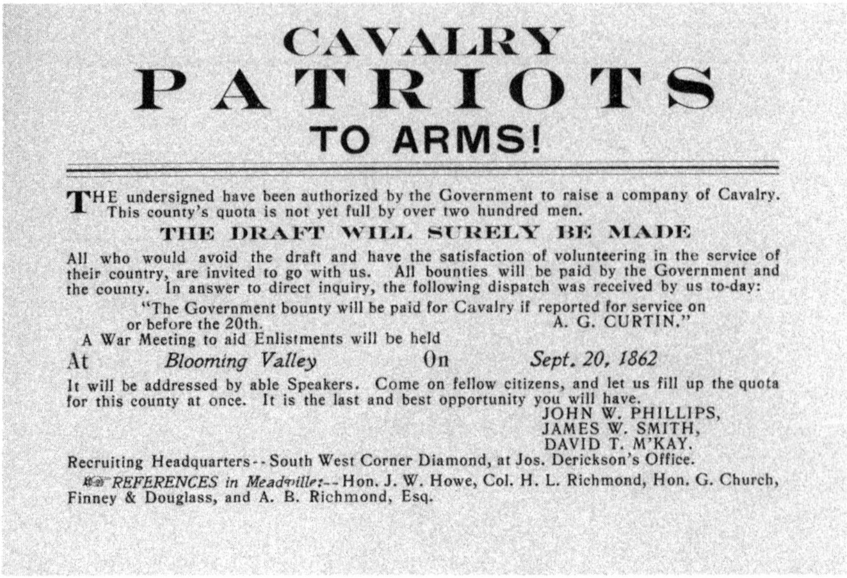

CAVALRY
P A T R I O T S
TO ARMS!

THE undersigned have been authorized by the Government to raise a company of Cavalry. This county's quota is not yet full by over two hundred men.

THE DRAFT WILL SURELY BE MADE

All who would avoid the draft and have the satisfaction of volunteering in the service of their country, are invited to go with us. All bounties will be paid by the Government and the county. In answer to direct inquiry, the following dispatch was received by us to-day:

"The Government bounty will be paid for Cavalry if reported for service on or before the 20th.   A. G. CURTIN."

A War Meeting to aid Enlistments will be held

At   *Blooming Valley*   On   *Sept. 20, 1862*

It will be addressed by able Speakers. Come on fellow citizens, and let us fill up the quota for this county at once. It is the last and best opportunity you will have.
                                        JOHN W. PHILLIPS,
                                        JAMES W. SMITH,
                                        DAVID T. M'KAY.

Recruiting Headquarters - - South West Corner Diamond, at Jos. Derickson's Office.

☞ *REFERENCES in Meadville:* - - Hon. J. W. Howe, Col. H. L. Richmond, Hon. G. Church, Finney & Douglass, and A. B. Richmond, Esq.

Fig. 3. Recruiting advertisement, 18th Pennsylvania Cavalry, Fall 1862. Recruiters traveled throughout Crawford County, PA, holding meetings to sign up volunteers. Weaver enlisted in Company B on his birthday, October 21, 1862. (Ernest Ashton Smith, *Allegheny—A Century of Education, 1815–1915*. Meadville, PA: Allegheny College, 1916)

nia recruits. A month later the regiment moved to Hyattstown, Maryland, and was attached to Percy Wyndham's Cavalry Brigade, Defenses of Washington. Receiving sabers and old carbines, they "drilled in the 'school of the soldier,' and in the customs of the service," and held their first mounted drill on Christmas Day. In early January, the 18th Pennsylvania Cavalry established winter camp at Germantown, Fauquier County, Virginia, where they constructed "log cabins with roofs of duck and chimneys built of wood and plastered with mud" and horse shelters with a "corduroy floor and pine bough roof" over canvas covers. The arrival of two additional companies completed the regiment. Mounted and dismounted drills and target practices continued, as individual companies rotated camp, picket, and scout duties.[6]

Northern Virginia was contested ground between Union and Confederate forces, and the poorly trained cavalrymen were vulnerable to surprise attacks and capture as they scouted enemy lines in the cold and rain. In January 1863, John S. Mosby's irregular forces twice captured picket posts of the 18th Pennsylvania, taking several prisoners. Mosby haughtily paroled some of them, taunting that "unless the men were better armed and equipped it wouldn't pay to capture them." A scouting party from the 18th soon returned the favor by seizing twenty-eight Confederates, but two months later Mosby's men, posing as Union cavalry, boldly rode between the Union infantry camps and captured a general and several enlisted men. Despite these early embarrassments, by spring the regiment had redoubled their training; secured new revolvers, sabers, belts, and carbines; learned how to train and care for their mounts; and gained military experience on scouting expeditions to Fredericksburg and Falmouth on the Rappahannock River and in Loudoun County, Virginia.[7] In early February the regiment was attached to Col. Richard Butler Price's Independent Cavalry Brigade in the newly created Department of Washington, XXII Corps, and two months later, to Maj. Gen. Julius Stahel's Cavalry Division, 2nd Brigade, in the same department. From their new encampment at Fairfax Court House, Virginia, the 18th participated in several raids and reconnaissances in the spring alongside regiments they would serve with in future campaigns that would test their combat readiness.[8]

One

"The Arts and Scenes of Active Warfare"

The Making of a Cavalry Officer, June 1–July 17, 1863

By June 1, 1863, when James Weaver's second diary begins, the 18th Pennsylvania Cavalry was a well-trained and equipped but untested fighting unit. Although the adoption of rifled muskets gradually shifted cavalry deployments from offensive to defensive actions, Weaver's regiment still engaged in reconnaissance missions; in sharp fights at Hanover, Pennsylvania; in mounted charges at Gettysburg and at Hagerstown, Maryland; and in aggressive pursuit of Robert E. Lee's forces as they retreated toward Virginia. By summer 1863, the Union cavalry had reached near parity with their much-vaunted Confederate counterparts, and the tenacity and endurance of the 18th marked their passage from raw recruits to battle-hardened soldiers, and the regiment eventually became known as the "Fighting Eighteenth."

As the Gettysburg Campaign opened, Maj. Gen. Julius Stahel's Cavalry Division, Department of Washington, was reassigned to Maj. Gen. Joseph Hooker's Army of the Potomac. On June 28, the transfer became permanent as the 18th, along with the 1st West Virginia, the 1st Vermont, and the 5th New York, formed the 1st Brigade commanded by Brig. Gen. Elon J. Farnsworth. This formed half of Brig. Gen. Judson Kilpatrick's 3rd Division, under Cavalry Corps commander Gen. Alfred Pleasonton. In early May, Col. Timothy M. Bryan Jr., a West Point graduate, took command of the 18th; earlier, Capt. William P. Brinton had been made lieutenant colonel. Weaver, eager for promotion, received appointment to sergeant major at regimental headquarters in January and a commission as second lieutenant, Company C, on June 18. As First Lieutenant Samuel Montgomery was ill, Weaver led the company.[1]

After a decisive but costly victory at Chancellorsville, Virginia, in May 1863, Lee decided to invade the North a second time, hoping to resupply his depleted

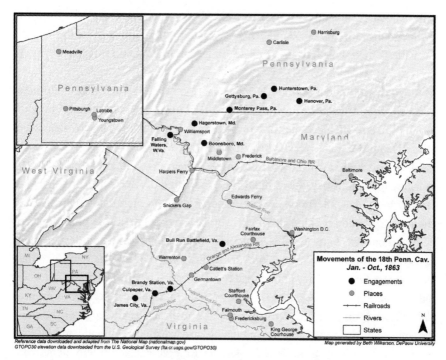

Fig. 4. Movements of the 18th Pennsylvania Cavalry, January–October 1863. (DePauw University)

army and depress Northern morale. Maj. Gen. J. E. B. Stuart's cavalry moved ahead to secure the gaps in the Blue Ridge Mountains in order to screen Lee's infantry as it moved down the Shenandoah Valley toward Maryland. Pleasonton's cavalry was unable to dislodge Stuart at Brandy Station, Culpeper County, Virginia, on June 9 and failed to learn the Army of Northern Virginia's location. The 18th was not engaged in these actions, but Hooker ordered Stahel's cavalry to move south from their Fairfax Court House encampment to the Rappahannock River on reconnaissance and then be the Army of the Potomac's rearguard as it followed Lee across the Potomac River. War's sounds—bugle calls, band music, drums, horses' hooves, tramping feet, and cannons' roars—left indelible echoes as the men of the 18th marched off to combat. Rumors of Confederate advances, like the reported sacking of Harrisburg on June 17, although later proved false, increased anxieties about their foe. After crossing into Maryland on June 26, the men of the 18th were greeted with "many smiling faces & plenty of banners" as well as an abundance of food. Four days later, as companies from the 18th guarded the 1st Brigade's rear and protected wagons and ambulances, they ran into Stuart's scouts south of Hanover, Pennsylvania. A Confederate charge drove them back into the town center where the rest of the regiment had been resting. The Pennsylvanians retreated in disarray only to be saved when the 5th New York Cavalry swept in and recaptured the town. Although the 18th "did not stand firm," Weaver admitted, and suffered the heaviest casualties—three killed, twenty-four wounded, and fifty-seven missing—they did delay Stuart's reunion with Lee.[2]

The 18th acquitted itself bravely at Gettysburg. At a July 2 skirmish at Hunterstown on the extreme Confederate left, the 18th turned the engagement by reinforcing the 6th Michigan Cavalry and preventing a countercharge by Brig. Gen. Wade Hampton's cavalry, which then withdrew. Brigadier General Farnsworth "said we had done a splendid achievement," Weaver proudly recorded. On the morning of the next day, the 18th marched southwest of Round Top on the Union far left. In the late afternoon, as Gen. George Pickett's men made their ill-fated charge at the Union center, Kilpatrick, over Farnsworth's strenuous objections, ordered a mounted charge northward across a field of woods and boulders, perhaps as a counterattack to turn the Confederate line once Pickett was repulsed. They faced the 1st Texas Infantry entrenched behind a stone fence piled high with wood rails. Incurring heavy fire at close quarters, the 18th never flinched but eventually retreated, dismounted, and set up a skirmish line at the edge of the field. Piecemeal attacks by the four regiments of Farnsworth's 1st Brigade and by four regiments from Brig. Gen. Wesley Merritt's Reserve Brigade briefly penetrated Confederate lines, but the Federals soon fell back, incurring heavy losses. The 18th alone reported twenty casualties. Farnsworth led part of the 1st Vermont's charge but became caught between the Texas and Alabama units and died under murderous fire. This was the US Cavalry's wartime nadir.[3]

Over the next two weeks the 18th faced unrelenting action in seven engagements as the Union cavalry pursued Lee's retreating forces. Despite nighttime attacks, coordinated light artillery and mounted charges, hand-to-hand combat, and captures of Confederate wagons and prisoners, the Union cavalry failed to dislodge Stuart's forces, whose successful parries provided Lee additional time to cross the swollen Potomac River. Marching through "mud & rain" on July 4, the 18th arrived at Monterey Pass on South Mountain in Maryland, joined a midnight attack on Lt. Gen. Richard S. Ewell's supply trains, and captured over a hundred wagons and more than a thousand prisoners. Continuing their advance, the next evening they encountered Confederate ambushers. Their objective was Hagerstown, Maryland, which protected Williamsport, Lee's intended crossing point. Supported by light artillery, the 18th charged into the town on July 6 and pushed out the Confederates. An infantry counterattack turned into dismounted hand-to-hand combat under steady artillery fire. The Federals withdrew while incurring heavy losses, including several officers. Unlike other Maryland and Pennsylvania towns, loyalties in Hagerstown were divided, and a female Confederate allegedly shot a sergeant from Weaver's regiment. Two days later, the 18th first engaged the enemy as dismounted skirmishers until dark and successfully repulsed Stuart's cavalry north of Boonsboro, then charged the Confederates after infantry reinforcements arrived. Union forces again targeted Hagerstown on July 12 and 13, and the 18th, held in the rear, engaged in skirmishing and picketing. Although Lee's infantry had escaped to Virginia the previous day, a successful attack on July 15 against Maj. Gen. Henry Heth's rearguard at Falling Waters on the Potomac captured two thousand prisoners. Company B of the 18th guarded the prisoners and delivered them to Berlin, Maryland, before crossing the Potomac on July 17.[4]

The exhausted men and horses of the 18th reported for picket duty at Snickers Gap in the Blue Ridge Mountains on the Loudoun-Clarke county line. Although they had failed to catch Lee, Weaver believed the 18th had acquitted itself honorably. "Amid these trials and difficulties, only a few murmurs were heard," he wrote, and "truly the boys acted bravely [at Hagerstown], for when death stared all in the face, they stood firm."[5]

Monday, June 1, 1863. Sent my diary home last night; also a party of 100 men went on a scout, having to report to Catlett's Station.[6] Various reports today of a supported attack but all official news are opposed to and contradict the report. Great talk of us being only nine months men and are to be discharged again 16th of July next, but all official knowledge favors our staying the three years for which we enlisted. Also got orders that no one should leave his post until further orders, owing to the report of that attack. Got two letters from Bro. Asbury, and from F. A. Arter[7] and wrote one to M. Keley. News concerning Grant are sparse but we are all in good hope that he is as well situated as he reports. Expected to have exciting times all around now as the time for activity has arrisen. Feel tolerably well, but not so well as formerly, having a slight headache but [MS page torn].

Tuesday, June 2. The Roster of promotions of officers was sent to the Governor[8] today having my name recommended for 2nd Lt. instead of 1st Lt. since 1st Lt. Montgomery's case had not been decided by the Court-Martial,[9] and he could not be recommended to Captaincy, but as soon as his case is decided, the former arrangement will be all O.K. Today was grand, and taking a ride enjoyed myself both grazing my horse and partaking of tame[10] strawberries, which grow in a desolated garden. The 2nd Pa. were paid off putting us in mind of that desirable individual's presence. The Scout came in, having captured literally "a variety wagon load" composed of guns, picks, spades, axes, clothes, sugar, salt, paper, tents, balls, powder, lead and in fact everything even secesh money.[11] This all inside our lines, showing that we are infested with rebels yet. They say they saw lots of gold and silver but did not consider that "contraband"[12] so they [MS page torn].

Wednesday, June 3. Today was pleasant having rained enough last night to lay the dust and make it cool. Had nothing particularly strange, and only little to do. Had my usual ride into the country and got quite a fine lot of strawberries. Got a chart[13] of Co. "B" with the Staff & Field, also the Non Commissioned Staff. Sent it home to my mother as a memento of the war. Got a letter from Hud. McCall, who has left the college and gone home to Leesville, Carroll Co., Ohio.[14] Wrote four letters, one to Frank Arter, one to Brother Frank, one to Frank Thomas, and one to Aggie Jack.[15] News but sparse from Gen. Grant and fears are entertained for his safety and indications are that part of the Fredericksburg [forces] have gone to reinforce Pemberton at Vicksb'g and what remain are trying to scare us, or they really mean an attack of which many around us are really afraid.[16] Health good and all [MS page torn].

Thursday, June 4. The morning as usual was pleasant, but toward noon the weather got very warm, making all seek the shade. Sick list: six officers and sixty-two men, being 1/10 of all present and matters in the Hospital are reported to be in a bad condition.[17] [God?] protect one from ever getting there. Got orders to hold the command in readiness to move in short notice, as the pickets had been attacked and are rather expected a visit from Moseby and maybe Stewart but the day passed and we were not called out.[18] But the orders are so strict, allowing no officer or man to leave his post that we can easily see that the authorities are expecting something. News from Grant not so encouraging, saying that he has fallen back to entrench himself against attack by Joe Johnson.[19] Wrote a letter to Hud. McCall and feeling well retired.

Friday, June 5. Nothing strange today. Not too warm having a cool breeze with occasional showers. Had a ride on the horse I traded "Fatty" for and decidedly pleased, as he is so easy, loping and racing but is not as strong as the one I gave. But sacrifice strength for ease. Got two letters, one from Jennie and one from Br. John, which I answered.[20] Good news from Grant that he is fully able to take Johnston and capture Vicksburg besides.[21] Reunion of Mosbey, having attacked our picket at Frying Pan,[22] but was repulsed. Still under marching orders, but no signs of moving. One man died in hospital, sixty-two on the sick report.[23] I am well and have no complaints but great reason to be grateful. Hear of the Draft or enrollment progressing prosperously so that soon we may expect a fight to crush secession.[24]

Saturday, June 6. Still pleasant, being warm but indications of rain. News from Grant as usual progressing slowly but surely. Excitement about is the same. Had a regimental review, and had orders for a brigade one at 4 P.M., which was countermanded and another order to go on a scout with four days rations. Got ready and was waiting orders to move, when at 4 o'clock P.M. got orders to detail 50 men and two officers to guard Brigade Head Quarters,[25] while the rest were on scout, as one Regiment would not be ordered out. So there is reason to suppose that they at Brigade Head Quarters are getting frightened. Got a letter from Sister Lizzie.[26] She gave me Forney's address: Hampton Battery, Gen. O. R. Tyler's Reserve Artillery.[27] Got a letter from coz [cousin] Bell,[28] answered both. All well and happy and hope that the future may only be so prosperous.

Sunday, June 7. Had a pleasant morning. Went to church at Fairfax [Court House]. Had a sermon on "Lead us not into temptation" by the Chaplin of 5th NY.[29] He spoke plainly and feelingly and it brought me to thinking and I secretly promised to resist temptation for the future with more energy. Oh that I may be successful. Got marching orders with four days rations and the whole command to go. The adjutant let me go, he being wounded and not caring to go along.[30] Waited and at dusk got word that we would start tomorrow morning at 3 A.M. Sat down and wrote a short note to my mother telling her of our intentions, also sending her home (camp) made rings for Mattie and Amanda.[31] Felt well and happy this Sabbath night. Feeling thankful that there are so many influences that lead to induce one to withstand any temptations to special vice that seems thick in camp. After all, there must be higher Power to the task.

Monday, June 8. Started about 4 A.M. with 150 men the Colonel and Lt. Col. going along.[32] Rumors are that we are going to capture all horses this side the Rappahannock [River]. The whole force of the Brigade in camp went out, also a battery of Artillery (6 pieces) of the Michigan making in all, I judge, 1000 men. Passed through Centreville through Bull Run Battleground (the eastern part) past Warrenton Junction, and at the R. [Rail] Road until near Catlett's Station where part of the Division was on picket duty.[33] Got dinner, lay armed waiting until at last encamped for the day and night in the grove waiting for forage and rations for [us] the command left there to go along. Had a good encampment and boiling my coffee and spreading my blankets I felt at home. Felt well. Reports of Stoneman being within 60 miles of us with 12,000 troops [with] whom we are to form and make a Richmond Raid, but of course, this only talk.[34]

Tuesday, June 9. Slept soundly, having a refreshing time. Got up, boiled my coffee and had my breakfast. Expected to move but was disappointed as now we find we are to do picket duty while the others do the scouting. Lay in the woods all day having a good pleasant time altho 'twas very warm. Saw Major General Stahel, a little dark man, but very sharp, also Colonel R. B. Price (our acting Brigadier) for the first time being a large tall man with strong shoulders also Colonel Town of the 1st Michigan.[35] The most of the regiment are out on picket, leaving only a few men in camp. The location is good being two miles west of Bristol Station[36] on the Orange and Alexandria R.R. and a strong place for strategic purposes. Rumors of fighting on the front but nothing definite. Prepared a lunch and a time with Lieutenant Beazell[37] and having a long talk in serious matters fell asleep.

Wednesday, June 10. Hear of heavy fighting being done at the Rappahannock [River] between Stewart (Reb) and Pleasanton (U) and with various success, but in the end our forces driving the Rebs for miles.[38] The loss on our side severe. Expect to be sent up as a reinforcement. The patrol last night captured a young Reb, a fine sharp fellow whose appearance is all dignity but his clothing desperate. Had a side wound. The Pickets getting cherries and looking at the country. 'Tis a hard looking place being the usual scenes of desolation, and all along the R.R. are remains of the many cars that our men were compelled to burn one year ago. Lay in the woods all day awaiting orders. Our men relieved from Picket at 3 o'clock. Weather pleasant, health good.

Thursday, June 11. Got up early having slept warmly on a large pile of hay with Captain Phillips[39] & Lieutenant Beazell. Soon had "Boots and Saddles"[40] and the "to horse." All got in line and made our way home but the not [way] we went. Stopped at Bull Run and fed. Getting home about 3 P.M. having a warm and dusty ride. Did not accomplish much this scout only capturing one or two Rebs, but may have been of service being a reserve for the Rap. [Rappahannock] Cavalry Battle. Found two letters for me at camp, one from Dr. Hunter saying "on behalf of the Faculty" that my certificate was sufficient.[41] The other was from Brother Asbury. He talks of moving. Also got a paper from home having the notice of two of my old college beau's marriage. Mr. Riley to Miss Norton, Mr. Hubbard[42] to Miss Tucker. It's so unexpected I think it is a ruse. Wrote home to sister Mattie, etc. Have expecting orders to move with 3 days rations, as they expect Stuart's cavalry to have got up or are [in] Maryland. The 2nd Pa. started; we will follow if they find anything.

Friday, June 12. Got no orders to move and found out that the excitement was caused by Mosby, who had made a raid into Poolesville capturing half of a Michigan Company.[43] Hear great excitement in Washington and Pennsylvania as they expect a raid from Stuart in Pennsylvania. They have called out the militia, under Generals Couch and Brooks.[44] Lt. McKay handed in his resignation; cause, a light hernia.[45] Got a paper from Greensburg, nothing strange.[46] Felt well today, having gotten over the fatigue of the Scout. The weather is dry and clear and long lines of smoke mark every moving object, man or beast. Sickness the same; occasionally one dying. How sad to see the soldiers laid in the cold grave so far from home and friends, and while his comrades discharge their shot over his rough mound, I cannot but regret a lot <u>so</u> unfortunate but borne.[47] Felt well.

Saturday, June 13. Got a letter from home. Mother, Amanda, and Mattie, being a good long one, which I relished gladly. Had Sargent Keys, Co "M," detailed as clerk instead of R. B. Fry who wanted to be relieved and expecting Keys to be Sargent Major as soon as I am promoted.[48] Adjutant Bryan[49] came to camp, being a fine little fellow social and possessing some if not many good parts. He intends to take to duty in a short time. The excitement about the raid of Stuart is still extant altho to us it seems of no concern. Had word the [that] the public item of the marriage of my friends at Meadville is all a hoax gotten up by the boys. Wrote a letter to Brother Asbury. Feel well and have but little to do the Sargent having taken most off my hands. The Colonel is trying to make us do the clear thing in sold[i]ering. This is right.

Sunday, June 14. Day pleasant. Health good. Activity increasing on the front, and Lee is threatening to cross to this side of the Rappahannock, while Hooker is watching him with his eagle eye,[50] but must be cautious since his army is diminished by the discharge of 2 years and 9 months men. Have quite exciting times sending out squads continually and increasing the camp guard. Captain Phillips and eighty men on picket at Chantilley.[51] Got orders for 50 men to go to Washington tomorrow for horses. Being a good change I have made arrangements to go along and see the city. Wrote a letter to Mother. Did not get to sleep being routed two other times until midnight, but this is soldiering and we must not complain. Feel grateful for good health. Did not go to church. Took a ride into the country with Lieutenant Smith and Lieutenant Grier.[52]

Monday, June 15. Got up at 3 o'clock and got ready to go to Washington. Started at six having a detail of 100 men from the Brig. Having rained last night had a pleasant ride getting there at 11 o'clock going by way of Falls Church. Had no time to stay having to come here today, contrary to expectations. The officers left the men, who got whiskey and with only a few exceptions all got on a big drunk, the officers not the least. Had a hard and dusty time coming home, having to leave many behind. Heard that Hooker's Army is moving, a good share passing through Centerville today, while a large amount of artillery came through Fairfax and now lies bristling in the moonbeams. The sound of martial music swells up as various localities and a thousand camp fires seem to fortel [foretell] a third Bull Run Battle. But, oh ye gods, shall the result be the same? Got eighty horses tonight.[53]

Tuesday, June 16. Got up and found the Twelfth Army Corps, command by Slocum, laying close to us having come up last [night].[54] They report the entire army on a move and from the columns of dust to be seen in every direction can see the truth of the report. Rumors dread and dire of the Raid of the Rebs into Pennia [Pennsylvania] and that they are within ten miles of Harrisburg. All things both here and at home are alive with excitement. The 2nd Corps (Couche's) and the Sixth are reported near Fairfax C.H.[55] Sent out a squad of cavalry to scout the surrounding country. Oh what a sound they made with the instruments of music, drums beating, fifes and brass bands blowing, horses neighing, and all things seemed so strange and exciting to me, a tyro[56] in the arts and scenes of active warfare that I could hardly restrain myself. Wrote a letter home.

Wednesday, June 17. The Army started at 3 o'clock this morning, making its usual amount of military uproar. All the Army is passing by, and miles of Army wagons dragging their slow lengths along for many hours. The Cavalry passed through, part of 1st, 3rd, 4th, and 16th Pa. but none that I knew, altho the old 4th was along.[57] Sad news from Harrisburg that the Rebs have sacked it, and are destroying everything in their path. The day was hot, very hot, and went out on a Regimental Drill, which lasted 3 hours. Got a letter from Jas. H. Thomas having written two before and sent two photographs, which I have never rec'd. He reports all things gay and promises a good time at Commencement.[58] Got over 250 horses this week; some good, others poor. Had a letter from Br. A. last night.

Thursday, June 18. The Army passing through yet, but report of affairs in Penn. much favorable, stating only a few Rebs in the state, not doing much harm. But many suppose we are going to have a fight here as Lee is reported to be in the Shenandoah Valley. Had the pleasure of putting on the Shoulder Bars of 2nd Lt. as Col. Bryan at the instance issued an order making me Lt. of Co "C." Also 6 others. All who had been recommended to the gov. [governor] but owing to the sad state of affairs in Harrisburg the commission did not come on. Brought into Fairfax nearly a hundred men and officers prisoners captured at Aldie of Moseby's band, but our boys were cut up in making the captives.[59] Paymaster in camp tonight; will pay tomorrow. Got three letters from sister Jennie, Ed McChesney,[60] [and] Aggie Jack. Wrote to Bro. Frank & Sister Jennie. Has been raining all afternoon.

Friday, June 19. Was detailed as Lt. of the guard being my debut on this branch of the military. Got along well, but found it tiresome work, going around so much to visit the guard. Rumors of Lee's forces approaching us becoming rife, but nothing is evidence of that. Still they, [the] infantry, are throwing up intrenchments. Got orders to move with light baggage having only one wagon to a company and all the extra clothing to be sent away, and extra arms and equipage to be turned in to [the] Q.M.[61] Had to be relieved of guard to take command of company as Lt. Montgomery is sick. Had gay times with our crabit[62] Q.M. during the whole time. Got pay for two months ($42) coming just in time. Got a letter from sister Kate,[63] a paper from Home. The tents being all turned in except one markee[64] for the officers; the men had to sleep out while the rain poured down in streams. Sent my valise home.

Saturday, June 20. Expected to start this morning but did not, spending all day in turning in old property and drawing new. Turned in 5 horses and drew 4, one of which I took. Also got 10 saddles (old ones). Lay all day waiting for orders but none came. Got a letter from Ed McChesney relative to college affairs. Wrote a letter to Aggie J. and also to Cousin Bell. Nothing but excitement all around, the infantry massing in heavy numbers and cavalry moving so that military matters are on the advance. All enjoying good health and feel well satisfied with the direction of my fortune. The company appears demoralized but can be brought to tune by discipline. Lt. Montgomery sick, and I am in command of the company which will turn out about fifty effective men.[65] Great excitement at home about the Reb Raid.

Sunday, June 21. Slept as usual, got up and had orders to turn in all the old carbins [carbines] and draw new. Turned in 36 Morrell carbines and 37 slings, also 1½ boxes of cartridges. Drew 37 sets Burnside Carbines complete with box of ammunition.[66] Got order to move as cannonading was heard all morning on the front; and getting in line having 49 men in my Co. [Company] started. Passed through Centreville, Bull Run B.F. [Battlefield] and passing through the 2nd Corps near Gainsville stopped on the north of Groveton when we bivouacked for the night.[67] Had the entire Division of Stahl's Cavalry being about 5000 strong with 4 pieces of artillery.[68] The boys expected [a] fight and may get it yet but all are eager to do their duty. In passing the B R. [Bull Run] Battle Ground saw the skulls and bones of the persons who fell in that battle who had been improperly buried. Health Good. Had luck scarce [as] the niggers in charge of our [baggage?][69] [MS page torn].

Monday, June 22. Got up getting in motion having breakfasted on two crackers[70] and feeling rather unwell having drank filthy water yesterday. We passed through Groveton, New Baltimore.[71] We came in sight of Warrenton. When we came in sight of the town, expecting the Rebs to be there, we charged with drawn sabers through the town in every direction but not a Reb was to be found. After scouring the country all around us, stopped for dinner but had as usual only having two crackers, but the niggers got many blessings. Sent out pickets all around and stopped for the day. Lay all day in the clover fields bating[72] our horses having no grain. For our supper bought two dozen biscuits of a secesh, paying 50 cts. a doz. in greenbacks.[73] I with the company went out on a small scout to meet Capt. Phillips who had gone to Waterloo, some distance.[74] 'Twas night and being between stone fences the thing looked billious[75] as the bushwhackers are reported there. Got back all right [MS page torn].

Tuesday, June 23. Nothing being found and the Rebels being supposed to be collecting in force in Maryland we started back. Got to camp of 2nd Corps where we dismounted, the wagons of our Reg. being there. Left for home and marching 'til 9 o'clock got back to the old camps, which look bad enough. Had a tolerably good time but did not see our accomplishment. Rumors of going to Harrisburg as the Rebs are reported there. The Company did well on the march and altho warm and dusty and dry they did not fall out without orders altho they had been used to do so, formerly. Felt well all day and endured the marching well. Getting around well to fatigue. Found our niggers with our blankets but they had eaten or lost all the provisions. Reports of Pleasanton whipping out Stuart at Ashby's

Gap when the firing was on Sunday.[76] Thus we seem successful altho the Rebs are trying to devastate the north but they are only grieving their own hearts.

Wednesday, June 24. Had a sound sleep as fatigue counteracted every adverse circumstance. Getting up, prepared for a march. Starting at noon with all the division, also one Corps of Hooker's Army passed thru Herndon's Station, and with a rapid rate charged through Drainsville[77] where they say there were fifty rebs but we saw nothing. Encamped for the night west of the town. The night was light and the sight was grand and all felt happy. Had the duty of taking charge of horse guard to attend to. This was not at all pleasing being an inconvenience. Hear we are going to march to H. F. [Harpers Ferry] but all these reports are unreliable. Wrote a letter to Sister Kitty. Feel well and am getting along well. Quite a number of the company were sick and have a good deal to suffer but generally they are getting along.

Thursday, June 25. Got to bed last night at 2 o'clock and slept until the bugle sounded "to horse." Started and passed along the Leesburg Pike within a few miles of Leesburg where I saw the "old eleventh." Saw Ed Gay[78] whom I had heard of but did not know. Crossed the Potomac at or below Edwards Ferry having a gay wet time the water covering the horses backs and are getting drowned.[79] Stopped for dinner. Started and what a column of Cavalry, Artillery and Infantry without number which I find are going after Lee who has made a raid into Penna. Passed thro Poolsville, Barnsville,[80] and stopped late at night (12) having come through delightful country and often rough enough. Saw and passed by the base of Sugar Loaf Mountain.[81] Rained nearly all day and the time was rough and having been on duty past night, sleep overpowered me. Also got lost and took a long time to get into right road. Many first lay down on the mud tying their horses to their leg or arms, thinking nothing of the rain and mud tho they were abundant.

Friday, June 26. Oh what a morning! The rain kept on and all looked like drowned rats and our horses had nothing to eat. But if we started saddly our ill such feelings were dispelled as the beautiful valley around decorated with its thousands fields of golden colored grain made us feel like at home. But when we passed throu Frederic so many smiling faces & plenty of banners made us really happy. They reported that 150 Rebs had passed through a few days before but suppose they are gone to Pa. as it is reported to be there with thirty thousand men. Passed thru a delightful country, getting bread, pies, cakes, and stopped near Middletown, Md.,[82] for the day. Sent out parties to forage getting plenty of food. Tied our horses to the fences having had orders to make ourselves comfortable. The army train of Hooker has been passing by and a hard fought battle may be the result.[83] Have not heard or written home since in the march. Health good, stood marching well.

Saturday, June 27. Went in the morning with a party for forage. Got all we wanted. Got breakfast, which was the only regular meal we've had for months.

Was detailed for picket, having Lt. Smith in command.[84] Had a good time as there was no danger from bushwhackers[85] and large columns of infantry and trains of wagons were passing through continuously. Also had plenty to eat: pies cakes, cherries, and all things needful. The people are very kind and give us all we want and seem happy to do all in their power. The weather is fine and the occasional rain prevents the dust from becoming troublesome. Reports of the Rebs being in force in Pa. and that Harrisburg is in danger, but that must be excitement. Feel well &c. and not being any use of watching, we on the reserve post wish [to] go to bed. Rather go to sleep, as beds are not, however, [for] us soldiers. May the high and holy one protect us and ours, also bring us all out of the difficulty.

Sunday, June 28. Had a good sleep. A courier was sent to inform us that the Division was moving. Called in the posts & Videttes[86] and followed after. Went back through Frederick and took the eastern pike running to Gettysburg but only went a few miles when we stopped with our whole division. Got a letter from Sister Jennie, which I was glad to receive and answered immediately. Got order for a review of the Cavalry as we were going to be transferred to the Army of the Potomac, having been brigaded with 5th N.Y., 1st Va. & 1st Vt. forming the First Brig. commanded by General Farnsworth having Gen'l Kilpatrick for commander of our Division (Stahel's old command) and Gen'l Pleasonton commanding the Corps.[87] Rumors of Gen. Hooker being relieved of command of the Army and Gen'l Mead put in his place.[88] Officers are angry about being brigaded with the 5th N.Y. but all will try and watch them so that they don't make anything of us.[89] Was in command of the Company today at review and think they did well. All well & getting along well. Stayed all night and slept.

Monday, June 29. Was wakened by one of the boys bringing me five letters from Mr. Lightcap, D. Greer, [Frank?] Thomas, Hud. McCall, & Bro. Frank, all [of] which made me glad to read. Heard of us being transferred to Gen'l Mead's army and being brigaded with 5th NY, 1st Va. & 1st Vt. Had marching orders at 10 A.M. Started and went in the direction of Little Forks where they say the Rebs are abundant. Passed the 2nd & 3rd Corps on the road. This was a delightful country and grain and grass abundant but the army pays no respect to such things tramples down all before it. Passed through Tawnytown, Md.,[90] where the cheering was lusty and all indicated their loyalty; but when we came to the Penna. line, long and hearty were the many huzzas for our Reg. Marched late, came to Littlestown[91] when the ladies favored us with songs. We all felt at home and happy.

Tuesday, June 30. Had a good sleep but very short and started again on the march. As we passed through the people fed us with bread &c and every house was busy in handing out water. Got to Hanover. Here were flags flying and all the demonstrations of loyalty and all forgot that we were in the vicinity of Rebs. But as skirmishing had been kept upon our right all morning, now about 80 charged into our rear among the baggage and ambulance train, also pack horses, and where the rear squadron tried to charge back they could not.[92] Consequently the men got excited and did not stand firm. They followed up through town firing and sabering our rear but at last the 5th N.Y. charged and whipped them. But we skirmished all day with artillery and dismounted cavalry and finally they left leaving in our possession 100 prisoners. They killed about ten or 15 and wounded a good number but in all they made nothing and lost a good deal.[93] This was my first initiation.

Wednesday, July 1. Had some sleep, sleeping on our arms, but nothing interrupted our rest save the tramping of our horses around our heads, as we have to tie them to our arms and legs. Started in the direction of Carlisle passing through Abbettsville and [East] Berlin where the Rebs had been reported to have come with a wagon train a short time before.[94] Marched late coming to within a few miles of Carlisle where either having run upon a force of Rebs too large for us or failed to catch the party. We are pursuing the latter I think most probable. We turned back and marched to Berlin where we encamped for the night. I with our Battalion was on Picket but being tired & hungry I lay down and slept. We had a large force along, the entire division. Rained a little enough to keep the dust down and, all willing, seemed to try on the Rebs and pay them back for what they did at Hanover. Health good, still command the company who are growing weak since Nov. and Dec. and several sick.

Thursday, July 2. Got my breakfast and horse fed at a farmer's house. Started on the march going back to Abbettsville and passing thru Oxford[95] in the direction of Gettysburg. Soon the booming of cannon and the bursting of shell with a dense smoke was heard and seen. But being in the center of the Rebs we had not force enough to attack. Just then the news that McClellan was in command went along the lines and was followed by deafening cheers showing that the Army have faith in him altho I never had since he had failed turning to the right.[96] Went toward Hunterstown and one squadron, Co. "C" and "I," was detailed to charge through the town to see if the Rebs were there.[97] We charged but found none. But citizens reported them just out of town. Soon the skirmishers began to fight and our squadron was sent to a hill to hold it. Could see the Rebs in abundance and in force. Got the Artillery in range and the Michigan boys charged but was met by a heavy force which drove them back, but not until they had done good work. The artillery since silenced theirs and the thing was done, leaving us the victory. Had some killed & wounded but the Gen. said we had done a splendid achievement. Got my boys together and encamped for the night.

Friday, July 3. Spending part of the night in sleep started about midnight and marched to Gettysburg, getting there about 8 o'clock. Here the Army was busy

Fig. 5. *Farnsworth's Charge and Death*, by A. G. Richmond, 1893. Richmond depicted the climactic scene on the third day of Gettysburg when Brig. Gen. Judson Kilpatrick ordered Brig. Gen. Elon Farnsworth to lead a cavalry charge against a line of Confederate infantry through woods and over boulders and fences. Farnsworth (shown in the front center of the scene) protested that the terrain put his cavalry at a disadvantage, but followed orders, losing many of his troopers and his own life from five mortal wounds. (Soldiers and Sailors Museum and Memorial Trust, Inc., Pittsburgh, PA)

Fig. 6. The monument to the 18th Pennsylvania Cavalry (1889) located at the southwest corner of the Gettysburg battlefield. (Elena S. Wilson)

and what a scene: Corps, cannon, wounded, and prisoners by the hundred and thousand. Rested awhile and started to the extreme right of the Rebs when we opened fire with Artillery. Had it hot all day having been under the heaviest fire, but now with much loss. Men ordered to charge the enemy behind a stone wall or fence and protected by artillery in which we lost our Brig. Gen'l Farnsworth. This was a daring exploit but was the end of many good men.[98] Cannonading was heavy on all sides and our seemed delightfully accurate. Held our ground till dark when we fell back, leaving the Regular Brigade to hold the field.[99] Commenced raining and rained most dismally, making soft muddy beds for us.

Saturday, July 4. Having spent a wet night, but sleep defying "wind & weather" we began the Fourth of July, and one that shall never be forgotten neither by us or many others. Went back to the main army when we heard of the enemy falling back being whipped, having lost thousands in killed wounded and prisoners, and many Gen'ls. We were congratulated by Gen'ls Mead and Pleasanton for the manner in which we had fought the enemy yesterday & were sent after the Rebs. Started & through mud & rain never before surpassed, passed thru Emmitsburg and made for Monterrey, a pass in South Mountain,[100] where we expected the Rebs to go through. Got to the pass again [at] 10 P.M. and found their train just passing. Attacted them & got them in a panic, when they went pell mell mashing up wagons & while the boys would run up and shoot a mule, capturing the team. They fought but did not amount to much. Followed them for ten miles when break of day dawned upon us.

Sunday, July 5. Counted our spoils and found we had captured 105 wagons with their horses and mules, also laded with baggage, wound[ed] men, [and] ammunition. Burned a good many we could not take away. Captured 12 or 15 hundred prisoners being as many as our entire force. What a motley throng & barefooted, bare headed and ragged in the extreme. Marched a few miles to Smithburg[101] w[h]ere we went into camp, and lay until evening when firing was heard in our front. Marched up into the mountain and fought the Bushwhackers for an hour but to no effect, but appeared as if we were surrounded but they fell back, and we marched thru Cavetown toward Hagerstown. Went as far as Boonsboro when we went into camp, sleeping and having limited rations.[102] The boys stand the campaign and are gaining a good reputation. A Lt. of Elder's Battery[103] was shot by a man supposed to be a maniac being unknown, and in our clothes.[104]

Monday, July 6. Started for Hagerstown where we expected [a] fight [it] being in possession of the enemy. Going through Funkstown[105] and came in sight of the city and opened the ball by the town with the 1st Battalion of our Reg.[106] They did nobly driving the enemy and soon for us a good reputation, but this was done at the sacrifice of many great men, loosing Capt. Lindsey, killed; Capt. Pennypacker, Lt. Potter & Laws missing. The Capt. is said to be shot by a lady in the upper window of a noted Reb house.[107] Throwing out dismounted skirmishers we fought a good share of the day, but the enemy was too strong, being infantry and plenty of it, so we had orders to retire, which we did, while they followed us and tried to capture our guns, but were repulsed with awful slaughter. Came near being surrounded as we fell back to Williamsport, where Gen. Bufort had been driven.[108] So we both turned to Boonsboro, getting off pretty safe. But we had a hard day and I wonder how we got off as we did, lost 8 or 10, and with a sad heart I look back on the acts of today and thankful to my God.[109]

Tuesday, July 7. Getting together we started for Boonsboro. Our Regiment was complimented by the Gen'l for their gallantry, and truly the boys acted bravely, for when death stared all in the face, they stood firm and made the evolutions[110] as cool, apparently, as if they were on the parade ground. Lee's many vacant places mark the result of yesterday but in all we have achieved great things in finding the enemy; attacking him in his strong hold, and getting away with less injury by far than we inflicted on the enemy, altho they were fine to crush. Report of Buford capturing a large portion of the Reb. train while we were attracting their attention yesterday. Also, that they are or were crossing the river, but too high for any success. Our Reg. guarded an ambulance train to Boonsboro when we went into camp guarding the mountain pass. The infantry was said to be coming up fastly & there is now no fear of any enemy.

Wednesday, July 8. Early in the morning firing was heard on the front and all were ordered out. The ball was opened by the Artillery and 3rd Division (ours).[111] Fought dismounted on the left; Buford's mounted on the right. The fight was severe, and lasted all day, heavy skirmishing being kept up on both sides. At dark our side made a simultaneous charge, and the Rebs broke running for miles, they leaving their wounded on the field. We lost but a very few men while that of the enemy must have been severe. I being dismounted followed them for 3 or 4 miles & was nearly given out when I got back to my horse quite out of the notion of infantry. Just then two Corps of infantry came up but too late to wrest from the Cavalry the glory of winning the day by chasing the Rebs. Feel well over today's labor and think the Rebs are sick of us.

Thursday, July 9. Having gone into camp I slept like the "Seven Sleepers" and did not waken until late.[112] Was detailed as Brigade Commissary and drew rations for the Brigade having a busy time and perplexing time till noon when I got thro. Moved our camp to the west of town getting a better position. The troops kept pouring in, the 6th, 11th and 12th Corps, and every indication is now for a heavy fight soon. Firing did commence but now ended. All reports and rumors are that Gen'l Lee is in a desperate condition and had no chance of getting across the Potomac. Also that Vicksburg was captured with all its prisoners on the 4 of July.[113] In general, all things are in a favorable condition and no doubt the Rebs are seen enough of Pa. & Maryland. Went to town and wrote a letter to my mother, being nearly two weeks since I have written before. Getting along well.

Friday, July 10. Had another night's rest. Lay in camp a good share of the day, but the frequent booming of cannon indicates that all are not so quiet.[114] Wrote to Ed. McChesney Wednesday being the third letter in so many weeks. Toward evening our men called into line and marched toward Hagerstown. Saw many marks of the day's skirmish, which resulted in driving the Rebs for three or four miles. We marched later backward and forward, having got lost from the Brigade, and failing to find it and being sleepy and weary we halted some 5 or 6 miles from Boonsboro. Encamped and laying on ponchos on the ground all were soon asleep. Amid these trials and difficulties, only a few murmurs were heard and these emanated from those of doubtful loyalty, even though they are in the ranks fighting ostensibly for our cause.

Saturday, July 11. Were called "to horse" early and marched a few miles until we found the rest of the Brigade. Went into camp. Got rations and forage, the wagon train having come up. But usually two days rations have to suffice for a week and the boys think it hard enough, but being among <u>friends</u> we have plenty to eat. Spent a good portion of the day in rest and sleep being now three weeks since we started on this campaign and the world knows that the 1st Brig. of Kilpatrick's Cav. Division has not been idle. 'Tis something to win a <u>name</u>, but the loss of many brave officers and men has been the price we paid, losing our Brigadier[115] and many staff and Line officers. When I remember what I have passed through, I thank my God that I have been an object of his care, not particularly for myself but for the sake of those who would lament my <u>fall</u> with unfeigned sorrow. May my lot always be so fortunate.

Sunday, July 12. Began the march early, our Regiment being in the rear supporting the Battery (Capt. Elder's). Advanced toward Hagerstown, held by the Rebs, and after some hard skirmishing drove them out capturing nearly one hundred prisoners, but found they had a large force back toward Williamsport and could see the intrenchments.[116] Found the citizens of various sentiments, a good many secesh. Found a good many of our men who had been surrendered on last Monday, and had hid from the Rebs. Found that then, altho we fell back, they were worsted, having been mowed down by scores by our guns. Toward evening, having only skirmished a little, our Reg. was sent on picket, all being dismounted; kept our squadron "C and I" and placed back of stone fences where they kept up a continued fire. One squadron was stationed in the street and had to remain up all night not knowing how soon the Rebs might dash in upon us.

Monday, July 13. Kept awake all night and was glad when morning came. Nothing occurred during the night, the lines being too far apart to do each other any harm. Got my breakfast at a Tavern, just by, but little was it they had to eat as the Rebs had stolen all their eatables leaving <u>them</u> to feel the disadvantages of <u>war</u>. I often think, 'tis a good thing for the union that the Rebs made this Raid, as the Copperheads[117] will see what they are doing, and get the fruits also. We did not get relieved until dark through the neglect of somebody, when the militia under Gen'l Couch came in and took the picketing.[118] Rumor says they pitched into the Rebs and captured two large guns. All things seem ready now, and all think tomorrow will be a hot day, if Gen'l Meade will leave us go into the Rebs. Gen'l Kilpatrick wanted to try them today but they would not permit him.

Tuesday, July 14. Was early on the march, as the news had come to Headquarters that Lee had crossed the [Potomac] River with all his force, playing us a grand slip. As we followed them we saw many signs of a hasty flight; wagons entire and in pieces, ammunition and guns being abandoned. They crossed at Williamsport on a pontoon, but hurried the men so much that a good many were drowned [and] also at Falling Waters where a few thousand were still having been cut off from the pontoon by their haste to destroy the Bridge. Our men, 6 Mich., charged them and captured them with little loss.[119] The rain had fallen all night & the mud was awful, making the prisoners look like a mass of dirt. So the old Fox has gone, and ma[n]y complain at Gen'l Mead for leaving him, but report says his Corps Commanders were not in favor of attacking.[120] Went in camp a few miles back.

Wednesday, July 15. Complaints and murmurs begin to rise since Gen. Mead has left [let] Lee get away. But report says his Corps Commanders were not willing to attack. Great are the Speculations as to the objects in view now for us. Some say beat Lee to Richmond, but our horses are so jaded with the twenty-four days marching & fighting and the Regiment is so dilapidated that we must rest. So they say we go to Berlin on the B & O R.R. to rest.[121] Started for Boonsboro coming through Hagerstown. Here we saw some of the new drafts [draftees] plump and fine as babies, but they will learn to lay aside some fancy stripes. Got to Boonsboro at dark and went into camp. Saw Jos. Coulter of 53 P.V. being in 1st D[i]v., 2nd Corps.[122] Report of Capture of Port Hudson by generals, Joe Johnson whipped and Bragg not to be found.[123] Appearances seem to indicate a speedy end of the war. Read of a terrible mob at New York concerning the Draft, but hope they shall all be sumarily dealt with.[124]

Thursday, July 16. Were aroused from our slumber before day to move. Started and passed through Rohersville and Buckittsville and within a mile of Berlin when we halted to feed.[125] Started again and went up the [Potomac] River to Harpers Ferry. This is the most romantic country I have ever passed. High hills, and jutting rocks hindered our way on all sides. Crossed the pontoon and put up at the ruins of the old arsenal for the night. But what a dismal place, muddy and dark and the vacant appearance tells full well what has befallen this once prosperous village. Report of the 2nd Div. of Cav. fighting at Charlestown eight miles from here, the place of John Brown's execution.[126] What a host of reflections spring into life at the mention of that name and these places.

Friday, July 17. Rained last night but slept well. Got breakfast in town, started on the march, crossed the bridge over the Shenandoah [River] and wound our way by twos down the river being the roughest stonyest road of the march. Saw green Paw Paws growing for the first time in abundance along the road.[127] Getting nearly to Berlin in fed. [federal] and turned toward Lovettsville[128] and marched through a delightful country, where the wheat fields were covered with abundance and old stacks yet remained showing that last year's supply had not yet failed. Got to Purcellsville[129] again crossing [the river] where we encamped for the night. Have now twenty men in ranks, when as I crossed the River into Maryland with 49. Still a good many are dismounted and following their horses giving out. Wrote a short letter to my mother also got a squad of papers and a letter from home.

Two

"Slept to Dream of War but Woke to Find All Quiet"

Campaigning in Northern Virginia, July 18–October 11, 1863

After crossing the Potomac River on July 17, the 18th Pennsylvania Cavalry went on extended picketing and scouting duties and engaged in small skirmishes in the Shenandoah Valley and at Amissville, Virginia, before encamping at Warrenton, Virginia, with the rest of the Army of the Potomac for recovery, resupply, and fresh mounts. Gen. Robert E. Lee, meanwhile, consolidated his infantry south of the Rapidan River in Orange County and sent Gen. J. E. B. Stuart's cavalry across the river into Culpeper County to keep watch on the Federals. The 18th spent the next two months patrolling and, on occasion, skirmishing in Stafford and King George Counties north and east of Fredericksburg to defend the Rappahannock River from Confederate guerrillas and army snipers. Poised between soft and hard war, Gen. George G. Meade's Army of the Potomac respected civilians but had little compunction about seizing forage and foodstuffs.

When away from combat, James Riley Weaver's entries, which he wrote by candlelight in the evening, often reflected on war's impact. A faithful correspondent, frequent letters from family and friends connected him to his prewar life. Like many soldiers, he mused, "Do they miss me at home?" Through an austere Methodist lens, Weaver regretted how military life often dishonored the Sabbath, a day that magnified the moral distance from his former civilian self, yet he also believed his faith would shield him from camp vices. Danger lurked from Confederate pickets, runaway soldiers, and irregular bushwhackers in the contested lands along the Rappahannock River frontier. Civilians' loyalties were fluid. Weaver dined with Unionists and with Confederates, describing the women as "half secesh, half union and profane to amazement," yet he also encountered deserters from the Confederate army and slaves fleeing their masters. He saw women's and children's faces etched by wartime poverty and combat's wrack in deserted

Fig. 7. The regimental standard of the 18th Pennsylvania Cavalry. Made January 1863, it was carried through the campaigns until captured by Confederate forces on November 18, 1863, and recovered from Richmond in April 1865 after the surrender. (Theophilus F. Rodenbough, Henry C. Potter, and William P. Seal, *History of the 18th Regiment of Cavalry, Pennsylvania Volunteers,* 1909)

encampments and battlefields. Despite war's inevitable sufferings, Weaver never wavered in the righteousness of the Union cause nor demonized captured enemy soldiers.[1]

After learning that Lee had sent two divisions of Gen. James Longstreet's corps to reinforce Gen. Braxton Bragg's Army of Tennessee at Chattanooga, Tennessee, General Meade's forces pushed south across the Rappahannock River and inaugurated the Bristoe Campaign. The Union cavalry's objective was to engage Stuart's cavalry forces at Culpeper Court House. On September 13, the 18th attacked the Confederates at nearby Brandy Station on the Orange and Alexandria Railroad and drove Stuart's men through the town under artillery fire. The next day they advanced to the Rapidan River and established a skirmish line at Raccoon Ford but soon withdrew to patrol along the Rappahannock River.[2]

Three weeks later Lee counterattacked, as Meade had sent two of his corps to the Chattanooga Campaign. Crossing the Rapidan River on October 9, Lee moved northwest of Union forces along the Blue Ridge Mountains foothills hoping to turn Meade's right flank. The previous day Stuart had left to seize a signal station in Union-controlled Madison County. Two companies of the 18th challenged the Confederate cavalry on October 10 at James City. After sustained artillery fire destroyed the hamlet, Gen. H. Judson Kilpatrick's men departed, and Meade withdrew his forces northward along the Orange and Alexandria Railroad. Crossing the Rappahannock River the following day, the 18th again engaged in heavy skirmishing at Culpeper Court House that became more intense as they retired toward Brandy Station. Serving as the rearguard for infantrymen, who were retreating along the rail line, Kilpatrick's 3rd Division became caught between cavalry units of Generals Stuart and Fitzhugh Lee. Although most of the division's regiments successfully charged through Lee's line to the safety of Brig. Gen. John Buford's forces at the station, some men of the 18th were captured. "After several desperate attempts to cut through we had to give it up," Weaver recorded, when he, three other officers, and thirty-two privates became Confederate prisoners.[3]

In the months following Weaver's capture, the 18th participated in the hard fighting of the war's final eighteen months in Virginia. They earned a reputation for fearless charges and sustained losses at Spotsylvania (May 9, 1863), Hanover Court House (May 31, 1864), Winchester (September 19, 1864), Tom's Brook (October 9, 1864), and Cedar Creek (October 19, 1864). At Buckland Mills (October 19, 1863), and at the Wilderness (May 5, 1864), enemy forces almost surrounded them, and in the latter engagement only a desperate charge through a pine thicket saved the regiment from capture. During the Kilpatrick-Dahlgren raid on Richmond in February 1864 to free Union prisoners, including Weaver, the 18th destroyed Confederate supplies and rail lines but failed to penetrate the city's outer defenses. As Gen. Philip H. Sheridan pressed Lee's right flank in the Overland Campaign, the 18th became embroiled in fierce battles, including Yellow Tavern (May 11, 1864) and White Oak Swamp (June 15, 1864). In August the regiment moved to the Shenandoah Valley to clear out Gen. Jubal Early's forces and lay waste to the abundant resources sustaining the Army of Northern Virginia. While at their winter camp near Winchester, the regiment learned of Lee's surrender to Gen. Ulysses S. Grant at Appomattox and fired off a hundred guns in jubilation. On April 11, the regiment joined local Unionists and ex-slaves to celebrate the war's end. They occupied valley towns until mustering out began in June. The process was completed in October 1865, which marked the end of their three-year enlistment. During this time, the 18th suffered 767 total casualties, killed, wounded, or missing, 39 percent of the regiment's total enrollment, with 135 prisoners of war among the regiment's losses.[4]

Saturday, July 18, 1863. Slept soundly on a brush pile as the ground was wet. The teams came giving us rations and forage, the horses look lank and worn out, many deserving a "discharge" from the service. Rested most of the day, making out reports of losses, wounds &c. and toward evening left for Snickers Gap with our Regiment to do Picket duty.[5] The 6th Michigan was on duty there, got to the place about dusk, finding it as [a] rough mountain pass in the Blue Ridge about 2 or 3 miles east of Shenandoah River. All dismounted and placed our selves among the rocks all along the pike, and felt no fear of thousands. My company being in the reserve we slept at intervals, and had a tolerable position. Rumors of the Rebs being across the Riv. (Shenandoah).

Sunday, July 19. After getting breakfast was detailed to go out to the front to relieve Lt. Tresonthick.[6] While there had the pleasure of finding a good blackberry patch and had abundance of berries all day. The boys enjoyed themselves and no Rebs being in close proximity had not to be very strict. A patrol went to the river, and found a picket post of the Rebs in a mill who fired on our men with no effect. Expected to be relieved but word came that we should hold the gap until further orders and that the Brig[ade] had gone on to hold the other gaps. This was partly pleasing, as it gave our horses a chance of resting. Health good, the very best, and nothing to complain of. By indications infer that Army is following the Rebs with hot haste, and will give them a good chase to Richmond. Weather delightful. No mail; hope for one soon.

Monday, July 20. Today was spent in the Gap at the old business varied by picking blackberries and killing sheep, hogs, and calves, believing that all things, even the cattle upon a thousand hills belong to the soldier when hungry especially when he can get hold of them. Wrote four letters, to mother, Mr. Lightcap, Bros. John & Asbury. Nothing new the Reg. being in the same position. One of Co "I" killed himself by accident having gone to a house and when sitting on a chair he drew his carbine up which caught and went off shooting him through the neck.[7] The infantry are massing down at Snickersville.[8] Am enjoying myself tolerably well but having only 19 men in the company now. I feel sorry but the horses failing is the cause.

Tuesday, July 21. Slept to dream of war but woke to find all quiet. There is something strange in the feelings experienced in going into battle and even in sleep the same feelings are felt. Some may say that they care not for the crash of war, the booming of guns and clash of arms but for me I [love?] not the sound. Getting scarce of rations but try to supply their place with berries and fresh meat without salt. Some complain but when I think what others have done and even the Rebs are enduring now, I feel ashamed of these petty complaints. Made a Reconnaissance to the Shenandoah [River] mounted & dismounted, finding all things the same. Have had no word from home, and I am getting desires of hearing from them. I have always dreaded the time when we should be thrown away from our mail communications. Health good and have easy times in the Gap.

Wednesday, July 22. Was relieved today by the 1st Vt. and had to march to near Upperville where the Brigade was lying only a short distance from Ashby's Gap.[9] Here we got forage and rations and found many infantry. In the evening had to move out, acting as rear guard for the wagon trains of our Division, and that of the 3 Corps. Had to wait long after dark to get in the rear and then we fell in about midnight, marching at a very slow pace and kept going till dawn when being near Manassas Gap,[10] the train stopped and we spread out blankets and fell asleep. While guarding the train I thought of the night we fell upon the Reb train and burned it, and how we would feel, would they return the compliment.

Thursday, July 23. Had only an hour to sleep when the hateful bugle sounded "to horse" and soon all were in line. Found the whole Division was on the march going through Piedmont Sta. at Manasses Gap, also through Orleans, and in the direction of Culpepper C.H. Came to Amissville where we stopped hungry, tired and sleepy and the horses were as bad as the men.[11] Yes, our Cavalry is gone up as it is so much reduced as to be beyond recruiting. Passed through some good country, but very mountainous & other rough and poor. Three more of our horses gave out and mine getting lame was left behind. Got one from Co "B." Felt something like Rheumatism in my limbs & heart fever is the result. Getting clear of duty would not suffice for the sickness. Head out to go on picket.

Friday, July 24. Started again in the direction of Culpepper C.H. and having gone 4 or 5 miles the 2nd Brig. being in front, run into the columns of Lee's Army.[12] The fight was brisk but short, where our forces fell back. The Rebs did not follow.[13] Our Pickets say that trains have been passing all day within a few hundred yards of them; also infantry, cavalry and artillery, so we may conclude that Lee's whole Army is passing. What a pity we had no more forces as we might have charged their train or shelled it and put the whole thing in a panic. What a great pity we did not get here before the Rebs as then they would be all over. Had to go on picket altho the 5th N.Y. has not been doing duty for weeks, but our acting Brig. is a N.Y. Col.,[14] and has a disposition as [low?] as to show mules ears beneath the [hind?] skins. But the time will come when this shall cease.

Saturday, July 25. Having stood my three hours duty, I went to bed to awaken with the high risen sun. Found the Rebs had drawn off their Picked [pickets] during the night and having gone out with a scout found nothing of what yesterday was an object of interest. A negro servant, who had been along with the Rebs in Penna., came to us and very intelligent. He gave us many interesting and amusing items, saying that Gen. Lee thinks we [had?] got in a habit of whipping them and we <u>will</u> keep a doing it; that Gen. Stuart says that all confidence in his cavalry has been lost and that they [illegible] worth a d__n [damn] anymore, &c. Had any amount of berries as the fields for miles are blue with them, every kind, size and quality. Tho soldier thinks them a big thing, and they make the hardtack much more palatable.

Sunday, July 26. Having spent another wet night on picket, the morning came clear and glorious. Nothing yet to be heard from the Rebs. Were relieved from duty by the 1st Vt. who came from Snicker's Gap. Col. DeForest [is] not in command of Brig[ade] and report of him being in arrest, so we perhaps may not be worked so hard. Went back to camp at Amissville where we turned in all the unserviceable horses, leaving our Co. 6, and sending the dismounted men to Warrenton Junction. Say we are going to get 800 of the drafted men from Pa. to fill our Reg., and three officers are appointed to go there so we may expect a full regiment yet.[15] Had the misfortune to be poisoned on the face, breast, arms, and legs and our surgeon having nothing to kill it.[16] I fear I shall have a nervous time. Wrote a letter to Sister Jennie. Toward evening they began as of old (last spring) to blow "Tattoo" & Taps,[17] and really those familiar sounds made me feel at home.

Monday, July 27. Had a good sleep last night. Today we spent in camp, having plenty of rations but no forage, the wagons being at Warrenton. Wrote two letters: one to Cousin Bell, and one to Sister Kate. Mail came in having three for me. One from Bro. John stating that he had been drafted but did not know whether he would go or get the substitute.[18] One from home, and the other from Sister Kate. Also got quite a quantity of papers. Felt a good deal out of humor having got the poison and nothing to kill it. The men started to barricks [barracks] but came back, not having the Vols. ready. This was as getting to be a big thing and we are now only getting to see it rightly. But the prospects now are brighter than ever of our success having destroyed within this month ¼ of the entire rebel Army. But, oh, what suffering, pain, & death are men brought to endure to subvert the ambitions of men, and to sustain our liberty.

Tuesday, July 28. Had "Boots and Saddles" at "Two" o'clock this morning fearing the Rebs might take advantage of our sleeping to fall at us, but we had no attack. 12 of the Reg. went out on picket leaving Sergt. McGlumphy, Corpl. Clutter[19] and myself to spend our time in camp, which we did variously. For my part I had to get up the pay Rolls and got one partly done. The wagons and forges left for Warrenton and rumors are that we will soon follow. The weather is pleasant being in the woods on a high knoll. Hear nothing of the infantry but expect they are trying to beat Gen. Lee to Richmond. Hope we may get to rest until the drafted men come on and we get horses. But even then the new men should be drilled or they will be little use. But we must be governed by our circumstances.

Wednesday, July 29. Had "Boots and Saddles" again at 2 o'clock but very few obeyed the call, thinking it only [a] fright. But they may get caught someday by their <u>thinking</u>. Spent a good share of the day making out Pay Rolls, having no Sergeant in the company to assist. But had "Boots & Saddles" again as a few men had been seen near a picket post. This stopped our working and the remainder of the day was spent in doing nothing. Rumors of going back to Fairfax to the old duty as Gen. Heintzelman has asked for us to be sent back, having only loned [loaned] us for 30 days.[20] So proof of this they say our dismounted men are sent to Washington and cannot get to us. I should be glad to go back and have rest and an opportunity of getting a change of clothing, and something refreshing to eat, having seen enough of the "elephant"[21] to satisfy the natural desire of seeing a fight. The poison is still spreading, but not much and I got along well enough. Health tolerably good not excellent.

Thursday, July 30. Finished my Pay Rolls congratulating myself on getting through as writing out here is no easy matter. Still, rumor of going to Fairfax and got orders to start from here at 5 A.M. tomorrow. Going to be relieved by Gen'l Gregg's Division.[22] He came offering to do something as heretofore he seemed to be only following up our rear, and usually doing nothing. Nothing seen or heard today of the Rebs, and I suppose they will remain quiet since they don't court combat with us, but did they know how run down our Cavalry is, they might safely fall upon us unless they are worse than we which may be the case. Feel well with the exception of the poison, which in these warm days, clothed entirely with wool is disagreeable enough. The officers started to Penna. for bringing in the drafted men. Hear of D. L. McCulloch's death, for which I feel sorry and it brings to my mind the remembrance of many things in the past, that are not "born to die." But this is a strange world, and many strange returns to him.[23]

Friday, July 31. According to order started with 104 men in line, looking slim enough, since this is not much larger than one company. After various stops & starts, we got to Warrenton. Passed the Sixth Corps on the way.[24] Found the cars running clean to Warrenton but how sad and desolate the places look. Not a store, nor any public [places] open, but glowing walls and dusty window shutters with the only few old gray bearded men bespeak how terribly Va. has suffered. Went to Warrenton Junction where we found many troops and all things were hustle, but as usual saw none whom I knew. After running around till dusk to find an encamping place, we stopped and making some supper we partook of U.S. Bounty, having been in the saddle all-day, making us tired enough. Thus far it seems as if we might get back to Fairfax, but hard to say nor do I care. Have plenty of forage and rations, the only two requisites necessary to a soldier's comfort.

Saturday, August 1. Spent part of the day writing letters and sent them to Washington with Capt. Cunningham[25] who took a squad of 30 men having unserviceable horses to the city for new ones. Wrote to Sister Mattie, to Bro. John, Frank Arter, Hud. McCall & Frank Thomas, having had to answer this for a long time. The day was extremely hot, and having encamped in the open field we had to build shelters to keep off the boiling sun. Got orders, about dusk to march. Got into line with our 70 men and started they say to Stafford C.H. 25 miles distant.[26] A part of our men just then came from Washington but were too tired to come along so they are to report tomorrow. Traveled all night, we being in front through a terrible rough and forest-like country, and again daylight found us 4 miles of the Court H. Here the boys made a raid on the farmers chickens and the mellee was laughable enough.

Sunday, August 2. 'Tis Sabbath came again, but who would dream of this being Sabbath and indeed the Soldier has <u>no</u> Sabbath. Started on and getting near found as few Rebs in the old burned buildings of the town, but they skedaddled instantly. Find we are to picket this place making a line with the other Regiments. Started out to find the picket post and having run all over the country to within a few miles of Falmouth,[27] without find [finding] the 1st Vt. we had to give up the trial and come back to camp. After dark tired enough, saw many new & strange sights. Old encampment after old encampment upon a "thousand hills," with all the old decorations that once graced them and still show, the taste of the occupants.[28] Saw a few Rebs but they skedaddled also, leaving our 70 men the undisputed monarchs of all. Saw some nice apples & peaches, being the first of the season. Got lost several times but by hunting got out. Seems as if the Fairfax report is all humbug, as this is in the opposite direction. The day was dismally warm, the warmest of the season yet.

Monday, August 3. Having spent a night in refreshing sleep got up finding all quit [quiet] nothing to be found of the Rebs. The command started again to try to find the 1st Vt. and succeeded joining our pickets with theirs. [They] Say the Picket is now extended from Rappahannock Station to Aquia Creek.[29] I did not go along, not being needed, and feeling tolerably out of condition for nothing. About noon the Rebs find [us] on the post and got us all on horse but they turned out to be only six or seven who I suppose were on a patrol. At night they were required to be very vigilant, and being too much so they fired twice on our own men but fortunately with no effect, but it succeeded in bringing all <u>to arms</u>. Had chicken for breakfast, and applesauce for dinner all being "contraband." Have no mail, nor word of the dismounted men who went to Washington. Health good, spirits ditto.

Tuesday, August 4. After repeated volleys of firing and bugle blowing, we found time to go to sleep, and slept till morning, and contrary to expectation found us unmolested. Sent a patrol to Aquia Creek, which found some oats & corn in a barn, which had been left by our army when leaving this locality. This just came to time as the horses were starving. They say they saw the gunboats.[30] Called in the picket toward night, as our force was too light to protect so large a territory. Had tolerably good time eating Hard tack & applesauce, as they are plenty. The day was hot, and seems as if August is going to be the "tug."[31] Expect to see the rest of our Regiment tomorrow, needing them badly. Have had no mail nor anything to read, and am getting lonely, but hope that from these circumstances [we] shall pass away, and we be brought back to civilization, where we can get something to read &c.

Wednesday, August 5. The rest of the regiment (107) came in, but only four out of 15 sent away from our company, the rest having staid to get horses & equipments. They brought in a mail having one for me from Bro. John, stating that he was not going to come to war, but was getting a substitute. Wrote two letters, one to Bro. John and the other to my Mother. The day was very hot, and had nothing to do but lay in the shade, which was hard enough. The Rebs are not making any demonstrations, and the likelihood is that they will not soon as two or three corps have gone over the Rappahannock [River] to give them something to do at Culpepper C.H. But after all there is but slight prospect of having much fighting to do soon. The drafted men had not come yet, and no prospects of them soon. Hear of the boys having a big time at Washington, having beat out all the guards and taken the city by force, until they were ordered out of the city.

Thursday, August 6. Was wakened at 2 o'clock to get out with the command to go on a raid down to Aquia Creek. Got out, and with 75 men of our Reg. & 75 of 1st [West] Va. and two wagons we started, going past A.C. Church,[32] crossing the creek, and winding through the pines, sg. [single] file, in one of the most desolate, and forest like country I ever saw, for the purpose of arresting citizen guerrillas. Went clear to the Potomac, getting several men & horses and find every amount of gov. property, but through the command of our notable Major Darlington,[33] could not touch anything, altho they had plenty of shirts, what we all need, and coffee and grain. Came back to where the 1st Va. had gone, to a mill where we fed our horses and got dinner. Then filled our wagons with flour, meal bran &c. and came to camp. Had a good supper of slap-jacks, potatoes, and other dellicacies. Had a good warm ride, the sun being as hot as hades. Poison played out, and am getting all right.

Friday, August 7. The day was warm and had to remain in the open field all day but the sun was counteracted by building shades of blankets [on] boards, etc. Got two letters, one from Sis. Kitty the other from Bro. F. A. W.[34] Both getting along gaily, the latter talking of coming to war. Wrote three letters, to Bro. Frank, sister Kitty & Ed McChesney. Spent the rest of the day in camp doing chiefly nothing. One detachment went on Patrol to Potomac Creek[35] saw nothing of hostile character. Things seem to be settling down to what they formerly were and being on Picket we have the same old monotonous duty to perform. This is to the soldier, very tiresome but preferable to hard hot marches. Thought of home and the many changes I have under gone since last I saw my friends. But I get along better than had supposed. May I always be so fortunate.

Saturday, August 8. Got orders early to go out and form a picket line between us and 1st Vt. Had seven officers & 50 men. Got on post with Capt. Hamilton[36] on the outpost. Had a pleasant time, having a good well, and shade being in [an] orchard. Had dinner of beans, potatoes, & corn bread, being the Staff of Life in this country. Saw a good many woman citizens who have a rough appearance and the most out-spoken that I have ever met, half secesh, half union, and profane to amazement. Had a quiet time, altho the patrol of the 1st Vt. was attacked twice today. Had three Sergts to take charge of the picket, and I have but little to do. The day was hot. Horses had but hay for forage. The location wild and gloomy, being the pine forest [in] ad[d]ition. But got along well. Had not news today.

Sunday, August 9. Today is the Sabbath and was spent as if <u>we</u> knew it not. I am often led to wonder what God thinks of the manner in which the sacred day is spent? But I feel thankful that I have feelings as grateful as I have and so much inclined to ever keep my God before my eyes. But I know the path by which I walk is and has been a devious one, and not the "straight" one spoken of by the prophets. Still on Picket, nothing strange only a few shots fired by our boys at the pigs & sheep. They shot one pig being the last one the poor woman had, and she complained so piteously and wept so bitterly at prospects of starvation, which indeed were not all imaginary that I felt angry at the boys and went out to find out the perpetrators, but did not until I found part of it cooked on the plate for my dinner, when I could not scold. Really, the people here are in a desperate condition, all widows but a few, and scarcely enough to cover the body.

Monday, August 10. Had a strange day as a good share of it was spent in visiting the citizens and seeing how they lived, and was truly astonished to see how low the "mighty" have at once fallen for starvation stares them in the face and as they say 'tis "sad living" and a pitiable one indeed. The day was hot exceedingly and spent a good share of the time riding around. Went on a Patrol with Capt. to Potomac Creek, and stopped at a reported union Lady's house, where there were three young ladies, tolerably interesting. Had good eating, having got rations and killed a large government steer. I am only now getting to see the horrors of war and nothing so moves me as to see women and children suffer for what they could not prevent. Yes, saw them clothed in nothing but old tent cloth and have only a dry corncake to eat. How I pitied them, but pity could not benefit them only as it touched my nerve-rack[37] sharing it with them.

Tuesday, August 11. This was the warmest day we have had yet, and we all were glad to seek the thickest shade. Rumors of the fever getting bad in camp and one darkey died, which is no doubt caused by the miserable water. We on the Picket

Post have splendid water and fear the day when we shall be called away. Capt. and I went down to the union Lady's house and had dinner. Got up as best they could having beans, bacon, corn-bread, turtle simmers, &c. Had also a gay time with the girls. Had given coffee & sugar to some widow women, and they returned the compliment by bringing us milk. Women, who once owned their tens of thousands, but now as dependant as the most lowly. Got eggs from a fine little woman, an exception to many I have seen. Rumor of a Regiment of Reb Cavalry being in our front and having given strict orders for vigilance we closed opperations for the day not certain but that the Rebs would visit during the night.

Wednesday, August 12. Although they had reported 800 Rebs on our front, we slept quietly and awoke the same, finding nothing to have occurred. Spent part of the day gassing with the secesh ladies and really they are an enigma to the sex. Finding we were going to be relieved I went and bid them good by and found them better <u>unionists</u> than I supposed. Had got a lady to make me some pies, but sorry for the men they never came to time. Left the Picket-Post and went to camp, finding all saddled [and] ready to move. They had caught 4 Rebs as the Scout had charged upon a Reb picket-post and captured them. Started for Warrenton Junction and marched all night, being 22 miles, and the sky being overcast by clouds and going through thick pines, the road was dark enough. Got to within five miles of Warrenton Junction when we encamped for the night, sleepy and weary enough.

Thursday, August 13. Having marched late, I went to the woods and prepared a bed and slept quietly through the rain and storm. Got up and found the Regiment had gone into camp. So we are here five miles southeast of Warrenton Junction. Found all the dismounted boys making over twenty now for duty. Got our tents and are now comfortable expecting to stay for some time. Had a letter from Lizzie M. C. breaking the silence that has existed between us for many months. Answered it in my best style, but the situation was so delicate that I could hardly do it to my satisfaction. Wrote home and to Lt. Montgomery sick in Washington.[38] 'Tis now dark, for a space of nearly two months the pleasant candle light and quiet camp has never graced the full of eve, and now as I pen these lines by the light of a candle I feel more than usually satisfied and thankful. Oh that I could be as I ought. Hear of Capt. Phillips being promoted to Major.[39] Glad of it, no other more deserving. Camp good but water scarce.

Friday, August 14. Had a good cool sleep as the nights are now cool and refreshing. Spent a good portion of the day in fixing up the company books. Also wrote a letter to the provost marshal of Greene County[40] to send back to the Reg. the deserters & captured of our Co. Found a good spring, having dug a sink in the field, which makes the water more plentiful. Lt. Golden says he is going to keep my account separate from the former commanders of the company so that I will not be connected with their responsibility.[41] Got a herald having the list of

exempt drafted men.[42] Ed. McChesney being among those paying the $300; also
A. G. Curtin, nomination for Governor.[43] We are all getting along well, and again
with the company very well indeed. Was ordered out on Brig[ade] Inspection but
getting out we were sent back. Had a pleasant [MS page torn].

Saturday, August 15. Was awakened early by the Bugler blowing "Boots and
saddles," and all had to pull down their tents and prepare for the march. Felt
quite out of humor having only got fired up and expecting a week's rest, but such
is not the fate of the 18th Pa. Cav. Got on the march and marched 12 or 15 miles,
when, about dinner we stopped near Hartwood Church, a few miles south of
Rappahannock R. [River].[44] Expect to lay here some time and reinforce the 2nd
Division now on Picket. Have tolerably good camp in the small pines, but water
for man and beast is very scarce. Hear of 2nd N.Y. Reg. (Harris Light) being attached to our Brig., making four Reg.[45] Got two letters, one from home, the other
from Ed. McChesney being at Meadville. Got the list of Drafted men from Washington Co.[46] and was amused to see some of the Copperheads drafted. Have got
one of the boys to cook for me, and it suits me much better.

Sunday, August 16. Today the sun shone brightly, the gentle breeze so swayed
the tall pines peacefully to and fro, and all nature seemed to point upward in
thankfulness to the great creator. But how different with those who alone should
be supplicants of the Deity. They seeming to forget for what they were created and
that the "Sabbath is the Lords" disregard his holy day, and never dreaming of that
injunction "Thou shalt keep it holy." Have felt well all day, and ever happy under
present circumstances. Wrote two letters, one home, the other to Ed. McChesney
feeling glad of the opportunity to correspond. The 2nd N.Y. came to the Brig. having about 500 aggregate 'tis said. Hear we shall stay here for a month unless some
general run be made and many other flying reports that only humble the brain
and perplex the soul. News are now sparce and so our mail of any consequence.
May we soon see the day when this shall not be.

Monday, August 17. Expected to have a wet night but no rain fell. The morning
was pleasant and had to get up early for Reveillie.[47] Nothing occurred during the
entire day to make it notable, and Reports of course would have to rise. 1st, no Lt.
could be mustered unless the company had eighty men, in consequence of which
Ben Austin tore off his "Bars." 2nd, Lt. Col. Brinton is said to be Colonel of 19th Pa.
Cav. and Capt. Wise a Major.[48] Both which are supposed to be false. Got orders to
change camp, and moved about a mile and encamped first at Hartwood Church,
in a rough looking place. Had the horrors,[49] wonderfully, bad feeling as if our Reg.
is imposed up, by being Knocked from post to pillar. Sent 9 men out on Picket at
the U.S. ford on Rappahannock River. Got a letter from Asbury rather thinks he
will not come to war. Got blank for Corpl Sanders'[50] description List.

Tuesday, August 18. Went to the wagon train and got our tent, also somebody's two blankets as the nights are very cold down here along the Rappahannock. Put up our quarters, had several details going on scout, guarding wagon trains, &c. One scout chased a party of guerrillas and retook two niggers and three horses, which had been captured. One Co. of 140 P.V. [Pa. Volunteers] came to the Church to erect a Telegraph between Gen. Kilpatrick's and Gen'l Mead's headquarters. Feel only tolerably well being troubled with the common complaint of Cavalrymen— Piles,[51] which are by no means a small affair. Got a letter from father of Thomas Polan asking of his son's where-a-bouts, but could only tell him the sad tale of going <u>into</u> fight at Smithburg, and not coming out.[52] Sad news for any parent. Nothing exciting. Sun very warm & ground dry. Water scarce, grub plenty.

Wednesday, August 19. Strange country this; day as warm endurable, and nights shivering cold, being, I should think, good ague country.[53] Dew fall like small rains and the ponchos above and below us are wet with heavy drops. Never saw "Yellow Jackets" so plenty, being like flies, and troublesome in eating. Today was a calm pleasant day and any man with health and a pure conscience must be partially happy at last and to the soldier who has the horrors, it would be a mighty impulse to throw off his melancholy. Toward evening, got orders to move with three days rations, as the Major had got the job of catching some guerrillas who haunted around. Started with fifty men and ten officers, (the rest being on picket) and went prowling around through the bushes charging upon citizens houses and after dark caught one runaway secesh who was at home enjoying himself. En- camped for the night, 6 or 8 miles from the old camp.

Thursday, August 20. Had a splendid sleep having plenty of hay for horses and beds. Continued our march, creeping through by roads and bushes, stop- ping at nearly every house capturing two citizens, supposed guerrillas, sending them to camp. Marched past Grove Church and in the direction of Bealton Sta- tion, O. & A. R.R.[54] but having encamped for dinner, we turned for camp getting in 5 o'clock P.M. Found all the tents torn down, and all saddled ready to move as they had orders to move, having heard that Lee was crossing the River with his whole force. But finally they found out that as yet it was only rumor. Had a good time on our scout so the Major threw off his stiffness and let the boys have some fun having stopped once or twice at orchards to get apples &c. Pitching our tents again and being tired I lay down to rest, feeling thankful for a lot as easy, and a future as promising.

Friday, August 21. Remained quiet all night and that yesterday's fright was caused by some Rebs coming across to give themselves up, and were followed by Stuart's Cavalry &c. Put up our tents again and prepared for a further stay, un- less something frighten us again. Was detailed as Act'g Adj't [Adjutant] in place of Act'g Adj't McKay, who was relieved to be Act'g Quarter Master in place of Lt. Golden, who was put in arrest.[55] Didn't care much for the position having been long enough in the Adjutants Office. The command went on Picket at U.S. Ford, leaving us in camp to attend to affairs &c. The mail came but nothing for me. 1st Vt. Cav. transferred to 2nd Brigade and Col. Davis appointed our Brig. Commander.[56] Day very warm indeed, but hope this will cease with Aug.

Saturday, August 22. Had but little to do all day, and consequently did but little. Had no mail. Wrote to Charley Hall and Prof. S. J. Hayes,[57] spending the rest of the time in talk with McKay who was a little sick. Had some green corn for dinner, pies for desert, but of such an inferior quality that they did not seem pies. Hear that Charleston has gone up; and the Rebs down at the [Rappahannock] river tell our boys that they are getting whipped, and a good many of them are swimming across giving themselves up. No rain but the day is warm and dry, which every moving object along the road carries with it a dense cloud of smoky dust. Slowly yet fastly the time creeps along, and when I look back ten months I hardly realize how much has passed in that length of time. No expectation of any move of our army soon, but it can move at any time.

Sunday, August 23. Another Sabbath has passed, but was spent much more quietly than many of late. All the boys nearly on picket, and a quietness lingers around that is musical. Spent part of the time in writing. Wrote letters to Sister Amanda, Aggie Jack, Jonas Ross, and to Post-Master at Washington. Felt well and happy all day, for why I know not; but the times have left me and I am myself again. Long to have a mail as this isolated condition is killing. The picket still report some of the enemy coming over the river and giving themselves up. Hope they will continue until the last rebel is a penitent upon the mercy seat.[58] But if they refuse to accept the offer of temporal salvation, may Father Abraham[59] withdraw his arm and say: "I shall not always strive with Rebels."

Monday, August 24. Pleasant warm day having its usual amount of dust & sweat, but as usual, having <u>nothing</u> to do but sit or lie in the tent I got dreadful lazy. Yes, this kind of life is too bad and is a <u>torture</u> [to] a man of any energy. Got letters from Bro. John, Frank Arter, Sister Matte, and a Paper. Wrote to Bro. John and Frank Arter and think it a pleasure to have anything to do, especially, the writing of letters, as "cast your bread upon the waters and there shall find it after many days."[60] Yes, I find some answers to my letters after <u>very</u> many days. Hear of 500 Rebs giving their selves up but <u>that</u> needs confirmation but really the demoralization is wonderful, as they are giving themselves up constantly. But one should think that now is the time to make the grand onslaught, but perhaps our army is waiting on the conscripts, hope they may soon fill our Reg.

Tuesday, August 25. The time is passing slowly along and I begin to wonder that nothing is turning up. For altho we hear of surrenders of the Rebs, they amount to nothing. Hear of Moseby capturing 100 horses from a detachment bringing them to the Division. Moseby is decidedly the boldest guerrilla that we have to deal with. The mail came but as barren as the desert, and I cannot but scold my friends who are lying in ease at home and have nothing of the hardships of war, to attend with. But 'tis pleasant enough to be a soldier, when in camp but when on a march 'tis endurance alone that can sustain the soul and body; [but] not the body alone, for the <u>soul</u> is often more oppressed than the body. 'Tis dark, and having hemmed in loneliness, "Do they miss me at home?"[61] I began to think of home and felt sad <u>enough</u>, but throwing off all these, I tried to feel merry, but 'twas hard work.

Wednesday, August 26. The Sergt. Major having been out and his horse falling upon his leg and breaking it <u>badly</u>, I have much to do, having no Sergt. Major.[62] Got a letter from sister Mattie, in which she propounded the serious question, how I would like to have more brothers, and not liking the kind spoken of, I answered her in the negative. A number of Rebs coming over the river for forage left at Aqua Creek, and our men were [the] 2nd Brig. [Brigade] were sent after them. Of late, somehow I am addicted to much serious meditation, and often when in the twilight of eve when nature seems about to give way to sullen night. I cannot but think of the contrast that exists between my present circumstances with that of my former days. But thought absorbed in thought is my portion, and I long to see the day when I shall find one to whom I can reveal my thoughts, and know that they can appreciate them. When these cruel wars are over, oh yes.

Thursday, August 27. The major is in from the picket line today and we have had Inspection by Captain Krom, Brig. Inspector,[63] who didn't think very much of our cripples. Was busy making out the Tri-weekly report, and the Tri-monthly. Had a big time in cleaning out the old papers, since the Sergt. Major is gone, and I want a clear row. Was also working at the muster rolls of the Company, trying to get them their bounty.[64] The weather is cool and has been for two days, so cool that we feel the need of good woolen clothing. How often do I think of the many camp meetings[65] I have been at, as I lie down here in my bunk, but the surroundings are quite different. But anything wakes up the memory of past days, and we would fondly wish the best of them to be reenacted again. May the present be so employed that its remembrance may be sweet and not one of sorrow.

Friday, August 28. Sent in a request to Capt. Cohen[66] of Gen'l Pleasonton's staff to be discharged as a soldier to be promoted to an officer, as I cannot get mustered until I get mustered out. But the document came back, not having my commission aby as Major Van Voorhis[67] has it away. Was busy making out the trimonthly Report, which passed muster. The mail was captured today and I am afraid that I have lost some valuable letters. Sent out scouts as all hands, but they could not find the Rebs, but they had orders to hang all they got. Business is beginning to be very active, and I expect to have a busy time. Also finished the muster rolls of the company. Capt. Kingsland[68] came into camp sick from the picket line. Nothing changing in the Army here but glorious news from Charleston and the entire South West. Hope that Sumpter's massive walls may soon totter and fall.

Saturday, August 29. Made out the Tri-weekly report but was not needed. Was also busy in getting the Company returns in for this month so that I can make them out tomorrow and expect to have busy times, even though it be the Sabbath, but in the Army Uncle Samuel's work must be done on all time and occasions. The mail came in having one for me from Sister Kate telling me of her going to teach at Grapeville[69] this winter. Also one from Bro. Asbury suggesting the strange idea of me becoming an Editor, perhaps jesting. Wrote a letter to my friend Lizzie of Latrobe, thinking she had not got my last or else the Rebs had captured hers. Toward evening we had a gay shower, which made the air fresh, and the night will be cold. Hear tonight, that the stars and stripes float over Forts Sumpter and Wagener.[70] Oh may this be the case for then another glorious victory shall be one [won].

Sunday, August 30. Began the labor of the day and <u>that</u> was not small, having to make out the monthly return, also the muster rolls of Field & Staff for the last four months. Wrote a letter to Sister Kate, and got a letter from Lt. Montgomery notifying us of having got a sick Furlough. Major Van Voorhis came to Regt. and had my Commission, which I was glad to receive. Went immediately to Headquarters to get mustered, but had to send my papers to Gen'l Pleasonton. Had a busy day, and a trying time and could not regard the Sabbath. Lt. Shields[71] also came to the Regiment, making the times seem as of old. Cold in the morning, but warm all day, but not so warm as formerly. Felt well, but tired of doing two duties. But when these reports are over, I hope to have some rest. News from Charleston and I hope that success may still be ours.

Monday, August 31. Was awakened by a Courier coming in to camp, telling us the sad intelligence that one of my Sergts., Martin Supler,[72] was shot, and badly wounded by a party of Rebs who came over the river & to Capture the post. But they found [it] a hard post to capture, and 4 of the six men were captured. The 2nd Corps came here today and we are going to be relieved. But the object is to give us a chance of making a Raid into Dixie. Saw Jonas Ross, Oliver Beatty, Ferguson (of Co. K., 23rd Pa.)[73] who gave me a visit the most of the afternoon. The muster did not come off having too much duty but sent in the reports, and got ready to move. Say we are going to move tomorrow at 2 A.M. to go down to Dixie with 1st Cav. Division. Hope success may again crown our business and another victory be inscribed upon our battle flag.

Tuesday, September 1. Was awakened at midnight to get ready for the move, but Maj. Darlington ordered me to stay in camp, so after getting the men out, and the Regiment started went to bed and a another sleep. Oliver Beatty came to my office and we had a good chat, and I find when one is away from home, he is glad to meet any one. Wrote a letter to sister Kitty, also to Brother Asbury. The weather is fine but not so warm as formerly. The Camp look[s] deserted enough, having sent all out. But the infantry being in close proximity is a comfort knowing that they will protect the unprotected. Health good but the general health of the Regiment is not the best having bad water and a poor camping ground. The Surgeons had a consultation and decided not to amputate Serg't Supler's Arm but they cut out the mashed part, allowing a new bone to be born. Hope they may succeed.

Wednesday, September 2. Slept soundly, but all had not slept as twenty rebs had come across the River, and killing two men dispersed themselves among the pines, and we suppose they are reinforcement for the Guerrilla Moseby. Hear of our Scout, consisting of the 1st & 3rd Divs. of Cav., being down at King George C.H.[74] some 15 miles below Falmouth, but had no fighting yet. News slim. Papers as silent as the grave about Charleston and some are beginning to fear that our good fortune has turned, but all my hopes are stayed in the valor of Gen'l Gilmore and his men.[75] Got a letter of Lt. Montgomery being at home on sick leave. My papers for Discharge have not yet come in and delay in this respect seems to be my portion. The infantry are running around half starved having come away with only short rations, and have to stay longer than they expected.

Thursday, September 3. Had to get up early to send out a guard for the Brig. [Brigade] Train going to Warrenton Junction. Various reports of the Cav. making a raid to Richmond, but toward evening they came in not having [but?] been across the River, but shelled and destroyed the gun-boats at Fort [blank in MS] which they captured of us but in all the thing was a failure.[76] Got a letter from Brother John also from Ed McChesney both being interesting, and spoke of war &c. The Regiment went out on Picket. I took a ride with Capt. Kingsland for peaches, but didn't get any. Had my horse, a fine bay mare, stolen night before last, and I fear she is gone. But I shall not get some old cripple that is not worth stealing. The Infantry started Back to Bealton Station as our Cavalry, they think, is enough to combat the forces of the enemy. Hope we may be, as the Cavalry now have all to do at any rate.

Friday, September 4. The papers came out with a high eulogium for Gen'l Kilpatrick stating that this last expedition against the gunboats was a decided success, also commending his gallantry in charging [our?] "gun boats." Wrote three letters one to Miss R_____d, of M_____e[77] being a new undertaking, also to Bro. John & Ed McChesney. Got the "Greenburg Herald." Nothing new but all worth reading being from home. Hear of us going to change camp going to river to the picket line. Rather strange idea taking Hd. Qrs. and Commissary

Stores on Picket line giving the Rebs an invitation to satiate their hungry stomachs by trying to capture our stores. Had another visit with Capt. Kingsland for Peaches, getting as many as we could eat for the 25 cts note in greenbacks. Yes these War Virginians are eager to amass these.

Saturday, September 5. Began to move early, but required a long time to get out the convalescents, and those trying to play sick, but finally got on the move with our whole train, getting to Ballard's Dam, on the Rappahannock River Between Banks and U.S. Ford, again [at] noon.[78] Sent all the men to the different posts thinking that the sick will be better off there than in camp. Are encamped along the banks of the River and can hear the rumbling of its waters. The Rebs are only on the other side but seem very quiet and social, but only to think of so small a natural boundary, separating the hostile forces, <u>once</u> friends and brothers but now deadly enemies: marauders and not erring brethren. Wrote to my mother, and feeling well and happy. I laid me down to sleep, not fearing Rebs or anyone else.

Sunday, September 6. Spent today in various duties, having a good deal of writing to do. Did not even think of it being sabbath until someone would mention it. The rebs are remarkably quiet, and they are said to be weaker along the line than yesterday. Reports are that Lee is in Richmond, awaiting the result of affairs in the south. Got a letter from home bearing all the news from Mother & Mattie. Had orders of the convening of a Board of Examination to examine some of the officers of our Division, having four of our Regiment, and there are those among them being as high rank as in the Regiment. Have a fair place, not too warm, some sick, others getting so. Have no fears as to my health as I am too busy to get sick. Am happy and contented.

Monday, September 7. Nothing special today. Our officers reported to the board of examination, but the Board was postponed until Wednesday. Hear of there going to be more of us drawn up, but I guess 'tis only a rumor. The old routine of business: writing notes, forwarding papers of all kinds and being troubled with Brig. & field officers of the day, who come around daily to see how we are getting along but leave as ignorant as they came. Spent a good hour of the day in getting the Company books in shape, the Clothing & Descriptive books. The weather is getting cook [cool], and scarcely any rain, so that the boundaries between us and rebellion is getting quite low, but 'tis the <u>Rubicon</u> and they dare not pass it.[79] Health tolerably good.

Tuesday, September 8. Had firing last night by our "enemy brethren," and found out this morning that they thought we were coming over, but they were deceived, we having no such intentions. See that the Reb Flag is still floating over the ruins of Sumpter,[80] but that our cause goes on well. Had a big spell with the Quarter Master, the Major giving him quite a going over as he had only given us half of the forage. Wrote a letter to Samuel Lightcap,[81] and long to get a letter as

I have now good opportunity of answering. But since Maj. Moseby has made so many requisitions for our mail, and got them filled 'tis hardly worth while answering or writing. Spent part of the evening in reading a novel called "The Conscript," and altho over drawn, and in some places ridiculous, 'tis a good thing.[82]

Wednesday, September 9. Had quietness last night and a good sleep this morning. The mail came in but I was forgotten and thought I would not write until I would get something. News are scarce, and from our front I am led to think nothing will be done but we will wait until the fighters of the South whip out the Rebs. Spent the day in reading and writing which generally make me happy as it gives me plenty to do. Sent in a Petition for a Furlough of twenty days for Serg't McGlumphy of my company, also various ones for mustering out of service those who have been commissioned. Got orders of a Foot Race going to be run at Div. Hd. QRs on Sat. This is rather gay soldiering and is a characteristic of our army.

Thursday, September 10. Got up early to send in our morning report. Major Darlington was ordered before the Examining Board. Got a letter from Miss Aggie J., which broke a long silence, as there had been several letters written without being received.[83] Felt for answering and sat down and returned eight pages full, of large size. But this to me in the army is not surprising. Spent the rest of the day making "descriptive Lists" for sick men, "Final Statements" & Inventories of dead men. Philip Gump of my Co. was returned today under guard having deserted July 14th 1863 at Falling Waters. I was ordered to map out Charges and Specifications against him for Desertion, which I did. It may go <u>hard</u> with him, but it will be an example for any of the rest.[84] Hear that our Division is going to Texas, but fear the truth of it, as have not such good luck.

Friday, September 11. Got up but did not feel well, so after breakfast I took a ride, going back to Hartwood Ch. with Capt. Kingsland, getting sutler[85] & commissary stores. Heard firing up the river but could not understand it. Got home feeling better of the ride &c., having been confined too closely of late. The examination of the officers still going on, none yet dismissed. Had glorious news, that makes the blood run warm, and revives the soul. That Forts "Gregg," Battery Wagner were surrendered; and that Gilmore would soon reduce Charleston if Beauregard did not surrender.[86] Also that Chattanooga was vacated and Bragg was routed from that stronghold.[87] Thus light again beams on the future and all goes on 'twas previously. Oh, soon the <u>Crocodile</u> will breath its last breath and die the most ignominious death recorded in the annals of fate.

Saturday, September 12. Had a busy day sending morning reports and muster rolls to Brig. Hd. Qrs. My papers for mustering out came back again waiting something new. Got orders to move taking all our effective force and falling back from the picket line as quietly as possible. Left 100 men on Picket and moved with the rest to Hartwood Ch. and with the Division in directions of Kelley's F.[88] going toward Bealton Station. Had a long dark ride and getting within ½ miles of the Ford, we stopped for the night in a low, ugly flat. Got 30 men of our dismounted men from dismounted camp. Don't know the object of the expedition but suppose we are going across the river to see what may be hidden beyond. Expect to have a hot time but seeing Gen. Kilpatrick at our head all is right and will be right.[89]

Sunday, September 13. Having stopped last night and lit up the surrounding country with its thousand campfires we supped and went to bed. Got up early and ready to start. Had a fine heavy rain just at daylight crossed the Rap. [Rappahannock] just at day with no opposition [and] captured some of their pickets. Moved due south. Turned to the west, then to the north and came upon the Rebs at Brandy Station where joining with Buford's division we drove them to Culpepper C.H.[90] The Fight was severe but our boys charged the Rebs driving them out and capturing four Pieces of Artillery and capturing 40 or 50 prisoners.[91] The boys took advantage of the opportunity and took what they wanted to eat. But what a sight. The entire Corps of Cavalry drawn out upon the Hills, it looked grand. Drove them two miles further and stopped for the night. Saw an old man and child killed in the cellar of his house by one of our shells. This looked hard but could not be helped. Lt. McKay was captured.[92]

Monday, September 14. Hear that the Infantry are following and that the move is general being to feel the enemy pretty hard. Started and firing soon commenced. But the Rebs made a bold resistance at Rapid Ann River.[93] We (18th) were drawn up in line, but the place was too <u>warm</u> and we had to withdraw to the woods, as our artillery was not suited to the distance. Gen'l Pleasonton thought we should go across and thinks we will. Perhaps we may if we get assistance as I think the resistance is only a <u>shell</u>. Fell back to go into camp. Wagon Trains came up giving us our rations being a happy thing for us. The future looks "mixed," sometimes all <u>hope</u>, then again <u>doubtful</u>, but in <u>all</u> prosperous. Had one horse in my company shot, but no men hurt. Have good luck having lost no men yet.

Tuesday, September 15. Had but a poor nights rest being broken by various wakenings to draw forage and rations which we were glad to receive. Expected to have a hard fight today but in this I was disappointed, as the Artillery only skirmished at a distance and the enemy being in force and having the advantage of the ground, it was thought policy not to advance too far. The mail came having a letter and paper from home for me. Answered it, but don't know when I can send it away. Hear of the infantry coming up in our rear and expect a general engagement. From here I see the Rebel's fortifications and their signal flags.[94] The boys seem happy and are dancing and singing around their campfires as if they were at home. Yes, they little care now whether they have to fight tomorrow or not.

Wednesday, September 16. Had various exciting orders and rumors last night, that the Reb Infantry had crossed the Rapidan, and we would have to fall back, that some of our Brigades had been badly cut up. But we stayed till near morning when we got in readiness for a fight, but no fight came so we went into camp again. But soon the firing of Artillery began, and we prepared again for the fray, but lay in reserve all day and had nothing to do, as the fighting was all or principally Artillery. The fighting was heavy and we drove the enemy twice back over the river, and finally they gave it up and staid on their <u>own</u> side. At dark the rumor was circulated that Meade's entire Army was coming up just in our rear and would be here soon. The boys again began their merriment, and I just thought that little they knew of the future but let them enjoy themselves as best they can. Feel well tonight and happy at my good fortune.

   Thursday, September 17. Had a quiet night, and a foggy morning. There was no fighting and all seems quiet along the Rapidan. The Infantry came in and relieved us so we shall soon be on the move. The greatest joke of the war is that the cavs [cavalries] now run out to the extreme front, and our cav. came into Culpepper not four hours after the Reb's train left. Surely they must feeled [felt] bored at, as [we are] now using their Telegraph and R.R. Got orders to move back to Falmouth to watch the movements of the enemy.[95] Started with the 1st Vt. and passed the 2nd Corps coming out to the front. Saw Oliver Beatty, Jno. Coulter & Jonas Ross. Marched through Culpepper, saw our whole army on the move wagons after wagons, and all things predict a speedy engagement. Went into camp for the night and the rain began its patter.

   Friday, September 18. Got up in good time and was on the march. Oh, what a day. For hours and hours the rain poured down as never rain has before, when some one remarked, only Kilpatrick's Cavalry would endure that. Passed through Brandy Station & Rappahannock [River] crossing the pontoon; then made for Hartwood Church, where we arrived at 5 P.M. wet and weary. Our men left on picket. They had left the day before, and as they passed along, Capt. Barker of the 5th N.Y. Cavalry being along was shot dead by a guerrilla.[96] How such base, low lifed villains should be made to suffer the punishment they so well merit. Divided our party, I going with Capt. Hamilton to within 5 miles of Falmouth where we went into camp. Had supper and prepared for bed. Feel well only tired and wet.

   Saturday, September 19. Slept cold and with but little satisfaction. Getting up, had breakfast and started on Patrol to Falmouth. Got there [but] found no Rebs. Got plenty of peaches. Heard of four Rebs being there last night. A citizen direct from Richmond came to us, also a negro, belonging to the 4 Va. Cav. They report only a few troops at Fredericksburg and none for thirty miles back. That Pickett's and Hood's Divisions have gone to Tenn. to reinforce Bragg,[97] and that the Rebs are almost starving and going to fall back and fortify, having begun a battery eight miles long. Affairs around here are slim enough having no rations, and nothing in the country to get to eat. Don't know how long we may stay, not long I suppose. Expect soon to hear of our men making a forward movement.

Sunday, September 20. Got up feeling quite well, and for once in a long time refused my victuals. Thought it was on account of eating so many peaches. A Patrol went to Falmouth and report that two Brigades of Reb Infantry have come into Fredericksburg, supposed to be there to prevent us from crossing, but this we did not intend. All this frightened the major once he moved back to Hartwood Church. The Detachment under Maj. Van Voorhis came to us with forage and rations, also brought the mail, having one letter for me from Ed. McChesney. Still find out how bitter some people around here feel toward us, and think they would not scruple to do the worst toward us. Feel better and shall be well soon. Hear our men here crossed the Rappahannock and now hold the highland.

Monday, September 21. In despite of the fright I slept as soundly as ever and awoke this morning all right. Major Wells or Hall of 1st Vt.[98] came with a small detachment and taking 90 men we started for Falmouth to see what may be there. Got there but found no fight so we scoured all through the country going along the river bank looking at the few Reb pickets that were on the other side. Saw the ladies of Fredericksburg, but at a distance and they beconed [beckoned] us over. This made all right and we sent a detachment to go to Falmouth to picket there. Major Darlington also went to Ballard's. Occasionally a shot is heard from across the river and fighting may be afloat. Shall not this be the glolden [golden] opportunity to crush the nefarious Rebellion? Shall not success now crown our efforts?

Tuesday, September 22. Nights as cold as ever, and the day was not far behind. Got a fine fatted Beef from a union man, which made rather happy hearts. Had nothing to do today, and got lonely by spells when I thought of that sentiment:

> Soldier brave will it brighten the day
> And shorten the march on the weary way.
> To know that at home the living & true
> Are knitting and hoping & praying for you.[99]

But after all we are not so bad off, and not so devoid of pleasure as many are the hours of mirth the [that] pass the heart of the soldier. Wrote a letter to Ed. McChesney, but being away from the Brigade we can have no mail either way. Hear of us all going down to Falmouth tomorrow, also to take a scout around by the Potomac Creek where my old acquaintance of former picketing reside. Feel well, having good health & plenty to eat.

Wednesday, September 23. Prepared to move today, but had inspection of arms first by Major Van Voorhis, who put on quite a style and for once became very military. Call the boys out suddenly to catch their arms dirty. He lectured all though. Moved our camp one mile further toward Falmouth to Borea Church (Baptist)[100] and have a middling site, but have plenty of peaches and chickeypins[101] all around. Went with a patrol to Falmouth, and stopped to graze the horses until dark, when we left for camp much to the satisfaction of many. But I was not pleased by any means to see so much style all at once, and now patrol night and day for no use, when it was not the intention of the General, being only here to watch the movements of the enemy. The nights are cold and the day warm.

Thursday, September 24. The Forage and Rations came today and with them the mail but my name was forgotten. The report is that our cavalry is driving the enemy, and that the Infantry under Gen'l Meade has got marching orders with eight days rations so I hope the work may be done soon. Rumor of Rosecrants having a hard fight with Bragg in Tennessee, and that he was worsted; but I hope better news.[102] But why or how can this state of affairs last long, that Gen'l Lee can fight Gen'l Meade and Rosecrants also. Remained quiet all day and the patroling has ceased for a spell. The people are constant visitors wanting safe guards, and usually they get them sending the sick, to get them out of the weather. Don't feel very well myself having eaten too much fruit.

Friday, September 25. Slept long but not sound. Got up and had a good breakfast. Had inspection of Arms. Had inspection of Horses, and all that had poor, or sore backed ones had to lead them three miles to pasture chagrining[103] them sorely. Went on a patrol, going toward Stafford C.H. two miles distant. Stopped at the houses along the road, and got acquainted with more of the Virginia Ladies, and flattering myself of being well acquainted with this part of the county. In our roaming we found a fine beef, which we brought in and butchered, making us a good ration of beef. Saw a Richmond paper, claiming victory for Bragg, and acknowledging the whipping of their cavalry at Madison.[104] All quiet, and we are enjoying ourselves well, but would rather rest than always patrolling.

Saturday, September 26. Last night was cold but had a good sleep. Had the boys to pasture their poor horses. Sent out patrols in all directions. I stayed in camp to take charge of it. Wrote two letters one to my Mother and one to Bro. A. Hear of one Lt. & eight men of the 1st Vt. being captured last night. This will make us more diligent, and made Maj. Darlington ask for 12 more men, so my company went leaving only one, my cook. Had a gay time around the officers around the campfire after dark. Capt. Britton[105] sang many good songs and all felt happy. Presently the rumbling of heavy feet was heard & all called out "Cavalry," so it was being the 9th N.Y. of 2 Div. to relieve us. They say Rosecrants is in a bad situation, and the Army of Potomac is going to relieve them, while we here fall back.

Sunday, September 27. Was relieved this morning and prepared for the march. Went to an old citizen preacher to call in a safe guard. Had a long talk with his black eyed daughter and exchanged cards. Got on the march about noon and began moving toward Grove churches. Then toward Kelley's Ford. Stopped about dark for supper but the rations were out. Still we fed the horses corn, and the boys ate the roasting ears. Moved on across the ford, past Brandy Station and toward Culpepper, but getting lost we stopped for the night around a cornfield, and having had a cold and long ride we built fire and went to bed. Felt good over the rumor of going to Tenn. so as the novelty of going so far would counteract every other opposing consideration.

Monday, September 28. Having got breakfast we pushed going through Culpepper C.H. and were going around to find the Brigade. After a long time we found it at or near James City,[106] ten or twelve miles west of Culpepper C.H. Rations were scarce, and only came up at dark. Mail came having a host for me from Sister Jennie, Bro. John, Miss R.[blank space in MS]d of Meadville, F. Arter; Chas. Hall, Mr. Samuel Lightcap, and Brother Frank beside a host of official letters and papers, so that I had plenty to keep me busy all evening. The boys were hungry, and they began to hallow [hallo] for "Hard Tack," when the Gen'l came along and gave the officers a severe reprimanding, which mad [made] the boys feel quite angry. The company is growing, having now fifty men. Had orders for a brigade inspection again tomorrow. Major Darlington ordered to Div. headquarters for getting frightened and drawing off his pickets while on the Rappahannock.

Tuesday, September 29. Had a busy day. Beside making reports of various kinds, I had to get the Regiment out for Inspection which was a hard matter, and required a long time. The paymaster came and payed all evening. Payed nearly all and many happy hearts were the result. I got nothing not being mustered as Lieut. and would not accept the pay of Sergeant Major.[107] Wrote a letter to Bro. A. [Asbury]. Major Van Voorhis in command and is making various changes. Got orders to have the monthly return in by noon tomorrow. This shall not work. Can't see any point in all the activity. I sometimes think they are niging [niggling] us up, and putting us thru a general inspection preparatory to going to Tennessee. May be. Felt well most of the time but by being troubled <u>so</u> much I grow impatient and wish for a change or an end. Hope long, hope ever sounds loudly, and I follow on.

Wednesday, September 30. The Major finished paying our Regiment and departed, leaving me to go into my report strong. Got it finished by one P.M. Had to make out a good many inspection reports. Maj. Darling [Darlington] got through with the Court-Martial, but I had to make out charges against six of my company for desertion and have six more. Got a paper from Lizzie of Latrobe, and it had many little sentences written on the inside margin. I sat down and wrote her a sililoquising [soliloquizing] letter, also one to Samuel Lightcap, also one to Mollie of M. Affairs are getting better, having a nice camp, and all goes merry as a marriage bell. Hope that we shall come make some effort to crush the Rebellion for to pass three years in this state and then look back and find nothing more done than shooting ball would be a poor boon.

Thursday, October 1. The morning set in very wet indeed, and the rain poured down all day without intermission, putting me in mind of the rains of last July. Spent part of the day at the rooms of the Court Martial, and am beginning to think some of the boys are getting tired of deserting. Was busy all day, but expect soon to get through the heaviest of the work. Hear nothing of our move of the Army, but still think the Army shall not go any farther forward. Sometimes I get lonely. I see how fastly I am falling away in morals and I fear the future but trust that all shall be well. Hope the election at home may turn out in favor of Liberty and Curtin, for the friends are making a gigantic effort against the super human energy of the copperheads.[108] May god prosper the cause.

Friday, October 2. Today was pleasant again. The warm sun shone out gladly and we are happy. Got a good supply of clothing for the men, and expect to get an overcoat for those who had to throw them away by order last campaign. Wrote a letter to Frank Arter. Got papers from home. Nothing new. All is quiet. But I have no doubt but that a storm is to be the result of this calm. Sent in my muster out papers, and hope to be successful so that I may be mustered. Had to spend most of the day at the Court Martial. But this is giving the boys such an example that they will not go home any more. Hear of Lt. Col. Brinton going to come back. Oh that he may, for then we should have someone who could command and not insult. But the latter is playing out and friends are forsaking.

Saturday, October 3. Having to be up late, I slept sound and long, and only awoke to get my breakfast. How fast the time flies by! When I look back over a year, I see but little done, so I expect it will be for the future. Had to make out a list of deserters besides the regular business. Had rumors of Buford and Gregg's Divisions going to Tennessee but it is only gunmen I think.[109] Lt. Smith[110] put in arrest today again for writing a letter to his old secesh friend Capt. Morris. Hear of Lt. Montgomery having resigned his commission.[111] Am not particular, what he does. Have orders for a Brig. Review tomorrow. Have great times to get the Inspection Reports. This life seems to grow wearisome upon me, nothing to read nothing to reflect upon and all things only point to the same thing. Killing of time.

Sabbath, October 4. Today is the Sabbath, but not much time to think what it is. Send morning Report to Brig. Hd. [Quarters]. Go to Court martial and not at Review in consequence. Don't know but that some move may result from the Review. Can't tell. Major Darlington in arrest to await the decision of the Court Martial, Major Van [Voorhis] in command. Wrote a letter to Sister Mattie. Got one from her. Wrote also to "Florette," Mass., Webster, on an experiment. Weather is cold, night chill and some are chattering with the Ague. Had a good inspection 'tis said and passed very creditably. Felt well, but rather lonely, as I now hear the boys far down the lines sing those old tunes that are to sooth my troubled breast when a boy. But my mother no more sings them but perhaps is now thinking of me as far away I roam.

Monday, October 5. The day comes and goes and leaves us the same as yesterday. Not quite the same, for one day has passed never to return, and it's good and evil past forever. Went to Div. Hd. Qrs. to get a man mustered into the Company. Hear of a General Review tomorrow. Saw the order discharging me from the service of the U.S. to enable me to receive promotion so that the past few months are right. The day is fair, and at Headquarters all things and people are gay, and happy. Hear many rumors, so many that my head swims, about going to Tennessee, falling back, & all the regiments whose time of service expires next summer have got the opportunity of going home for sixty days to recruit. Several of the Regiments have expressed their desire to accept.

Tuesday, October 6. Had to get up early to prepare the review, which came off at Div. Hd. Qrs. at 10 A.M. Had a gay time, seeing Gen'l Pleasonton and his staff. The Review passed off nicely pleasing the general who returned the same by complimenting us. Had a severe headache on account of being without dinner so long. Lt. Guy Bryan going on duty as Adjutant. I was relieved from duty as Actg. Adjt. Wrote a letter to Angelina, Webster, Mass., trying as an experiment. Changed quarters down to center of camp, but sleep in Adjt's office. Am glad to get back to the company, as it needs my care. Saw Lt. Montgomery's resignation, and I am glad something is being done to arrange niceties. Cold evenings and good weather for taking fevers.

Wednesday, October 7. Getting my Discharge I did not feel <u>so</u> well in being a citizen that I would forgo the idea of leaving the service and loosing nearly four months pay. So I went to Div. Head Quarters with Lt. ~~Montgomery~~ McCormick[112] and was mustered into the service as an officer for three years by Jacob Briston, 5th Michigan Cavalry.[113] The Adjt. also got mustered, and relieved me greatly to my satisfactions. Report of the Pickets being attacked last night, two captured, one killed.[114] Gen'l Kilpatrick says we cannot fall back, being too many Rebs in front. Sent my Commission & Discharge home to my mother, also a letter. Wrote to Sergt. Supler, to Peter Polan [Poland], father of one of my men being lost at Smithsburg,[115] also to Charley E. Hall. Commenced Raining and rained gaily but almost too cold to be <u>very</u> gay. Happy am I tonight.

Thursday, October 8. Was aroused last night by the Genl's orderly bringing orders, but did not find out till morning what they were. Reveille was blown one hour before day and all ready to move. The tents were torn down and soon all were ready for a march. But we waited all day but no move was made, so the tents were put up again and affairs assumed the same shape. The rumor was that Lee was making a move against us with his entire force. But two divisions of 3rd Corps came out to support, and we felt a little easier.[116] But this I suppose is only a feint, and we intend to hold the front until the Infantry fall back. Wrote a letter to Eps. [Ephraim] Brunner giving him the News. Felt well all day. The weather pleasant and the boys generally in good spirits.

Fig. 8. Edwin Forbes, "Brandy Station, on the Orange and Alexandria R.R., Light Artillery Going to the Front," September 15, 1863. A portion of Weaver's unit was surrounded, cut off, and captured by Confederate cavalry here on October 11, 1863. (Library of Congress)

Friday, October 9. Having spent another night in the old camp, arose as usual without any excitement. But all things indicate a change soon, and Rumors say the Army has all fallen back. That Lee is over the Rapidan, and we must fall back, but Gen'l Kilpatrick says no fall back without "fight." So we will go in, no matter what the issue may be. Wrote letters to Dennis Murphy and Sergt. Supler of my company being in the Hospital.[117] Had another excitement toward evening and all the cry was to arms, but this too was a feint. But the first Battalion went out on Picket some 10 or 12 miles to see what may be the reason of all the noises. Am getting tired of this excitement and hope that they will soon move out, or get to fighting. But this thing of waiting and waiting, oh this suspense it torments me. Health good.

Saturday, October 10. Were early called to horse and on the move, but instead of going toward Washington we went toward James City and found that the Pickets had been fighting, and they reported some of the Infantry captured. But the cavalry got to fighting and the Infantry fell back. The rumor is that all the Reb army is on the move, going toward Martinsburg.[118] We fought all day skirmishing hard. Our regiment was in reserve except Co. I and C, which was detached to aid the 5th N.Y. We had to stand mounted, expecting a charge. The swift winged messengers of death flew thick and fast but Fortune was ours as none was injured but some of the 5th N.Y. was wounded. The firing stopped at dusk, and we were again put on picket for the night. Felt quite angry; think that we were imposed upon. During the day we had spent in listening to the boys calling out to the Johnnies[119] to "come on if your dare" &c.

Sunday, October 11. Just as day dawned we were drawn off Picket and fell back. Found all the road clear and affairs looked as if we really meant to fall back. Stopped for breakfast a short distance of Culpepper. Started and came to Culpepper, but here we waited for some time to get the trains out of the way, when we commenced to fall back. The Rebs came on in our Rear, all cavalry. We had to fight them and hold them back. But soon we found to our surprise that they had flanked us and got in our rear at Brandy Station, Ftz. Lee on our Right, Hampton on our Left.[120] The charge was ordered and the 2nd Brig. of 3rd Division cut through.[121] Next came our turn. We were ordered to charge. We did charge, and drove the 1st N.C. Cavalry, but not being supported, the 7th & 12th Va. Regts.[122] closed on our rear and after several desperate attempts to cut through we had to give it up. So Lt. Tresonthick and myself with about thirty men were prisoners of war, and Major Van Voorhis wounded.[123] My horse shot twice through the neck. The fighting was desperate, being Kilpatrick's Division against the entire Cavalry Corps. Camped with the 7th Virginia for the night.

Three

"What a Little World in Itself Have We in Libby"

Libby Prison, Richmond, October 12, 1863–January 16, 1864

On October 13, 1863, two days after his capture, James Riley Weaver entered Libby Prison, where some nine hundred Union officers were incarcerated under increasingly overcrowded and unhealthy conditions. A cartel signed in July 1862, which had provided for prompt paroling of prisoners at set exchange points and emptied most prisons, had all but collapsed by fall 1863, as each side accused the other of violating its terms. Confederate prisons in Richmond refilled as that summer's protracted fighting sent streams of Union captives to the Confederate capital, straining the city's food resources and increasing civilians' fears for their safety. Brig. Gen. John H. Winder, provost marshal of Richmond and overseer of Confederate prisons, had only limited authority to coordinate prison administration and, by necessity, adopted piecemeal approaches, leasing commercial buildings and open land, securing home guards as wardens, and purchasing rations and supplies with inadequate appropriations. Libby was one of a half dozen prisons located in Richmond's commercial district near the James River and the canal.[1]

As a ready-made warehouse in a secure location, Winder thought Libby an ideal choice for a prison, but its physical shortcomings became apparent during Weaver's captivity. Libby was composed of three connected buildings constructed between 1845 and 1852 for a tobacco factory; in 1854 Luther Libby rented the building as a grocery store and ship chandlery. Anticipating more prisoners as war resumed in spring 1862, Winder leased the building from Libby in March to incarcerate Federal officers. The brick structure was three stories tall; inmates were housed on the second and third floors in six rooms, each 45 by 105 feet, with interconnecting interior doors. About 150 prisoners would have greeted Weaver when he arrived in his new quarters. Wooden bars covered the small windows and left inmates exposed to summer heat and winter cold, but admitted little

53

light. Three rooms on the ground floor were used as a kitchen (middle), a hospital (east), and for administration (west). Slave quarters, a carpenter shop, and dungeons were in the cellar.[2]

The educated officers confined in Libby compiled vituperative wartime exposés and postwar memoirs that accused prison officials—Maj. Thomas Pratt Turner, prison commandant, and, especially, Col. Richard R. "Dick" Turner (no relation), prison warden—of causing needless suffering and even delighting in tormenting their captives. Weaver's diary affirmed the prison's harsh physical conditions, but he hurled more invective toward Richmond's pro-Confederate newspaper editors than against the guards. The building had running water, but limited bathing facilities and privies created unhealthy sanitation and hygiene. Vermin infested everyone and many prisoners suffered from diarrhea, dysentery, and typhoid. Furnishings—tables, beds, blankets, clothing, cooking equipment, and eating utensils—were sparse, and inmates either improvised or did without. In theory, prisoners of war were to receive soldiers' rations. In reality, both the quantity and the quality of food varied but always included corn bread and either rice or beans and, occasionally, salt pork or beef. Officers with money supplemented their diet by arranging with the guards to exchange Union greenbacks for Confederate dollars at below-market rates to purchase food from city vendors. As word of prisoners' deprivations reached the North, the Union government, the United States Sanitary Commission, a private relief agency, and inmates' families and friends sent blankets, provisions, and personal supplies to Richmond. While these alleviated some suffering, many prisoners believed prison officials arbitrarily delayed their distribution, pillaged the boxes, or diverted them to Confederate soldiers. Relief, like the exchange cartel's breakdown, became another front in the sectional propaganda war.[3]

Prison diaries like Weaver's, which were written with no plans for publication, not only reveal incarceration's daily rhythms but also its psychological impact, especially after early parole became less likely. In the face of extended confinement, officers self-organized to provide internal order and some semblance of community that was independent of but did not directly confront prison authorities. Messes of twenty or so men shared provisions and rotated cooking chores; French classes and lessons on military tactics continued their education; card games, chess, and cribbage filled the hours; practical jokes and ribaldry released tension; books and dances ("trip the gay fantastic toe") provided amusing diversions; and the *Libby Chronicle,* an oral newspaper, and the Libby Minstrels, a troop of musicians and jokesters, satirized their guards and Confederate leaders. Debates over the accuracy of exchange rumors (even skeptical Weaver occasionally succumbed) or the latest war news gleaned from Confederate newspapers or from newly arrived "fresh fish" preserved some measure of free speech and con-

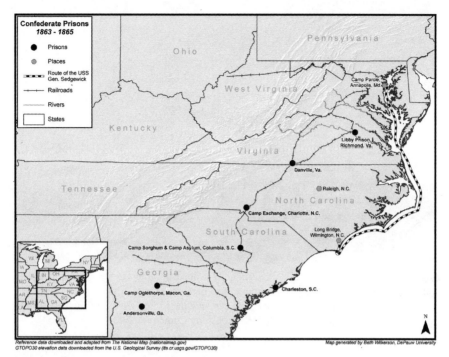

Fig. 9. Confederate prisons, 1863–65. (DePauw University)

tact with the outside world. Weaver rarely questioned the Lincoln administration's calculus in not resuming general exchanges, astutely noting that "were our
private[s] as well off as we officers, it would be policy to stop exchanging, since
one man is of more worth to the Confed. Gov. than to us, being so much harder
to have his place refilled." For the prisoners, diary-keeping created private space
in noisy crowded places. In solitude, amid inmates' constant jostling, feet tramping on wooden floors, and a cacophony of voices, Weaver was able to objectify
his imprisonment and reflect on his previous life's meaning and on his future
hopes. Through his diary, he imagined himself free.[4]

Monday, October 12, 1863. Having spent the night, partly in sleep partly in reflection on the past and future thinking of Libey Prison &c. I got up but had not
breakfast as usual being out of rations, as well as the most of my clothing and
ten dollars of green backs the Rebs forced from me. We saw Major Van Voorhis
being tolerably badly wounded.[5] Passed on to Culpepper <u>under guard</u> and found
Lt. Wilson[6] and some more of our Regt. making 4 officers and 32 men of our
Regt. and 11 officers and 299 men in all being the Prisoners for a week past. Got a
dinner in town. Saw one Brigade of Rebs passing through, they cheered as lustily.

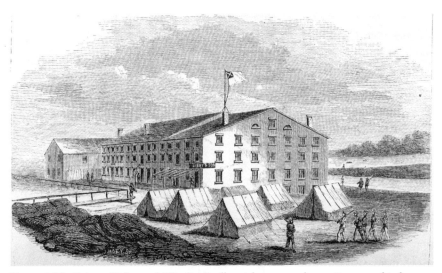

Fig. 10. Libby Prison, Richmond, VA. Originally a tobacco warehouse it was used to house captured Union officers. Weaver was imprisoned here from October 1863 to May 1864. (Willard W. Glazier, *The Capture, the Prison Pen, and the Escape: Giving a Complete History of Prison Life in the South.* New York: U.S. Publishing Company, 1868)

Having got on the [rail]cars to go to Gordonsville[7] we heard the report of cannonading on the front, and soon the flash of Artillery was seen on the hill near town all of the boys looked for Kilpatrick.[8] The Rebel dead and wounded came in thick and they began to be frightened. But the firing ceased. We started at dark, being on the top of cattle cars, and cold to the extreme. Passed through Orange C.H. and got to Gordonsville at 12 at night. Were put into a hard old shanty to sleep. But we fell asleep and knew no more till morning.

Tuesday, October 13. Awoke and were taken to a Major's office [and] for the third time they took our names and sent us back to wait till noon for the cars. Got permission to go for breakfast, under guard. Got one not so good in quality, but we ate eagerly being very hungry. Was astonished at the prices having to pay $1.00 and 50 cents for a pie or cake. But they preferred <u>ours</u>.[9] Started in passenger cars for the city of Richmond. Saw nothing scarcely but bush, and desolation, all the road being desolate of vegetation except in a few places. Got there, being surprised to find the city so free from fortifications but the land was so marshy, that it would be impossible for any army to approach that way. Found the long famous "Libey" and after giving our names again we entered its precincts to meet our friends Lt. McKay, Lt. Potter, Lt. Leslie, Lt. Laws of 18th P. C., Ed. Gay Lt. of 11th Pa. and many of our Division being over 900 in all.[10] They gathered around us like bees to hear the news, and we were welcomed. Liby is not so bad as I expected but the idea is <u>hard</u>, as Exchange is not in the program now.

Wednesday, October 14. Having spent the night in a good sleep, began to look around. Found many strange things. The grub slim enough but sufficient to keep from want, getting 20 ounces soft bread and a small bit of meat per day. But the officers having money can buy anything extra they want. We had to give up our greenbacks, and they give us seven confederate dollars for one of ours. Prices are wonderful high but when divided by seven they don't appear so desperate.[11] The officers are all anxious to be exchanged, but there is no hope. The Rumors are that there is hard fighting going on at the Rappahannock, but they are not to be relied upon. A lot of prisoners came in, no officers. Wrote to mother and Lt. Mc-Cormick,[12] having to leave open the letter. The Prison seems very healthy, but the officers complain of the "grey backs"[13] being troublesome. They also say the men on the Island (Bell)[14] are very sickly and dying fast. But what a set of people at any rate. It seems a Hades for sure with its sinks[15] all filth.

Thursday, October 15. Am getting to see what "Libby" is, & learn its ways. Officers cook their own meals in messes, having 22 or 25 messes. Three of each cook each day. I belong to "Mess 4," eating at 7 A.M., 1, & 5 P.M. The day is spent in sleeping, eating, walking the floor for exercise, together with other athletic exercises and the nights in dancing and games of chance. They have got a violin and forty or fifty "trip the gay fantastic toe" and thus drive dull care away. On all sides the chess board and the deck of cards meet the eye, but 'tis hard to sensure <u>any</u> amusement in a situation like this. Another lot of prisoners came in, being from the Rappahannock and they Report Mead's Hd. Qtrs. at Centreville.[16] Expect to hear of hard fighting soon or else of Gen'l Meade falling back on defenses of Washington. I am thankful for <u>life</u> and <u>health</u> and sorry that it has been the lot of so many to be here.

Friday, October 16. Today was spent as usual nothing occurring to change the monotonous tramping to and fro over the floor that to the uninitiated seems oppressing. A few more prisoners came in but no officers. One Doctor exchanged by special exchange. But altho I wish for that looked for day, I would hail with equal joy the day that liberates our enlisted men from their dark lot, as they have not the advantages we have. Having recitations in tactics and French.[17] I should enter the class had I books, but how could I study here. 'Tis hard enough to endure the time by spending it in every conceivable way. News of fighting on the front that Gen'l Meade is falling back to Arlington Heights, but only rumors are of but little importance. Feel healthy but the grub is limited, and one would surely starve did not we have something to buy extra bread.

Saturday, October 17. Having eaten my piece of bread and drank my cup of rye coffee began to walk the long isles for exercise. Spent a part of the time in playing cards with the others for amusement. Had a meeting of the inhabitants of Libby to hear the "Libby Chronicle" read being a paper published by the officers and serves for amusement and instruction.[18] It was read and took well having good hits &c. at various subjects and persons. At night had a Exhibition in the lower room, a negro concert giving us plenty to laugh at and a large crowd.[19] The Rebel officers were present and they seemed to enjoy it, altho frequent hits were made at the manner we were treated and the southern Confederacy. But all part of pleasantly [pleasantry] and gave us a good opportunity to "laugh and grow fat" being now essentially necessary since the grub we get could signally fail in securing that object.

Sunday, October 18. Today was pleasant indeed. The warm sun shown out, and the balmy air fanned the brow reminding one of many happy days spent under circumstances quite different, but altho we are refused the liberty that makes life pleasant, we enjoyed ourselves quite well. All news and rumors died away and for one day we had nothing to harp upon. The Chaplains having all been exchanged we had no preaching but there was prayer meeting in the evening.[20] Have nothing to read, nothing to do, and the time hangs heavily, and when I think of passing many days thus, the future looks dark, and we are apt to complain at our government for not relieving us of this bondage, but they must have some just cause for not making the exchange and we must submit. But much feeling is felt on this account, and especially on account of special exchanges. My health is good and appetite better.

Monday, October 19. Felt well today, and the morning paper made me feel much better stating that all the "Rumors of great victories were nowhere, but that they (the Rebs) had suffered badly at Bristow Station having come upon the 2nd Corps and Gregg's Division of Cavalry.[21] The day past as usual, the "Flag of Truce" Boat came up but no exchange, and Gen'l Meredith[22] went back empty to the sad fortune of us all. But many boxes of provisions and clothing &c came for the officers, which made the hearts of many happy as now something good to eat is a real Godsend. Bishop McGill[23] of the Catholick Church preached for us in the afternoon dwelling on his beloved theme "No salvation apart of the (Catholic) church." Thus we pass days, weeks and months.

Tuesday, October 20. This morning the papers proclaim as [of] the escape of the notorious Dr. Rucker who they say has been in the way of our Exchange, as the Confed. authorities demanded him for trial for horse stealing before he entered the service.[24] Our Government was not willing, so Exchange was stopped. But he is gone and the rumor of exchange has received an impulse. The day was fine. News of the movements of the Army scarce, and we just stay here, without knowing what is going on. Everything scarce, no paper, pen or ink and correspondences must be few and short. Am happy because I look back and see how many dangers I have past [passed] through and as yet am scot-free from scar or maim. Oh may our cause so prosper that soon this war will close.

Wednesday, October 21. Today one year ago I, upon my 23 birthday, became a soldier by enlisting as a private. How many changes has past [have passed] since. I look back with a good degree of pleasure to see what success has filled my path. To look forward for one year to my twenty-fifth birthday I dare not, and were it possible for me to lift the curtain that enshrouds the future I would hesitate before I would glance at a destiny so uncertain. Quite a lot of Prisoners came in some 12 or 15 officers and near 1000 men, being gobbled up on the falling back. Capt. Penny-packer[25] of our Reg't also came in, we gave him a joyous reception but no <u>feasting</u>. I am sorry to see <u>so</u> many of our men coming here, and misfortune seems to be our lot. But we must trust the future, hope that there lies our deliverance.

Thursday, October 22. The land of Secessia is truly blessed with delightful weather as scarcely a cold rainy day has crossed our path since I arrived at this Mausoleum. But today as usual the pleasure created by a pleasant outside was broken by the unfavorable news in the papers. But they are so grossly sectional that nothing can be believed. The [They] report Genl. Banks with Staff & 15 Regts captured.[26] Hear of four of our men breaking confinement from Castle Thunder,[27] and shooting one of the guards, they skedaddled. Quite a lot of boxes of all descriptions came in, also a good number of letters but nothing for me nor did I expect anything. Wrote three letters to Bro. Frank, Sister Jennie and Ed McChesney. Spent part of the day reading and playing chess and the remainder sleeping, ruminating and walking the floor to and fro, up and down, back & forward. Health good and am getting along [as] well as expected.

Friday, October 23. The boxes of provisions and books are still coming and we has [have] great need of them, as threats are made that no more bread may be bought extra to what is furnished us, as the people are about starving in the city, and every paper speaks pathetically of the state of affairs, as scarcely a day passes but that some thieving is done. Tobacco is to be stopped also as the officers spit on floor and out of the windows. For my part the future of the confederacy is gloomy, and I begin to fear for my own account least in their poverty we starve also. As usual all the "good news" of Banks' capture was contradicted, and Genl. Lee has given up pursuing Genl. Meade having fallen back of the Rappahannock. Gov. Curtin and Brough are elected by large majorities being a strong arm for the administration.[28]

Saturday, October 24. The rain began its fitful splashing, and in making the external world more undesirable, it made me the more contented with this seclusion, and as I stood looking out of the third story window of our <u>palace</u> upon the dimpled and broken surface of the James River just by I thought of the past, and all its many changes seemed to flip through my mind as the changing surface of the swollen River. Nothing past [passed] today and it was spent as the nearly two weeks that have preceded it. Rumors of all kinds, the monotonous tramping of many uneasy men keep the old tobacco factory or warehouse being now christened "Libby" or "Confederate States Military Prison" in its constant uproar. Threats of cutting of all privileges are made, and the authorities seem to try to stress us out. But from such people what could we expect.

Sunday, October 25. Today the day of rest was only a day of excitement, as two officers having escaped last night from the hospital we had to give up our eating room for a more secure place, as Hospital and the rest of the sick officers were confined there and starved to make them tell how the others got out. Had an indignation meeting to try a surgeon of our Army who had written a secesh letter to the Reb authorities and he was surely dealt with. But, by explaining the matter to his own dishonor he was let go free. Fourteen officers came in, being captured by Gen'l. Imboden at Charlestown, being nearly all infantry.[29] News of the President calling out 300,000 volunteers this fall. This is good; may our friends at home see the necessity of responding promptly. Wrote a letter to Bro. John. The weather is very cold, and many having no blankets they have a cold time. I have only an overcoat, but do not suffer.

Monday, October 26. Last night was very cold and many slept cold, and the coming winter has no charms for us, but rumor says that our Government is going to send clothing and blankets for us. But still our men on Bell[e] Island must suffer since they have no shelter from the cold rains that have been very frequent of late. But the Rebs say they are going to give them shelter. Wrote two letters, one to "Lizzie of Latrobe" and one to "Mollie of Meadville." The prospects for exchange have entirely died away, since our Government has notified the Rebs that she will not exchange any more. But many officers look forward with strange feeling to an imprisonment such as we have for many month or years during the war, and such a fate as this may well awaken our fears for the future. Got some tracks [tracts] and a testament sent us by the Christian Commission[30] at Philadelphia. They were eagerly picked up.

Tuesday, October 27. Were notified at Roll Call that we should having nothing but bread today for allowing the officers in the lower room to burst open the door and get among us. So we had almost a <u>fast</u> day, but no praying, at least to any extent. Had a job of washing my underclothing, being a new and arduous job, and I thought many times of those who could accomplish this much better than I. A lot of our sick and wounded prisoners were sent north for as many sick Rebs. The men are said to be dying fast, and loads of coffins go past our Hades daily. Skirmishing after "grey back" has to be done daily and proves more successful than fieldwork, but not as dangerous [on] our part. Chess playing, card playing, checkers, &c. continues the same, but having cut off the Gas the evening sports has to be discontinued. A lot of letters came in but none for me yet not old enough.

Wednesday, October 28. Feel tolerable well today, but having a severe cold I am not as I wish to be but thankful that I am well as I am. The Exchange question is not entirely dead as the Papers speak of its possibility. They (the Rebs) seem anxious to get us away since they say we have eaten up all the beeves and are now commencing on the sheep. But they have many other reasons of getting us away, as then they could reinforce Gen'l Bragg & trouble Gen'l Grant.[31] Had the Ethiopian concert[32] tonight but it did not amount to much, being pretty well worn out. Still they sang some beautiful songs, other[s] comic enough to get up a laugh. Long to hear from home or get a letter from any friend, for this life is very lonesome, and to break its monotony is our whole aim, but only partly do we succeed.

Thursday, October 29. Selfishness is a strange temperament of the mind and under circumstances like these it exhausts and destroys nearly all the little happiness we might have. Yes, every little occurrence seems to be an insult, and for the most part those imprisoned become more and more sinical [cynical]. Was appointed as cook today having with Lt. Potts, 115th P.V.[33] to cook for three days. But having only a dinner of Beef and rice to cook each day for our mess of 24 men we can get through and it be only exercise. The coffee is played out, and our victuals are now dry bread for breakfast and supper and beef and rice soup for dinner. A lot of boxes came in also letters. Clothing & blankets are sent to our men by the Government in care of Gen'l Dow.[34] This is a good thing as our men were freezing, and will be much better off now. Had the visit of some secesh officers and ladies.

Friday, October 30. Still on the cooking committee and have almost graduated in the culinary department, but having only the one meal to cook per day the labor is small. The Rebs are complaining more than ever because of our Government not exchanging. But they have great reasons, wanting to get off from feeding us, and their men to reinforce Genl. Bragg who now stands in great need of them, but I feel confident that there shall be no exchange until the summer campaign is over, and we shall get out about Christmas. Have a good lot of literature sent by the Christian Com. and all eagerly picked it up being glad to get something to read. How contemptible, how low are these who have by misfortune got possession of us, even slandering the Bibles & testaments sent us from home. The day fast approaches when all this scale will change and we [are] free.

Saturday, October 31. Today finished my Administration as Cook for mess &c. and am glad of it. The papers say old Genl. Joe Hooker has attacked Gen. Longstreet down in Tennessee and is driving him, which gives us all hope that success may secure Chattanooga for us without fail.[35] The Richmond Inquirer[36] says, "Altogether too many prisoners taken in this war." But I would like the brave Editor to practice his idea of no surrendering for only once and see how it fits. Show these sit-in-an easy-chair warriors are big things and bold as chained Lions. The clothing sent to us by the Sanitary Commission[37] was distributed, but as usual, those who least needed got, being <u>selfish</u> enough to see others go naked to gratify themselves. I with the majority got socks and drawers. Many got shirts and all wanted. I was astonished to see how childish some men are and even those holding high positions. So unconstrained were many that it was almost impossible to issue them for the crowd of "seekers" homing around. Thank the Lord I am not so blind as to sacrifice honor for the sake of a shirt.

Sunday, November 1. The day passed as usual with all the uproar of our thronged pallace. Spent the day in reading Baxter's "Saints Rest"[38] and tracts sent by the Christian Commission. The blankets were distributed to those having none. I got one; also the rest of the boys being with our mess, for which we were a thousand times thankful to friends at home who gave them and the Government who sent them. Report of part of our men going to be sent away from Richmond to the interior where they may freeze, but this would only please them as they would do anything to compel our government to exchange prisoners. The day was pleasant, cool in the morning and more comfortable in the afternoon. As I eat by the window and looked out upon the waters of the James River, and saw the sun go down in majesty as I have seen it a thousand times, I thought of <u>home</u> and strangest feelings arose, and the sound of Prayer from the upper room broke the revery [reverie].

Monday, November 2. The faces of many brightened by the information that the authorities were going to give them some money in exchange for the "Green-Backs" taken from them when they came in, which they began to fear they were going to loose [lose]. They got seven Confederate dollars for one greenback and fifty dollars each month is to be the monthly amount. In consequence we had some good eatables, but a few dollars don't go far, paying three dollars for a small cup of butter, one dollar for six apples, or twenty crackers or four sheets paper & envelopes. Wrote two letters, one to Mr. Lightcap and one to Epr. Brunner[39] and would have written more but had no paper. The Handkerchiefs were distributed, I getting one. The officers then certified to what they got & how much they were willing to pay the Sanitary Commission when getting exchanged which would amount I should think to $5000. The weather is delightful, but the night[s] are cold and a heavy frost marked the boards outside this morning. Have good health.

Tuesday, November 3. The papers report this morning heavy fighting at Chickamaugia and that our forces are driving the Rebels. Oh how we look with interest to that place, and should Genl. Grant [have] early success in whipping the Rebs all will be ours. Exchange is again agitated, and the papers say our authorities have broken the "Cartel" and will not exchange any more prisoners, and that in retaliation, they ought to feed us the least possible allowance that would sustain life, and here after take no more prisoners. Nearly 200 boxes came up on a flag of truce boat for the officers making many happy with a good lot of clothing, eatables, reading matter, &c. The weather is so pleasant outdoors that I would fain step upon the mother earth again, and enjoy a ramble among the desolate looking streets of Richmond. But this I cannot, and I must be content. I am really thankful for my present position when I reflect what I might be and how many dangers I have gone through.

Wednesday, November 4. Still good news from Gen'l Grant, and Joe Hooker with the 11th and 12th Army Corps are doing wonders in their new field of labor.[40] Every thing seems to predict a forward movement of our Army, which is devoutly wished by most of us. I felt very lonely all day and with a melancholly turn of mind not usually my fate. Had but slight amount of bread, and having eaten my crust with unusual relish I sat by my window and followed my mind's vagrant thoughts. But soon the concert began in the lower room, and I went there to break the spell which it did wonderfully having excellent music, good jokes and plenty of mirth, so that all thought of sadness took wings and gave place to better feelings. How I would love to be with the Company for they are left now without any officer to see to their wants.

Thursday, November 5. Report from the south good, that we had gained advantages that <u>must</u>, if possible, be overcome. But the siege of Charleston hangs on and Genl. Gillmore fires away, by the hundreds of shots per day.[41] How we hope that that "nest of Rebellion" may fall a prey to our forces! One Doctor exchange by special today and his Esculapian[42] brothers feel badly that they are left behind. Also Dr. Pierce took his leave of Libby having gotten a pass from not only Libby, but this vile world of sin. He died in the evening.[43] A lot of letters came but none yet for me, being yet to[o] "fresh"; or, as they say, say "fresh fish."[44] Had games of chess with Lt. McKay, &c. Had some thought, a good deal, and got rid of the melancholly mood that had brooded over me for many hours. Felt well.

Friday, November 6. Having bought a few sheets of paper and envelopes I wrote to Sisters Kate, Jennie, & Mattie, also to Cousin Bell and Adjt. Byran[45] but having to leave the letters open for the perusal of both the Rebs and our Government, letters loose most of their pleasure having to be confined so strictly to generalities, and what all may know. Every day seems to add some new insult to our prisoners, and increases my hatred to the Rebs. Genl. Dow was over at Bell Island and reports our men starving, and the mean low-down officers don't allow them to go near the river to wash for fear of them escaping. See that they are guarded by several pieces of artillery. I hope in God the day of retribution is nigh at hand. To hear the[m] speak of their high estimation of humanity and then treat men who are helpless in such a manner is worse than barbarous. I hope our authorities will do all they can to exchange us as soon as practical.

Saturday, November 7. A very heavy frost this morning and a cold day with high winds, made us rather uncomfortable. Papers say Col. Irwin has been appointed Asst. Com. of Exchange of Prisoners,[46] and as he has been here not long since, many think he will do something to get us out. A large quantity of boxes came again, also letters, but none for me. The day being boisterous the cooks failed to get the fire to burn and so we had no dinner, which was lamentable enough to <u>us</u>. Had an exhibition in the evening, gotten up by the East end of the Prison consisting [of] forensic, dramatic, and comic performances, being tolerably good. Have a good string Band, extemporized by the officer buying the instruments of the Rebs. News from the front scarce, and the Armies seem quiet, but Kilpatrick is said to be in Falmouth. I would he were in Richmond.

Sunday, November 8. Today was a busy one, but by looking around you would not judge it to be the Sabbath. You see men engaged in their daily amusements, and some go so far as spending the day in shuffling their cards <u>for gain</u>. This is too bad, and prosperity cannot follow such a course. I wrote two letters to Bros. John & Asbury, read some, heard a sermon in the evening. An officer came in just at dark and tells the good news of the capture of Hoke's and Hay's Brigades at Kelley's ford, having been cut-off.[47] So we see that the idea of "we surrender" won't do, but they are also glad to save life by hoisting the white flag. All things indicate a forward movement of General Meade since President Lincoln tell him "'go in' and if you succeed the glory is yours, but if you fail I'll take the responsibility."[48]

Monday, November 9. Oh how the Rebs squirmed in their papers this morning, having to come down to the capture of two Brigades and the[y] begin to cover their loss by reporting <u>our</u> loss in killed as dreadful. The authorities at Libby also felt sick and tried to seek some comfort by misusing us, and old Genl. Dow who formerly was allow[ed] to remain seated during Roll Call had to stand this morning but he only said, "Every dog has his day." The News from Tennessee is good, as Grant has obtained successes that rendered him secure, and will compel Bragg to fall back, as they cry out, "must we stay here any longer in the mud." Felt unwell all day and could not relish what little corn bread we get, but I hate the idea of going to the Hospital although they say they get better usage than we do. But "Time at last makes all things even,"[49] and I hope the time will occur soon when we may turn the scale.

Tuesday, November 10. Felt worse today and eat nothing at all, but making a bed I spent most of the day there. A lot of Blankets came for the Privates on Bell Isle, and Genl. Dow was refused privilege of going over to distribute them, since <u>they</u> say he violated his former pass by meddling into the Commissarial department, which he denies but says they all hallooed "for bread" and they were starving, &c. Good news from the North as all the States have gone in the elections for the Union. New York gave a majority of 19,000 Republicans where it went 1,000 last year for the Democrats.[50] One officer from the 2nd N.Y.[51] came in saying Meade was coming on and was in the vicinity of Culpepper C.H. and that a hard fight is to be had. Genl. Averill has also gained a victory over Jackson,[52] and our forces are said to be active down on the Peninsula.

Wednesday, November 11. One year has rolled away since I left the land of my parentage and began the life of a soldier. One month also since my capture and I look back upon all these scenes with interest. Then an anniversary of my departure from home has passed, and with anxiety I look forward to the day when I may again get free and be on my way homeward. The signs of a speedy fall of the Confederacy has come upon us. Today no beef and nothing but corn bread, and they have to acknowledge that they can get none. Preaching by a Bishop out of the Episcopal Church of the City.[53] An exhibition was given by the "Libby Prison Minstrels," which took well, as they usually make some good hits at the low life Rebs. Oh how sick I grow of their gassing in their papers about Southern Chivalry and Northern Trash since every day exhibits them the more hateful. Feel better.

Thursday, November 12. Affair in Libby are beginning to grow to a point, as today they have given us sweet potatoes instead of beef and but a few of them. Rumors of the Surgeons, some 80 or 90, going to be Exchanged, which will leave a hole, but 18 or 20 officers more came in from Burnside's [army][54] and we don't get much smaller. Strange Place is Libby, and stranger yet to the uninitiated for as he came in, he will hear "fresh fish," "fresh fish," "close up, close up," then, "give us air, give us air," while he is surrounded by as many as can hear to learn the news. Well do I remember the first evening of my arrival! Expected a fight by Meade but nothing yet. One thing is solved: Grant is safe at Chattanooga. I am getting to feel better but not entirely well, and I doubt if any of us get along as well for the future as in the past, as the Prison is left dirty and the grub getting more inferior each day.

Friday, November 13. The cornbread loaves have gone into corn flat cakes, and the two sweet potatoes into one, so that our diet will be light today. Seven hundred of the Prisoners are gone to Danville, Va., today and seven each day until they have 4000.[55] The papers say there are 930 off. [officers] and 12, or 15000 men of ours here. Some two or three hundred boxes came and as many officers expecting were disappointed. These had to be guarded strongly to keep the citizens from stealing them. Read an account of "Libby," having been given in the Phil. Inq. by one of the Chaplains, who was here and exchanged, being a graphic and truthful description of the nefarious Rebs.[56] Today was fine and instead of the cold blasts of wind that made us "walk the floor" for exercise we have the balmy days of June and apparently it infuses spirit into all. But like caged birds on the opening of spring be [we] beat the bars of our cage and sigh for freedom. Still I am thankful that I am alive and as well off as I am.

Saturday, November 14. All things have again grown quiet, and Gen'l Meade is said to be waiting for "the opportunity." The Surgeons are getting very uneasy and fear their delay may grow into an entire disappointment. 'Tis said that the Government is sending thousands of rations and clothing for the men so that it seems as if we may remain all winter. The mail came in, and I had the good fortune to get one from Bro. John, being the first since I came here. It seemed a happy receipt as it was the only assurance I have that they at home know of my where-a-bouts. The rain toward night began its fitful falling and thickening toward dark gave Lts. McKay and Tresonthick[57] plenty to think about and plan. But it cleared up about 9 o'clock, and all remained the same. The rations of beef was resumed today, but 'tis <u>horrid</u> to see what a quality of corn bread we receive.

Sunday, November 15. Another day has gone with its usual amount of excitement and noise. Nothing today of a religious nature but prayer meeting in the evening, while many spent the day in play, "poker" and other games of chance, to the disgust of the more moral. Had our usual "white stone" bread, and rice soup. Wrote a letter to Brother John in answer to his of yesterday. I am beginning to feel myself again as [I] relish my eatings, as the homely adage is "Hunger is good sauce." A great many boxes came and being usually padded with papers we have more now to read, this keeping us busy and "whiles away the lonely hours." But when I think of spending the war here, I get the horrors[58] as so long a time would only seem to be a blank in my life. Oh had I some interesting books. Had I some scientific books or those on the [illegible], and I could spend the time both profitably to myself and my government. I fear to send for them least we be exchanged too soon.

Monday, November 16. The time passes fastly by and although 'tis not the most agreeable place to spend ones spare hours yet they are passing, and leaving no trace of anything we have done. News from Meade and Grant but everything is so contradictory that we can find out nothing. Many times are the Doctors made the but[t] of some joke by some one raising the report of their "leaving in a few moments" and often at the dead of night someone call[s] out "Fall in Doctors," "Fall in," and when about out they find they are not gone to the Land of Liberty, but made the butt of some joke. Health good, and by eating the solidest cornbread ever baked, the stomach gets pretty well filled.

Tuesday, November 17. A good lot of boxes came and Capt. Turner[59] thought he would not issue them but after consultation he let the owners have them. The men are daily going to Danville and those on the island coming into the houses vacated. Owning to some delay we got no dinner to [until] dark when it was too late to cook and we had to go to making our own supper. Rumors of the Army fighting at Gordonsville and the [that] Meade is driving Lee out. It gains but little credence. The weather is again delightful. The sun shines warmly and the warm southern breezes feel very pleasant to the pent up prisoner. Grub still getting dearer and scarcer, but the most difference seems to be in the depreciation of their currency, gold being worth 15 dollars of the Rebs money while greenback is worth 8 or 10 dollars.

Wednesday, November 18. The contentions about exchange seems to be growing warmer, the Rebels charging our government with breaking the cartel, showing that they (the Rebs) are loosers by the [their] own exchange principle. Oh how they squirm and advise their men not to take any prisoners, nor be taken, but still they love life too well not to except [accept] the alternative, to <u>death</u>. The papers get very rampant and advise the feasting of their lank stomachs on the bodies of the union prisoners, made lank enough by their short rations. But all this is only the foam of their wrath. Soon they will be <u>cooled off</u>. Today was pretty indeed, and as quiet as pretty as there was not [naught] to break the pleasant feelings that only occasionally fall to our lot. I felt well and think I enjoy myself better than any times from the begin[ing].

Thursday, November 19. This was a fortunate day for me, as the mail came having three letters for me and a lot of paper. One from home, one from Bro. John, and the other from Chas E. Hall, which was a type of his big soul. I thought myself fortunate in all, but sorry to hear of the Diphtheria being among the family at home. Wrote two letters, one to "Aggie" of Salem[60] and the other to Chas. E. Hall. Had an Exhibition of the Libby Minstrels but did not attend; think that the crowding was too dear for all I got. Felt happy all evening and having had additional rations through the boys that got boxes from home. I also felt better on that account. The day was fine, warm and sun shining in all his beauty.

Friday, November 20. The Rebs reported the capture of a Penna. Reg. of cavalry this morning and we all said there goes the 18th Pa. and sure enough in the evening in came Adjt. Bryan, Dr. Withers, and Lt. Herrington, saying that the <u>Colors</u>, Camp, and 36 men of our Reg. was gobbled up, being surrounded by 1500 Rebs near Ely ford on the Rapid Ann.[61] Oh how angry we felt and how chagrined to think of the <u>Colors</u> being captured, but from all accounts the Reg. was not to blame as headquarters was sent out on the Picket line, some four miles from the Brig. [Brigade]. We gave them a welcome warm and interesting and kept them talking to 12 o clock at night and made their <u>misfortune</u> our fortune by way of hearing news.

Saturday, November 21. The boys tell us of Major Darlington being dismissed [from] the service with little or no sympathy of the Regt.[62] Lt. Jones also, Lt. Shields for Disability.[63] Lt. Montgomery of my company the same, leaving me the only officer in the Co[mpany].[64] That Lt. Sellers, Co. "A," was shot in the fight and Capt. Kingsland, commanding the Regt was wounded, and many other things interesting to us all.[65] The day passed fastly by and looking around I see eleven officers of our Regt., which makes me think that I am with the Regt., while the 2nd N.Y. (Harris Light) still keep us in the shade[66] they having over a dozen.[67] Rained nearly all day. A load of government rations came to the Prison and we are to get a portion of U.S. Provisions which may aid us considerably.

Sunday, November 22. The day was fine and passed off quietly and nothing to distinguish it from any day of the week. The Rebs have taken a great notion of washing and scrubbing the Prison, being at it all the day, or, rather, making the

Niggers do it. The meat has played out and we have potatoes in place, but having a good quantity of cornbread, we dispel the hunger. The Doctors not gone yet, but are looking to go soon, and Dr. Withers is very anxious to get off. Have felt better since our officers came in giving us so much to talk about. Having sent a letter to my mother yesterday I forgot to notice it until now. Nothing of a religious nature except a Bible class and prayer-meeting which but very few improve. Health very good &c.

Monday, November 23. Little passed today worthy of record, and, in fact, the quietness was the most surprising. The papers report and contradict the capture of Knoxville with 2200 prisoners[68] and the Rappahannock quiet as Genl. Meade is resting on his already won laurels. But the canvassess of the Rebs make us think that they have met with some reverse, as this is the usual precursor. They even threatened to pen up Col. Strait's men by themselves.[69] The Flag of Truce boat came up having a lot of boxes, and, many think, the Confederate Surgeons. Did not feel very well having a touch of dyspepsia[70] as carried by inactivity in spite of course corn bread.

Tuesday, November 24. The surgeons were rejoiced this morning to see that one hundred and twenty one Confederate Surgeons had come to City Point[71] and that they would get out. They were soon ordered, "Get ready" when all was "Hurrah for the Exchange." Ninety odd left and Major White[72] managed to go along in place of a sick surgeon, but some one was so traitorous as to tell the authorities, who telegraphed after him, and had him brought back. Such treachery! Sooner would I see such are all hanged high as Heaven, than the worst Reb in the Confederacy. The Rebs informed us that we would not get anything to eat until we would tell who had staid [stayed] in his place. But all cried out "Starve." The Surgeon stated the affair and all was dropped. 'Tis said they would not give our officers their greenbacks but meanly pawned off eight of their worthless rags[73] for one of ours.

Wednesday, November 25. As we expected, the paper came out giving us hark[74] advocating that we should be starved, that the authorities should not allow anything to come from the North, as we can now live better than they. Adding many horrid stories told by the Surgeons, &c. The guards got very cross and would cock their pieces at every head that would look out of the window, and all say they have surely been defeated, since this is a sure criterion. Mead is quiet but he will move surely and give Lee a trial and I have no fears as to the result. Have better living by reason of the boys coming in having a good amount of Confederate money, by which we buy butter &c., but the Rebs only give us bread, corn bread. Have a slight touch of heartburn and I have almost concluded to quit drinking coffee.

Thursday, November 26. The papers gave us the joyful intelligence of the defeat of Bragg's Army as he telegraphs: "The left center of the army gave way, soon the entire left, and I have withdrawn all back to Chickamauga Creek." This makes our cause the brighter, as fears of Longstreet pressing Burnsides were rife.[75] If only Gen'l Meade pushes Lee big things will result. Despondency seems to take possession of the Editors and they bear out their wrath on the prisoners who seem now cursed by the continual execrations that fall upon us. Had a good dinner, having gotten U.S. rations sent from the North. Had an exhibition of the "Libby Minstrels" being good, having some dull scenes of "Libby." Health middling good, weather comfortable.

Friday, November 27. News of Gen'l Bragg's defeat grow into positiveness while the papers give forth a <u>howl</u>, <u>painful</u> but pleasant to hear, and with additional news of Gen'l Meade making a forward movement from the Rapid Ann, one side of this momentous struggle seems to brighten.[76] And I am compelled to think that in this struggle depends the life or death of the Confederacy. The boxes came in. Leslie got one. The letters were distributed. I got five, one from Bro. John, two from mother, one from Mollie of M., and one from Ed. McChesney. This was a happy time for me, and I gloated over my letters with the fondness of a miser for his money. Had a little trouble with the Dyspepsy, but think it only a slight attack.

Saturday, November 28. News of Gen'l Mead's advance, and also of Gen'l Butler who was put in command of Gen. Foster's command at Norfolk, who is said to be advancing,[77] while the news of Gen'l Grant pushing Genl. Bragg and threatens to drive him out of Georgia. The rumor of Gen'l Burnside's surrender is turning out false, and he says that he is able to hold Knoxville for twenty days. Military affairs have taken quite an excitement and the result of this fall campaign will no doubt change the aspects of the so-called Southern Confederacy. Gold coming down in the North quoted at 147½;[78] this portends good. Wrote two letters: one to mother and one to Ed. McChesney. A lot of prisoners, one officer came in tonight, and as usual we gave him a noisy reception, while the many surrounded him calling for the news and thousand inquiries.

Sunday, November 29. Today was one of excitement, both to Libbyites and the Rebs, as the news was that Butler had made a landing at Harrison Landing while the Homeguards went down early many taking umbrellas along to screen them from the rain falling fast. A Lt. Col. came in telling us of the advance of Gen'l Meade, and that Lee would have to fight or fall back, while the men made for great jests by calling out "Killpatrick is coming" since we have an idea that he will come after us.[79] All things seem in fine condition and had this rain kept away the sanctity of this day would be forgotten by the contest of armed enemies. Wrote three letters, to Bro. John, Mr. Lightcap, and Mollie of M. glad to have opportunity of the mail. The weather is cold, health as good as expected. Rations the same consisting of Reb cornbread and U.S. pork.

Monday, November 30. The rain ceased and all expect that Genl. Meade will give Lee fight, something devoutly hoped for. All day the cold breezes have been blowing and the [this] is pronounced good for fighting. News from Gen'l Grant good. He being in pursuit of Bragg who is fleeing, while Longstreet will have to give up the idea of capturing Burnside. The papers still hold out and try to keep their coverage up by big talk, as a "cowardly boy whistles going through dark woods." The poor yankey prisoner gets hait [hate], and the authorities are recommended by fire eating Editors to starve us the more. Thanks to men who have better sense, as they know how to treat us. The cold blasts make us gather around the stoves, whose frail heat bearly [barely] suffice[s] to warm the nearest.

Tuesday, December 1. Today was very cold, and with all the fire that could be mustered, we were cold. News exciting sometimes in favor of us, then on the side of the Rebels. Ten officers and 100 men, prisoners, came in from Burnside. A few officers from the Potomac, causing an excitement by reporting Gen'l Butler coming up the Peninsula with Gen'l Schenks and the 22nd Corps,[80] while the papers say that Grant is hanging on the rear of Bragg with <u>bulldog</u> tenacity. Bragg has resigned and Gen. Hardee but in temporary command.[81] Some officers very sick in the hospital, and noise being made above, the officers had to be removed. Should the weather get much colder, we shall suffer here this winter.

Wednesday, December 2. Not so cold today, the sun shines out warmly and you hear the remark "What a good day to fight." All look to Meade and wonder why he delays so long, some censure, other excuse, but the papers say still no fighting and many doubt Meade's intention to fight. A <u>few</u> days <u>must</u> decide. The Exchange is again agitated, and the Rebs offer to exchange man for man, rank for rank, (Niggers also) parolling the excess, but our government doubt their good faith, and having been embezzled once, they don't care about trying again. I often think that were our private[s] as well off as we officers, it would be policy to stop exchanging, since one man is of more worth to the Confed. Gov. than to us, being so much harder to have his place refilled.[82] But the idea of remaining here for years is too dark to endure and I cannot but dismiss all such conjecture.

Thursday, December 3. Having nothing to read but novels I grew tired and went to whittling a set of Chess-men, being of late a follower of Paul Murphey.[83] Got three letters, one from Bro. John, from Eph. Brunner, and Frank Arter, the latter being a famous large one of <u>four</u> pages of <u>largest</u> size. Boxes are still coming by the hundred and we are beginning to live fat, and by the sight of pieces of meat and bread lying around, no one is in danger of immediate starvation. The eating is much improved, being mostly rations from the North. Did not feel very well, having sick headache but only lasted a short time. Nothing of fighting from Meade. Reheard rumors of Burnside's capture, also that he is to be relieved by Gen'l. Foster.[84] Got one monthly payment of Confed. rags for greenbacks, getting 50 dollars per month.

Friday, December 4. Today the papers seem to try and make the picture as dark as possibly by saying that Meade has fallen back, which we cannot understand. Grant falling back; Burnsides captured, John Morgan ran off from the Northern Jail, &c.[85] But this is too much and shall apt to be all untrue. Still, the news are hard to be understood, since we all thought Meade was in for a fight, but perhaps only to keep Lee off of Grant. Wrote letters to Eph. Brunner, Frank Arter, & Frank Thomas. The exchange question forms a standing subject of conversation and speculation, but nothing nearer the accomplishment. Have gotten quite a lot of tin dishes and having gone into a private mess with Lt. Wilson & Adj. Byran we are getting along finely. I cook dinner, Bryan supper, Wilson the breakfast. All well and happy.

Saturday, December 5. They have changed the tune again and say Longstreet has fallen back and is apt to but [be] cut off or will at least have to fight for his position with the main army, so he has not captured Burnsides but is in danger of capture. Mead has really fallen back, as prisoners came in stating his intentions to cross the Rappahannock.[86] Got a letter from the Island of Corpl. Gregory of my company, who was captured at Hagerstown on July last. He and Johnson the only ones of my company there.[87] Wrote two letters, one to the Regt. to Sergt. McGlumphy,[88] the other to Corpl. Gregory's friend. The time rolls fastly by and soon two months will count the time of my imprisonment. Health good.

Sunday, December 6. Having no paper today we have peace and quiet, being no rumors to excite. The day was very fine and the sun shone out warmly and all were gay. The Rebs seem anxious to create exchange, and say they are willing to exchange niggers [and] parole all giving surety that none shall go to duty until the difficulty is settled. But our government will not be apt to trust them since they have been so faithless heretofore. Tomorrow both Congresses meet, and no doubt some influence will be brought to bear upon our government maybe even to except exchange at a sacrifice of principle, but I hope that the Rebs shall have to give in first. Nothing religious except prayer meeting. Health good, eating good enough, and spirits lively.

Monday, December 7. With the usual amount of gas the papers speak of successes &c., how the members of Congress in session should act being active and not going off in bombast. Nothing new. Charleston is still being bombarded but with nothing of any consequence, but the most surprising thing is that still that detestable fort holds out. The niggers are busy at our "Hotel" and having began white-washing. They shall have labor for a week. A "Flag of Truce" boat came up bringing many boxes &c. to the disgust of the Editors who, no doubt, are piqued because they can't have "ham & eggs." They are trying hard to have this stopped asserting that Libbians are "feasting" whereas they should starve. The armies have settled down and shall go into winter quarters I suppose.

Tuesday, December 8. Being very cold last night we slept soundly, and only awoke with the sun. Not often do we pass so quietly as many seem to go to bed only to have fun, laughing and singing to the discomfiture of many. Mail came having a letter for me from sister Jennie, being short, but I was glad to hear from her. See many accounts from the surgeons who have gone north and they seem to be creating quite a feeling for us, on the part of our friends.[89] The picture is sad indeed but no doubt the reality is far worse, as nothing can be represented bad enough to imply "starvation." Glad am I that the hands of hunger have not gotten hold of me. This day is pleasant, the weather as fine as summer and were it not for this confinement I would be happy.

Wednesday, December 9. Adjt. Bryan got a large box from home, and I being in his mess had the pleasure of partaking of the many good things he got. The rumor is that the boxes and money are stopped as the Rebs assert that our Gov. prohibits their prisoners from having these things. Read President Davis' message trying to smooth things very much, especially the Currency & late Chickamauga fight. Also read Gov. Lecher's. They seem despisable, fancying they are the proto-type of our forefathers and fighting for the same object, asserting that we forced them to fight. But how false![90] The day was fine; cold, but sun shining. Spend the day in reading and the night in the same with some amusement.

Thursday, December 10. Congress seems busy gassing and Senator Foote in speaking of the Exchange of prisoners is said to have proposed to inquire into the rumor of ill treatment. He also goes into the President with a vengeance.[91] Wrote a letter to sister Jennie. Felt happier that [than] usual partly caused by the good thing we have got to eat. 'Tis when shut up here, we are foolish enough to set our hearts upon what we eat and drink & feel disappointed when these fail. Truly my mind has changed materially on the estimation of human nature since I came here, as all seem so selfish and cynical that many quarrels are the result. In myself, I observe the change, and for this reason I particularly now pray for speedy change. A lady soldier was discovered on Bell Isle Friday. She will be sent North.[92]

Friday, December 11. The weather has been delightful and the air today as soft as Spring. Hear of Gen'l Wagner being captured by the rebs and will soon be the inmate of Libby.[93] We are surely throng enough, but no matter to them how thick we may be. Boxes and Barrels for the Off. [officers] & men are coming con-stantly, notwithstanding the report of their going to stop them. Two Boatloads tonight. Tonight makes two month since I was captured and I look back with in-terest to the many changes that have come to pass since then; but fastly the hours have flitted by! And soon the old year will go by on swift wings, no doubt, leaving us the same as many days has found us. 'Tis a hard thought when combined with that of home and friends, and often makes a topic of thoughtful converse.

Saturday, December 12. Wrote a letter to Captain Casy, Com. at Fortress Monroe, for a Box of provisions. Both Lt. McKay and Lt. Wilson got large boxes of good things from home, and we are living well. Had a supper of Soda Crackers, Ham, Beef's Tongue, puddings, (white and head) cheese, condensed milk, sugar and tea, besides the little delicacies such as peaches and prunes, making no doubt better eating than half the families in Richmond could afford. We are getting along very well so well that should the boxes be stopped we would hardly know how to go to eating the rough cornbread, which now lies around in profusion. Felt sad to see it least many of the privates have to suffer and would willing eat of our cornbread.

Sunday, December 13. Bryan got a box of clothing and getting two new blankets, which give us the handsome bed of six blankets and two overcoats, since he and I bunk together. The usual din continued during the day, the constant sweeping and scrubbing that grows a nuisance continues and the day after dragging its slow length along passes by with but little to break the monotony of prison life. The small pox that were reported in the brick building among our men are said to be dying out and only two in three cases are left. Happy for them and us. I am truly thankful for such good health, which has been still improving of late. The prospects of speedy exchange is far in the future.

Monday, December 14. Read Pres. Lincoln's Message[94] in the Reb papers being a good thing, but of course was the object of derision by the Editors of the Reb Sheets. Read the order preventing the Gov. [government] or our friends from sending more provisions to us beyond what was received at City Point. The authorities also informed us that this is the last day anything can be bought in the city, so there was a general reckoning and settling up sending out for over $10,000 of provisions merely to get rid of the money which will be useless to us. These objects formed the topic of the day and complaints and threats were the result, should ever the opportunity be afforded. We have good eating so far and enough to aid for a month.

Tuesday, December 15. With the day began the bringing in of vegetables and commissary stores something like Noah did before closing of the Ark. As we expected to have no more chances to send out for anything, this being stopped. Nothing of interest past today, the amount of rumors was slim and most have concluded that Exchange is not in the order of things for many months. Have nothing now to do but cook and eat, with some reading and occasionally writing a letter. Wrote one to sister Mattie. Have roll call at 3 P.M. instead of 9 A.M. The day was fine, the air pleasant, and for the most part all are enjoying themselves, but look hard at the stopping of Boxes. That is a cold pill.

Wednesday, December 16. Two officers are said to have escaped last night, bribing the guard before the Hospital.[95] Say our private boxes are not stopped, only the Gov. Sanitary and of the Christian Commission. Mail came in. Three letters for me, two from Bro. J. W. & the other from Sister Kate. Answered both, speaking freely so that the Rebs may not send them. Rumor of General Averill threatening the "Virginia & Tennessee R.R." having a body of 4500 mounted infantry & cavalry.[96] Hear of Col. Byran being with the Regt., but cannot hear of its whereabouts.[97] Health good, weather pleasant.

Thursday, December 17. Rained last night and this morning, but the weather not cold. News of Gen'l Averile bringing a train of cars near Salem on the Va. & Tenn. R.R. [and] that our Army is going into winter quarters about Culpeper C.H. All those in the Hospital who could walk were sent out, since some of them bribed the guard. The guard was arrested and he shall have the worst of it. The Reb Congress is fighting, trying to pass a Conscription to force all into the ranks but those detailed by the President. The papers oppose this and sometimes hint a dislike even to the president. Sometimes I feel lonely and allowing my mind to go back to the past, when surrounded by friends, and all things worthy of living for. I wonder off until I grow lost in reflection.

Friday, December 18. Today passed with but few variations, spent in cooking and eating, reading the news, scanty enough, and playing games of cribbage. The correspondent of the "London Times"[98] and the artist of the Illustrated, made a visit to Libby, and thought our situation very good, which offended many. Had to give the list of names, rank, company and Regt. of the officers, being thought to try to find out the names of a few officers of nigger Regts., who have denied their regiment through fear.[99] Charleston still holds out and, by the news from that point, is [it] seems destined to withstand all the naval and land forces that can be brought against it, either by power or stratagems. 'Tis dark, not cold, and no comfort essential to partial happiness is wanting but hoping for our release we try and be as merry as we can.

Saturday, December 19. Last night Col. A. D. Strait and Capt. Lee tried to escape by bribing the guard, but the Rebs were ready to intercept them and they were captured and put in the dungeon.[100] News of Averill trying to get to Danville to liberate the prisoners there, which I hope he may succeed in. The James River is very high, higher than my time since I have been here, occasioned by the recent rains. The air is damp and cool but we are tolerably comfortable. The bickerings of [Confederate] congress are growing more frequent and like the disturbed ant nest its members are running into every whim trying to get some way of filling up the Army, and restoring their bankrupt currency, but all their efforts only seem to show their imbecility.

Sunday, December 20. Today seemed to pass more quietly than it usually does, and being cold, the most gathered around the fires, and contented themselves over their book, usually novels (Bulwer's, Scott's, etc.),[101] while a few [are] still so low as to go to gaming. The report of Averill succeeding in releasing the Danville prisoners. Thought the water was going to fail, as the river got too high for the engine to work in pumping the water into the basin. Felt well today. Have good eating, and felt thankful for so good a time in the land of secession, but long to change this sedentary life for the field since with the latter comes the idea of freedom and revenge. But fastly the time passes by and surely the day of retribution is at hand.

Monday, December 21. Last night was cold and this morning the canal had a coat of ice on it.[102] Cold all day, making us draw around the fires. Expected news but nothing important. Saw the account of the Death of Genl. Buford in Washington of Typhoid Fever.[103] The Cavalry has lost in him a gallant Brave. Read with interest the proceedings of the court on the case of Mrs. Allen who is being tried in Richmond for Treason.[104] Got three letters; one from Mother being the fifth to me and recei'd [received] none, so that I fear my letters are not passed. Got one from Bro. John and Bro. Asbury seeming as gay as ever. The report of Averill releasing the Danville prisoners is premature, as he is reported to be in Salem yet, and the rebs think they can capture him but I doubt it. The capture of 2 companies of Reb Cav. on the Peninsula confirmed.

Tuesday, December 22. The night was cold but the day warm and delightful so that the outer world seemed to contrast so strongly with the inner as to make us long for freedom. Felt-sick with a Headache, not bad. Three officers, Captains, were chosen by lot from the N. England States to be put at hard labor at Salisbury, N.C., for the retalliation of three Reb. Officers used in the same way, for officers of Negro Regts., who have been unaccounted for by changing their rank when captured. Capt. Litchfield, 4th Maine In., Capt. Chase, 1st R.I. Cav. and Capt. Kendall of the Signal Corps were the unfortunate ones.[105] They bear it well. Were left in prison yet. Wrote three letters to Mother, Bros. Jno. and F. A. W.[106] Hear of Kilpatrick making a raid up the Shenandoah valey, his task to aid Averill. Stewart is said to have made a raid on the O[range]&A[lexandria] R.R. at Bealton.

Wednesday, December 23. Day unusually pleasant while the time was spent very indolently being nothing on hand but to try to amuse ourselves. ~~wrote three~~ A load of boxes came up from City Point, and some say the private boxes are coming still. Also sent out again for private dishes, among which many turkeys and chickens for Christmas while great preparations are going on for the Libby Minstrels going to give their last exhibitions tomorrow night. Averill is said to [be] safe, having illuded his pursuers and got off with but small loss. The Commissioners are met in solemn conclave trying to come to some agreement for having us unfortunates go home. Hope they may succeed and that New Year may see us once more free.

Thursday, December 24. Active operations for tomorrow and the Libby Minstrels have got their Programmes out &c. Strange work indeed for Prisoners of

Fig. 11. Playbill, the Libby Prison Minstrels. This performance occurred on Christmas Eve, 1863, about two months after the group was organized. (*Journal of the Illinois State Historical Society* 56, no. 2 [Summer 1963]: 330. Courtesy of Joseph O'Brien, Washington, PA)

THE
LIBBY PRISON
MINSTRELS!

MANAGER,	·	·	·	·	LT. G. W. CHANDLER
TREASURER,	·	·	·	·	CAPT. H. W. SAWYER
COSTUMER,	·	·	·	·	LT. J. P. JONES
SCENIC ARTIST,	·	·	·	·	LT. FENTRESS
CAPTAIN OF THE SUPERS,	·	·	·	·	LT. BRISTOW

THURSDAY EVENING, DEC. 24th, 1863.
PROGRAMME.
PART FIRST.

OVERTURE—"Norma" ....TROUPE
OPENING CHORUS—"Ernani"..........................TROUPE
SONG—Who will care for Mother now..............Capt. SCHELL
SONG—Grafted in the Army.....................Lieut. KENDALL
SONG—When the Bloom is on the Rye........Adjt. LOMBARD
SONG—Barn-yard Imitations.............................Capt. MASS
SONG—Do they think of me at Home................Adjt. JONES
CHORUS—Phantom..TROUPE

PART SECOND.

Duet—Violin and Flute—Serenade from "Lucia,
             Lieuts. Chandler and Rockwell
Song and Dance—"Root Hog or Die,......................Capt. Mass
Banjo Solo..Lieut. Thomas
Duet—Dying Girl's Last Request......Adjts. Lombard and Jones
Magic Violin....................Capts. Mass, Chandler and Kendall
Song—My Father's Custom............................Lieut. McCaulley
Clog Dance ....Lieut. Ryan

RIVAL LOVERS.

JOE SKIMMERHORN...............................Capt. MASS
GEORGE IVERSON................................Lt. RANDOLPH

PART THIRD.
COUNTRYMAN
IN A
PHOTOGRAPH GALLERY

PROPRIETOR..................................Capt. MASS
BOY...Lt. RANDOLPH
COUNTRYMAN ....Maj. NEIPER

MASQUERADE BALL

MANAGER...Adjt. JONES
DOOR-KEEPER....................................Capt. MASS
MUSICIAN......................................Lt. CHANDLER
MEMBER OF THE PRESS............................Lt. RYAN
MOSE..Lt. WELSH
BLACK SWAN....................................Lt. MORAN
BROADWAY SWELL..............................Lt. BENNETT
RICHARD III.................................Capt. McWILLIAMS

THE WHOLE TO CONCLUDE WITH A
GRAND WALK-AROUND

Performance to commence at 6 o'clock.

ADMISSION FREE—Children in Arms Not Admitted.

Adjt. R. C. KNAGGS,
Business Agent.

war. Many think the future is full of hope since Major Mulford, commander of Flag of Truce, says that he is confident that we shall soon be exchanged.[107] Did not go to the Minstrells since I could enjoy the time as well playing cribbage and reading. Averill is safe, but part of the 14th Pa. Cavalry is reported captured, but he has destroyed millions worth of property. Genl. John Morgan is reported having got safely to Columbia, S.C., so he is now beyond the grasp of our government which he has so treasonably deserted. Warm today, health good. Scrubbing going on as usual.

Friday, December 25. After the Minstrels were through last evening and the most had gone to bed, some of the officers feeling patriotic began to sing, "Rally around the Flag boys,"[108] and oh how sweetly it sounded contrasted with the current place. Today was "merry christmas" and all tried to do their best on having good dinners and most succeed having turkeys, chickens, and all the delicacies of northern states. The authorities failed to give us wood but the boards, and tables were broken up and burned, but I expect we shall have to pay for it. Had a grand Ball after night and looking over the living mass and seeing nearly one hundred officers dancing at once, the delight at this time was greater than I had ever dreamed, and I would have joined "tripped the gay fantastic toe" myself had I been able. Major White left for Salisbury as a Hostage. Being very influential at Harrisburgh, he thought he was going to be specially exchanged.

Saturday, December 26. Yesterday the papers say a company of the cavalry was captured by us on the Peninsula, while they (the papers) are howling at the ill success of their Cavalry. This morning no new [news], having no papers, but rumor was never more rife about exchange, apparently coming from high authority. The canal was frozen over and several little boys got on to skate, when the ice giving way they went under. Three got out. Two sunk and perished. 'Twas a hard sight to see the fathers and mothers mourning and wringing their hands in agony while no help was nigh and tonight these hearths are desolate. The weather continues pleasant having no snow, but pleasant days and sharp frosty nights. Health good, and with the many thing to speculate about the time is passing swiftly by. Roll on old Time, the future is pregnant with interest.

Sunday, December 27. Great excitement today as the exchange Cartel is reported to be renewed, and three officers left for the north, also more than 500 privates. Sent two letters with the Chaplain, who came in night before last, captured on the Averille Raid,[109] to Bro. John and Mother. Oh what a time, all are happy in prospects of some going home but there is a certain fear of it being only a mistake that keeps up the excitement. The rain kept falling slowly and the outer world seems cold and drear. Gave my name to Col. Northcut who is going to write a book, The History of Libby, with the names of all officers here, while others are securing the autographs of the officers among which there are many hard ones.[110]

Monday, December 28. All eagerly waited for the morning papers, expecting to see the exchange proclaimed, but all were disappointed, as they seemed to know nothing of it which made some think the whole report false, but by all accounts the exchange is progressing, so that the longed for day will soon arrive. Mail came but nothing for me, which seemed hard. Kept issuing Boxes slowly. Saw Averill's report of his Raid being a good thing, destroying a large amount of property, while he got off from all the generals who tried to surround him, which brought out the severe indignation of the Stay at home generals, the Editors. The mist from the river kept flying all day and the weather was rough. Health good, and hope buoyant.

Tuesday, December 29. This morning the papers put a damper on the exchange question as they say Genl. Ould has refused to receive Genl. Butler as Commissioner of Exchange and that no more prisoners will [be] paroled is [if] the Cartel is not resumed in lots by giving all the surplus. This latter is a hard point, the former one that I hope the Rebs will have to give in to.[111] But as heretofore we had so bright anticipations of going home, the future now looks dark indeed and time hangs heavily. Lt. T.[112] got a box with Northern papers, also books among which he had many interesting ones, which will be a pleasure to read. The autograph question is growing and as we say, all have "Autograph on the brane [brain]."

Wednesday, December 30. Several officers getting up work on "Histories of Libby," I agreed for "two" of Col. Cavanders' and five of Col. Northcott, which we expect to be luminous affairs.[113] Commissaries are being distributed by the U.S. Sanitary Commission, but they am't [amount] to but a small affair, being distributed as usual to favorites rather than the needy. Weather gloomy, and the humours[114] are quite catching, and should the time thus spent last long so will be the affliction. The time is passing by and a blank seems to be growing in my life that shall never be filled. But reflecting that 'tis the will of our government that we have sworn to serve, we will try and count it only gain. Thank [Thankful] for health.

Thursday, December 31. Again the edition of the Examiner gives forth a howl calling the past year, an "Annuis miserabilis,"[115] and acknowledges the many defeats they have endured during the past year. The Senate (Reb) have also passed with the House the bill, stopping all substitution and exemption which is causing many to flee from the land of Dixie.[116] Various rumors of exchange excite us daily. Tonight Capt. White was put in the cell for trying ('tis alleged) to bribe the guard. Am going to burn our light to 11 P.M. instead of 9 A.M. [P.M.] as usual, being the <u>Old Year</u> night. While the old year passes by silently but surely and I naturally ask the question, where shall next old year's day find us. Echo answers "where?"

Friday, January 1, 1864. The old year passed leaving us in Libby. But last night was spent in Singing the old year out and the new one in. Often have I felt patriotic but when under circumstances similar to these, the depths of those old patriotic songs was greater than ever in my experience. As usual upon such occasions the papers try to forget the push and hope for the future advising that all beyond puberty be married and raise up a generation to fight the Yankees for years to come. The evening passed away in a ball in which many whirled in the "giddy dance" and all apparently felt happy. Wrote a letter to mother. Day was cold the rain kept falling and in general the weather was the most disagreeable for many days past. Exchange gone up, and we have come down to the plane [plain] thing stay "ad infinitum."

Saturday, January 2. The night was bitter cold and hard the fortune of the soldier who had to bear the blast. The River got to high for the water works supplying the water for the prison and the "negroes" had to carry the water. The day passed with the addition of dancing all day to keep warm, besides the exercise, which makes it one of the most commendable of amusements in Hotel de Libby. Lt. Laws is said to have the varioloid,[117] and two cases of Small Pox are in the officer's hospital. Read Gen. Smith's of Virginia Inaugural, while the editors hope the state may not be cursed on again with such a Gov. as Letcher.[118] John Martin did not get to the city owing to the sickness of his wife &c. Health good. Happier than usual.

Sunday, January 3. Day cold but moderating so that we enjoy the cool breezes again. Nothing to cause excitement and the usual cry Exchange has grown into an unnecessary bore and most, or at last many, begin to doubt any exchanges at all. Had preaching by a capt., but as usual the men cared little for religious exercises that they play cards, write, read, and even talk at the speakers elbow. Got acquainted with Lt. Krepp of 76th Pa. In. of West Newton, Pa., being a gay, fine little fellow and an intelligent officer.[119] Was glad to meet him being from my old county and we had many exchanges of opinion &c. He belonged to [the] Army of Cumberland and was captured at Chickamauga, Ga. My good health continues and give me good spirits.

Monday, January 4. The weather has so moderated that the water has been put on again and it seems much more handy. The letters came having two for me, from sister Mattie and Bro. John. Glad to hear all well. Lt. McKay is sick with symptoms of fever and unless he acts more wisely in his method of eating he will entail some disease. Read part of "The Strange Story" by Bulwer and it seems so far really as its title would indicate.[120] Spent part of the evening in drilling on the steps used in dancing, thinking that the exercise would repay. Felt well and again we are stirred up for the exchange question by the rumors of a boatload of prisoners.

Tuesday, January 5. Spent most of the day reading the "Strange Story" and I was a good deal non-plussed with its ideas of clairvoyance and mesmerism, and brought to mind many thoughts that I have formerly had as to the supernatural but usually in all matters of this kind the "deeper the darker." News again waned and we are left alone to try and spend the time as best as possible. But how the mind grows tired of itself and in vain tries for something upon which to meditate.

The weather is tolerably pleasant for the month and sometimes I feel thankful that we are not out among the storms and rains, but still all would willingly accept the latter in preference to this confinement.

Wednesday, January 6. Papers say that lists of the off. [officers] in Libby have been sent North proposing to exchange them "man for man" providing such arrangements can be made which gain another impulse to the exchange question, since this seems all that our government wants. It was still augmented by the authorities get[ting] us all in part of the Libby and calling our names, sending us to the other part, thus verifying their Rolls. The day was cold and snow fell upon the ground to the depth of one inch, making it look indeed similar to the happy homes in the North its white purity well contrasting with the gloomy aspect of this depraved City. How fallen and now how full yet deserted.

Thursday, January 7. Began the day with the labor of the wash tub getting allong as an adept. Guy Bryan got a good supply of eatables from the Sanitary C. [Commission] Stores, being in good play just at this time. News of Ben Butler threatening the Rebs, that "if they injure one hair of the union soldiers he will put the whole Confederacy in mourning." He is a good one and equally hated and feared by the Rebs, and after all their gassing they appear willing to secretly accept him as an Agent of Exchange although under their ban of authority. Hope shines bright and the future not entirely wanting signs of a success in favor of the Union, and sanguinary hopes promise great things before one year has passed its rapid cycle.

Friday, January 8. Snow upon the ground and the jingling of sleigh-bells brings to my mind the thought of my happy home in the colder regions of the North, but with the snow comes the pain and sorrow, both bodily on the part of the men and sympathetically on the part of us, since the poor fellows on the Island will suffer & many no doubt die of freezing.[121] Wrote two letters to Sister Mattie and Bro. Jno., but report says the U.S. Gov., on the refusal of the Rebs to accept Gen'l Butler as Agent of Exchange, has not favored them with a Flag of Truce; also that the Rebs are going to send a Boat to Fortress Monroe.

Saturday, January 9. Had considerable excitement as the Committee appointed to distribute the San. [Sanitary] Stores, after issuing to some of the officers, decided to sell the remainder at auction, highly incensing the off. [officers], since some of the party are charged with grand mistakes. An indignation meeting was held and the passed resolution to request a new Committee. Genls. John Morgan & A. P. Hill, C.S.A.,[122] were in Libby, but I saw them not. Read part of Dicken's "Little Dorrit" and was partially pleased with it.[123] But his style is so strange that it seems to require a long time to become accustomed to it. The evening was very cold and the ground seems frozen almost. But what is the condition of the men on Bell Isle?

Sunday, January 10. This morning the mushy ice ran thick upon the River (James) and 'tis reported to have excelled anything for the place of many years. Rumors of the rough treatment of our prisoners by Col. Sanderson, who has been appointed to distribute the clothing, is creating a good deal of dissatisfaction, and if the rumors be true, he is digging a grave so deep that shall never see day-light when we get home.[124] Poor Boys! They suffer enough, and many I fear last night have been placed beyond the taunt and brutality of him who in the same circumstances may be no better than they. Sabbath passes quietly and happy am I.

Monday, January 11. The weather delightfully pleasant, the hard, cold weather passing by leaving the sun to burst forth once more in beauty. The Flag of Truce being up for more than two weeks the Rebs are getting uneasy wanting evidently to exchange badly, and if our government only show a little Backbone, they will come up to any proposition we may dictate. Eleven officers from Foster's (late Burnside's) Command came into the Libby. Spend most of the time reading, but the day seems so short that but little progress is made. Health good, spirits buoyant.

Tuesday, January 12. What a little world in itself have we in Libby. Men from every class of society, high and low, rich, and poor, and from every country and clime, so that one practiced in reading human nature has plenty to exercise his faculty. Today pleasant again, portentous of rain or snow. Nothing new, and the day passes so succeeding each other in rapidity so that we hardly notice it and seems impossible that three months have passed over my head since a capture. Speculation of the future is wild and none can come to any conclusion, but everything executes the gradual decay of the hopes of the Confederates.

Wednesday, January 13. Today was a day of excitement caused by an indignation meeting to consider the actions of Lt. Col. Sanderson, being charged with cruelty toward our men on the Island and divers complaints, but they grew so fearce that they overdone the matter and killed themselves. Had a new Committee for the distribution of the Sanitary goods, the first one acting unsatisfactorily. Flour was issued us getting 5 lbs. a piece. Rumors of exchange growing better. The weather chill and winter passing swiftly by. Spent most of the time reading "Little Dorrit" and enjoy myself better.

Thursday, January 14. Capt. Metcalf and Capt. Gregg were exchanged by special order. A Major (Reb) was sent down to exchange for Major White but the authorities would not accept him so the Major had to go back to Confinement.[125] News from the North say that the Gov. [government] will not appoint any other one but Genl. Butler as Com. for Exchange, and in addition he is to have the control of most of the Prisoners and treat them accordingly as we are dealt with. We hail this with pleasure, as it seems the Gov. has at length learned that the only way to bring down the rebs is to hold them with a firm hand.

Friday, January 15. Additional news from the north is that Genl. Kilpatrick is recommended for Major General. Burnside going to take command of the Cavalry in the West. Hear from the Regt. being at Stephensburg yet and on picket duty. Had hoped that they would be relieved to recruit but no hope of any rest. Long to hear from home but as a boat has been signaled today we hope for a mail soon. The time passes pleasant as could be expected, but with hope of exchange we could endure anything. Good health, good spirits, and good prospects.

Saturday, January 16. The Flag of Truce came up but the papers say "No mail." Congress (U.S.) is coming down strong of [on] the war question, tabling with large majorities all propositions of treaty, and even shows a disinclination for exchange, which may be the policy of [the] government after all. Hope that some good thing shall terminate from this confinement, as that thought would releave us greatly. Got some Sanitary Stores. Read part of "Children of the Abbey," being desirous of knowing the contents of that ancient novelette.[126] Exchange has gone down and the boxes coming again, a boatload today. We are now having to stay all winter.

Four

"Our Happiness Is Alloyed by the Fear of Being Disappointed"

Libby Prison, Richmond, January 17–May 6, 1864

Life inside Libby turned bleaker by the end of January, as hopes for early release faded and prisoners' health declined from the cumulative effects of stinted rations, poor sanitation, and winter's blasts. Some inmates lashed out by taunting the guards, defying the rules, or plotting escapes. In retaliation, prison commandant Maj. Thomas Turner ordered more frequent roll calls, sealed the doors between rooms and to the stairs between floors to restrict movement, limited correspondence to a single letter of six lines per week, delayed delivering boxes or pilfered or destroyed their contents, ended the privilege of purchasing food in Richmond markets, threw troublemakers into the dungeon and wooden cages, and even forbade looking out the windows newly barred with iron. Sudden shots from nervous guards, many poorly trained men and youths from home guard units or disabled soldiers, ricocheted inside the building, wounding two men and killing an Ohio soldier. The deteriorating conditions escalated tensions inside Libby and increasingly divided the inmates. Group activities such as minstrel shows, the *Libby Chronicle,* and dances ended as individuals and factions devised their own coping strategies. Some men withdrew into listlessness and rarely left their blankets; others whiled away time in gambling and cards; one group, derisively labeled the "Kings and Barons," bribed guards for extra food; others, including Weaver, withdrew into solitude and read books; a few obtained civilian clothes and walked out the prison doors; and Colonel Thomas E. Rose, 77th Pennsylvania Volunteers, plotted a mass escape.[1]

Tensions boiled over in February. During roll call on the morning of the tenth, authorities found that over one hundred prisoners were missing. Turner initially blamed the guards, assuming that, as with earlier escapes, they had been bribed or tricked. A general search soon revealed a tunnel in the basement. Rose's earlier escape attempts had failed until he discovered that the kitchen chimney provided access to an unused basement room. For several weeks, five-man teams with chisels slowly dug a narrow passage toward a tobacco shed over fifty feet away, hauled away the dirt in a wooden spittoon, and buried it in the straw-filled room. Suffering from stagnant air, fending off rats, and almost sabotaging the project when they came to the surface near several guards, the conspirators kept their project a secret—Weaver was "ignorant of the escaping"—until the tunnel was completed on February 8. The next night 109 men fled, scattering in small groups in different directions. Fifty-nine eventually reached Union lines, forty-eight were recaptured, and two men drowned in the flooded James River.[2]

At the end of the month news reached Richmond that two Union cavalry columns, led by Brig. Gen. Judson Kilpatrick and Col. Ulric Dahlgren, were advancing toward Richmond to rescue the prisoners at Libby and at Belle Isle, a stockade prison for enlisted men on an island in the James River. Kilpatrick reached the city's fortifications on March 1 but retreated after encountering home guard units and Maj. Gen. Wade Hampton's cavalry. Dahlgren, blocked by the swollen James River, failed to join Kilpatrick and died an in ambush on March 2. Although the plan failed, Richmond citizens panicked. To prevent a prison uprising during the raid, Brig. Gen. John Winder ordered Turner to undermine the building with two hundred pounds of gunpowder and threaten to set it off if anyone attempted an escape. A few days later, Richmond newspapers reported that Dahlgren's orders had allegedly included burning the city and assassinating President Jefferson Davis and his cabinet. Citing this as proof of Yankee perfidy, editorialists denounced the supposed coddling of Union prisoners at the expense of suffering civilians and their safety, demanded hanging all captured cavalry officers, and rejoiced in the public mutilation and secret burial of Dahlgren's body. Union officials declared the "Dahlgren papers" a forgery; inmates lamented how close they had come to rescue.[3]

Despite these blighted hopes, contacts from the outside world cheered Weaver's spirits. Letters arrived more frequently, books were available for reading, care packages sent by family and friends supplemented meager rations, and Weaver's health remained strong. Realizing that release now depended on Union victory, he avidly followed the war news. Meanwhile, he perceived prolonged imprisonment as a test of his moral character by providing opportunities for self-improvement through reading, infantry drill, sword exercises, and dancing lessons, and, most of all, for reaffirming an unwavering patriotism. Weaver tempered his own trials with sympathy for the sufferings of the enlisted men on Belle Isle, who had only canvas tents for shelters and meager provisions and blankets, and for the poor women and children outside Libby who begged the inmates for cornbread.

Yet, as weeks stretched into months, Weaver often became gloomy when his daily routines of "reading, roaming around, playing, chatting, et cetera" no longer fended off bouts of chronic depression. I "can hardly confine my mind to any one point for more than a few minutes," he lamented, as "without variation man grows tired of even himself." When the prospects for a general exchange brightened in March, Weaver became obsessed with "the thought to be free once more." Still, he was never among the hundreds of released prisoners, and bitterly accused some men of obtaining their freedom with bribes or special influence. Exchanges resumed in mid-April 1864 but were limited to the sick and to convalescents By the end of the month Weaver's spirits languished further: "Felt lonely and sad, and am almost worn out in expectation of going home."[4]

The great Libby escape and the Kilpatrick-Dahlgren raid convinced Confederate authorities of the folly of concentrating Union prisoners in Richmond, and Winder secured new prison sites in Georgia. In late February 1864, the first enlisted men were moved from Belle Isle to an unfinished prison camp near Andersonville, and the next month officers from Libby began arriving at a stockade prison outside Macon. Commencement of the Overland Campaign suspended all exchanges after May 6. The following day Weaver was among the prisoners evacuated from Libby to Danville, Virginia, the first of several removals to prisons in Georgia and in the Carolinas.

Sunday, January 17, 1864. Today was passed as usual with its attendant variations, familiar to Libby life: some devoting the time to reading and writing while a few still endulging in gaming, a practice so low as to excite pity rather than disgust. A Secesh Minister favored or cursed us with a Sermon, but being engaged I did not attend not caring much for his effusions. Happy am I today in prospect of a mail, and flatter myself that I shall have a goodly number of letters. Rumor grows no less bold than formerly but being duped so often I have learned not to trust its various and contradictory rumors.

Monday, January 18. Spend most of my time in reading and find the day passes fastly, if not pleasingly, by. And if nothing else results from this, seeing misfortune of being a prisoner, this fact, the having read many interesting works will be a matter of happiness. Wrote a letter to sister Jennie. Hope the day shall soon come where this troublesome medium of communicating thought will be unnecessary. But still how delightful when cloistered within Brick-walls, and guarded by glistening bayonetts to have the opportunity of saying to those we love, "I am well" &c.

Tuesday, January 19. Papers tell us that all the U.S. Sanitary Stores (some 36 tons) have been confiscated by the Rebs, but the papers are so faithless that we dare not believe them. The mail came, I got two from Bro. Jno.; one from Sister Mattie. Was glad to hear from them and the happy Christmas &c. that was

Fig. 12. Interior of Libby Prison, showing the rooms and the living conditions of the prisoners. Men prepared meals on the lower floor. (Willard W. Glazier, *The Capture, the Prison Pen, and the Escape: Giving a Complete History of Prison Life in the South*. New York: U.S. Publishing Company, 1868)

spent. I long to be at home and have the pleasure of enjoying the pleasant snow of which they speak. Hear of Senator Wilson of Mass.[5] introducing a Bill in the Senate to lower the officers' wages while they are in Libby, which seems to cause a good deal of feeling. Why not begin on <u>civil</u> offices to economise.

Wednesday, January 20. The remainder of the letters came having five more for me, one from Lizzie, one from Bro. "FA," one from sisters Kate and Jennie,[6] also one <u>Business</u> <u>one</u>. Got a good lot of news and was especially glad to hear of my letters getting through. Report concerning the Confiscation of U.S. San. [Sanitary] Stores contradicted as we had reason to suppose. Now gotten quite interested in the "Children of the Abbey," but feel quite disappointed to see the young "Amanda" so innocent yet subject to such horrid treatment. But I suppose the fancy of Miss Roque would have it so.[7]

Thursday, January 21. Finished reading "Children of the Abbey" and after many disappointments was pleased with the winding up. Wrote to Sisters Kate and Jennie, to mother and Bro "F.A." coming at length to the conclusion that I had used the Weaver name fully enough for once. News of Jeff Davis's house being tried to be burned down, also that his fourth servant has run away, showing something wrong or some dislike somewhere. The day really fine and although the dead of winter it is wondrous fine. Had no meat for a week from the Confeds, and those who live on Confed. rations alone had dry work.

Friday, January 22. Wrote to Sister Lizzie and Bro. Jno., to the latter for a Box of clothing and food, having thought that we are going to stay here for a long time. The Rebs refuse to issue the boxes down stairs until they are satisfied that their prisoners in the north get what is sent them. Hope they may soon get the desired information since a few days will throw us entirely on Reb. rations. Col. Strait's command was shut off from the rest of us cutting a little hole in the door for the privilege of talking through.[8] Some of the officers last evening got liquor from the guard and were quite merry or even drunken.

Saturday, January 23. The weather is delightful with the din of Spring, on such a Spring as I have been used to. One of the Committee from the Reb. Senate appointed to inquire into the treatment of Prisoners came in today and was introduced to Gen'l Dow.[9] Being shown the rations he said they were <u>too</u> small; and being told that we could not get what Boxes had been sent to us, he promised that it should be attended to. About dark, a lot of officers got in the dining room and began promenading, singing patriotic songs, and cheering and making noise generally, when they were surprised by the guard and made [to] stand "in line" for three hours. I was nearly caught with the rest being cooking at the time but elluded the guard.

Sunday, January 24. The most surprising affair of the day was the issue of <u>a</u> <u>meat</u> ration, being the only one for nearly two weeks, and we had a good dinner thereby. Had the front door open and had the pleasure of standing on the pavement, which is a rare thing. As usual on Sabbath, a good many people came around and it is a pleasure to see a citizen's face, altho hateful to the reflection. The sun is just going down. The air <u>mild</u> and under other circumstances I should be very happy. Yet when I think of all things I have passed thru I am very thankful. Hear Lt. Laws is dead, dying of Small Pox.[10]

Monday, January 25. The weather is still delightful being warm as Spring, and altho the winter in the north is very severe, being 10° & 20° below zero, still we have suffered none. All things seem to point to our stay here for some time, which is a gloomy aspect, since there are fears and doubts least the boxes never be permitted to come in. Remarkably quiet and nothing passing to break the lazy spell that has fallen upon us. Oh how I fear some evil may grow upon us either bodily or mentally though this confinement. Sword exercise, still progressing. Infantry drill increasing, the dancing class continuing and rations as slim as ever.

Tuesday, January 26. Today a prototype of yesterday in quietness and do-nothing. ~~Rebs.~~ Two men came in today, having been recaptured after escaping from Columbia Prison[11] and wandering about four weeks, finally captured within a few miles of our lines. They are nearly naked and are a sorry sight. For a change of diet, accidentally got some beans and mess pork for dinner, and baking cakes of the grated bread we fancied we had a gay dinner. Got a paper from the North and astonished to find how far we are growing behind the age. All things from home are prospering and there is a good hope of soon overcoming.

Wednesday, January 27. Another Flag of Truce Boat is said to be up, with boxes &c. The Rebs began barring the windows with strong iron bars, either because they are afraid of us getting away or to lighten the guard. It makes our confinement more like imprisonment, for we appear to be cut off from the entire world. Still the officers are sanguine enough to suppose they are only fixing up quarters for themselves; may they "dig a ditch into which to fall." The day comes and goes leaving nothing by which to be remembered, and so we expect to pass many months. Gun Boats has made a Raid up the James River doing a good deal of injury, burning provisions, &c.

Thursday, January 28. Was shocked this morning to read in the "Enquirer" of our boys on the Island eating dogs and yet more so to hear the editor jest over it by saying "it was the taste of the Yankees to prefer dog to the meat, beans, and soup of the Confederate Commissary." How sad and how low must we have fallen, that could jest at the suffering of even an enemy. Gen'l Lee has issued an order to his men, praying them to bear up under the scanty rations they get, being a good evidence of scarcity, as Gen'l Lee speaks not when not needed. The day fine, wonderfully pleasant, balmy as Spring and all the windows are thrown open to exhale the new air of Heaven. Had a long chat with Lt. Potts of Pottsville, Pa.[12]

Friday, January 29. Felt rather badly today and had I given up to feelings I would have been melancholy enough. This added to the constant smoke that filled kitchens and "parlor" [and] made our abode almost hateful. Two officers escaped from the west room by getting Reb clothes and passing the guard unhailed.[13] Hear of Moseby capturing a wagon train of our forces by passing himself off for one of the 18th Pa. Cav.[14] The conscription act of the Conf. [Confederate] Senate has been made public and excites a good deal of controversy trying to put all in Army except special exemptions.[15] Our boxes remain below and no hope of getting them. Have got a bad cold and the weather being so pleasant the contrast is disagreeable.

Saturday, January 30. Today was a disagreeable one both outside and in. A load of boxes came from City Point. Five officers escaped by passing the guard in citizen's dress, which caused a general count and calling of the name to find who they were.[16] This required the most of the day. The morning had been occupied in guarding a Squad of officers in the Kitchen for insulting the guard, and this prevented many from getting breakfast. So late night found us eating a little beef and cornbread with rice. Had the officers all crowded into the kitchen and the smoke was blinding, showing the dirty disposition of the Rebs who try to incommode us as much as possible. Retaliation would be sweet. Got the lone [loan] of Virgil's "Aeneid" and had a good hours reading. Want to study it.

Sunday, January 31. Today was spent in roll calling having to file through a door while two clerks on either side counted, putting me in mind of the farmer counting his sheep. After getting through some negro persuaded the Clerk that one had been on the roof while calling, and this caused the hatch hole to be nailed down and a repetal [repeatal] of the roll call. They at length found they had a few dozens too many and come to the conclusion that the citizens had slipped in to evade the draft. But one thing is sure, they keep their books in a wretched state, and as the clerk says a thousand Yankees are too much for one head.[17] Had the headache pretty badly and was quite out of humor.

Monday, February 1. Papers say Gen'l Butler[18] has notified the Rebs that if they don't confer with him upon the exchange question, all flag of truce will be stopped. Major Turner, Commandant of Prison, issued an order: that "no Federal prisoner shall send to the <u>so called</u> United States but one letter of only six lines on each week, Monday." When read the "so called" was hooted openly. Got our letters. I had two, one from Bro. Jno. and my mother. The latter informing me of the marriage of Miss Lizzie of L. [Latrobe], a fact which once would have astounded me, but today feel nearly regardlessly of than ever. But I must repeat how many change[s] one single year has brought to pass. Had roll call twice, by daylight and at 3 P.M., and the boys call out whenever they see a Reb, "roll call," "roll call." Weather sultry, warm and a slight mist falling.

Tuesday, February 2. Roll call began the day and had to be repeated once or twice before perfected, while the interval was filled up with cryes of "so called" &c. Capt. Cupp[19] was recaptured about thirty miles from the city so that it seem almost folly to try and get away. The Papers (Inquirer) had a communication concerning Libby in which was portrayed the condition of its inhabitants, being jumbed [jumbled] in by the score and none ever leaving and said that all who pass its portals never returned. Sad thought! Almost might that strange sentence be written about the door, "All who enter here leave hope behind."[20] The day cool, but indication of pretty weather. Health good and mess of meat for once. Matters are growing severe.

Wednesday, February 3. Weather colder and more disagreeable. Had to pass through the regular sheep driving roll call getting to be quite a bore. Rations playing out, getting nothing but cornbread, which by dint of mixing with rice makes more, and burning the crust forms our coffee. Too bad, since plenty of boxes remain below, but not to be issued as the Rebs affirm their men North do not get the boxes sent to them. Three officers (Naval) came in and they really thought they had got into a den to [of] thieves by the demoniac cries of "fresh fish" "give him air" "look out for your pockets" that greeted their ears. They with 150 men were captured off the "Smith Briggs" which was burnt by the Rebs at Smithfield.[21]

Thursday, February 4. News from the North say Pres. Lincoln has made another draft for five hundred thousand with those obtained by last draft. Am glad to see this and hope that the quotas may be filled without drafting. The Confed. Congress passed a resolution to request the U.S. Government to enter into Treaties of Peace with them. They boast highly of the Patriotism of their troops reenlisting for the war, when in fact they past a Bill to hold them against all will in the matter for the war. Strange patriotism. Weather colder, the wind being high and disagreeably cold. Great rumors of exchange. The Reb's Congress having gone into Secret Session concerning the Exchange and rumors of a Flag of Truce being up.

Friday, February 5. Began calling roll by name at daylight, and kept it up till <u>noon</u>, before the most of us had any breakfast. Had some "fresh fish" from Newburne, N.C., who give a dark account of the prospects of that post. Since Gen'l Pickett has attacted it, [with] 15 thousand men, it having a force of 3 thousand, and it will in all likelyhood be overcome before it can be reinforced.[22] Exchange news in assendency. Judge Ould[23] having been at City Point since Monday, and every little rumor is magnified in huge dimensions. The day cold and disagreeable. Had a ration of refuse turnips today.

Saturday, February 6. Had a day roll call today as Capt. Johnson who is said to escape last Monday was missed.[24] Capt. Ives, 10th Mass. Infantry, and Capt. Reed, 3 Ohio Infantry, were drawn by lot to be put in irons and sent to Salisbury to be put to hard labor during the war in retaliation for two Confed. officers caught recruiting within the Union lines in Kentucky and were punished with ball and chain.[25] They left for Salisbury. Retaliation is assuming a dark phase and 80 Cav. Offs. are said are going to [be] put in cells for like treatment of Morgan's men.[26] Exchange question gone down. Judge Ould having come back and said there is no hope.

Sunday, February 7. Excitement was the order of the day, as rumors of various characters ran hot through the prison of our forces advancing up the Peninsula. Soon the home guards straggled past the Libby who were hooted by the Yankeys. Two mounted howitzers drawn by mules with two attendants filed by also amid the shouts of "Jackass Battery."[27] "Look out for old Beast."[28] &c., and we were answered by one making the form of a noose with a rope. The rebs are excited and some great consternation has fallen upon them, as the "Alarm Bell" has been dinging frequently. The Committee from Congress to examine the prison passed thru the Prison. Did not hear the estimation they had of the inmates, or the opinion they formed of our treatment. The day was cold but fine and dry and splendid weather for action military movements.

Monday, February 8. The fright of yesterday seems by the papers to be well founded as two columns by way of Rapid Ann and Peninsula are making for Richmond.[29] Our cavalry is said to have tried to pass the Chickahominy River but did not succeed. Activity prevails all through the army and it seems the campaign is open. News of a plot to liberate us incarcerated in Richmond and a good number of citizens arrested. Rumor of a committee sent to City Point to meet a similar Committee from North to try to arrange the Exchange. A Flag of Truce Boat came up on Sat. last. The freight on provisions said to be ten tons, came here tonight but I suppose it shall receive the fate of the former to lie in the warehouse and rot, sooner than deliver them to the owners, through false protests, evidently trying to starve us.

Tuesday, February 9. The force on the Peninsula turned out to be only a reconnaissance of a few cavalry companies and are reported to have fallen back. Several Officers got their Boxes but in so mutillated a form that there is a great dissatisfaction, and altho they report that the boxes are going to be delivered yet there is little confidence in the rumor. The Newburn affair turned out but slight, the capture of a few men.[30] One officer came in last evening from Army of Potomac. He relates something about Gen'l Hays being wounded;[31] news of Col. Rosser (Reb) capturing a large wagon train &c, &c.[32] Wrote two letters yesterday; one for Ed. McChesney, one for mother. The day was very cold but the weather dry. Have begun the rice soup again, and suppose are all only beginning to see hard times.

Wednesday, February 10. Was awakened at dead of night by men falling over me and making a terrible noise all through the house. Found this morning it was a stampede of the men who were trying to escape and were frightened. But to our satisfaction roll call proclaimed 109 officers absent, who had escaped by cutting or digging a hole under the wall into a yard nearby, a distance of twenty ft. Eleven Colonels, seven Majors got out. Col. Streight being gone with a large party. The Rebs were surprised and hunted around till they found the hole. The rest left behind had to pass the day in roll calls. Toward evening several rebs came in dead, and the supposition that they run against some [of] our men. I was sorry that I was ignorant of the escaping, as I would have cast my lot among those going. But the hole was kept full till dark, and many of the original designers failed to get out.

Thursday, February 11. Up to six o'clock P.M. only 22 officers were recaptured, one being a major. Two were said to be dead, refusing to surrender by names of Freeman and Clifford, 15th U.S. Infantry.[33] Rumor says Streight is mounted and armed and will get away and more than half of our forces are up the Peninsula as far as Bottoms Bridge.[34] Several naval officers off the "Underwriter" captured at Newbern came in, also a Paymaster.[35] A few infantry officers also. G. Bryan[36] got his Box or part of the perishable articles. But this seems to be the way of the Rebs to do fancy robbing. Weather cold. Health good.

Friday, February 12. They report 32 of the officers escaped to be recaptured; Freeman Gay and Frank Krepps and James F. Pool the number.[37] Having gone down the James in a Boat, and getting men ashore had to give it over. Still the thing is very fair yet and acknowledged by the Rebs to be fairly done. Rumors again of our Army advancing and Meade getting in Lee's rear, while the guard is being relieved around the prison and sent to the front. Capt. Polluck, 14th Pa. Cav., Adj. White, 4 Pa. Cav., Lt. Daly, 8th Pa. Cav, Major Henry, 5th Ohio V., Major Walker, 73 Indiana, Col. Spofford, Freeman, Lt. Small, [and] Col. Ely have been captured among the rest.[38] Had a good dinner of Tomatoes, Turnips, and confed. cornbread and meat. The issue of boxes still goes on with the same peculation.[39]

Saturday, February 13. The officers recaptured were sent up from the cells today to give room for others. They tell great stories of their pursuit, having got nearly to our lines. Some by the last Picket, while others had to give their selves up being starving and freezing. Some were hunted down by "Blood Hounds," an old method for the Chivalry to pursue the fugitives. The mail came having six letters for me. Two from Sister Kitty, one from Bro. Jno., and Frank, one from Sergt. Burns,[40] and one from Capt. Curry, Post Commissary at Fortress Monroe, informing me that he could not send me the supplies sent for, as the Confed. authorities would not receive them. The Killing of Lts. Freeman and Clifford by the Pickets turns out faulse. Health very good, weather pleasant.

Sunday, February 14. Col. Rose, 77th Pa. Vol., was recaptured, also a Capt. Ross of Streight's command, being 44 in all.[41] The day was very quiet. The men having grown more quiet than formerly and all seem to prefer solitude, and getting a book up will see many retiring to some lonly corner and there spend the weary hours. Wrote three letters, to Sister Kate, Bro. Frank and Sergt. Burns of my company, getting those to hand two of them in, who had none of their own. How I long to be free! But the uncertainty of getting out, any ways soon makes the contemplation sad but the strong love of country sustains me, as I am satisfied to do anything or be anything for my country's good. Have a severe cold. The day tolerably pleasant.

Monday, February 15. The winds blow cold, and appearance of snow, again brings to mind the fact that winter has not yet passed by. Nothing very strange. Reb Congress has stopped all Blockade running, trying to throw their people upon their own resources, and thus make them ingenious [so] that they may be independent. Their troops seem to be moving down the Peninsula taking early measures, perhaps, to prevent surprise by our forces, as 'tis thought that Col. Streight will attempt something in this line. Rumors of going to be put on half rations, by way of retaliation but guess 'tis all rumor. Retaliation is talked of much, but although sweet at first, grown bitter soon and affects the retaliating most. The recaptured officers now am't to 52 being less than half.[42]

Tuesday, February 16. The weather getting very cold so that comfort is out of the question, and suffering, at least on the Island, [in]evitable. Beside the small fires, the officers keep them[selves] warm by quick stepping around the dining room, some being long enough winded to make two laps. Hear of Gen'l Scammeron being captured on a Boat on the Ohio;[43] of Gen'l Rossers (Reb) capturing a large wagon train in western Virginia. Reb. Congress will soon close, and the three great Bills, Currency, Tax, and Conscription, are the great theme, and being discussed in secret session and exciting a good interest while their soldiers are foolish enough to reenlist after having been conscripted for the war.

Wednesday, February 17. Last night the wind blew fierce and cold and many of our boys suffered assuredly on the Island. Our rations instead of getting smaller as anticipated are getting larger, with a little cabbage and a few turnips. 'Tis said 55 officers have got off of the 109 who escaped, being more than half, but the papers think they have gained by getting Gen'l Morgan for Colonel Strait.[44] If so, all right. Both are satisfied. The day is still cold and tonight will be the same. The issue of boxes goes on as usual, the owners getting the "perishables." Exchange has gone down low and is hardly ever mentioned all seeming satisfied that that period is far distant.

Thursday, February 18. Today very cold within a few degrees, six or seven, of zero, being the coldest weather this winter. Gen'l Scammeron with his two aids [aides] came in. Also a Capt. from 5th Corps, who states that part of our Regt. is at 5th Corps yet.[45] Gen'l Sherman is moving on Mobile, and there are strong hopes of its fall.[46] The Reb. Congress closes its first term today to resume next May fancying they have done wonders. Flag of Truce Boat up with 30 tons of provisions for the prisoners. Hope that some satisfaction may be had respecting the matter of issuing. Gold appears on the increase in the North, going at 161½ being higher than for some time. Rebs are sending away daily 400 of our men to Americus, Georgia.[47]

Friday, February 19. The weather still very cold the river being nearly bridged. Papers state that it was the intention of Gen'l Butler to try and capture Richmond and liberate the Prisoners, thus obviating the exchange. Grant is about moving and they indicate something grand. The issue of the Boxes continues in the old style. Spend the time in reading Virgil, playing, and cooking and eating. Got a whole loaf of bread. Had a dinner of potatoes, turnips, and ham. Have a dreadful cold, and sore throat. A telegram announces the arrival of quite a number of our officers who escaped into our lines. Glad to know that so many have got away, but sorry I had not a trial of my luck.

Saturday, February 20. Cold weather still continues and many think last night the coldest one this winter. Yesterday as was intended Spencer Deaton was hung by the Confederates, being convicted as a spy, and was caught recruiting in Tennessee which the Rebels affirm to be their territory. This is following the example that Burnside gave them last summer and our government cannot complain.[48] Cruel War! Many times I find myself brooding over its sorrows and have to exclaim: Could not independence be maintained without so much bloodshed? Does the benefit reaped by the subduing of the rebellion repay all this suffering? This answer comes back, altho not to the present generation, future generation shall reap the reward. Saw Lt. [Joseph] Smith, 67th Pa., from Latrobe Pa.

Sunday, February 21. Today was not so cold, and the moderate breezes make our lonely, altho filled to overflowing, mansion more pleasant. As usual on the Sabbath the Citizens gathered around the Prison, at a respectful distance, eyeing us as Jail Birds or as harmless beasts caged. This is hard to endure but the language of Shakespeare comes to mind, "But all these woes shall serve for sweet converse in time to come."[49] Hope that coming day may not be far distant. Wrote a letter to Bro. John of the allowed six lines. Was perplexed by the rumor of the exchange of 1500 privates, knowing it to be false, but serving to remind us of our situation.

Monday, February 22. Washington's Birthday finds us safly [safely] esconsed in Libby with bolted doors and barred windows. But little display was made altho no doubt many of our hearts dilated at the name, and hoped that soon the success that followed his armies may follow ours. But singular the Rebs will affirm that they are fighting for freedom and Robt. E. Lee is second Father of his country. Altho they may be as deeply in earnest, yet they lack the one great principle. Nothing new. Day pleasant. Rumor of Flag of Truce, let it come, let it come.

Tuesday, February 23. Last night a large coffee warehouse caught fire and burned down, the steam boiler inside exploding with terrific noise and being near "Libby" shook the building. The issue of boxes entire began today causing great delight and satisfaction to us. The weather is growing delightful again, the balmy air and warm zephyrs fill the soul with delight. These shall hasten the movements of the Army, when slaughter shall be renewed and a shedding of blood a greater than which there never has been. Feel happy, and thank my God for life and as much cornbread as I desire.

Wednesday, February 24. Continues very pleasant, all excitement in receiving boxes as the Hall below exhibits [a] scene as auction room in our large Northern cities. The Rebs report Sherman to be falling back to Vicksburg, but don't know his object. The most of the escaped officers who have not been recaptured have got to our lines and are <u>safe</u>. Cornbread is again growing plenty and soon will be a burthen, and go out of the windows to the animals that linger around, or to the little boys and girls of the city who often gather around for the purpose of getting some to eat. Still spending my leisure moments on "Virgil's Aeneid."

Thursday, February 25. Had a mail today. Got two letters from Bro. John, the last of 7th inst. Nothing strange at home. A Flag of Truce Boat up again with boxes of eatables to the amt. of 10 tons. Got Northern news from the papers in the boxes delivered, being a relish as reading Reb news all the time grows tiresome as well as sickening, and like the continual dropping of water so continually reading their bombast gives a subverted shade to everything. Had Roll Call last night at 12 P.M., the guards receiving an alarm falsely. But what a time! All the men driven in upon us before we had time to lift our beds.

Friday, February 26. The papers intimate that Gen'l Dow & Capts. Sawyer and Flinn are to be exchanged.[50] Got news from the North. All in good heart expecting soon to quell the Rebellion. Got two letters, one from Mother, one from Sister Jennie. Mother writes Lizzie of L. is <u>not</u> married, the notice being a ruse, which news struck me about with as much surprise as the first. The Rebs fixed the stairs that leads to the first story so that they can take them down at night showing plainly that they are afraid of us. Spent the morning with Freeman Gay having a pleasant time.[51] The day was pleasant and health good, and feel very well. Strange the developments of last. How momentous the facts.

Saturday, February 27. Were all driven down into the kitchen before many had breakfast, in order to have a search made for arms and weapons of destruction. What a mass! Nearly a thousand men on one floor. We had to stand or sit if possible for many hours. I crouched down in a corner and my mind ran away to home and wondered what my friend[s] would think if they saw me. The Rebs made search taking away files, knives, saws, hatchets, used for making bone work and splitting wood, but found no arms as I heard of. A boatload of boxes came up and altho they are issued, 'tis done in such a manner as to create much dissatisfaction, being mutilated in search after money and half the valuables filched often by the guards or the authorities themselves. Each day they grow meaner.

Sunday, February 28. Very pleasant day, getting warm and delightful. Capt. Bartum is said to be exchanged but may be as others only a rumor.[52] Maj. Gough of Va.[53] is held as hostage for a Reb Major who they seem to think is held in close confinement. Wrote two letters one to Mother and one to L [Lizzie] of Latrobe being done, this the information of last letters. Frequent rumors of the Army advancing, of hard fighting and a thousand stories of exchange being all gass. Read of Miss Richardson speaking on the subject of Emancipation in the Senate hall, Washington, to a crowded and intelligent house.

Monday, February 29. Slow nasty rain fell today, but few boxes were delivered but what were were filled with Harper's Illustrated Magazine,[54] making a literary feast and were eagerly devoured by all. A Petition is said to have been sent to Gen'l Winder concerning the delivering and filching of our Boxes and 'tis also reported that there is to be a change in the "modis operandi." Was surprised at the basket of letters that was handed in, being fully an average of two to each officer, whereas their orders are <u>one</u> to each. Finished read[ing] Seventh Books of Virgil.

Tuesday, March 1. A Raid is on hand again. All Richmond is in excitement and fear Kilpatrick from coming in and relieve us.[55] Orders are very strict, not being allowed to look out the window, in fear of being shot by the guard. But the only result of this strict order was the killing of one of the Reb's detectives in Castle Lightening being in the building at the time.[56] In the evening, excitement grew intense and from information received, we expected our forces to enter the city tonight, and in consequence organizations were being affected for escaping, and joy light up the countenances of all in anticipation of being freed from this imprisonment. All the Army seems moving and communication between this city and Lee's army is cut off. Oh, may success <u>smile</u> now.

Wednesday, March 2. Morning found us still prisoners although our forces had got within a few mile[s] of the city and firing could be heard. Still, altho it seemed the intention of our forces to come into the city, some delay or misfortune prevented & they fell back. There was some hard fighting and 139 of our men were made prisoners, with 3 officers, Lt. Col. of 7th Mich. Cav., Surgeon, 2nd N.Y.C., besides a few killed.[57] Half of the city Battalion (Reb.) ~~was~~ captured and a goodly number of militia. Rumor of Burnside advancing and Meade crossing the Rapid Ann. We were notified by authorities that they had 1,000 lbs. of powder in the seller [cellar] of the Prison and they could blow us all up should we attempt a revolt.

Thursday, March 3. Had a mail today, but I got none: unfortunate event! The fright occasioned by the raid is still at fever height as they say Kilpatrick had made a junction with Gen'l Burnsides who is moving up the peninsula with 12 Regts. of Infantry. The Powder question was thoroughly discussed and altho disbelieved by many at first, was proven to be fact, but all knew they dare not do such a barberous act, but what a light it put [on] the these traitors. They continue issuing boxes but punch all the cans thusly spoiling them, and confiscating the whole where anything contraband is found. They are also issuing so slowly that they shall always have four or five boat loads ahead, spoiling the whole. Their actions are getting so mean and disgusting as to astonish even their own people, when they hear of it.

Friday, March 4. Find that we were so near being released and Richmond destroyed, that disappointment altho coming late, sickens the heart. Col. Dahlgren who was in charge of one detachment and intending to charge in the city from the South side of the James River was killed during a charge, which seems to have discouraged the whole. The papers showing the entire program were found on his body. Oh! How bitter the papers open! [opine] wanting his body hung in the street for twenty-four hours and all the officers caught hereafter to be hung![58] When on Raids, the officers captured are in solitary confinement, put there by the decision of the Cabinet, but if our Gov. [Government] serve John Morgan so, we cannot find any objection to this treatment since we have acknowledged them a bel. [belligerent] power.

Saturday, March 5. Rumors still of the Raiders being near the city, and something like the reflection of Artillery was seen in direction of City Point at and after dark. Lt. Hammond was shot at by a guard for putting his head out of the window and the ball cut a piece of his ear, close enough![59] Rumors of a substantive character say 800 men and 82 officers of the Rebs are at City Point, and as two Flag of Truce Boats have gone down, the whole building is in an excitement about exchange, and the Rebs say that they look upon it as the beginning of a general exchange. Hope it may be. Oh what a happy day it be.

Sunday, March 6. All excitement today, as eight hundred men and sixty-four officers (Rebs) came from City Point, and rumor has it that a general exchange on parole has been affected, by giving the Rebs one-fourth of the excess, we holding the remainder.[60] The Rebels were "fat as pigs" us all remarked and were well dressed having usually valisses [valises] full of supplies from the North. But Look at our poor fellows, nearly naked and half dead, sickly, and pale. Two parties of Cav. came from the Island, one for Americus, Georgia, and the other for City Point, 'tis said. Wrote a letter home to mother. Oh, is this a general parole! How happy I feel even in the hopes at almost any sacrifice.

Monday, March 7. Forty odd officers left today for City Point, those being chosen who have been favorites and were the most importunate in asking the favor of the Rebs. This was about ¾ of what was sent to the city. But all things look favorable for the most or all of us leaving shortly. They say that no more boxes are to be issued; thus leaving in their hand about 100 tons. The Editors can't quit breathing "fire and sword" upon the last raiders, wanting them hung or put in dungeons, while the body of Col. Dahlgren was buried ignominiously by cutting off his fingers to get his diamond rings, leaving no coffin, and the place kept a secret to prevent his friends ever finding his corpse.

Tuesday, March 8. Looked all day long for a Boat of Officers to come up from City Point but were disappointed, and there are doubts beginning to arise as to the probabilities of Exchange as a load of Boxes came up and there are men being sent to Americus yet. But the boxes may have been there for some time, and the prisoners sent to Americus maybe exchanged there. Still doubt hangs over the entire thing and I grow uneasy and discontented, having the subject continually before me. The weather delightful and spring has set in fully. Major Cook, Kilpatrick's Staff, [61] is a prisoner and confined with 4 or 5 niggers in the low cell, an indignity heaped upon him for being a Raider. But time will make that good.

Wednesday, March 9. Still no Boat, and from the News outside we need not expect one for three or four days. But still the general supposition is that the Parole will continue. Feel happy in the thought that soon we will be free, but should it be false, Oh, the disappointment! The day was pleasant. The sun shone brightly and all nature was gay and joyous. A number of the Paroled Rebs visited Libby and they say that they were generally used very well in the Northern prisons, a confession impossible for us to make. They find fault with our mode of warfare in destroying all the provisions, &c., possible.

Thursday, March 10. Rain fell thick and fast, all day and River rising, but in all 'tis yet pleasant. Made me a seat out of a barrell getting the tools of the workmen making a pen in the kitchen for the confinement of Kilpatrick's Raiders I suppose. Had a shave also, the <u>second</u> during the 5 months nearly I have been here. Exchange quiet. Grub consisting of cornbread or meal. Got three new stoves making <u>sixteen</u> cook stoves in the building, which would be plenty should we have enough of and the right kind of wood, both [of] which we lack. Quite excitement as to whom are going [on the] next Boat, and many officers are looking to request the Rebs to send them before others.

Friday, March 11. The officers of Negro Regts. were called down early this morning and put into the pen built in the Kitchen with the Raiders, and two Negro Soldiers caught in last Raid. Their names are Lts. Titus, Brown, and Coleman.[62] But the thing is so low and disgusting, and the pretended "retaliation" so sham like, which, taken in connection of putting the Negros with them, makes them appear the more asses. The papers still cry out for the life of the Raiders, breathing the most Horrid threatenings, giving a true exhibit of their chivalry. Boasting of the ignominious death of Col. Dalgran, also his brutal burial. Washed today. River rising, the day pl[e]asing. Harry left mess to cook for Lumbard.[63] Good health, and prospects of a Boat load of Rebs soon to be up. Still sending out men to Americus, as it would seem that they have no idea of Exchange.

Saturday, March 12. Rumors of a Boat being up, but nothing definite. Several letters were received from the officers last sent away, and they present the matter of exchange in various lights some regarding it all settled, others as gloomy enough. Miss Bell Boyd, Gen'l Stewart's Scout, was in the Libby today but I did not have the opportunity of seeing her.[64] Gov. Brown of Georgia[65] has spoken very freely and disparagingly of the Acts of last Congress in the cases of Conscription Bill, Currency Bill, and the one suspending the writ of "Habeus Corpus" saying that the faith of the people is being shaken in the authorities and will eventually be entirely lost. Slowly and surely they seem to be drifting to internal dissentions. The time hangs heavy and this week has passed slowly by. Good health, and hope buoyant.

Sunday, March 13. Pretty weather again, and the renewal of exchange excitement & 'tis said that a Boat is up at City Point with 40 or 50 officers and 800 privates, so that exchange stock runs high. Preaching in the morning by the Episcopal Minister, at night by a Chaplin. Got meat yesterday, once in two weeks, and it was so spoiled that the Commissaries of the messes rejected it. Had they not offered such to us 'twould have saved their credit, but to give us spoiled meat for the purpose of <u>having</u> it, to say we get meat rations, shows their low meanness. This shall all be rectified someday and woe to him upon whom it falls! River swollen. Feel happy as hope of exchange.

Monday, March 14. Exchange high today and the arrangement for a general parol said to be completed. Forty officers left the Libby, Gen'l Dow, Capts. Sawyer and Flinn among the number. Some 800 hundred privates also. The matter of exchange has got to be a matter of favor and some men are so low as to pray or even buy their exchange of the Rebs in advance of others entitled to go home. What excitement! All seem merry and happy but still a lasting dread of being left fearing some interruption of the parole. The Rebs still affirm that Butler has nothing to do in this arrangement but that it has been completed through Major Mulford of the Flag of Truce Boat, "New York."[66] Wrote a letter to Mother, telling her of our prospects. The men filed by our prison, and what a sight: some scarcely able to walk, the most horrid pictures of humanity conceivable, being starved outt by the damnable Rebs.

Tuesday, March 15. The Confederate Prisoners in return for those leaving yesterday arrived today and the Rebs tried hard to have an ovation. Rumors still continue to increase, and Boats are on the way to take us home! Yet little confidence is placed in all such, and fears are entertained least Gen'l Dow will fire up our authorities so that they will seek retaliation in place of exchange. Were notified today that we might write one <u>page</u> instead of six lines in each letter as usual. Maj. Beers of 18th Ill. Cav.[67] was put in the cell for some act as yet unknown to us or in retaliation for something. See the notice of the capture of one of our Gun Boats on the Nansemond[68] and the crew put in Castle Thunder. Kilpatrick has gone to Alexandria on transports. The army of the Potomac going to be increased. Gen'l Halleck, Chief of Lincoln's Staff. Grant a Lt. General in total command of the entire Army.[69]

Wednesday, March 16. Day cold and disagreeable. A number of Reb Exchanged officers were in the Prison, and the discussion in some instances grew warm. A certain Colonel Greenwood made a fool of himself by his expressions, calling the officers here thick headed Dutchmen and ignorant Irish being worth nothing whereas he was born with thousands. The others were gentlemen and talked and acted decently. They said they were well treated in the North; that the Parol they thought all right &c. A load [of] more boxes arrived up, seeing a strange thing if we are going to be paroled also. Six hundred men sent daily to Americus, so that there are only 4000 men here now, 957 officers. The time hangs heavily, and reading ever grows tiresome. Had a trial and court, also debating society all having to get something to pass the time.

Thursday, March 17. The weather still continues very cold and disagreeable, and the strong winds blow fiercely. Got a ration of meat today, the second one this month. But this one was eatable, hence, we had a dinner of rice soup. Released Reb Prisoners came to visit Libby, Col. Davis of 10th Va. Cav.[70] whom our Regt captured at Hagerstown Md., was among the number and he refered to recent incidents [which had] transpired then and since in his usual brusque and jovial manner. Say he was well used in the north, in general being recipient of the <u>most</u> courteous and careful treatment possible, remarking that to find a person fit to take charge of prisoners you must choose him that has "swallowed powder"! Such is the truth on both sides. He is said to [be] paroled specially for Col. de Cresnola, 4 NY Cav.[71] Our Cols. are going out fast leaving only 4 or 5 remaining. The cause of the tardiness of exchange is said to be the facility of the Rebs to receive their men.

Friday, March 18. Weather still cold, but indications of a change. All things remarkably quiet, and Rumor weary of herself talks herself to rest. Heard of the issue of the boxes but 'twas false as they are being hauled away for some purpose. But they act so secretly that we know nothing of what is going on. Spring is coming on and shortly the grass will come forth and hail us as jail-birds. It seems so long, that as I sit and think of the past, and the prospects of freedom, the shadow is so dim that the heart grows faint. The sight of beef again gladdened our eyes. Spend the day partly in reading, most of the day in musing. May the day soon come when these sorrows may cease.

Saturday, March 19. Had a mail today. Got two letters, one from Mother, of 28th ult. [ultimo], also one from Ed. McChesney, who states that Haskins is Val., Hall, Greek Sal., Pierce, Latin Sal. Of our Society: Bales, Val., and Hubbard, Reply of Allegheny; Val. Hall and Reply [of] Knox; Of Bibs [Biblical Studies]: Pierce, Val. and Painter, Reply. Thomas (J. H.) and Mechem and McCall, gone to the Army.[72] Our folks at home [are] going to run to the "Jack," now Welty Farm, to Farm it.[73] So many changes are taking place at home that a strange[r] I shall be when permitted to again get there. Today is warmer; the sun is gaining strength and having now passed the winter in the balmy country of the South I long to go North.

Sunday, March 20. Another cargo of prisoners up, consisting of 1000 enlisted men and sixty officers: Four Colonels, Four Lt. Cols, &c. Wrote a letter to Mother, consisting of a closely written page. Lt. Cupp[74] got shot in the face with a buck-shot by the guard. They are getting so strict that we dare not stand by the window. Card playing and chess is the object of the day even Gen'l Scammon participating for which Capt. Whiteside gave him a lecture.[75] Incendiaries and all kinds of depredations committed in the city and the editors recommend none to be put in guard but Southerners, least they be treacherous, showing the fear that exists in the city.

Monday, March 21. Another party of Officers left today to the amount of 64, 6 Colonels, 5 Lt. Cols, leaving only one Col. and 8 or 10 Lt. Col. in Libby. Lt. Tresonthick[76] through the influence of his friends in the city, got away, also being the only representative of our Regt. Rumors of the Parole going to be stopped unless the terms be man for man, rank for rank, and we lay [rest of sentence unclear]. Hopes of soon getting away as but few privates are now left in the city, being mostly sent to Georgia, and 1,500 Confed. off. [officers] have been sent to Point Lookout.[77] Spent a good portion of the Day playing chess, getting to love the game. The day was delightful, the warm sun shown out brightly and only needed our freedom to make us extremely happy.

Tuesday, March 22. About noon the snow began to fall and again [at] dark. Measured the depth of several inches, verifying the adage "Since March came in like a lamb." The stoves in the Kitchen smoked and the fires were put out by the Rebs, making us cook all upon one, being impossible. Boxes were issued, and a load of 15 tons more came up for the "Generals" as the papers stigmatize us. They say that only about 2000 Yankey remain in and about the city including nearly 900 officers, and only 300 remaining on the Island engaged in making shoes and skins.[78] Col. Sanderson, Capt. Forbes, Lts. Knaggs, and Jones have been arrested since going north for their actions while in Libby in regard to the distribution of the clothing sent us.[79] Rumors of good prospects of speedy exchange and indications seem as if the Rebs were paroling man for man instead of 7 for 10 as at first. Health good, eating slim enough.

Wednesday, March 23. This morning the snow was five or six inches deep and very cold, so that looking out one would fancy he was in the frozen land of the North instead of the South. The sun came out brightly and the snow began to melt, leaving but a trace against night. Got news from the officers who left on last boat who say the prospect of exchange is bright and the papers, especially the "Whig,"[80] recommend that Butler be recognized as Commissioner of Exchange intimating that their men will take the "oath of Neutrality"[81] if not released soon. Charge the officers and men who, being in confinement, prefer to remain as prisoners rather than recognizing Gen'l Butler, as desiring the confinement to the dangers of the Battlefield. Expect soon, now, to be free and how the heart dilates at the thought to be free once more, and call yourself a free man. Health still very good, meat today again.

Thursday, March 24. Snow still upon the ground, but not so bitter cold, a blessing to the many poor women and children in this city, destitute of clothing, victuals and fire and the children who gather around the Prison on waiting for the refuse cornbread daily thrown out to them. The "Enquirer" thinks Butler should not be recognized under any circumstances. Papers usually fight among themselves, finding fault with the President, the Congress, and everyone. May confusion and contention prove their overthrow. Reading the letters of Napoleon Bonaparte to his bro. Joseph, which gives a good exposition of that great man's mind.[82] Daily we hear many rumors of every nature, but not to be depended upon and the longer we remain here, the longer the time appears. Still when I look forward, hope grows strong, and the anticipation of having a good time when free make me happy in prospections. Good health for which I am thankful.

Friday, March 25. The day was mild and the snow disappearing fastly so that only a trace is to be seen. The prison is undergoing improvement by having the sinks and water closets refited and placed <u>inside</u> the Libby in place of <u>outside</u> as formerly, as they fear it gives us too much chance of escaping. All things still point to the exchange as immediate and from the ardent desire exhibited by the Rebs there is no fear. 'Tis said the officials are going to be removed from the "Libby" and sent to the front, and they were taking an inventory of the Stores &c. looks like [this is] reliable. Had a fun day upstairs, having some fun and exercise, all being happy and as contented as possible. No operations (military) are the topic, but all seems quiet but this cannot continue long.

Saturday, March 26. Got letters from Bros. Jno and F.A., the latter being at Nashville, Tenn., and describes the country and his experience in his usually glowing style. Speaks of Mumfordsville, Bowling Green, and the Barren River in Ky. that empties into a cave and is seen no more. Also of Mammouth Cave.[83] He seems to like the Cavalry service better than the Infantry and is getting along swimmingly.[84] Bro. Jno. will soon start to Conference and has sent his last letter from Fayette Co.[85] Scarcely anything new. "Inquirer" opposes the recognition of Butler, saying that Lincoln might then impose upon them a negro for Commissioner of Ex. [Exchange] and does not (the Ex. [*Richmond Examiner*]) consider his recognition necessary to exchange any men thru parole, since the <u>old</u> cartel would allow them to exchange paroled prisoners by giving equivalents and sending notification. But 'tis understood that the <u>old</u> cartel is dead.

Sunday, March 27. Very pleasant today, the sun is warm and the balmy air of Spring gently fans the brows bared to its refreshing influence. Eagerly are the windows sought to breath[e] its fragrance, even at the risk of an unlucky bullet from the musket of the surly guard. When I think of the dastardly order that has consigned <u>some</u> of our prisoners to speedy death, revenge burns within my bosom and "crys aloud for vengeance." Coming as it does from a man who has never "smelled powder" but been in fat, easy positions all his life, may be palliative, for no man being a soldier would act as he does. Spent the day in reading. 'Tis Easter Sabbath and I reflect the many happy beings that have enjoyed it, while we pass it by as so much time desirable to be forgotten.

Monday, March 28. Reb money depreciating as again the 1st April it will only be worth 2/5 value by act of last Confed. Congress, and the Authorities refused to receive the money sent out for extras unless 1/5 should be deducted. Gen'l Grant at the Army of the Potomac having a review. Gen'l Smith appointed Chief of Staff; Gen'l Seigle has appointed Gen'l Stahl as Chief of Cavalry in Western or North W. Virginia.[86] Fort DeRussy in Red river reported captured by our forces.[87] The Rebs report that they captured two of our G. Boats. No Boat[88] up yet, and being unusual, many are want to interpret it as unfavorable to parol. Wrote a letter to Mother. The day is fine and having good health I am comparatively happy. Spent the day cooking, reading "Napoleon's Correspondence" and studying "Cavalry Tactics."[89] Roll on weary moments, roll on.

Tuesday, March 29. Rain fell fast all day and the wind blew fiercely, so that 'tis said no boat can land at City Point. Rumors of the stopping of the Parolling, as our Government has demanded that the mooted question about the Parolling of the Vicksburg, Port Hudson, and by Lee at Gettysburg.[90] But from the tone of the Papers, they seem as willing to investigate the matter and continue the matter of parolling. Gen's Burnsides is collecting a force at Annapolis for some unknown destination. He seems as odious almost as Butler. Capts. Campbell and Utter of our Regt is said to be discharged, dismissed [from] the service for disorderly conduct.[91] Issue of Boxes continues slowly; but all having anything contraband is confiscated. Very quiet no prisoners arriving and nearly all men have left for Georgia or for home.

Wednesday, March 30. The River is very high and promises to be higher than I have ever seen it. Great Rumors of Exchange since no boat has been up for more than a week, but the Rebs are so anxious of Exchange that they will come down to acknowledging Butler. 1st, 3rd, and 6th Corps are to be consolidated as [the] 6th and the Army of Potomac to be in their Corps, 2nd, 5th & 6th, consisting of 2 divisions.[92] Gen'l Pleasanton relieved from commanding the Cav. Corps, to report to Rosecrantz. Gen'l French to Philadelphia.[93] Issue of Boxes continue and they say all will soon be issued. The authorities ordered to the front the City Battalion [and] leaving today. Got half a loaf wheat bread today instead of cornmeal. Did some washing. Bryan being cook had time to play <u>chess</u>. Felt very well, but long to be exchanged as my feet are growing bun [bunions], the boots worn out.

Thursday, March 31. River wonderfully high being equal to, 'tis said, to the freshet of '62, occasioned by the fall of heavy rains upon the snow in the mountains. The Navy Yard is covered and some of the streets. Injury will be done. Gen'l Bragg, Commander in Chief of the Rebs, was in the Libby but I failed to see him.[94] The little boys, black and white, who have frequented the front and rear of our dwelling, were roughly handled by the men of the Chivalry, being caught and tossed in blankets to their great fright and consternation, so that they shall forgo the opportunity of getting the refuse corn-bread, suffering hungry stomachs, rather than the shaking process. Markets high, corn quoted at $40 a bushel, flour $250 per bbl. [barrel], but really higher as a pk. [peck] of meal costs $16.

Friday, April 1. "All Fools" day came and with it all the "sells"[95] and jokes practical, but being in expectation they had to be couched in unusually cautious terms to make them take. River fell to its milder position, had orders not to throw anything out of windows on penalty of getting shot at a risk. The "little girls" took the place of the "little boys" who got the tossing yesterday. Owen Lovejoy is reported dead.[96] Active movements on the tapis,[97] and had not this storm or succession of rainstorms come on movements would undoubtedly have been made sooner. Began raining toward evening and the petulant drops rattle upon the roof with no disagreeable sound. Had slight head-ache, with many others. McKay got a Box.[98]

Saturday, April 2. Rained most of the night and in the morning began to snow, and snowed heavily for several hours seeing a contradiction to southern climate. No news of exchange and as Judge Ould has been down to Fortress Monroe to see Gen'l Butler we expected to hear something reliable, but nothing is heard, and we are left in suspense bordering on desperation. Better [to] know that there is <u>no</u> hope that [than] to be continually swayed between hope and fear. See the Raiders and the niggers working together sweeping the streets done to make us sick of the "Everlasting Nigger,"[99] but retalliation shall only sting the one retalliating. No boxes today. Rations of bread and rice but having coffee and tea we get along. Find it possible for humanity to endure almost anything, and still be happy for among all our sorrows we have many happy times. May they increase.

Sunday, April 3. The weather continues drear with rain. Hear the good news that the Cartel is resumed, Judge Ould getting back from Fortress Monroe and all difficulties settled, &c. News of Paduca, Ky., being attacked by Gen'l Forrest and 5 or 6 thousand Rebs., which was gallantly held by our troops, 800 in Fort and on Gun Boats, killing 300 and wounded one thousand.[100] Rumors of a Mob in Illinois acting very badly, having to call upon the soldiers to quell it, being good news for the Rebs.[101] The Rebs are busy in refunding the old currency and issuing the old [new]. The say they have got 900 million in currency. The day unusually quiet, scarcely noticing it to be the Sabbath.

Monday, April 4. Had the comfort of the confirmation of all yesterday's rumors of Exchange by the Papers, stating all things settled and a Boat to be up the

6th or 7th inst. [instant] with wounded prisoners. Judge Ould had had an interview with Butler, recognizing him and the papers drop the epithet "Beast" and call him "Mr." or "Gen'l Butler." Oh, what a fall was that! All feel happy and merry on account of our prospects of getting home, but still our happiness is alloyed by the fear of being disappointed. For the first time since I have been here we got a ration of molasses. Read "Orpheus C. Kerr Papers," second series, and was amused and pleased at the many happy hits he gives the Conservative party of 1862, also the "little Hero," Gen'l Cundy, the "Mackeral Brigade," Gen'l McClellan.[102]

Tuesday, April 5. Rain, rain, nothing but rain, so that we fear that the River will be too high for the "flag of Truce Boat," to come up being by now our greatest desideratum. Gen'l Dow has got home to Portland, Me., and was escorted through the city by the military and martial music. The 11th or 12th Corps are said to have joined the Army of the Potomac. Sergt. George (Reb.) gave the number of deaths of Union Prisoners in Richmond since last July at six hundred and sixty, a goodly number. Began to read "Gil Blas" translated from LaSage's French by Molletts, being a strange affair, but wonderfully true to life, and altho the evil may sift evil out of it, yet to the good there are many lessons of wisdom and virtue.[103] Feel unwell this evening, having overcharged my stomach with too great a feast of ham-bone and turnips & parsnips. Long for clear weather and the day when we may quit this lonesome place.

Wednesday, April 6. Cleared up and rain ceased to fall giving us pretty weather again. Rumor of a Boat being up at City Point but no Confederates. Still the sick have had orders to "pack up" going to leave soon. The River is said to be to high for the Boats to pass the obstructions and Torpedoes, so that the elements have conspired together to protract our stay. Felt unwell all day, having a dull head-ache with bilious stomach. Am growing restive and can hardly confine my mind to any one point for more than a few minutes, and the order of the day usually continues, reading, roaming around, playing, chatting, et cetera.

Thursday, April 7. Pleasant day, warm and comfortable. A Boat said to be up with only four Con. [Confederate] Officers; our sick to go down soon. But 18 tons more of provisions have come from the North, and it would seem our authorities expect us to stay some time yet. Read "Klosterheim" a German Story, ending with good effect.[104] Water gave out, and a great rage for carriers. Lt. Scudder[105] got a box and <u>our</u> mess came in for a share through his benevolence. Saw an advertisement of a Capt. Ayers of Co. "I," 18th Pa. Cav., for recruits in the Phil. Inq. so that there had been promotion or he is bringing a new company into [the] Regt.[106] Good news from the North abt. [about] the success in recruiting and the strong determination to put down the rebellion. May Heaven hasten success.

Friday, April 8. Today is the day appointed by Jeff Davis as one of "Prayer and Fasting," not willing to give up the confidence in the Deity thinking, perhaps, or endeavoring to persuade the people that the lord has his traitorous undertaking as an object of care. In the day of disaster the Devils themselves believe in God and cower, so the traitors fear for the future and would fain pour out libations for mercy. May they learn to respect not only God but his ordained government. The day was pretty and warm and was spent tolerably happy. Expect the sick to leave soon. The time creeps on slowly and soon six months will have passed since I became a prisoner.

Saturday, April 9. No papers today on account of yesterday being a day of "Fasting &c.," hence no news except those of Rumors. Some one tried to perplex the credulous with the Rumor that Stanton had vetoed the Exchange and we were here "ad bellum."[107] The day was spring like and in the evening the Rain fell in copious showers, and high waters shall again prevail. No officers left yet as the rains prevented 'tis said. But really all things are very inexplicable indeed. Read part of "Gil Blas" and am getting disgusted with it, being so frivolous and pointless. Have given up the idea of reading it through. Have come down to eating cornbread alone for breakfast, dinner, and supper, no enviable diet surely. Have hope for speedy relief or else the knowledge the [that] we have no hope for exchange, the suspense being too hard to endure.

Sunday, April 10. Rained all last night and the water is high, swelling over the banks of the river into the canal higher than at any former time since I came here. A gale of wind came on and what a sight, the water framed and pile up into mountains. Two Steamers left the warf [wharf] and anchored opposite Libby under the protection of the Island.[108] This gave an opportunity for spirited calling out "Two boats Up," "All exchanged," "Pack up," &c. Lt. Timony,[109] the Regular Officer who made himself so ridiculous by asking for private quarters from the volunteer officers, has at length got them, being sent to the cell for insulting the surgeon having but few to pity him. Read part of Bunyan's "Holy War" but did not admire as much as his P. Progress, being the result of his imprisonment.[110] How few improve the time as well.

Monday, April 11. Three years this morning at 4 A.M. have passed since the traitors fired upon fort Sumpter and compelled Major Anderson to haul down the "Red, White & Blue." Oh, what blood has flowed since then! Six months have also passed since I was captured. The river was desperately high submerging half the lower part of the city being higher than the memorably floods of '62 & '47. An officer, Lt. Stevens, 104 N.Y., died in hospital today of Chronic Diarhea.[111] The Exchange said to be all right and as soon as the river admits we shall take our course "homeward bound." Northern papers saying all is right, the exchange being "man for man." The morning clear, but clouding up again, and more rain set to fall.

Tuesday, April 12. Lt. Forsythe, 100 Ohio Rgt., was shot by the guard; said to be accidental while loading his musket opposite the prison. The gun went off while he was priming, but he enjoyed the joke so well that many think he played it purposely. The ball went through his head scattering his brains in all directions.[112] The blood flowed freely and to those who under other circumstances looked unawed upon blood now shudder at the sight. So near release having contended so much, to fall the victim of negligent awkwardness or hatred is a fate deplorable enough. Had a meeting of the Officers. A committee consisting of one from each state, also one from Regulars, and navy was appointed to draft resolutions to be sent to his home Regt.[113] The day was gloomy but promises to be better weather soon.

Wednesday, April 13. The river has fallen into its former chanal and the Steamers, which were lying opposite Libby left for their former positions. It was expected that the Convalescents should start to City Point but did not, and are expected to go tomorrow. The day is fine, and the air warm so that spring is fully set in, and the rain storms gone. 'Tis said our men at Americus are dying fastly, at the rate of thirty a-day, and that the prisoners at Danville are going there to be exchanged. It seems a hard lot to be so far from home and friends with no hope of ever seeing them and then lie down and die.

Thursday, April 14. The day mild and comfortable. The River falling and low enough for boats to run but the Boats did not go down. The fisheries opened, with slim success as far as we could see.[114] Many are getting heartily sick of the many rumors that distress us, which others delight to raise for effect. Read part of "Don Quixote," but although laughable, is not much of an affair. Don't think I can read it through. The water was turned on again much to our comfort, and we had scrubbing and washing all day. Feel well, and wait patiently for Exchange.

Friday, April 15. The day fine, Rumor of the Boat going to lan[d] "tomorrow." A Capt. coming from the Army of Potomac says they are ready to move, that the army is 100,000 strong. All the Commanders of the Cav. Corps changed: Gen'l Torbert, the 1st Div., Gen'l Wilson the 2nd, Gen'l Sheridan the Corps. Gen'l Kilpatrick released from the command of the division and is to command a Brigade.[115] Gold has gone up to 175 in New York. Had a Resolution in the House trying to expell Long of Ohio for Treason and resulted in Harris of Md., giving vent to words traitorous as Fernand Wood.[116] The sick are being loaded on the Boats to leave tomorrow. Well and hopeful.

Saturday, April 16. The convalescents left today for City Point, also the Surgeon and Capt. Doten, 14th Conn. Capt. Chase who was at Salisbury was sent back to Libby.[117] Looks well and reports the rest getting along well. Capts. Reed and Litchfield have escaped but were recaptured.[118] Have good hopes of exchange soon, as the Rebs want to close the James River before our Army attacks. The day was wet and cold, raining slightly most of the day. The Rebs are busy on the fisheries. Were notified to apply for any money left with the authorities, as it would be refunded.

Sunday, April 17. The morning cold and chilly. The Flag of Truce Boats came up from City Point, have a load of Boxes, which were stored in the common receptacle, scarcely ever coming forth. The fisheries were busy, irrespective of Sabbath. The Roads are getting dry and information from the Army of the Potomac says they are ready to move having eight days rations. Grant it appears is going to take Richmond by close siege, being his fort[e] yet many hard battles will take place. All cavalry orderlies ordered to their Regts., so our regt. is likely together. Health good, cornbread and tea.

Monday, April 18. Today cold, but indications of getting warm. Nearly all the Prisoners at Danville have gone to ~~Salisbury~~ Americus Ga., some few to City Point via Petersburg. Exchange wavering, a Reb. Capt. reporting no arrangements made for a General Exchange. Finished "Headleys History of Napoleon Bonapart" liking it extremely well, being the mean between the partial Histories of "Scott" and "Abbott."[119] With all his faults I cannot but admire the man and sympathy for him remains throughout the whole. Weather dry and expect Grant soon. Health good, rations slim.

Tuesday, April 19. No Boat up yet, but expecting one. Boxes were issued. Had orders last week to apply for money, but it has not made its appearance. "Fresh fish" came in, Capt. of 16 N.Y. C. and Lt. of 157 Penn. captured by Moseby.[120] They report Mead on the eve of moving. Everything looks like speedy movements. Longstreet is said to be making a junction with Lee. Gold in New York is very fluctuating, seemed to be made the sport of speculations. Not long since was quoted at 179 and in one day went up to 189 to fall immediately to 171, where it now remains. Sec. Chase is said to have made a loan of 3 million of England.[121] Forrest has taken Fort Pillow, deliberately murdering hundreds of our men, bayonetting them after surrender. He has also made another attact on Paduca.[122] The day fine and dry. Health good, and hopes variating.[123]

Wednesday, April 20. The sun shines brightly but the air is cool. Activity is increasing, the Rebs making preparation for the Reception of Grant. The lady Clerks of the city have been ordered to leave the city for more southern, and safer climes, also the women. We got money getting $100, if they had enough greenbacks, a good share of which was sent out, for provisions. Fishing continues but the prices, indicating poor success, paying $5.00 per small shad. Exchange fluctuating as Dick Turner[124] says we must eat thirty loaves of cornbread yet, and Col. Cesnola thinks that we shall soon leave and all together. The Boat is expected up on Friday with sick. Burnside reports of moving, thus taking most of the transports. Health good. Had no meat for many weeks. Thanks to Northern friends, for meat.

Thursday, April 21. The day was delightful, the sun shining brightly and the air came so pure through the iron bars that I long to roam the free earth again and enjoy its comforts. Got mail, two letters from Sister Kitty and Eph. Brunner, Jr. Good news of both. Gen'l Kilpatrick has been relieved from command of our Division (3rd) and ordered to the West to Sherman.[125] The Rebs captured Plymouth, N.C., with 1600 prisoners guns &c also a lot of negroes.[126] Part were negro soldiers. They seem to have very bad luck. Fort Pillow is destroyed, evacuated by the Rebs. Our forces seem incensed at Forrest's acts, and want to shoot all his prisoners for his murderous deeds. Health good.

Friday, April 22. Weather very fine and dry. Some active operations in the Army must take place, and oh, what destiny hangs upon the success of this campaign! Read the speech of Long from Ohio in Congress, which I fear indicates the growing sentiments in the North for the recognition of the Rebs.[127] If this be the policy, why such blood shed, why so many lives lost in vain. No Boat up yet and we are growing quite discouraged. Sent out $20 for soda and potatoes. Fishing poor as only a few are caught. A good size shad costs us $15. Health good.

Saturday, April 23. The day fine, warm and dry. Nothing occurring to break the monotony of this life. Hear that Gen'l Averill is not expected to live.[128] See that Col. Bryan had captured some Rebs on the Rapid Ann being with the Regt now.[129] The day passes slowly as we have been disappointed so often in expecting exchange. Hope has grown sick and the very repetition of this word sickens. The Government is growing warm on the "Fort Pillow" Butchery and retaliation is going to be the order of the day. But to us this looks gloomy enough, since we may be fortunate enough to hang before we get out of the Rebs hands. But to the Gov., thick or thin.

Sunday, April 24. Very pretty day and the bipeds of the city kept quite a parade before our domicile, displaying all sorts of colors and characters, from the highest to the lowest. The evening was wet but very pleasant, being warm and airy. An "old Grey haired gentleman" came in and said exchange was all right and a Boat was hourly expected. Wrote two letters one to Kitty and one to Eph. Brunner, Jr. Felt lonely and sad, and am almost worn out in expectation of going home. Have very little to read, and existence seems void. It need not be thus, but to feel otherwise requires Herculean efforts. Feel well physically, and hope for the future.

Monday, April 25. Day fine, News scarce, but expect something soon. Dr. Roger Lugo and Sterling King have been arrested by spies, the former on the Rappahannock, the latter by Longstreet's detectives.[130] Our forces are said to be landing at Yorktown in force, but the Rebs are at a great loss to know when the onslaught is going to be. Banks is reported to be repulsed on the Red River Expedition in Texas, losing a good many men and gunboats.[131] Fire at Rockets[132] yesterday the fire Brigade passed Libby in double quick. Cavalry made a demonstration at Germania Ford but retired. Over two millions is said to be enlisted and conscripted in our Army since the war. Chase is at New York and trying to break up the gold gambling among the brokers. Have good health, Capt. Pennypacker got a box; Capt. Craig gave us coffee.[133] Feel well and live in hope. No Boat up.

Tuesday, April 26. Rained last evening. This morning pleasant. Air warm, and refreshing. The Gen'l and Staff captured at Plymouth came in: Brig Gen'l Wessels, two Colonels, two Lt. Cols, two Chaplains &c about a dozen in all. The[y] report 120 officers and 2000 men captured, 30 guns, one "two hundred Parrot," two gunboats sunk by a Ram then [that] came down the Roanoke [River].[134] Provisions &c. being a disaster [and] disgraceful. The 101 & 103 Pa. Regts., 16th and 15th Conn. Regts. with detachment of Cavalry held the Post. Anticipate movements upon New Berne now. Gen'l Butler sent word to the French vessels at City Point on Sunday that the time granted for putting out their tobacco had expired and they left without the tobacco, indicating that active movements are about beginning. No Boat up yet. Health good. Had roasted turkey for dinner. [MS illegible]

Wednesday, April 27. River rising, preventing the fisheries. The day clear and beautiful. No news. The "Examiner" was withheld from us and we surmise something in it not for us to know and rumor says 'tis a fight on the Rapid Ann with ill success, but nothing indicates anything of the kind. Gen'l Averil is said to be on a Raid. The Rebs can't understand Grant. The gulf states think he is going to make the attack in Georgia and they deplore it, while the Virginians say his attack will be on Richmond. No Boat up and a good many doubt the probability of the "Exchange." Had preaching by the Chaplin who came in from Plymouth.[135] Feel well and try to be happy.

Thursday, April 28. Felt unwell all day having the headache, occasioned by too free use of the ugly water we have to use. Our forces are again reported in the vicinity Barhamsville,[136] 30 miles down the River from Richmond. Moseby attacked our forces in Fairfax county yesterday, A.M., [but] was repulsed losing two Lts. Our expenses said to be 1½ million per day, entire debt $3,000,000,000. The debt of Great Britain $3,912,669,792. Gen'l Wessels appears to be an ordinary man, a Brig Gen'l of Vol., Major in regular Army. The Examiner wants more "Fort Pillows." The stay at home Gen'ls are for the Black Flag.[137] Let him enter the field and his tune will be trimed.

Friday, April 29. The day very fine indeed. Rumor of a Boat coming to City Point loaded with prisoners. Excitement runs high, altho none scarcely believe the Rumor. News from the North are various. Banks has had a hard fight in the Trans-Mississippi Department, but loss not so bad as the Rebs thought. Indication of our forces attacking Richmond by three fronts, the Rapid Ann, Shenandoah Valley, and the Peninsula or Petersburg. Grant is moving slowly but surely and as the destiny of the Nation seems hanging on the success of this campaign it behooves him to move securely. Plymouth officers not yet arrived. Health good, but long for exchange.

Saturday, April 30. No meat issued this month. Boat came up and thirty four officers left including Col. Rose, Col. Birch, 16 Conn. captured at Plymouth, Two ~~Surgeons~~ Chaplains, Three Surgeons, Major Henry,[138] eight of the "gofers" (who escaped through the hole and were recaptured), [and] 350 Privates left. The Papers say a large number started from Point Lookout, but the "Express" gave out and only part got to City Point. Exchange stock is more lively. The Raiders were put in the lower cellar for cutting the board that let them out of the cell in the kitchen. The Board fell down at night and gave the alarm. Gen'l J. E. B. Stuart was in Libby a pretty good-looking officer. Weather very pleasant. Health good, nothing to read, and feel lonely. Without variation man grows tired of even himself.

Sunday, May 1. The Rebs came up from City Point last night, 40 officers and about 400 men, all sick or convalescents. A Flag of Truce Boat is to be up every week. All prisoners received at City Point up to 20 April declared exchanged. Dr. Mary E. Walker confined in Castle Thunder was not sent North by last Boat.[139] Four of the men in the brick [prison] opposite Libby escaped last night. Rebel Congress to meet tomorrow, when they intend to repeal the "Bill Suspending the Habeas Corpus." Rebs expect our forces to attack this week, and great consternation seems to be among them. They took to large guns, 8 or 10 inches, down the river, probably for the Gun Boat in Iron Clad Ram building down at the Navy Yard.[140] Wrote two letters to mother and Bro. Frank. The day was fine and the usual parade in front of the Prison. Health good, Grub consists of corn bread.

Monday, May 2. Burnside is reported to be reinforcing Grant or Meade, having loaded up at Alexandria. The "Inquirer" says a Flag of Truce is to come up every week, seeming too slow for us. The men at Georgia[141] dying at the rate of twelve per day: soon there will be none left to exchange. Why does our government delay so long? Read Gilmer's speech upon the "Suspension of the Writ of Habeas Corpus."[142] How they howl at the prospect of the President having so much power! Had a heavy gale of wind, which nearly lifted off the roof of the West Room. Rained very hard, thundering and lightening. The Plymouth officers are hardly coming to Libby. The officers in the cell were put in their old quarters on the kitchen floor. Have very good health but not very strong on corn bread diet. All these things make me pray for Exchange.

Tuesday, May 3. Read Jeff Davis message; was a short and small affair. Says he don't know anything about Exchange. Our Authorities stopping at any time without any apparent cause; says the men are dying fastly in opposition to the humane treatment received. Major Goff, Capt. Fry and Lt. Manning were confined in the cell for retalliation. The Major for the confinement of a Reb. Major caught recruiting within our lines.[143] 'Tis said Grant has asked for the privilege of assigning McClellan and Fremont[144] to Command in the Army of the Potomac. No movements particularly, some forces are at West Point &c. Reb. Congress trying to expel Senator Cob from Alabama, thinking him a traitor.[145] The day was very fine. Could see the farmers in a distance planting corn. Oh the days of the past.

Wednesday, May 4. Fine day, dry and pleasant. The Armies on all sides seem to be on the eve of moving, as Grant is said to be crossing the Rapid Ann, and maneuvering for position. Soon a heavy battle will evidently be fought there. Rebs seem buoyant and hopeful of success and gold has got down to $20 for $1

[Confederate currency]. Hon. J. T. Leach of South Carolina said in Congress that he was for peace, if not by their immediate independence, then by anything but subjugation.[146] Dissatisfaction is growing since apparent, as a good portion of the officers think the necessity of us staying here is gone by. Then why not give us the benefit of freedom. I grow almost out of patience.

Thursday, May 5. Lt. Duchesney, Capt. Markbright and two of Straight's Command were put in the Cells, said to be retaliation for the confinement of four officers at Johnson Island.[147] Got a mail, one letter from Sister Jennie, says Sister Kate is married. She [is] going to teach at Adamsburg.[148] Gen'l Garibaldi had an over whelming reception at London.[149] The Danes had a very heavy fight and defeat.[150] Grant is moving slowly but surely. A Fleet has made its appearance in James River near fort Darling, thought to be Gilmore from Charleston.[151] All things look bright to us and should the fort fall into our hands, and the Gunboats come up the river, Richmond is gone under. A Flag of Truce with 60 Off. [officers] and 352 men came to City Point last night. The day is very fine and excitement is growing so tense. Have the headache.

Friday, May 6. A Boatload of Officers (28) and men left for City Point, but was met by Judge Ould who sent them back, as active operations have commenced and the boat could not be received. Excitement grows intense. News coming from Lee of a battle raging, two of his Corps engaged. Reports the Capture of 4 Guns and some prisoners, also the Death of Gen'l Jones (Cav) and wounding of Gen'l Stafford.[152] Great operations are going on to repulse our Army, coming up the Peninsula, sending all the home guards and Jackass Battery to the front. Indications of having to leave Libby, as rations have been brought in this evening and the guard lies at a short distance. Great excitement among us, and conjecture as to where we shall go. Anything may be as good as this. May Grant capture Richmond.

Five

"Think of Home and Wonder When the Space That Now Separates Us Will Be Traversed"

Macon, Georgia, May 7–July 27, 1864

Weaver happily left Libby Prison, but traveling on the South's deteriorating railroads only added to prisoners' ordeals. Stuffed into filthy cattle cars and flatcars with little room to sit or to lie down, the men suffered from hunger after a day or more without food and from exposure to rain during forced marches and at transfer points. A few prisoners escaped into the bushes or jumped off the slowly moving cars, prompting shots from the guards posted on top and pursuit by bloodhounds. Yet, these trips provided opportunities to observe the Southern countryside and towns and to interact with free and enslaved civilians. Most whites came to jeer the Yankee prisoners, but a few offered comforts. Compared to prison's monotonous routines, the novelty of travel through a wartorn Confederacy left indelible impressions in many prisoners' narratives.

Weaver's first stop was Danville, Virginia, a town of six thousand people and tobacco factories, Confederate depots, and hospitals about 145 miles southwest of Richmond. The prison complex was established in November 1863 and consisted of six tobacco factories of three stories each, stripped of furnishings. Prison No. 3 housed some five hundred officers, who were cramped on the two upper floors and the garret with about twelve square feet of space per person, Weaver calculated. He thought the rations an improvement over Libby, but meals had to be cooked outdoors and water carried under guard from the Dan River, about 1,200 feet away. Fortunately, he arrived after a smallpox epidemic the previous winter had ended and left before mortality resumed in the fall from inferior rations and disease.[1]

After four days, Weaver and the other officers were marched through rain and mud and loaded into flatcars. Five days later, on May 17, they arrived at Camp Oglethorpe, a prison stockade in a former military camp and the state fairgrounds outside Macon, Georgia. A plank wall twelve feet high enclosed some three acres of ground with a small stream and several one-story buildings, including the former floral hall now serving as the hospital. Guards patrolled the camp along platforms set ten yards apart and four cannons aimed at the prisoners deterred rebellions. A three-and-a-half-foot picket fence placed sixteen feet inside the stockade marked the deadline as any prisoner caught between this fence and the wall could be shot without warning. Weaver found outdoor confinement less onerous than gloomy Libby. He noted the temperate weather, his good health, religious services on Sundays, space to roam among the 1,400 imprisoned officers, and decent rations of cornbread, bacon, molasses, bran meal, vinegar, and salt that he supplemented with purchases from licensed merchants, or sutlers. Inmates formed two divisions, each subdivided into squads of one hundred men. Twenty men constituted a mess, which rotated cooking duties and, under guard, left the stockade to gather firewood. Lumber and building materials were issued for making shelters, and Weaver kept busy during the first month helping construct a shed and a bedstead. Using prisoners' labor reduced costs, but it also provided planking used to hide tunnels. Despite threats of retaliation by Captain George C. Gibbs, the camp commandant, the prisoners frequently attempted to escape.[2]

Physical activity revived Weaver's spirits despite an absence of letters and reading material. Although aware of enlisted prisoners' extreme suffering at Andersonville, he opposed a proposal to send representatives from the Macon camp to Washington to plea for resuming the exchange cartel as only playing into the hands of the Union's antiwar opponents. Weaver followed military events closely, as newly arriving prisoners gave generally favorable accounts of Ulysses S. Grant's Overland Campaign in Virginia against Robert E. Lee and about William T. Sherman's Atlanta Campaign against Joseph E. Johnston. A quick raid by Sherman's forces outside Atlanta rather than a general exchange seemed the more likely path for release. Weaver's hopes were not misplaced. In late July, General George Stoneman Jr., commander of the Army of the Ohio's Cavalry Corps, supported the Atlanta Campaign by leading his forces deep into Confederate territory, intending to destroy railroads and factories and free the Union prisoners at Macon and at Andersonville. Although Stoneman failed and was captured outside Macon and held for three months, the approaching Union cavalry forced Camp Oglethorpe's hasty evacuation. Half of the prisoners went to relative comfort in Savannah and the rest, including Weaver, to Charleston, where they faced new dangers from poor prison conditions and from Union artillery bombarding the city.

Saturday, May 7, 1864. [We] were aroused by 12 midnight and ordered to be ready to leave for <u>Petersburg</u> in an hour. Few believed we were going there as it really turned out. Took till daylight to call our names when we started and got aboard

Fig. 13. Officer's Prison No. 3, Danville, VA, where Weaver was briefly held in May 1864. (MOLLUS-Mass Civil War Photograph Collection, United States Army Heritage and Education Center, Carlisle, PA)

of the Danville & Richmond R.R., which disclosed the policy of Dick Turner. We were crowded into cattle box cars and having only one door open with two guards in the door, and many men on top, taking extra precautions to prevent us escaping, not allowing any one for whatever cause to go out of the cars. But they failed after all, as three or four jumped off, but don't know whether or not they got safe. We spent a terrible night and got to Danville about 3 A.M. next morning. Slept but little but looks gloomily for Exchange.

Sunday, May 8. Morning found us at Danville, Va., 140 miles south west of Richmond on the line (almost) between Va. & N.C. and south of Lynchburg. A fair town of considerable size but much scattered. We landed, happy to get the fire and being dirty enough we marched to our quarters, put 500 of us in one building to occupy two floors and the garret of 37½ by 76, making about 2 ft. by six [ft.] per each man. Water scarce; have to carry it from the River (Dan) ourselves. Have not the privilege of cooking ourselves but our privates do it for us. Get better rations than at Libby. Getting plenty of cornbread, and some bacon, but still all would soon go back to Libby in point of comfort. Can't get any news, but it seems we are getting the better of them, and a fleet large enough to clear the James is ascending. 'Tis exceeding warm and wear nothing but underclothing. Have roll call by the old system, in four ranks. Amid all, I feel well, and pray for the future.

Monday, May 9. Affairs continue the same, with the news that our forces had captured Petersburg with immense stores, Arms, &c. Grant progressing with hard fought battles, but getting only an occasional paper, we are ignorant of the true state of the case. Exchange is still going on slowly making "Aiken's Landing" on the James above City Point the place of delivery.[3] The papers at Richmond complain severely at the officers destroying their extra stores when leaving. About 50 of us at once get out into a small yard 20 x 100 ft. to wash or cook extras or a little coffee. Water has to be carried from the river, 80 Rods distant, by us and the privates. The privates are to police our building, preferred by them and accepted by us to get to see them. Hear from our Boys, they are getting along well. Hear of a goodly number escaping from here. Our condition remains the same but hope for move soon. Eating abundant.

Tuesday, May 10. The news of the taking of Petersburg was premature but the Railroad is cut at Chester Station and the decisive battle about to be fought.[4] Grant is fighting stedily loosing some Generals, Wadsworth, Hays, Carr, while the Rebs suffer fully as badly.[5] Two of our Gen'ls[6] & 2000 prisoners said to be captured with 150 officers. Cavalry doing good service cutting the Central Road.[7] Rumor of going to Geo. [Georgia] and the rations were brought in but countermanded. Had plenty of bacon and cornbread. Cook coffee occasionally. The Exchange seems to be in vogue and occasional, big excitement burst out. Health good, &c.

Wednesday, May 11. Day pleasant and as active as ever. News of the Battle progressing in Virginia but the Rebs claim to repulse our forces at every point. Still the statements show that Lee is only fighting the 5th Corps and we expect the others to turn up somewhere. Cavalry doing good service, cutting all the railroads, the one south of Petersburg also west of Lynchburg.[8] Expect to leave this [place] tomorrow, and the rations have been issued and great speculation is going on as to our destination. Most say Macon, Ga. This looks good for us, as Grant is likely successful. Feel well and have hopes of getting to the land of better days soon. Exchange is as usual, subject to great excitement as the papers say it is all "Right" now. Still we don't put any confidence in any such reports. The weather is warm, the grass and trees all green, the corn up, and all things [illegible] happy. And with a sad thought I look upon these things as I am [able?].

Thursday, May 12. Were wakened at daylight. Raining fastly. Got out and marched to the train through the mud, and being delayed then four hours standing in the rain, we got loaded on open flats or wood cars on the Piedmont Rail Road, crossed the Virginia line into N.C. and coming to Piedmont Station; had to walk 5 or 6 miles over the unfinished part.[9] This was a sorry road and by dint of much puffing and sweating, at last tired and sore got to the next station. We got supper and about midnight loaded and went to Greensboro. Was astonished to see N.C. look as well, it having large crops of corn planted but little wheat. The ground looks poor and worn out, the expected result of Slavery but Yankey farmers can make something of it. A good portion is wilderness and swamps. Very few people along the road, many niggers being blacker than Virginia niggers.

Friday, May 13. Greensboro[10] is a pretty, small place but nearly deserted as usual. Crossed the Yadkin River. Passed thru Salisbury but could see but little of the place. Saw the building in which our men are confined &c.[11] Made good speed, getting to Charlotte, N.C., about 4 P.M. Landed and got rations, 9 hardtacks for 3 days rations. Some ladies came out to look upon "live Yankeys" and we greeted them with "Star Spangled Banner," "Rally Round the Flag Boys," &c, seeming lively enough and no doubt awakened thoughts of the past. The officers are very haughty and their actions were as mean toward us boxing us up in dirty, filthy cars placing four or five guards in each car and nearly a dozen on the top so that a little negro remarked: "Why you guards must be afraid of the Yankeys. They are nervous them Yankeys." But with all their vigilance a few are escaping but what a prospect before anyone roaming wild through the swamps of North Carolina. Many times I debate the prospects and looking at my bare feet my reason cautions: "attempt it not." Raining slowly.

Saturday, May 14. Got aboard the train at midnight amid wind and rain, and the cars leaked so badly and were so dirty that we got so completely wet and covered with dirt. No sleep for me and I had to stand up and sit cradled down alternately till morning. Anxiously we waited for starting. Passed [blank space in MS] River[12] into South Carolina, Chester, Hillsboro, and arrived at Columbia at dusk having passed through a horrid country and miserable day. Notice that the farmers are planting large crops of corn. No cotton planting. We changed cars and made way for Augusta, Ga. Have no news as to what the Armies are doing, and we appear to be shut out of the world, thrown about like pigs driven in and out and get dressed more like thieves, convicts, than prisoners of war. All these things fire the blood and demand vengeance. Oh, that the day may come which shall make all things even.

Sunday, May 15. Slept a good portion of the time last night being covered over with limbs of others, having 50 or 60 in each car. But sleep overcame all difficulties. Ran very slow, having all the officers instead of half as the two trains consolidated at Columbia. Passed through a village in which some ladies throw a good number of bouquets to us for what reason I know not for otherwise no union sentiment is observed. Got to Augusta at 4 P.M. when a large crowd of ladies, soldiers, and negros waited to gaze at us. The people of this city are the most civilized of any I have seen in the Confederacy and I should not wonder should there be a union sentiment here. The guard was changed. The home guards taking possession of us being all grey-headed men over the age of 45. Strange sight. Staid all night lying in the cars. Slept middling but too close not knowing where my own limbs were. Thus pass the Sabbath here.

Monday, May 16. The morning found us in Augusta. The guards were kind and our situation was better than any time during the rout[e]. We started and moved out 10 miles where we halted, until 4 P.M. We had coffee, chance to dry our wet blankets, and "skirmish" since the cars were desperate[ly] lousy. Doubts we had concerning our rout[e], as some were sanguine enough to hope we were going to Savannah, to be exchanged. But we got to the junction[13] and headed for Macon, when all expectation of that kind disappeared. The day was warm, but I cut a board out of the car, which gave me view and air. What an amount of corn the Rebs are planting. Fields after Fields, Negros, women and men do the plowing, using only one horse to each plow. Saw as many as 6 plows going at one time. The country is low and swampy but not as low as S.C. Felt well, and try to be as comfortable as possible.

Tuesday, May 17. Running all night we got to Macon at 8 A.M., stopping at the outer depot, not getting to see the City. Were put into Camp surrounded by a stockade with sentinels mounted, also a picket fence inside of this. Have no buildings, but made tents out of our blankets. Have plenty of water and good accommodation, so that I prefer it many times to the Notorious Libby. The Plymouth officers came in, also some confined in the Jail, making nearly 1000.[14] On the rout[e] 'tis said that fifty-one officers escaped, but a good portion were Tennesseans, who knew the road. We are divided into two divisions, commanded by Gen'ls Wessells and Scammon,[15] also into squads of 100 commanded by Lt. Cols. Get cornbread, and bacon being better than Libby but not so much as at Danville. But then we are in the air, and can roam around the camp in size about 5 or 6 acres. At night it seemed like a large encampment. Day warm.

Wednesday, May 18. Pretty weather, but very warm, especially for us who have not felt the sun for so long. Have to do our own policing and cooking. Getting boards for barracks. Hospital in the middle of the Ground. Have a good many sick or those who pretend. Have the opportunity of sending out for anything except liquors, but the money being left behind at Richmond very few have any to send out. Lt. Smith, who escaped from the train, came in having given himself up, unable to get through the swamps. Gen'l J. E. B. Stuart was killed or mortally wounded near Richmond, 'tis said.[16] The nights are cool, and have good sleep, but the guards keep up such a noise calling the Corporal and at night, the hour and half hour, that it worries me. Have nothing to read, and 'tis weary and lonely. Hope success may soon fall on our arms, that we may leave this place. Have excellent health.

Thursday, May 19. The day clear and warm. Our grub continues the same being very good in quality if not in quantity of meat. Have three days of rations issued at a time except bread: that daily. Getting boards and expect to have sheds. Capt. Van Buren, 6th N.Y. C., was recaptured escaping off the train.[17] He was at Andersonville, Ga., and saw our men, some 10 or 12 thousand shut up in a camp of 6 acres having no shelter and very little clothing. Get but little food and are dying fastly, having 1189 died since the 4th March. This is a crime to be accounted for some day, and woe to him upon whom it falls! Capt. Mason was also recaptured.[18] News from the Armies of various kinds but most rumor. Sherman is driving Johnson to Atlanta having occupied Rome and S ____.[19] Banks has not surrendered as reported. He is at Alexandria, La.[20] Grant is driving on Lee, and hard fighting is the result. Have good health and spirits.

Friday, May 20. Warm and clear as usual scarcely a cloud to break the rays of the scorching sun. The men wear as few clothes as possible, being nearly nude. Some of the goods came in sent for, and the prices are worse than at Richmond, paying $32 a gal. for Molasses, $5 per tin cup, $15 per quart tin bucket, $15 per wooden bucket &c., but it is supposed that the Rebs charge us 100% for their trouble. Capt. Tabb is in command of the camp.[21] Greenbacks are not so good here as at Richmond bringing only 4 or 5 for one.[22] A guard shot at an officer and it being proven that the latter was not disobeying orders, the guard was put in arrest, and punished. The trains run nightly and 'tis said they are bringing wounded to the City. Gen'l Wessells is making himself very disagreeable, by assuming much authority, ordering our chaplain "not to make reference to the war." Exchange rumors is not dead but the old citizens trust not.

Saturday, May 21. The sky as clear as ever and the sun equally warm. We are getting pretty well satisfied with our Camp but complain considerably about our Government keeping us here so long. Squads 1 & 2 built their sheds, 100 ft. by 12 ft. Wrote two letters to Jennie and to Mother, paying $1.00 for two sheets of small paper, and $1 for three miserable envelopes. News from the front conflicting but Johnston is undoubtedly getting the worst of it. Got the papers today. They say our men at Andersonville are dying at the rate of 20 to 30 daily. Gov. Brown has ordered out all the militia.[23] Very few "fresh fish" come in, and we interpret this "good for us." Washed having hard work. Am learning to sympathize with the washerwoman. Oh, how I long to be at home to leave this hateful place and be myself again. The past is leaving a blank in my life never to be filled.

Sunday, May 22. Felt unwell today, having a bilious spell,[24] but soon got well. The days passes very sluggishly, having nothing to read, not even the bible. Had preaching by a chaplain. Felt happy for the opportunity of attending while most disregarded the call. How reckless soldiers get neither regard God or man. "Fresh Fish" say Sherman is seven miles from Atlanta, only 100 miles from this place, shoving Johnston with impetuosity [and] that Grant has placed 25,000 of Lee's men hors de combat.[25] An officer relates a dream in which "Old Abe," Stanton, and Butler, 10 yrs. after the war, meet in a saloon at Washington. Feeling well, they recount the war past, and suddenly "Abe" has an indistinct recollection of some prisoners sent to Macon during the last year of the war. Stanton don't know anything about it. Butler remembers and says, it is so, for the Rebs would not recognize him and he would not exchange. Says it is all past now as they all died many years ago.[26]

Monday, May 23. Very warm today and I was busy in helping to put up our shed. Got good protection from the sun, but not so good from the rain. Had not boards enough to cover all the squad, but I was among the fortunate, getting under cover. We have frequent visits from the Ladies of Macon, but I then think of Gen'l Butler's remark, "the poison of the he and she adder is the same."[27] Rumor says Johnson is leaving Atlanta, and we consequently expect to be removed from this [place]. Rations are growing slim, but it may be better for us not to eat too heavily. Have very good health and thankful for life.

Tuesday, May 24. No rain since we came here, very dry and warm. Lt. Wood, 82nd Indiana, died in Hospital of Chronic diarrhea.[28] Gen'ls Seymour and Shayler with 110 officers from the Army of the Potomac came to camp today captured mostly on the 5th, 6th & 7th. Capt. Zarracher, who has been appointed to my company being mustered April 23, came among them.[29] He says four new captains had been assigned to the Regt. The Adj't. made Capt. I made Adj't. Major Darlington was restored to duty and wounded in the fight, [and] left in the hands of the enemy. Major Phillips with the Regt. Lt. McCormick is 1st Lt. of Co "L." Lt. Nieman is thought to be killed.[30] The Regiment is filled up but at dismounted camp. Col. Bryan commanding [the] Brigade.[31] So they are going, and irrespective of right they trample on us absent. I had the promise of the Captaincy of my Co.

Wednesday, May 25. Had a fine rain last night, the sheds keeping out the rain very well. Today is pleasant not so warm as heretofore. Nothing very definite from the front, but the Rebs fear the issue. Johnson is slowly falling back and we all hope for success. Cannot hear anything from Grant. The "Daily Confederate" gasses loudly about repulsing our forces at all points, but strange our lines are advancing at all points.[32] Grant being at Warren Junction. The more I hear concerning the doings of our Reg. Officers the more disgusted I get, and am persuaded that the entire thing was caused by wire pulling. If my rights cannot be guaranteed in my absence, I take it, they don't want my services. Have very good health, for which I am thankful.

Thursday, May 26. The day passed as usual, having a pleasant rain, to settle the dust. The sick left for the new Hospital, but came back for some unknown reason. The Editor of the "Richmond Inquirer" Pollard is said to be captured by our forces, and is now in Fort Lafayette.[33] Oh that he may reap the reward of his treason. Have the most of the shed finished. Our situation is very good considering the treatment of our enlisted men. A rumor says they overpowered the guard at Andersonville last night and escaped. Can hardly believe it. The Rebs got the date and place of capture of the Officers. Exchange quiet.

Friday, May 27. Warm today, sun shining brightly. The rumor of the escape of our men at Andersonville was incorrect. The sick have been sent again to the outer hospital, being parolled and not guarded. Nearly all that escaped have been recaptured, some getting as far as Savannah. The Officers stand the change of climate tolerably well, but a good many sick. I am well and thankful that amid so many misfortunes I am still alive. The Gen'ls that came in seem fine men not cowering to the Rebs as Wessells and Scammon.

Saturday, May 28. Very pretty day, with cool breeze yet still very warm. Had all to form in continuous line for roll-call. They found a tunnel that was digging, which through carelessness was left uncovered was found, and Capt. Tabb made quite an ado about it threatening to tear down the sheds if any more tunnels were found. He brought a guard of twenty men into camp at roll call, ordering them to fire upon any men who should leave ranks. All counted. All bosh.

Sunday, May 29. Had preaching twice by the Chaplains, two being among us. Was very happy to attend. They speak so patriotically, and spoke of home and friends, so tenderly as to move the feelings, and bring to mind the days of gone by. Capt. Tabb thought he found a hole or tunnel in shed no 4 and made a horrid splutter, bringing in 60 guards and threatening to shot [shoot], even striking a major with a musket, and finally took him out of camp for refusing to dig or fill up the hole, being only a soldier. He (Capt. Tabb) will find all ends eventually.

Monday, May 30. Weather pretty and warm but the nights cool. Twenty eight fresh fish came in from Grant. Twelve or fifteen escaped on the road. They represent all flourishing, but heavy fighting, and have not a doubt as to the issue. The Army stretching toward White House.[34] Had a roll call by name commencing at 4 P.M. taking till dark, when I doubt w[h]ether they know anything more than at first. Have the diarrhea. Getting along very well.

Tuesday, May 31. The day warm as usual and nothing strange excepting the mounting of two cannon (8 or 10 pounders), upon the stockade bearing upon the camp. Capt. Tabb says he had to mount them to satisfy the citizens. Exchange news on the rise, as the rumor is that Gov. Brown sent Pres. Davis word that Georgia could not feed so many prisoners. But otherwise our Gov. [government] notified the Rebs that no exchange could take place until they recognize the negro soldier. Fresh fish coming in speak very encouragingly of our Army. May the most sanguine [hopes] be realized.

Wednesday, June 1. Had roll call by being filed from one side of camp to another having to pass through three times before they got the count correct. Capt. Tabbs is said to be relieved and Capt. Gibbs takes his place to the satisfaction of all,[35] as the former is so small a man in all his actions as to deserve the lasting hatred of us all. He tried to steal and [an] officers watch, and when the latter threatened to report him, he "bucked" him for two hours.[36] Get 4 days rations at a time. All meal, a little.

Felt unwell today. Rained a little making it more pleasant. Capts Ives & Kendall got here: Maj. White, Capt. Litchfield &c escaped in [rail] cars.[37]

Thursday, June 2. Rumor got afloat that our Cavalry got to Columbus, Ga., and, 'tis thought, to be to liberate the Prisoners both at Andersonville and here. We trust it not, but still think of the success of joy that we would experience if such to be the case. Lee is said to be in his fortifications and Grant closing around. Atlanta is thought to be unsafe. Capt. Gibbs, they say, is to command but I saw him not. Good health. A slight rain, all hopeful.

Friday, June 3.[38] Pleasant, cloudy day. Nothing new ere the raid. 14 officers from Grant came in reporting hard fighting and good success and rumor from in that says terrible fighting is now raging, and many good officers killed. [Illegible] [Conty?] has been arrested from sutler shop. The officers [rest of sentence unclear]. [Illegible] happy but only this [rest of sentence unclear]. Good heath, living on corn cakes, having enough meal to bake the cakes.

Saturday, June 4. Very quiet indeed. Had a pleasant rain, which made the weather delightful. The Magnolia and Catalpa trees are out in bloom and make the air fragrant with their perfume. The evenings are serene and the fireflys light up their butts in divine circus. The Negro seems to be the bone of contention, as Senator Cobb says they never will exchange their slaves.[39] If not, we are in for the war. And speed the day when Grant's troops may possess Richmond and Sherman's Atlanta.

Sunday, June 5. Very pleasant day. Had preaching morning and evening. Felt happy for the opportunity of hearing the sound of the Gospel. Various news from the Armies, and Grant is said to have repulsed an attack of Lee's, and gained the outer line of fortifications. Six gunboat men came in from the Savannah [River], captured from the "Water Witch."[40] Had a slight headache but past of soon. Very healthy, very few sick, and diarrhea subsiding, getting acclimated. May fortune be ours.

Monday, June 6. At morning roll call, 61 new officers came in, being collected at Libby. Gen'l Heckman with his Brigade of Butler's forces among the number.[41] They report Grant succeeding nobly, and have implicit confidence in his being able to take Richmond. Wrote a letter to Mother, having a mail to send away. Have had no mail since we came here and hardly expect any. Sherman is very quiet, no officers coming in for more than a week. Camp is getting filled, having 1250 or more officers here now. Day warm, evening pleasant. Often think of home and wonder when the space that now separates us will be traversed.

Tuesday, June 7. Was cook today, which gives me plenty to do, being very warm. The Rebs have put up some cooking places, and one little oven for our squad. As the Republican Convention meets today at Baltimore to nominate a candidate for next President &c., we took a vote to ascertain our choice, and found the officers preferred Lincoln almost unanimously, since few could go McClellan,

Frémont &c; For V. Pres., Andy Johnson, Hamlin, &c.[42] Borrowed $25 dollars of Capt. Zarracher in conjunction with Adjt. [Guy] Bryan [Jr.]. Cloudy and expect rain. A few "fresh fish" came in from Sherman's Army. They say all is right. Feel well and am contented.

Wednesday, June 8. Very pretty day, with scattering clouds, and slight breezes making our shanties very pleasant. Three "fresh fish" came in from Butler's Army. Grant is said to be within four miles of Richmond, going to make a junction with Butler. Sherman is coming on slowly, and the citizens of Macon getting frightened. Spent part of the day studying Phonology, more for something to do than for its benefit, but it in perfection must be a sublime af[f]air.[43] Feel happy tonight. The buzz of activity or restlessness sounds in my ears. The light flickers on the sight, I think of home far, far away.

Thursday, June 9. The mornings are delightful for, before the rising on the sun, the birds sing so sweetly and the air feels so pleasant that I am happy. Spent most of the fore-noon making a pair of moccasins out of my overcoat cape. A few gunboats [men] came in from Savannah who usually with all fresh fish, think exchange all right, but for us, we look not for this, unless by a Raid of our Cavalry. Good news from Sherman, and the Jews in the city are giving $30 in coin for $1 gold. Feel well, and contented.

Friday, June 10. Had excitement again as 50 ranking officers, 5 Gen'ls; 11 Cols, 25 Lt. Cols. & 9 Majors, were ordered to leave at 4 P.M. leaving us in the dark as to their destination.[44] Many surmised a Raid being made as the guards began drilling on the Guns. But others think it is an exchange as Gen'l Heckman still affirms we shall be out in a few weeks.[45] This gives matter for a thousand rumors, and the fresh fish bite eagerly, but with the older ones, it passes as but little. The quartermaster says he has to furnish transportation for 1500 privates tomorrow. Why do they excite our hopes if it be but to crush them?

Saturday, June 11. Rained very hard a good portion of the day. Cleaning up our camp, but it must make the camp at Andersonville very disagreeable. The guard, Pri. Belger, Co. 'C,' 27th Ga., Shot Lt. Gerson, 45 N.Y., while at the spring for no provocation whatever, and seemingly in murderous intent.[46] He died at Midnight. One more cowardly act to avenge. One more man's blood spilt by a villain who dare not to assault an armed foe. Have dug two wells, getting water in both. Nothing new on exchange, but 'tis generally thought the officers left yesterday for Savannah to be sent North.

Sunday, June 12. Rained nearly all day. So the sunny south had turned out to be the frigid north. Had preaching in the morning, more in the evening. [Lt. Harry] Wilson had come back to our mess, giving us 3 days rest and one apiece to cook. Various rumors about the killing of Lt. Gerson, and, 'tis said, the Commandant sent in word that as much investigation has been made as was usually made by the officer at Point Lookout when Negros shot the Rebs.[47] If this be the game, let it be practiced by both sides.

Monday, June 13. Rain continued all day with uninterruption. Very cold, so that all wear their overcoats. 'Tis hard to cook being difficult to keep fires burning. The Exchange is still a matter of doubt the rumor being that the officers that left went to Richmond via Savannah and Charleston. Got rations for four days, 4 lbs. meal, ½ lb. pork, ½ pint molasses. This weather is difficult to endure.

Tuesday, June 14. Rain has ceased but still remains cool. Got boards to finish the sheds, and completed our bunks. Got a mail from Richmond having to pay $24 Express charges. Got two letters, from sister, Mother, and Bro. Jno. [dated] May 6th. Saw an old "Greensburg Herald" (Jan 3 or 4) and had a pleasant time perusing it. Saw the proceedings of the Lancaster County Institute with all the old names bringing me back to days of other years.[48] Felt tolerably well. Hope the time may soon come for a change. 44 fresh fish from Libby.

Wednesday, June 15. The day was fine, not too warm nor too cold. The squads were busy completing their sheds. Wrote two letters to Mother and Bro. Jno. W. Sent out for eatables, getting onions at 50 cts a piece and other things in proportion. Gen'l Poke of La., formerly Bishop of New Orleans, was killed a few days ago in Johnson's Army.[49] 'Tis ascertained that Lincoln and Andy Johnson have got the nomination for P. & V.P. Indications of Grant taking the south side of the James.

Thursday, June 16. Very pretty day. Wrote three letters to Eph. Brunner, Bro. Frank and Mr. Lightcap. The "Daily Confederate" says the 50 officers who left here were put in the Mills Hotel at Charleston in range of our Guns, and advises us all to be taken there.[50] If this be true, when can a parallel of barbarity be found. It shall undoubtedly call for retaliation. Gen'l Dix, and Howel Cobb are said to be Comm. of Ex. and that Judge Ould is in Macon.[51] Exchange rumors busy. Grant is making some new movement. The Rebs can't find him. Our Cavalry nearly took possession of Petersburg. Staunton is in our hands.[52] Had preaching in the evening. The preacher speaking of profanity ask any one to write all his words during today on a paper and like a true soldier sent it home. How many would blush for their friends to see or hear.

Friday, June 17. Rained nearly all day, making the camp disagreeable. The Rebs complain of so much rain as it spoils the grain that is shouck [shocked], having been harvested, but not hauled in. The peach crop is said to be a failure. The papers were prevented from coming in, and the officers coming from the hospital say Sherman has taken Atlanta. Grant has captured Petersburg, and Hunter taken Lynchburg.[53] Capt. Gibbs issued an order stopping all trading in "Green backs" or selling private effects to the dissatisfaction of many. An officer, Lt. McCully of Ohio Regt., died on yesterday of the Diarrhea.[54] Have good health, thankful for it.

Saturday, June 18. Not only rained but poured a good share of the day. I was cook having a heavy time. The papers mention the death of Gen'l Imboden,[55] and the capture of Wise's Brigade at Petersburg; that Lincoln got 427 and Grant 22 votes at Baltimore for Pres.; Johnson 462, Dickinson 17, and Hamlin 9 for V.P. Nearly all the states were represented, excepting the Carolinas, Ga., Miss., Tex., showing the narrow limits of the Confederacy.[56] We had an exciting rumor of Sherman having whipped Johnson, and occupying Lossing Mountain, and that our Army was occupying Atlanta.[57] The Rebs acknowledge that our forces hold 75,000 enlisted men and we must have now 5,000 officers.

Sunday, June 19. Continues wet, but our camp is still clean, being so sandy that the rain only cleans the ground. Had preaching in the morning and at night. A good many attend, but the majority disregard all religious services and refuse to listen to the word. Capt. Tabbs got back from Richmond assuring us, the Exchange would take place in 15 days, but all laugh in derision at his opinion. He says Lee has made a Raid toward Maryland leaving Richmond. This is as likely as the other. Felt sadly, as the dusk of evening gathered round me of the thankless life I am spending here. The time moves very slowly.

Monday, June 20. The day pleasant, the rain ceasing. Washed once more. News unimportant, but Lee is not going into Maryland, but is on the South side of James River. Forty officers came, captured at Guntown, Miss., by Forest, they relate the circumstances as disgraceful. Gen'l Sturgis, with Grierson's cavalry and several thousands of Infantry, went to tear up the Mobile and Ohio R.R. but got so intoxicated as to get his men in a trap and then forsook them, loosing 18 pieces of Artillery, 150 wagons loaded with provisions, and about 1000 prisoners. The nigers, two Regts, fought well, but were all cut down.[58] Another crime added to the long list caused by intemperance of our Gen'ls.

Tuesday, June 21. Began to rain again and made a wet day with a windstorm. News of little import, since all in report, and being mistaken <u>so</u> often one would almost doubt his own existence. Petersburg is not yet taken, and rumor says Grant is on the South side of it, going to shell the works.[59] Get tired awaiting the completion of his Campaign, and was it not for the confidence imposed on [him] I would grow despondent. A Catholic Priest from Macon came into camp, and having been at Andersonville, describes as horrid the treatment of the enlisted men. They have not room to lie down, no shelter, no clothes. One beg[g]ed the guard to shoot him. Some had taken the oath of Allegiance to the Con. [Confederacy] and who could blame them. They claim to have 30,000. The camp 13 acres long.[60]

Wednesday, June 22. A pretty day, and indications of a clearing up. News of partial engagement on the Ga. Front leaving our forces in possession of Kennesaw Mountain.[61] Grant is battering at the gates of Petersburg for entrance. A few fresh

fish came in from Forest's capture, making 1359. The project of sending a committee from our number to Americus or Andersonville and thence north to give the
government the facts about our treatment and urge the necessity of exchange produced a great deal of excitement. Two were chosen from each squad to select three
for the Com. [Committee]. They chose Majors Beatly and Marshall of Ohio, and
Owens of Ky., also Act. Master Pendleton of the Navy.[62] Many opposed the matter fearing it would only embarrass the government since we are unable to inform
them of any facts they are unacquainted with and will give an opportunity for the
Oposition to misconstrue it into the opposition to the Administration. I reined
myself with these.[63]

Thursday, June 23. Very pretty day, the rain clouds passing away and the
warm sun shining brightly. No news from Richmond (telegraphic) but correspondents try to make it appear that Sheridan with his 2nd & 3rd Divs. has been
whipped.[64] Fresh fish (4) came in from Sherman. One of 7th Pa. Cav. reported
success and is sanguine of the capture of Johnson's Army or at least its destruction. The excitement about sending the committee North grew intense and indignation meetings were held, holding forth these ideas. We have not the right to
assume the responsibility of urging and [an] exchange of prisoners, least [lest] it
embarrass the Gov. and give the enemy a pretext to throw the section[al] blame
on it [by] charging our Gov. with ignorance of our condition or neglect should
they be acquainted with the facts. For me, I oppose the matter.

Friday, June 24. The weather has cleared up finely making the day very warm.
Twenty two "fresh fish" came in from Mead's Army, 4th Brig., 1st Div., 2nd Corps,
having made a charge on the works around Petersburg, and through a mistake
failed. Three Officers of 53rd P.V. [PA Vol.] among the number [and a] Lt. Col.
of 145th P.V.[65] They are all very hopeful, and say Grant can take the place at his
option, but is trying to get Lee's Army along with it. The negros charged the
works at Petersburg and captured 9 Batteries and 450 prisoners, giving evidence
of their fighting ability.[66] Hear of the 9th Ohio Cavalry being at Athens, Ala.,
some time ago. Three officers of the Reg't one Capt. [blank in MS] and Lts. Cook
and Nape.[67] Health very good.

Saturday, June 25. Very warm day, the sun shining out bright and clear. The
Surgeon informs us the season of the year for malarias has arrived and urges
cleanliness. Capt. Gibbs is sick and Major Chas. E. McGregory [McGregor] is in
command. Seven "fresh fish," the remnant of Forest's capture, came in. Lt. Col.
Von Helmrich[68] who left "Libby" last spring was among the number, and what
a reception we gave him. All took him by the hand shouting and halloing and
in unison to call questions; he in german accent pronounced the word "Miserable." Good health, fair, passibly good, and under other circumstances I would be
happy. Had prayer meeting in the evening.

Fig. 14. Camp Oglethorpe, Macon, GA. A prison stockade in a former military camp and state fairgrounds where Weaver lived from May to July 1864. (MOLLUS-Mass Civil War Photograph Collection, United States Army Heritage and Education Center, Carlisle, PA)

Sunday, June 26. The day was oppressing warm with not a cloud to intervene between us and the sun. Had roll call by squad. Nothing new, and all feel anxious as it was reported that heavy fighting was going on at Atlanta. Altho the Rebs have been bolstering up their people with the idea of success yet occasionally the papers make a candid statement and says so far this spring they have been driven to the wall. At 10 P.M. a shot was heard at the sink, which aroused the guard and proved to be someone escaping. Orders were given for no one to leave the sheds on any account, and soon the howl of dogs sounded through the adjoining woods, after the trail of the fugitive. Hope he or they may succeed in getting away.

Monday, June 27. Had an Examination for tunnels which resulted in finding three, two complete and the third 58 ft. long, two ft. square, having 20 ft. yet to complete when the camp was expected to be emptied. From all their accts [accounts], 'tis plain some one of our number has been base enough to divulge the matter and could he be found he would hang high as Haman.[69] Bitter are the curses pronounced against him. We were ordered to take out all the bunks we had put up, but this was rescinded and a threat of cutting down the trees and pulling down the sheds if this should be attempted again. The[y] put a piece of ordnance in position on the rear of camp. Thus the hopes of many have been blasted. News of hard fighting at Richmond.

Tuesday, June 28. Thirty fresh fish came in making over 1400 in camp. They are of the 2nd and Sheridan's Corps. None from our Division. They report Grant doing good work, keeping the Rebs busy. The papers are getting dispiriting saying that Atlanta is about to fall, calling upon the citizens of Macon to relieve the guard and send them to the front. Really they seem to be approaching the last ditch. Had some rain, but the day was very warm, scarcely endurable. Capt. Dushane left for the hospital, with symptoms of Fever.[70] One officers [blank in MS.] died in the hospital of Consumption. Still we are very healthy considering the number confined. Health tolerably good.

Wednesday, June 29. Continuous showery and cloudy, not as warm as yesterday. Got letters from the officers at Charleston, S.C., saying they have a very good posish [position] being on their parol[e], having good quarters, good grub, and plenty of it. Four refused to take the Parole and are in the Jail. Two fresh fish came in from Hunter's Army.[71] News from Richmond are very meager, and of doubtful import, but they are getting very tired of Grant's <u>continual</u> fighting. We look wishfully for the day of victory, believing that therein alone lies the power to deliver us. The pump stocks were put in the wells. Capt. Gibbs is trying to arrange the money matter of the officers. He gives $4½ for $1. Health good.

Thursday, June 30. Was cook today, having corn bread and flower [flour] gravy for dinner and breakfast, and "slap jacks" and molasses for supper. Drew five days rations, getting cornmeal, bacon, molasses, beans, vinegar, salt, and soap in moderate quantities. No "fresh fish" and we are desirous of hearing from Grant. But it seems that Grant is getting possession of all the Rail Roads around Richmond, when doubtless he will rest at ease forcing Gen'l Lee to surrender of [or] come out and fight. Lt. Bader, 17th Mo. putting on a Reb uniform, walked out with the guard at Roll Call and has not been heard from since.[72] Five cannons still point on the camp but 'tis the distance that dissuades any outbreaks.

Friday, July 1. Very pretty day, bright and warm. One year ago the Battle of Gettysburg began and well do I remember the part our Division played. This is the anniversary of the capture of a good many of our officers. News unimportant. Rumor good, as 'tis currently reported the [that] Beauregard with 15 thousand has surrendered to Grant. Oh can it be true. How I would love to see Richmond fall on the 4th. Capts Litchfield, Johnson, & Wilson were brought in having been recaptured. Major White, Capts Reed and Barse escaped in the road, making the 5th time for some of them.[73] Lt. Kennedy, 9th Ind. Cav., walked out of camp with a pick on his shoulder, with a fatigue party who had been filling up the tunnels discovered.

Saturday, July 2. The day was very warm and in the evening threatened rain thundering and lightning terribly. A few fresh fish came from Johnson's captures, and the 25,000 reported by the Rebs as lost has turned out to be only two officers and 100 men. Richmond entirely cut off giving us no news of Grant's movements nor saying a word about Beauregard's capture. Lt. Bader is said to be recaptured at Atlanta, having got on the cars here and caught up when he got that far. All the captured say our Army is large enough to take Johnson and Lee and can get more men whenever they want them. Health good, and with the exception of an occasional attack of hems [hemorrhoids], I get along very well.

Sunday, July 3. Very warm day. Quietness reigns all around. Preaching twice, the sermon in the evening being very good. Wrote a letter to Corpl Jno. Ashbrook of my company now at Andersonville.[74] Rumor of Capt. Tabb being captured while on his way to Richmond. No news and rumor has grown disgusted of itself. Tomorrow shall be the 4th and what a place is this to be on that glorious old day. Oh I long to break away from this confinement, from these indignities, and be free. The best philosophy I can muster fails to reconcile me to remain so long, but hope of being recaptured or released keep me in tolerably good spirits.

Monday, July 4. Felt melancholy and sad in the morning, thinking of our situation and the chances of remaining in the same for some time. But at roll call, someone displayed a little union Flag and "The Star Spangled Banner" was heartedly chanted to the breeze. A meeting was held in the building and many mounted the stage. We had a good time till noon when as Lt. Col. Thorp, 1st N.Y. Dragoons, was holding forth beautifully, the Officer of the day came in and stopped us, and Lt. Col. Thorp, being senior officer in Camp, was relieved from command.[75] Gibbs suggested that we better be quiet, &c. Pretty day. Rumor of fighting in Ga. Such is our confidence in the prestige of this day that we confidently believe success soon be ours if they are fighting. Had $4 worth of potatoes for dinner.

Tuesday, July 5. A fine day, but very warm. Have no papers, and scarcely ever get any of late. All the news we get is Rumor, and very unreliable. Reports of McPherson's getting in Johnson's rear cutting off from Atlanta.[76] That all who have been here as prisoners for six months will soon be paroled as 'tis feard the Scurvy will get bad. But all this yammer only disgusts. Got rations for the 5 days. Have vegetables of all kinds coming into camp. Black-berries plenty for $2 a quart, squashes, onions, tomatoes, & but at fabulous prices, and being alowed but $4½ for greenbacks we cannot support it. Have no reading matter, but spend part of the time studying phonography. Health good. May success be ours.

Wednesday, July 6. The news from Sherman is good as the Rebs acknowledge Johnson to have fallen back six miles from Marietta, leaving this place and Kennesaw Mountain in our possession. They now say Johnson cannot cope with Sherman and urges every citizen to go to the front. The people are fortifying Macon, and the four pieces of artillery to rear of camp left for the front. A Reg't of Cavalry came and are encamped near our Camp, and all things show their fear of a raid. One officer, Lt. Wilson, 5 U.S. C., escaped by hiding in a box of the cart bringing in vegetables.[77] Day warm, and dry. Getting along well. Wrote a letter to Mother, but don't expect it to get north, all communications being cut off.

Thursday, July 7. Had two roll-calls one by name verifying the list. Two fresh fish came in from our Div. (3rd of Cav. Corps). They represent Grant as doing finely, being entirely around Richmond. The Div. burned 30 miles of South Side R.R.; 30 miles of R&D R.R., 5 trains of commissary stores on the road to Richmond.[78] Gold was 195, last of last month. Capt. Reed and Lt. Barse were recaptured and brought in. Also, Lt. Wilson who escaped yesterday. Activity among the Rail Roads and it appears as if the Rebs were bringing their machinery from Atlanta, also their rolling stock. The Cavalry still remains within hearing, putting me in mind of old times. Health very good, appetite the same.

Friday, July 8. Was cook today. Eat three meals. Weather very warm. The cannon taken away a few days ago was put to the rear of camp. Hear the Cavalry yet in the woods. Great activity on the R.R. and eight Locomotives came from Atlanta in one train.[79] Fresh fish came from Charleston. The Col. Hoyt and Lt. Col. of 52nd Pa. V. being among them.[80] An attack was made on some of the forts and, 'tis said, Johnson has sent 10,000 reinforcements. Lt. Brooks 6th Wis., who was released from Libby last spring, came in.[81] He says the Army has had hard fighting but have been equal to the occasion. He eulogizes the Negro troops highly. Lt. McCormick is killed, Capt. Tresonthick (Capt. Lt.) was wounded in the knee joint.[82] Had not his leg amputated. Sorry to hear of these disasters.

Saturday, July 9. Hot day, felt unwell with headache. Fresh fish came in from our Division, which was roughly handled by the Rebs at Stony Creek [while] cutting the railroad.[83] Our Regt was not along so they for once have got off [without] disaster. Capt. Robinson, Act. Mas, U.S.N., who was captured in the "Satellite," died in Hospital.[84] It seems so hard to lie down here and die. His gray-haired father, a Virginian, was confined by the Rebs at Salisbury for his union sentiments until he breathed his last. The news of Early going toward Washington, and Burnsides being sent after him is doubted.[85] Get no papers and have no news. Had a <u>private</u> talk with Free [Freeman] Gay.

Sunday, July 10. 107 fresh fish came in from Libby some from Sherman. Col. Hewey, 8th Pa. Cav., Col. Frazier, 140 P.V., Col. Stoughton, 2 U.S. S.S., Col. Sherman, 88 Ill., Major Dweese 13th Pa. Cav., Capt. Elder 2 US Artillery, &c, were among the number.[86] Our Division got a hard knock at the last Raid, but did good cover destroying the Rail Roads badly. Col. Covode, 4 Pa. Cav., was killed; also Major Kirwin, 13th Pa. Cav.; Col. Bartleson, one-armed Col., who left Libby.[87] This has been a bloody campaign more spilt, I should think, than in all heretofore. 'Tis the bloodiest campaign of the Bloodiest war of modern ages. Had a delightful rain than [that] cleaned out the camp. It now contains 15 or 16 hundred officers. It is a consolation that more are going the other way. Good health.

Monday, July 11. The day was warm still the heat is not oppressive and we can feel tolerably happy. Boards were brought in for more bunks and sheds. Many got one and make a bunk above us. Camp is getting filled up, and 'tis said they are going to enlarge the camp but no signs yet. News from Sherman was good, coming gradually on, having large army, plenty of rations, but the men worn out. Nine months ago, I was captured, and how little I then thought that today would find me a prisoner! The future holds out but little hope, as most fresh fish say prisoners are forgotten, and non-exchange is the policy of the Government. How long! Oh, how long!

Tuesday, July 12. The papers had a super abundance of news. That Ewel's Corps had gone to Maryland and occupied Hagerstown &c., and Grant was going to go after him, and abandon Richmond campaign. But Grant will doubtless say: "Northerners take care of yourself and I will of Richmond." The "Alabama" has at last gone up being sunk in an engagement with the "Kearsage" commanded by Capt. Winslow. Semmes escaped and is in the hand of the English.[88] We have an exchange rumor, as Mr. Cobb informs the Commandant of the Guard that in four weeks all shall be exchanged. Sherman has crossed the Chattahoochee on the right.[89] The wounded are said to be coming into Macon by the thousand. Health good.

Wednesday, July 13. News today the same as yesterday with a slight modification not so favorable to the Rebs, since they doubt that Ewel has got into Maryland, having only gone up the Valley to forage. The[y] advise the holding of Atlanta at all hazards, since if they lose that they loose all Georgia. The Exchange news is verified by letters sent from our officers at Charleston. The Rebs making propositions to exchange man for man, they holding the slave Negro soldiers, we the excess. The day was very warm. Stay closely inside shelter during the day. Fresh corn is brought to camp, selling at $4 per dozen ears. Berries are plenty but too dear to buy as most vegetables are.

Thursday, July 14. The weather continues very warm. Indications of rain, but very little fell. News few. Rumor of going to leave this place soon for either Mobile or Hawkinsville, 40 miles south of this place. The Suttlers have orders to settle up their businesses.[90] The Rebs were practicing their artillery on the fortifications, which they are erecting fastly. It is thought Johnson will fall back this way. Have nothing to do, nothing to read and the days come and are whiled away aimlessly. May they prove no worse than a <u>blank</u> in our history. Had preaching with a good many auditors. Good health, eating the same with vegetables at high prices, rice, potatoes at $4 per quart.

Friday, July 15. Had pleasant showers in the evening cooling the air and making it delightful. News from the Raid into Maryland are unreliable, and the Rebs doubt whether Ewel has gone into Maryland, still they telegraph "Baltimore's capture and the shelling of Washington." Hear of the "Journal of Commerce" in N.Y. City being suppress[ed] for publishing a false order by the Gov. [Government] and Gov. Seymore calling out the militia to prevent it.[91] "Freedom of the Press," once a grand principle, cannot be allowed by a people trying to suppress a Rebellion. If you suppress the Rebellion, suppress the papers that encourage the Rebellion. Good health, no signs of moving.

Saturday, July 16. Was cook today; got five days rations, as usual. Had some apples to eat, the first this summer. They seem pretty plenty. The suttler says he was robbed of $1000 Confed last night. Some doubt it. He is fond of the gaming table. Three officers escaped in Reb clothes walking out of the gate. One was brought back, and put in confinement. News of no importance. Rebs in Maryland between Baltimore and Washington. Had a skirmish but [at] the N. Central R.R. Couch and Hunter at Frederick.[92] Day pretty but warm. Exchange quiet but are enduring hope that a few month will see us free. Health good.

Sunday, July 17. A pretty quiet day without the many Rumors that disturb our peace. Had roll call twice and then by name occupying the most of the forenoon. Lt. Fish came in recaptured at Savannah where he had been hiding for nearly a month. Three gun boatmen off the "Water Witch" came in also, having their heavy loads of flitting,[93] which they usually are permitted to bring along. They report Ewell retreating from Maryland. That Johnston is in danger of giving up. Had a sermon in the evening. Feasted on Blackberry pudding for dinner. Health good, as is the general health of the camp.

Monday, July 18. Had two Roll Calls and an examination for tunnels, which resulted in the finding of one in Squad 8, nearly completed. Having a new Commandant, the matter was past over without any excitement. Capt. Gibbs is Col. Commanding the Post, and Lt. _____ Davis is [in] command [of] the camp. News as usual. Cavalry raids on the increase, one going in the Direction of Columbus or West Point. The Rebs boast of Capt. Winslow's being a <u>Southern</u> Traitor, being born in one of the Carolinas. The day fine and as warm as comfortable, but the evenings cool. Good health and getting along well as can expect. Got wood, the first for more than a week.

Tuesday, July 19. Was awakened by Capt. Meany and Lt. O'Shay fighting—this disgraceful habit.[94] Had three roll calls occupying the most of the fore noon. The new Commandant is very active and trying to put on style having been in a Yankee Prison some time ago. Gen'l Hood has relieved Gen'l Johnston of command of the Georgia Army.[95] Those who know him say he will fight, which is what Sherman wants. A Raid is being made on Columbus and Montgomery, Ala., and the same to be heading for Andersonville.[96] "Fresh fish," 3 Surgeons, came from this place saying they were dreadfully frightened and fear the release of the prisoners. The surgeon says 70 died yesterday, 2000 last month.[97] Oh what a waste of life; what suffering.

Wednesday, July 20. Was cook again. Got part of 5 days rations. The papers were prevented from coming in but one was obtained, otherwise preventing us from thinking that there were good news for us. They say Gen'l Grant is dead, the Gunboats on the James having the colors at "half-mast." Expect a fight at Atlanta since Hood had taken command of the Army. The Raiders cut the Montgomery and West Point rail road.[98] Had a new style of roll call, forming in home ranks. An officer blacked himself and tried to pass the guard and escape but was caught.

It was a very foolish conception. Fresh fish came from Sherman. Most of the Army across the river and in possession of Aug. & At. R.R.[99] Health good.

Thursday, July 21. The day fine, with a slight rain in the evening. Got no papers but by strategy, still the news are unimportant. Grant is still alive, the report false. Fighting expected at Atlanta. The raiders still around Montgomery and Columbus. Early is said to be out of Maryland. Lt. Apple was recaptured, getting within 40 miles of our lines.[100] Got the rest of our Rations, but soap is very scarce, not enough to wash our clothes. Rumor has been busy today, and the Exchange is hacknied again, giving food for the fresh fish. Saw a few ladies on the stockade looking down at us wild animals in this cage. 3 years since 1st Bull Run.

Friday, July 22. Twenty four "Stale fish" came from Libby compricing all the Raiders. The Cal. Off. and Hostages were left behind, Lt. Cols. Litchfield and Cook among the number.[101] Col. Crook, 22nd N.Y. Cav., came in with them being in Libby a short time.[102] Hear of our Regt Colonel[103] is commanding it and the others doing guard duty. It was not on the Raid, but Lt. Col. Brinton was.[104] Rumors plenty, being pretty certain that a fight is going on at Atlanta. 'Tis said we are going to move. Weather warm. The day passes slowly, nothing to read. Tired of this kind of life. Health good and hope for the future. Conscripts are collecting at this place.

Saturday, July 23. The day comfortable, the papers state heavy fighting has been done at Atlanta and intimate that that place has gone up. Camp full of Rumors of death of notable Gen'ls on both sides. The wounded are coming in. The city Authorities wanted to take our Hospital but the Commandant refused. We are getting to like Davis as a Commandant, being very accommodating and trying to sympathize more than anyone heretofore. Our Surgeons find fault with S. [Surgeon] Walton for serving in the Hospital, showing their inhumanity. Hope is strong and expect to hear good news from Sherman. Health good, and getting along well. Capt. Dushane got in from the hospital.[105]

Sunday, July 24. Last night was cold, verging on frost and all day cool so that not only coats but over-coats became desirable. Strange weather for July especially in the sunny South. All rumors from Atlanta; at one time it is ours, again, it is contradicted. One speaks of our victory, another of our utter defeat with death of many General Officers. The Rebs remain very quiet and all are wont to interpret this into good news for us. Got very tired and thought a great deal of home making me uncomfortable. Had preaching in the evening. Health very good for which I try to be thankful.

Monday, July 25. Last night cold but today very warm. Excitement on foot, as troops were massing all last night and it was feared that Lee was sending reinforcement to Hood, but the rumor is now that a Raid or Riot taking possession of Milledgeville, and the conscripts were leaving for that place.[106] Nothing definite from Atlanta, although a thousand rumors stir up the camp. Yet it is partly certain no fighting is going on. Got six days rations. Read Szabad's "Theory of War."[107] Two fresh fish came in. Gen'l Winder was in camp, being in charge of all prisoners in Ga. He is a gruff looking old man destitute of pity or humanity.

Tuesday, July 26. At Roll Call got orders to be ready to leave for Charleston by tomorrow evening and bake or cook all our rations. 600 men (1st Division) are going. Many doubt that they are taking us to Charleston, but all seem to wish it. Fresh fish (12) came from Sherman, who say McPherson is dead but all is progressing well.[108] Lt. Byres who escaped in Rebel clothes was recaptured, having been at Atlanta three days, and was captured between our pickets and the Rebs.[109] He represents Atlanta evacuated, and probably in our possession again now. All busy. Clay & two others with Early's Raid asked if they would be received as Commissioners for Peace from the Southern States.

Wednesday, July 27. Was busy baking rations as if we had to bake four days rations, making many poans.[110] Began to call the roll at 4 P.M. and took to dark crowding us between the dead line and stockade, not having room to sit even. Waiting till 11 P.M. we were taken in charge by Lt. Strong with 200 guards who marched us to the depot of the G.C.R.R.[111] and carried by 50s to a car. All the field officers went along. After singing patriotic songs, those who could lie down, tried to sleep, the others nodding and keeping watch, till morning. News from Sherman is few giving us the comfort that Hood is doing nothing dangerous. 'Tis said, Longstreet has reinforced him.

Six

"They Go High Like a Shooting Meteor and Fall Abruptly as a Star"

Charleston, South Carolina, July 28–October 5, 1864

The three-hundred-mile-journey from Macon to Charleston took over twenty-four hours. The exhausted prisoners were herded into the Charleston prison yard, as the building was already filled with anti-Confederate inmates. Constructed in 1802 and enlarged in 1855, the jail occupied a four-acre site that included a work-house for runaway slaves, a hospital, and a poorhouse. Six hundred officers and three hundred white and African American enlisted men crowded the masonry-walled yard, which soon became a sinkhole of misery with shelters of overcoats and canvas, overflowing latrines, biting mosquitos, and few implements for chopping firewood or cooking food. Still, the prisoners were not without hope. Rations often included fresh beef or bacon, their first meat, Weaver noted, in four months. The guards treated them respectfully, and nuns from the Sisters of our Lady of Mercy, a Catholic religious order established in 1829, tended the sick and provided medicine. An exchange of fifty officers, who had preceded them to Charleston, raised hopes of imminent release. After three weeks, the officers moved to nearby Roper and Marine Hospitals after signing paroles or pledges not to escape or talk to civilians. Weaver was among the two hundred men in Marine Hospital, a three-story building designed by Robert Mills in the 1830s with a double piazza along the front, a large yard, and a good water supply. This was the most comfortable accommodations during his imprisonment with eight to twelve men per room, funds to supplement rations with outside purchases, visits to Roper Prison next door, gas lights for nighttime illumination, a supply of books and newspapers, and sea breezes and city views from the hospital roof.[1]

Charleston was a city besieged by the Union guns on Morris Island at the harbor's entrance. Almost daily, shells screamed across the skies "and burst in profusion," causing fires and civilian casualties. Confederate authorities reportedly had removed the Macon prisoners to Charleston to serve as human shields against further bombardment and to pressure the Lincoln administration to resume a general exchange of officers and enlisted men. Maj. Gen. John G. Foster, Union commander, Department of the South, retaliated by requesting that six hundred Confederate officers be transferred from the Union prisoner-of-war camp at Fort Delaware to Morris Island where they would be exposed to the Confederate guns at Fort Sumter. Despite their endangerment—several shells fell nearby but inflicted no bodily harm—Union prisoners welcomed the frequent fusillades as demonstrations of the Federals' proximity and military power and as fitting retribution against the city where the conflict had begun. Weaver's faith in the war remained unshaken as he excoriated those Democrats who sought "peace on any terms" over Unionists who were waging a "war to honorable peace." Encounters with African American soldiers softened assumptions of their racial inferiority. After visiting them in the prison, Weaver noted that they were "fine looking men, who talked intelligently." He cheered news of Atlanta's fall to Union forces on September 2, and decried the suffering of the "thin, dirty, sickly" men arriving from hastily evacuated Andersonville prison. In late September an outbreak of yellow fever required removing all Union prisoners from Charleston: the enlisted men went to Millen, Georgia, and the officers were sent to Columbia, South Carolina. This would be Weaver's final prison site, but he would not be released until February 1865.[2]

Thursday, July 28, 1864. Started at break of day for Savannah being 205 miles distant, passing over the same road to Millan that we came. The remainder of the road, 205–126 miles,[3] was varied with fields of corn, rather poor, and potatoes, &c. Got within two miles of Savannah when we changed cars, taking the Charleston and Savannah line, 90 miles. Orders were "not for any to leave the cars," but when night approached, some slipped off to the woods. Had expected the train to be captured but failed to the sorrow of many. Slept part of the road and morning found us near Charleston, when we could see the flash of guns in the distance, and hear the boom but we still prisoners. The last ray of hope has gone.

Friday, July 29. Got off the cars and marched across the Ashley River two miles through the city land at the yard of the State Prison. Saw a few marks of Gillmore's shells but the bombardment is a humbug.[4] The city is partly deserted but many yet remain and the ludest [lewdest] yet. They look low and dirty. The prison is in range but no danger. It is filled with niggers, deserters, Yankees, and lude women, a horrid place. 72 escaped last night and more would if they had not expected a general escape. Severe sensure rests upon the leaders. Six of the escaped were caught. Col. Hoyt, Sherman, Hewey, Thorp, &c, all escaped.[5] Have

Fig. 15. Charleston Jail yard. Weaver was imprisoned here for three weeks in July and August 1864. Constructed in 1802 and enlarged in 1855, the jail occupied a four-acre site and held six hundred officers and three hundred white and African American enlisted men. (Willard W. Glazier, *The Capture, the Prison Pen, and the Escape: Giving a Complete History of Prison Life in the South.* New York: U.S. Publishing Company, 1868)

to use our over coats for tents. Pretty good oats, Hard tack and bacon. The Roar of Artillery continue at intervals. Health good.

Saturday, July 30. Had a rain storm last night but did not get wet. Bombarding continues night and day, but none reach us. Got a few wall "A" tents, and rumors of going to Marine Hospital to quarter. 'Tis said we can send home for clothing and money, but no eatables. This is a hard place being daily mixed up with the dirty prisoners let out to attend to their wants. All are wishing for an alteration and would like to accept a parole such as the Generals gave. Cols. Sherman, Hoyt, and Thorp were recaptured getting nearly to the coast. Some represent the coast as heavily guarded other say it is only lightly, and public sentiment sencure [censure] those who lep [leapt] the cars before it was decided not to <u>Act</u>, showing their cowardice. Health good.

Sunday, July 31. The booming of guns still continues, irrespective of Sunday. Nothing of our surrounding would look as if [it] were a day of rest but chopping, buying, and selling goes on. Got some 60 tents. The rest to come soon. Expect to leave this soon as they are taking a new list of names for the papers. 'Tis a horrid place here, lying in dirt and sand mixed up at times with niggers, convicts, and Rebels to the disgust and inconvenience of all. The day continues warm the evening cool, but the musketoe are very bad leaving my flesh perforated with holes.

Fig. 16. Union battery on Morris Island, SC. Weaver could hear and see the bombardment
of the city from his Charleston prisons. (Library of Congress)

Rumors plenty but nothing reliable. Hear nothing from the Army. Health good,
and am trying to be contented and thankful for life.

Monday, August 1. Got flour and fresh beef for rations, the only fresh meat we
have had for 4 months. Get good rations. Exchange excitement on the wing, as the
50 officers sent here first are said to be exchanged and going home Wednesday. Col.
Lasale[6] took a list of our names to publish at the north. It is hope[d] that arrangements will be made to see us home like wise. Great news of cavalry raids around
Macon and it is hoped they will release the prisoners. They cut the C. R. R. at
Gordon.[7] Col. Hewey with 20 others were recaptured leaving but a few to get away.
The[y] represent the swamps as terrible, hunted by dogs as usual. The officials are
very kind, the guard gentlemanly, bringing in many things for our accommodations. This is the "mother of Treason" but we have been treated better than at any
other place.

Tuesday, August 2. Heard solid shot flying past our camp last [night] and
today the shells burst in profusion all around, but none came into camp. One
struck in the yard where the Genls are quartered; hurt none. These are going to
the North tomorrow as they transferred all their effects to us. Hopes are now had
that we shall be as fortunate as they. Got soft bread instead of flour, a loaf per
man, with good rations of meat, which with a few vegetables bought by private
funds, we have plenty to eat. The guard were stopped from bringing in articles for
sale, and the commissary is going to make out bills as at Libby. Rumor of Gen'l
Stoneman's capture on the last raid around Macon.[8] Kreps[9] with a dozen of them
were recaptured leaving only 10 out yet. Poor success.

Wednesday, August 3. The officers left this morning (52 in number) and the same number returned to this place. They have not yet visited us. We are still in the dirt, without any conveniences to chop wood or police the ground and general dissatisfaction prevails. Better by far be in a penitentiary, where you can be clean at least. The shells keep whizzing by as thick as yesterday, but it seems our gunners have a knowledge of us being here, and the shells go to our right and left. The day was very hot and had we not the hope of getting away soon, our situation would be disagreeable enough. Have no paper to write letters and can't succeed in getting any. Rations the same as yesterday. Exchange active, but we have been sold so often none are taking stock. Hope we may all be disappointed and soon get home. Have good health. Hope I may continue to have.

Thursday, August 4. The day was very warm and amidst the sand and filth of this hole we have very little comfort. Gen'ls Johnson and Jeff Thompson, exchanged Rebs, came in to see us.[10] They said our Gov. holds 4100 officers at Johnson's Island and Point Lookout, while the Rebs hold only 1600.[11] Others came in. Some satisfied with their treatment north others not. Wrote two letters, to Mother and Ed McChesney. Rations the same as before. Vegetables getting scarce. The Shells getting plentier but none doing harm to any prisoner. The officers coming in think there is a good prospect of us getting out. Hope we may. Health good.

Friday, August 5. Warm as usual with an occasional breeze from the Bay. The Bombarding continues, the shells, 30 lbs., parrot,[12] passing on all sides, some bursting in air. They come 4 miles, acquire a height of two miles, assending at a[n] angle of 30° and descending at 50°. A Petition was sent to Gen'l Jones, commanding post, requesting a removal from this place, objecting to being confined with convicts, and in such a "Calcutta" as this.[13] Wrote two letters to sister Jennie and Mr. S. Lightcap. Rations continue the same, but are light enough getting only a light load of bread, and a piece of meat. Buy potatoes at $1 per qt. Water mellons, shrimps, & crabs are plenty but bring high prices. Health good &c.

Saturday, August 6. Hot as ever. Bombarding not so brisk, but they fell on all sides. Grub the same, getting two days rations to avoid issuing on Sunday. Still we remain in this hole. Never were officials more indolent. News confirm Gen'l Stoneman's capture, saying he is much dejected, being captured by an inferior force. Our forces are shelling Atlanta at times. Grant is at a standstill. Early is threatening another Raid into Penn. Foster has sent word that 600 Reb. officers had been sent forth but under fire in retaliation for us. This may bring about an exchange. The time passes slowly and drearily. Am happy for good health and enough [to] satisfy appetite.

Sunday, August 7. Got one ounce of lard in tin of meat, which with a small loaf of bread is hardly enough to sustain life. The day was warm, a few drops of rain but the sand still flew through the air. Was in the Prison, which looks dark, dirty, and constructed strong. Saw a good many negro soldiers, fine looking men, who talked intelligently. Got some figs, the first fresh ones I have had. Not moved yet and all complain. Some betting it is retaliation. Nothing of a religious nature goes on in camp, but the day passes as if we knew it not. Oh, I grow tired of this life. No news but all speculation as to exchange and hopes are getting brighter as our treatment darkens.

Monday, August 8. This was the roughest day upon us since our arrival in Rebeldom. Getting nothing to eat but an ounce of lard and a pint of rice. The Commissary refused to take the rice, being wormy, full of weevils and mouldy. The inspector condemned it, but nothing else came, and hungry stomachs pled for even that so near evening, it was issued. Thanks [to] fortune we had money. They taunt us still by telling us we are going to move tomorrow. The Rebs have burned Chambersburg.[14] This calls for retalliation in kind. Faragut with his fleet have past the forts Morgan & Gains commanding entrance to Mobile. We captured one ironclad—Tennessee—sunk one, tracked another and captured Buchanan, the Reb Commander.[15] No shell of the city today being the 396 day of the siege. Good health.

Tuesday, August 9. Rations better than yesterday getting cornmeal and bacon. Capt. [George] Lodge sold his coat for $60 giving the mess some change, and we appropriated some already. Good news from Mobile, as Fort Powel has been blown up and evacuated, Fort Gains surrendered with 600 men to our forces. Still promising to move us, but that is all it amounts to. The day not so warm with indications of rain. No shelling of the city today and the batteries seem very quiet. Nothing new from the Armies. Grant, it seems, is mining the Rebel fortifications of Petersburg while the Rebs countermine.[16] Sherman is holding on, working slowly but certainly. Get the horrors[17] badly, when I think of chances of staying here for many months.

Wednesday, August 10. Rain today, making camp very disagreeable, but the air more pleasant. The field officers with their messes left at noon for the Building next our yard.[18] Said to be the Penitentiary, being large enough to hold 400. Some of Squad 1 went also, and enough will go tomorrow to make up the compliment. We have intentions of going, thinking the grounds must be cleaner altho. the rooms are 4 x 7 cells for one or two and but poor ventilation. They say a shell has come down through the center of the building. Foster is quiet as scarcely a shell fell upon the city today. Our bright hope of being used as the 50 officers before us have vanis[h]ed into air and of even getting a half decent habitation. The day comes and goes, and leaves us the same and no brighter hope of exchange. Health tolerably good.

Thursday, August 11. Contrary to expectation, no more left [the] yard, but it is much more comfortable since the others left. The Field Officers got the matresses of those officers who went home. Sherman[19] is housed in a well-supplied room, with burners, tables, and chairs. The Provost Marshal tells us [we] are in prospects of Exchange as Foster's Adjt. Gen'l informed the Reb authorities that he was authorized to exchange all prisoners in the department man for man. This gave an impetus to exchange and various opinions were expressed, some thinking it likely. Few shots were fired today. News from Mobile the same. Nothing from Sherman or Grant. The day fine. Health good. Rations of corn-meal and bacon. Trying to be contented.

Friday, August 12. Fine day, not very warm. Got pint of rice and three tablespoons full of molasses for our rations, part of which was eat[en] with curses instead of blessings. This thing is growing to a point very fast. They took a list of our names, Rank, Regt., &c. Wrote a letter to mother. Capt. Lodge wrote to Hilton Head[20] for provisions for our mess, we paying shares. Rumor of us going to Roper Hospital, as officers are on the way here from Macon. We deplore this, as they cannot feed us, even now. Anticipation of a fight at Atlanta. Nothing from Mobile. Health good, but getting tired of being tired.

Saturday, August 13. At daylight the officers were taken out of Penitentiary Building and sent to Roper Hospital, on parole of the size of the yard. 300 officers came from Macon via Augusta and Branchville. Gen'l Stoneman was among the number. Major Harry White came along having been recaptured. They felt buoyant on exchange, more so than we. 32 enlisted men came along. 'Tis said we would have been taken to Roper H. had not Col. Sherman objected, thinking he had as many of his friends there as comfortable, for which many cuss him. Got pint of rice, and few spoonfulls of molasses and tea spoonful of salt. The guards were prevented from bringing anything in to sell so we had rice all day. Day warm. Exchange declining. Health tolerably good.

Sunday, August 14. Warm day, rations—¼ lb of bacon and one pint of grits, very course ground meal. The day passed without excitement till evening when some 20 or 30 officers were notified to be ready in the morning to go north, mostly being chosen from the officers of Gen'l Foster's department. Many regard this as a bad omen, thinking that this manner of selections and special exchanges will result in the same as last spring. Consequently many sad hearts and gloomy countenances mark the result of this hateful practice. 300 officers came from Macon, going into the Pen. [Penitentiary] Building. Potter and Airy escaped off the train.[21] 600 off. [officers] are at Savannah, 1200 here, leaving only a few sick at Macon. We are not allowed to communicate with our officers in the Buildings. Health good.

Monday, August 15. The officers notified yesterday left by Flag of Truce for Port Royal Ferry.[22] Col. Hoyt, Lt. Com. Pendegrass, U.S.N., Capt. Manning were among the number.[23] The papers think there is a prospect of propositions being proposed that will secure the exchange of all. Some fifty more left the yard for

Fig. 17. Robert Mills, Old Marine Hospital (1833), Charleston, SC, ca. 1933. This building provided Weaver's best accommodations of all his prisons from August to October 1864. (Library of Congress)

Roper Hospital. All are promised to be taken out tomorrow or next day, if we take a parole not to try to escape or communicate with citizens.[24] News unimportant. It seems a fight is expected of the Upper Potomac. All our Cav. is there under Sheridan. Scarcely any shelling for many days; none thrown into the city. Got 1 pint grits, and spoonful of lard, a piece of soap as large a solid inch, a teaspoon of salt. Got a few articles brought in but 'tis difficult. A guard shot at the men in the Building but missed. The Lt. of [the] G [Guard] was censored.

Tuesday, August 16. At 10 A.M. began paroling the officers to go to Roper & Marine Hospitals. I was among the latter, taking a parol not to try to escape nor to communicate with citizens by word or signal other than thru the military authorities. It was a hard pill taking parole for what we are rightly entitled to but they say it is for our health, &c. We left the yard at dusk and about 200 that were left went into Marine Hospital. It is a large building, with large yard and plenty of good water, so that all are satisfied they came here. A shell has passed nearly through it coming from S. E. direction. Got pork, ½ pt. flour, ½ pt. rice & ½ teaspoon salt. Roper has now about 400 officers in it. Health good.

Wednesday, August 17. Slept on the piazza, the muskitoes singing and biting alternately. Got up at daylight and examined our habitation. 'Tis a large building of 3 stories, 10 ft., 15 ft. & 12 ft. high, respectively, with many rooms. We are 8 to 12 in each room. House dirty, but expect it cleaned. Went on top and had a view of the city, looking from Ashley to the Cooper River. Could not see the Harbor. Some crossed the fence to "Roper" say it is a fine building superior to this. The officers who left for the north came back all but three and 9 privates, as Gen'l Foster had no officers at his department to exchange but they expect a large number soon when the hopes are that we may be the fortunate. Was cook. Cook in the yard. Got very tired, not used to running up and down stairs. Got fresh beef and 5 days rations, 3 qts. of meal, 1 qt. flour, 1 qt. rice, 1 tablespoon salt, and small piece soap. Have the chance of buying things at the gate. Only a few guards on the front of the building.

Thursday, August 18. Very warm day, and although in the shade, the perspiration is abundant. Feel unwell, having an attack of billious stomach occasioned by eating too heartily yesterday. About 200 officers from the workshop were put in the Jail Yard, preparatory to offering them the parole for better quarters. Intercourse is still kept up with Roper Hospital and is allowed by the authorities. Capt. Belzer[25] is Commandant of our Building and makes a good one. We got brooms and do our own policing. Got pans and buckets. News of our Cavalry having a fight north of James [River]. Mosby has captured another train at Perryville.[26] The Gen'ls going north are beginning to talk hard of their treatment while here. For this, we are prevented from getting any provisions from the north. No firing in the city since Monday where they bursted a gun at Battery Gregg.[27]

Friday, August 19. Pretty day, not so warm as yesterday. Nights warm and the musquitos bad. News of no importance, being mostly rumor. Kilpatrick is said to be in the field after Wheeler who has cut the R.R. in Sherman's Rear.[28] Admiral Dalgrin makes a proposition to exchange some captured citizens for naval officers.[29] Gen'l Jones refuses, but says the gov. [government] is ready to exchange man for man prisoners of war, giving a chance for various rumors of exchanges. The papers north and south talk a great deal of an Armistice of 90 days to try and make peace. That is beyond possibility I fear, and the only remedy now is to back down ingloriously or fight it to the end. Wrote a letter to mother. Got fresh meat. Good health &c.

Saturday, August 20. Had a pleasant sleep as the air was cool and delightful. The day very pleasant. Went with Lt. Potts[30] to Roper Hospital. It is a gay place looking out upon the "burnt district" of 1861,[31] and from the roof the Harbor can be seen but we were prohibited from going up. The rooms are cleaner than ours, but they are more in a room than with us. Visiting got so frequent that Capt.

Hall, commanding us, stopped it, putting a line of sentinels in our back yard. He charged us with breaking the parole, we charged him of ignorance, which he confessed. A list of our names &c was taken again, to be sent north, 'tis said, concerning exchange. Some of the officers got gold sent to them from Hilton Head. No news of any importance. Sherman's Report of the Battle before Atlanta on 22 ult. [ultimo] makes the Rebel dead more than our entire loss.[32]

Sunday, August 21. Rained last night driving off the Piazza into the rooms. Rained most of the day to the delight of us all in the buildings, as the cisterns were giving out, but it gave the officers in the Jail Yard a wetting. Cooked under the Piazza, having a good dry place. Nothing of a religious nature going on as no Chaplins are in our building. So I spend a good share of the day in reading the Bible, having a good supply in the Building. No shelling today, and quietness reigns supreme. The guard is still in the yard, and would only leave but one go to the sink at a time, to the bringing down of many curses upon the head of Capt. Hall. Have good health and some prospects of exchange. Beef for rations, but not much opportunity of buying things of the huxters [hucksters].

Monday, August 22. Warm day, sultry and oppressive and I am thankful for the shade. A Flag of Truce today, hope to hear something favorable. The officers are busy making ovens in the yard out of old bats and chains, table and bunks out of old lumber, pans of the tin roofing of a torn down outbuilding, cups or tumblers out of bottles cutting the tops off by drawing a rope rapidly around the bottles until they get warm by the friction, when being put in water, the[y] break off square. Had the yard cleaned up, and plenty of wood. Got ten days rations of proportionate quantities with addition of few beans. Capt. Raymond, Gen'l Jones' I.G.,[33] says there will be a change concerning the guard, &c., now in the yard. Shelling continues but not rigorous. No shells come near us. Read Life of William Baxter. What a good, and great man! Read 1st Chronicals taking a course.

Tuesday, August 23. Weather continues warm and sultry, making us all seek the shade. The Rebs came into our Building at daylight, looking for tents, which the officers carried out of the Jail yard. They found a few, and some were cut up into clothing &c. This looks badly for officer of the U.S. and may get them into difficulty. News are the same. Kilpatrick on a raid around Atlanta, was surrounded, but cut out.[34] Fighting on the north side of the James, by 2nd Corps. The Mexicans have taken up arms again and threaten the French. I would be glad to see Maximillan defeated and expelled from Mexico.[35] Shelling began at 3 o'clock P.M. and continued all night to the disturbance of sleepers. Many shells fell within a short distance of our quarters, a few bursting. Got fresh beef. Hooker is in the command of the Valley, being relieved of command of 20th Corps.[36] Health good—and passing the time tolerably well.

Wednesday, August 24. Had a heavy rain in the afternoon, flooding the yard but we were nicely esconsed [ensconced] in the dry. The shelling continued most of the day. Some 50 coming over the city, a good portion time fuze shells, burs[t]ing high in the air and on the tops of homes. At dusk we began to see the shells by the fuze burning. They go high like a shooting meteor and fall abruptly as a star. The[y] presented a beautiful sight. Nothing on exchange. News of none import and as the novelty of exchange is wearing away time is beginning to grow heavy. Read "Bible not of Man" by Rev. Spring, D.D., New York, and was pleased with the work.[37] Health good, although the rations are beginning to make a good many sick, having so much fresh beef at a time and not accustomed to this.

Thursday, August 25. Pleasant day. Rumors of Exchange as the Courier says "Exchange is about to be resumed on a new basis, the excess to be held by either party, the free negros exchanged, the slaves returned to their masters."[38] The commissioners at Port Royal have not yet agreed to any propositions. News from Petersburg good, as our forces are now entrenched along the R.R. and repulsed the enemy capturing the most of Haygood's S.C. Brigade.[39] Atlanta remains in "Status quo." Occasionally a shell killing a citizen or soldier. Bombarding on this place was fierce, mostly time fuse shells. Was cook today, getting fresh meat. Have pretty good rations. Great talk of an Armistice to be proposed soon. 'Tis said the peace Democrats will nominate Millard Fillmore for President.[40] Paper says 58,895 Confed. soldiers have died up to June 1st, 1864.

Friday, August 26. Day fine and spirits very good since the news from Petersburg is _very_ good since the correspondent says: "For the first time during the campaign has the Army (Reb) of Northern Va. suffered disaster and repulse." The fleet fired salutes and hoisted the Colors in rejoicing for some unknown victory. The N.Y. Herald says on the 18th that in a few days 500 officers would leave in a few days for Charleston Harbor in retalliation for us.[41] We all hope we may be exchanged. Got rations of corned beef. Have the opportunity of buying from huxters in the lower room. Shelling is going on as fiercely as ever, most of the shells bursting high in the air, the _time_ being too short. Getting along comfortably, and had we clothing and a few victuals from the north, we would be more comfortable than any time during our stay in Secessia.

Saturday, August 27. Slept soundly altho the shells flew howling through the air and bursting with terrific noise. Washed clothes, white ones having a Job. A terrific rain storm passed by in the evening nearly drownding the offices in the Jail Yard. It would doubtless give the fleet [a] gay time. Got 3 days rations of bacon, tolerably good one in quantity but poor in quality. News of Fort Morgan, Mobile Bay, surrendering with Gen'l Page and 583 men making about 1200 prisoners captured then by our Navy.[42] Read many items copied from Northern papers of what the "Peace Party" under the name of "Democrats" are doing. Vallandingham[43] is splurging all through N.Y. and one would think that "peace on any terms," what this party avows to be their hue and cry, is the prevailing sentiment of the North.

Sunday, August 28. Very pretty day, calm and clear. Foster was busy all day, and one shell bursted near enough to throw a piece of the shell into the yard of Roper striking an out building. It seemed as if it were coming for us, and a great skedaddle was gotten up from off the piazza. Had news of a battle at Petersburg on last Wednesday and extras came out having a despatch from Lee claiming to have driven Grant from the P. R. R. capturing one Gen'l Cutler, 9 pieces of Artillery, and 2500 prisoners.[44] They also said a proposition had been sent to Washington to exchange officer for officer, man for man, leaving us keep the excess. Hope this may bring about an exchange. Health good; our ten days rations growing slim.

Monday, August 29. Pretty day, tolerably warm. No shelling of the city today. Reports say he is mounting guns for more extensive operations. The papers speak of the success they achieved at Petersburg but are not at all buoyant on it so that doubts are held of any very great victory. Col. Jaques and J. R. Gilmor ("Edmund Kirke") have had an interview with Jeff. Davis to search him in regard to peace, but he distinctly says there can be no peace without the recognition of the confederacy and they would sooner be annihilated than back down.[45] Still the copperheads of the North cry "Peace, Peace." Got a barrel of Artesian water brought to the yard to drink as the Dr. says it has medicinal purposes qualities. Very few liked its taste. Good health. 41 officers came from Macon yesterday, a few more today.

Tuesday, August 30. Foster began shelling again this morning throwing them farther than heretofore. The guard said one soldier was killed up at by the exploded pieces. News of very little importance but it seems now that the success at Petersburg dwindles down to nothing. Exchange is quiet, but the commissioners at Mobile are said to have made arrangements for general exchange. A committee was sent from Andersonville to represent their case to the government, &c. Gas was put on tonight making it much more pleasant, and having a chance of spending the long nights in reading. The situation is more desirable & endurable. Got a little molasses of bad quality. Good health and getting on slowly.

Wednesday, August 31. The day clear and comfortable and cool in the evening. But a few shells were thrown, some bursting far up in the city. Washed my clothes, a disagreeable job. Got ½ oz. of lard being the last of the ten days rations. All is quiet. Saw the items from the north, which now fill southern presses about peace and armistice. The Democracy[46] will undoubtedly nominate a "peace man." Read a work entitled "The Right Way" a "prize essay" written by Rev. Collier of Geneva,

N.Y., and treats of the evils of war. It is handled so well as to make me blush, for <u>this</u> war, and pray for its speedy termination and ask the question "Cannot it be stopped by convention?"[47] The Cruiser Tallahasse is doing sad work among the Ships burning & destroying about 30 in this month.[48] The Blockade runner "Lillian" was captured 24 inst. [instant].[49] Chaplins said to go away tomorrow.

Thursday, September 1. Cold last night, the wind blowing hard and cold. Today is pleasant and comfortable. Got ten days more ration of corn and wheat flour, two rations of bacon. The commissary Serg't says he has issued the last rations to us as we are going to be exchanged in a short time. Discussion on the merits of the different ones proposed for nomination for Presidents & V.P. grow exciting. While McClellan's name is discussed thoroughly; some admiring him no matter what he does or with whom he associates but the most reject him. Hope we may get home for this campaign and prospects bid us <u>hope</u>. Good health, with all the rest.

Friday, September 2. Good news in papers of 600 Reb officers being at Port Royal for either exchange or to be put under fire in retaliation for us. McClellan is nominated by the Chicago Con. for President, to be supported by Vallandigham, Wood, and all peace men. This will make the contest for peace on any terms, or war to honorable peace.[50] A fire broke out near our quarters at 7 P.M. making a great smoke and light. The fire companies were soon on the grounds, and Gen'l Foster celebrated the affair with additional shells. One piece fell near us in the Med. [Medical] Col. [College] Yard. The non-com [non-commissioned] butternuts[51] are to leave tomorrow. Exchange stock advancing. Gold: 232½ in N.Y. 30 ult. [ultimo].

Saturday, September 3. Pretty day, clear, but not warm. Pendleton of Ohio of the Vallandigham school has been nominated on the ticket with McClellan as V. President. The Chaplins and Surgeons with a few officers and privates went to the Harbor by Flag of Truce for exchange. The officers and men came back. Could not be exchanged. Fighting was said to be going on at Atlanta yesterday, but no news. All is quiet. Was unwell having a bilious headache. No shells till evening when a good many solid shot were fired. Rumor says the Rebs intended to move us, had they (our folks) kept up the time fuse shells. We still expect to be exchanged soon.

Sunday, September 4. Very fine day. The sun shone out brightly and to us in the <u>shade</u>, the day was comfortable. Good news of Atlanta being in our possession and a good portion of Hardee's Corps made prisoners.[52] This made us all feel jubilant. Exchange is also buoyant as the officer of the guard says we shall be exchanged in a few days, and sent a dispatch north. The shells, timer fuze, came over plentifully screeching through the air. Read "Universalism why rejected" by Rev. Hawkes, a good thing convincing to my mind at least. Had good health, and passed the day pleasantly. Wrote letter to mother. A few letters were received from the North none for me.

Monday, September 5. Was rejoiced to hear the news from Atlanta confirmed. Atlanta is in our possession. Hood blew up his trains and retreated, losing six guns, besides having his Army crippled badly. The Rebs feel very sore, and begin censuring the Generals. Morgan has been relieved, his command, divided among others.[53] Gen'l Winder has been relieved for incapacity and inhumanity to prisoners.[54] Twenty officers came in from the Jail Yard, 20 to Roper. The Rest went back to work-house. The papers are opposing special exchanges of officers as it leaves the privates in confinement &c.

Tuesday, September 6. Had a stormy, rainy night. The 6th, 7 & 8 are said to be noted for squalls in this place. Not much from Atlanta, but the Rebs feel so sore over its fall that they keep quiet. They have lost very severely. The "Courier" advocates the release of enlisted men prisoners but close confinement of officers, and hope no more special exchanges. Gen'l J. H. Morgan was killed and all his staff captured at Greenville, Tenn., a few days ago.[55] Thus enduth another of their bright lights. Last quotation of gold: 244. Got fresh meat yesterday & today. I was cook. Wood issued, the first in ten days, and all the out buildings have been burned. Good health.

Wednesday, September 7. The nights remain cool, and the day not disagreeably warm. The "Sisters of Charity"[56] came to the marine today with grapes and other things, giving them to the officers. They attend the Hospital, being of great service to our sick. They truly are a worthy association. Felt unwell having headache. Bombarding continues, the shell going far up in the city. The papers think all communication should be stopped with Foster until he stop[s] his barbarous shelling. News from Atlanta are quiet. Sherman is not advancing fastly. The Rebs are building up on the Peace Party; all regard the success of McClellan identical with theirs. The Draft is reduced to 300,000 made 6th inst., I suppose.[57]

Thursday, September 8. Weather cold. Calm altho this is the stormy season. The 600 Reb. officers at Port Royal have been put in confinement on Morris Island guarded in a stockade by 16 sentinels. The shelling continued about 40 shell[s] falling in the city. One white man and two children wounded. Sherman is said to [be] retiring to Atlanta, stopping to recruit his army. Great rejoicing in the North in consequence of the fall of Atlanta. Fresh meat continues. Our rations are not large of meal & flour, and the greatest economy failed to make it last the 10 days. The rice is all that is left. Saw ripe pomegranates. Felt well. Sat up late.

Friday, September 9. Nights cool, day pleasant. Bombarding continues the shells going up farther into the city. One negro Barber was killed & the barber that comes into the Marine [Hospital] says the people are very much frightened, and conveyances to the country are in demand. The Rebs are getting frightened about the Andersonville prisoners as Sherman has said he is going there to release them. Another Reb. Craft, "Georgia," was captured a few days ago.[58] Their navy is playing out fast. Health continues good. Have fresh meat and rice for rations. Flour and meal played out.

Saturday, September 10. Pretty day. Last day of the rations, having only a little rice left. But at dark got part of 10 day's more. Meal, bacon, rice, beans, soap, salt. About a thousand enlisted men came from Andersonville and were put in the Jail Yard. They were told they were going to be exchanged to prevent them from escaping. They look bad, thin, dirty, sickly, and made me feel like sacrificing anything to get them home. Why are they not exchanged? Oh, War is a cruel monster! A few special exchanges have taken place from "Roper" of late. A few boxes and many letters are coming from the north, but strange not even a letter to me.

Sunday, September 11. Today is said to be a day of "Thanksgiving and Prayer" in the North for our recent successes. Foster kept it pretty well, but threw enough of shells to kill one white man and one colored woman. The "boys" in the Jail Yard seemed revived at the sight of the shells and shouted loudly. They have a throng[ed] place, and still are lively, singing songs patriotic, &c. None of our Regt. among them. An officer came into Marine having been at Andersonville as a private for 5 months. He tells of 6 prisoners being hung by a court formed of 12 of their number. They were thieves and traitors, 3 from Pa. Reg'ts, 1 N.Y., 1 R.I.[59] They seem more successful in detecting traitors among them than us. The Catholic Priest visited us.

Monday, September 12. The weather continues fine, and cool. Health good, rations moderate. Got fresh beef, and lard for tomorrow. Sherman has made an Armistice with Hood for ten days to dispose of the citizens at Atlanta, sending all who take the oath to the rear, and those who do not into the Rebel line, being unwilling to feed them or see them starve.[60] The Yanks had a ball there, and some of the ladies attended much to the chagrine of the Rebs. The enlisted men prisoners were taken out of the Jail Yard and sent to the Race-Course preparing a camp there.[61] Some thousands more came from Andersonville. The men so ragged and haggard looking they were ashamed to bring them into the city till after night so says the guard who condemn the inhumanity of their own men.

Tuesday, September 13. Today was a contentious one as the papers say that Gen'l Butler has notified Judge Ould the [that] the exchange of Slave Negroes is necessary to exchange. This news made many crabit [crabbed] and they found fault with the Government, some even cursing the Administration from which two fights resulted. The 600 officers came from Savannah and were lodged in the Jail Yard. They look well and intimate that they have been well treated. Capt. Freeman of 101. Pa. was not shot by the guard. Potter and Airy who had escaped came along being recaptured.[62] Washed. Had bean soup for dinner. Spent most of the day in amusements.

Wednesday, September 14. Had a mail yesterday, getting two letters, one from sister Jennie and Bro. John. All well and I was glad to hear again from home not having heard since 28th Apr. Wrote to sister Jennie and Lizzie of L [Latrobe] now at B. [blank space in MS] News better than yesterday, as the Naval officers all said to be exchanged and Sherman and Hood are discussing the matter. Gold on 12th at N.Y. 219 being a healthy decline. McClellan's star is declining, and Vallandigham has forsaken him, as being to war like. Great rejoicing all over the north. No shelling today. Foster has likely strained his large guns. Pretty weather, dry and warm. Good health, hope still alive.

Thursday, September 15. Warm, dry day, no rain for some time. A few shells fell upon the city today. Rumors of the last lot of officers going to leave the city on Friday. Also that many sick enlisted men are in the hospitals here. A train loaded with our prisoners ran off the track in Ga. smashing up eight cars, killing and wounding many. The papers say the Yankeys are stealing all the private property of the refugees sent from Atlanta. The Courier urges the release of the enlisted men. Hood and Sherman are trying to arrange an exchange of the prisoners in the department. Got half rations of fresh beef each day. Health good, and slight hopes of exchange growing brighter.

Friday, September 16. Weather continues fair, not very warm. Had a mail but nothing for me. The official correspondence between Sherman and Hood was published concerning Exchange. Sherman was willing to exchange man for man for as many as he had retained at Chattanooga (2000 men and 120 off[icers]), but was not willing to take any others than those captured during this campaign in his department. This blocked the matter. Our officers are loud in the denunciations of his acts. A Flag of Truce is to meet in the harbor on Monday. Gen'l Jones was notified that the Rebs on Morris Island would be fed on rations as nearly as possible to the C.S. [Confederate States] Ration till every prisoner should be taken from Charleston. This may stir up something.

Saturday, September 17. Weather the same, very pleasant. Had a great excitement in town a fire breaking out near the Roper Hospital. Foster seeing the smoke began pouring in the shells, one striking a large building far up in the city setting it on fire. The Roof burned entirely off, but the fire was put out. The first fire spread, burned all afternoon, getting near the Work-House. The shelling was close, two pieces falling in our yard, one in Roper, hitting an officer in the arm, not serious.[63] The fire got so close [to] our buildings that Foster ceased firing. The firemen kept up a howling all night, clearing and hallering. Letters came in but none for me. Health good and rations [of] beef, rice, & cornbread.

Sunday, September 18. Fires appear to be the order of the day. Early this morning before the firemen left the scene of yesterday's fire, another broke out between us and the Channel. Being in range of us Foster did not shell. Shells flew thick today, some bursting farther up in the city than any I have yet seen. Nothing new today. Great dissatisfaction on account of the exchange as the Rebs seem willing to exchange on <u>any</u> terms except <u>slave</u> <u>negros</u>, but our gov. [government] could hold all the excess as hostages for them. Rained nearly all day, filling up the cisterns. Water is getting scarce, the wells not fit to drink. Our rations growing to a pint. Reading the bible in course. Health good.

Monday, September 19. The papers say that Saturday's fire was the most destructive one since the great fire of '61 burning down some 20 buildings. The day was fine. Nothing new. Hoped to have exchange news but got none. Wrote to Bro. Jno. Hood and Sherman are going to exchange 2000 men and 120 officers captured during this campaign. Wilson is in the Shenandoah Valley.[64] A correspondent says "Early's Infantry disregards the Yankey Infantry, but respect the Cavalry." An Englishman is buying "gold checks" from the prisoners at $5 for $1. A good many will purchase at even this sacrifice. Greenbacks are worth $7 in Confed.; gold from $20 to 25. Health good.

Tuesday, September 20. Rained most of the day, nearly flooding out the officers in the Jail Yard. A Flag of Truce to go to the fleet on Friday. Expect the Surgeons and Naval officers to be exchanged there. Two Brokers were in giving $5 and $6 Confed. for one in Gold taking checks on orders on any firm North. They could buy more than they wanted at even this reduced price. Our mess will take some next opportunity. Rations out. Some have nothing since yesterday noon, hence their eagerness to get money at any price. The Yellow Fever is said to be in the City. Not many cases. The Blockade Runner "A. D. Vance" has been captured off Hatteras first of this month. Said to be a very fast craft.[65]

Wednesday, September 21. The Bankers did a heavy business today, one buying 'tis said notes payable in gold to the amount of $10,000 at 5 for 1. I got $20 at six. Each of the mess ditto. Sherman and Hood are keeping up a heavy correspondence between each other criminating and recriminating. Sherman gives the latter many good hits. No rations today till dark and those who had no money were starving. We (4) had a dinner of Sweet Pottatoes ($4 worth), Bread ($2 worth) and "<u>Shrimps</u>" ($1 worth). Some spent $50 for an egg nogg, others $50 for a few pounds butter or ½ gal [souse?]. The money came from Richmond and was turned over to the owners in kind, Gold, silver & U.S.C.[66]

Thursday, September 22. Pretty day, warm and airy. Got rations for ten days, a good deal short of what we usually got, but had more beans and some molasses to make up. Marketing was [a] throng, everything cleaned out as fast as brought to the fence. Prices running high. Potatoes $16 a peck, Sweet potatoes cheeper. Wrote two letters to Sister Lizzie and Ed McChesney. Capt. Airy and Potter got transferred from the Jail Yard to Marine. Fighting has been going on at Winchester in the Valley. Rebs lost two Gen'ls killed, Rhodes and Godard, two wounded, Fitz Lee and [blank in MS], leaving the field in our possession.[67] Sherman's armistice ended at daylight. Butler gives Judge Ould a caustic letter about exchange, showing the in[ju]stice of the delay on our Gov. not to exchange, &c.

Friday, September 23. Pretty day. Exchange buoyant. Eighteen Surgeons and Chaplins are exchanged by way of the Channel and rumor says nearly official that the naval officers and all prisoners captured in Sherman's Campaign will go soon. Exchange is also going on at Richmond, including men by the hundred and one general. The battle in S. Valley was a success. Sheridan captured 2500 prisoners, 5 Guns, 7 colors, and all the wounded. McIntosh of our Brig was wounded, lost a leg but capturing the 8th S.C. entire. Gen'l Russel of U.S.A. was killed.[68] Col. Moseby was wounded in an engagement near Washington. The peace Democracy have called another convention to nominate another president bolting McClellan. Felt quite unwell, having the cramp cholic, but took opium and camphor. The Bankers still seeking our men who spend it at the gambling table.

Saturday, September 24. Felt unwell all day, bilious headache the complaint. Yesterday's Flag of Truce brought up 150 boxes from Sanitary Com. of N.Y. Four hundred Reb officers were added to the number of pris[oners] on Morris Island. Sherman and Hood are to exchange Four Cols., Three Lt. Cols., Four Majors, Thirty-Eight Captains, and Eighty-Eight Lts. which were chosen in the evening from the officers captured this campaign and afterward the Western Army. Some 20 of the maimed were selected. President Davis and Gen'l Lee are in Georgia. They likely fear that Gov. Brown will bolt the Confederacy.[69] Gold at 225. Got Fresh beef. The last was unfit for use. The Draft is ordered to come off immediately. Excitement high on account of exchange.

Sunday, September 25. The officers left this morning for Atlanta, mostly recent captures. It seems that Sherman has captured more officers than Hood or his Predecessor since the Rebs had not enough of fresh fish to exchange for those in our hands, altho., 'tis said, one whole Regt took the oath of Allegiance (Rebel) at Atlanta. It seem discouraging to old fish to be left again. Got letters, one for me from Bro. Jno. Wrote two to Bros. Jno. and Frank. Nothing today beyond the usual rumors. Some believe the rumor of 700 going to be exchanged this week. A Fire broke out at 9 P.M. near the palce [place] of the last big fire and caused a furious shelling. Bombardment continues very rapid.

Monday, September 26. Weather continues cold and windy. Still sleep out on the Piazza in preference to the sultry rooms. Shelling was kept up fiercely all day. News of Sheridan whipping Earley at Fisher's Hill in the Valley, capturing 12 cannon.[70] Great rejoicing north. Gold down to 200. Davis is still in Ga. Made a speech at Macon, so puerile as to be disowned by the Charleston Papers. Some think he is afraid of Gov. Brown taking Ga. out of the Confed. but he says it is to organize the Army. The most of the officers in the Jail Yard were paroled, sending them to "Roper," "Marine," and "Mills" house; when [where] the Genls were. Health tolerably good but not good appetite.

Tuesday, September 27. Weather continues fair. The shelling of the city on the increase. A 200 [lb.] Parrott Gun was opened today. One with [a] man killed, while [a] woman wounded. The shells flew over our building but fortunately they did not burst till beyond us. Bought butter at $11 per lb., Eggs at $6 per dozen. Got wood issued, said to cost $45 per cord. 'Tis thought more Confed. prisoners were brought to Morris Island. News from the Valley still good, but little going on at Atlanta. The Rebs threaten hugely and are to make Sherman's defeat more than a "Moscow."[71] Got positive knowledge of the Yellow Fever in the city. A good many dying with it. Feel better, but not entirely well.

Wednesday, September 28. Day fine. Bombarding fiercer than at any former time. 88 shells fell upon the city from three guns in twenty-four hours, at times one in every three minutes. Wounded a good many, 3 men & 4 women reported. The Rebs talk a great deal of some movement that is going to frighten Sherman, &c., cut his communications likely. All news from Richmond indicate that the final struggle for that city as well as Petersburg will shortly come off. They talk despondingly. News from the Valley still good. Wrote two letters to mother and Mollie of M. Had a subscription for buying a violin and Banjo. The evening was past by some in dancing. Health getting good.

Thursday, September 29. Pleasant day, health good. Lt. Stahl, 2nd U.S. Cavalry, died of Bilious Fever in Roper today.[72] Gunboat officers on a visit, going to leave tomorrow via Richmond for the North. The shelling was furious, 110 falling on the city last night. Major White, 67 P.V.[73] has succeeded in going with the western officers for exchange. He is from Milroy's Command. A Flag of Truce by way of Port Royal ferry was had to exchange papers & letters. Rumors of going to be sent to Columbia S.C. We all fear we shall as all would prefer Charleston with shells and Yellow fever than Columbia.

Friday, September 30. Rained heavily last night. Shells flew thick and fast. None reported killed. Capt. Soule returned from P.R. [Port Royal] Ferry. Major Fontaine (Reb) came along to be exchanged for Major White, who has gone to Sherman's bosom. Capt. Goyen, Provost M[arshall], has gone to Columbia to prepare Yankee quarters, but whether for us or the enlisted men is uncertain. The boxes were delivered, but one horridly mutilated, getting nothing but a few pieces of clothing and old papers. Still they have the cheek to raise subscriptions to send eatables to their officers on Morris Island. Capt. P. got a valise with a few Northern Papers.[74] Spent the evening reading them. Finished reading "Willis" poems, think them fine.[75] Health good exchange drying up.

Saturday, October 1. Rained last night. Warm today, sultry and unpleasant. Unhealthy weather, bad for the Yellow Fever. One case out of Roper. A Reb captain died in the city. The "Gun Boats" left yesterday. Rumor still of moving, some have it that only the excess above the number of Rebs on the Island will be sent away, the rest exchanged. Some of the officers got out in the city & got drunk. Likely to stop all advantages of buying extras. Spent part of the day in reading northern papers. Find I am getting full a year behind the age. How long will this confinement continue? Felt unwell. Capt. Zarracher has been unwell for a week or two.[76]

Sunday, October 2. Continues warm. Water scarce. Got part of our rations, but they seem to make us depend on our private purse for the most we get. Capt. Sheldon is sick, said to be Yellow Fever. Capt. Mobley is in command. Had two roll-calls. Hear that we shall leave for Columbia this week. Rumor says Col. Lay will make Foster a <u>final</u> proposition to exchange man for man for all on Morris Island, and remove the rest from the city. Finished reading the Old Testament, by course, since we came to the Marine. Health good. Got very much disheartened at times by reflecting on the probabilities of long imprisonment.

Monday, October 3. Rather cool today but still a sultry air makes it unpleasant. Rained last night. A "Flag of Truce" went down the Harbor. They took a large quantity of provisions &c to the Rebs on Morris Island. Said to receive some for us, but they will purloin the most of it as before. Forrest seems to be doing damage in Sherman's rear. Grant is moving. Had a hard fight last Sat. taking Reb. works.[77] Gen'l Hardee is to relieve Gen'l Jones of Command of the City.[78] No more talks of moving. Had only one day's rations now in three. Had we not got money we would be in a starving condition. Wrote a letter to Major [John W.] Phillips. Health good.

Tuesday, October 4. Day clear and warm. News of none importance, all rumor that we have had a reverse in the Vally, that Hood hold[s] the R.R. in rear of Atlanta, and the Rebs in high glee, in prospect of Sherman evacuating Atlanta.[79] Had a slight mail, no letter for me. Rumors that part will leave the city tomorrow on account of the Yellow Fever. Nothing was accomplished by yesterday's Flag of Truce and the future looks gloomy. Good health and good appetite. Got rations of meal and molasses, rather inferior.

Wednesday, October 5. The most of the officers left this morning for Columbia leaving but 180 in the Marine. Guy Bryan of our mess left. They were cheered lustily as they passed. The citizens regret our leaving, as they fear that Foster shall shell the city more furiously. The building seems quiet since for [those] left. But the day was spent as usual. A few letters and boxes came, none for me. Quite a lot of Sanitary Stores[80] were sent to the officers in this place. The "Sisters of Mercy" say the Yellow Fever is on the increase, and it is high time that we were leaving. One or two cases has taken place in Roper. Had a dance for the last in Charleston as we go tomorrow. Good Health and spirits as buoyant as ever.

Seven

"Escape Has Been the Order of the Day"

Camp Sorghum, Columbia, South Carolina,
October 6–December 11, 1864

The hastily evacuated prisoners from Charleston and from Savannah, about fifteen hundred in all, arrived in Columbia, the state's capital city of about eight thousand residents. With little advance warning, local authorities were unprepared for their new charges, who were herded to a four-acre open site that lacked housing, wood, water, cooking utensils, latrines, or even a stockade or guards. Improvisation was the order of the day: cadets from a local military academy watched the prisoners, pine branches marked the deadline, and pine boughs formed rude shelters. "We dug a hole in the ground, propped sticks over it and covered it with sod and dirt," Lt. Henry C. Potter, 18th Pennsylvania Cavalry, recalled, and "in this hole Captains Pennypacker, Airey, Weaver, Fortescue, and I slept at night." Small groups under guard were allowed outside the prison's bounds to fetch water, gather firewood, and use the latrines. Meatless rations of coarse cornmeal, flour, salt, and large quantities of sorghum molasses caused many cases of severe diarrhea. The prisoners dubbed their new home "Camp Sorghum." Drafts on back pay purchased meat and vegetables at inflated prices from sutlers, and intermittent supplies sent from the North provided much-welcomed clothes, blankets, money, reading material, and provisions. Weaver, after going barefoot for many months, gratefully secured a pair of boots from a dead prisoner. Cold, rainy weather delayed improving their shelters, and not until late October were axes and shovels issued so they could go with the guards to gather timber. Slowly, log cabins with chimneys, fireplaces, roofs, ovens, and daubing gave the camp a more settled appearance.[1]

Angry over their mistreatment and aware that Union soldiers were in Atlanta, in northern Georgia, and along the Georgia coast, small groups of prisoners frequently fled the poorly guarded camp. "The officers think <u>any</u> means of getting away from the horrid place legitimate and honorable," Weaver noted approvingly. They bribed the demoralized guards with greenbacks, ran the deadline at night, constructed tunnels, claimed to be paroled to perform outside work, forged passes to the hospital outside the stockade, wandered off when gathering wood or water, and walked away wearing Confederate uniforms. Although civilians and bloodhounds returned many escapees, and the guards killed one soldier as he dashed off, the prisoners remained undeterred and took courage from the stories of slaves' assistance and poor whites' disaffection from the Confederacy. By November's end, the camp's population had fallen to under a thousand prisoners. Even the ever-cautious Weaver succumbed to escape fever by answering "present" to the name of an escapee who was included in a group of men about to be exchanged. When his doppelganger returned, recaptured, the next day, Weaver ruefully noted, "I felt badly, but not having built up very buoyantly on the matter I did not take it to heart."[2]

Weaver's diary entries at Camp Sorghum became longer and more reflective as October marked the one-year anniversary of his capture and his twenty-fifth birthday in the midst of a seemingly interminable incarceration. "One year ago I little dreamed of this day finding me in the confederacy," he mused on the latter occasion, "But 'tis so, with but little hope of getting free again this day one year. Oh, the length of weary days; how slowly it passes by!" The fall elections provided some diversion. Weaver was pleased that Lincoln received a seven-to-one majority in the camp's mock election in mid-October over George McClellan, the Democratic candidate who ran on a platform calling for a negotiated end of the war. He anxiously awaited the results of the actual contests the following month that would determine, he believed, whether "our Government will be established anew or the Confederacy will be a success." Although encouraged by the frequency of special exchanges and paroles of wounded prisoners, he resented being deceived with false hopes and, especially, that new arrivals with political connections were released before "old fish." A satirical poem, "A Psalm of Prison-Life," found on the camp letter box, captured Weaver's sentiments about the prisoners' mistreatment and their own government's callousness: "We've been treated more like cattle / Than like heros of the strife." Most of all Weaver took comfort in signs of civilians' waning support for the Confederacy. Some of the guards were temporarily placed in the stockade after threatening mutiny, and even unsuccessful escape attempts, prisoners believed, lowered Southerners' morale. One recaptured officer reported that a doctor had told him that it would be better to "send all prisoners across the lines, than to have them escaping and mixing among the negros and white people, as all the negros talked about now is 'freedom,' 'the war,' &c., feeling [and] appreciating the struggle on hand for their Emancipation."[3]

Fig. 18. Camp Sorghum, Columbia, SC. Named by the prisoners for their meatless rations of cornmeal and sorghum molasses, it occupied a four-acre sloping field. Weaver's home from October to December 1864, the open site initially lacked housing, wood, water, cooking utensils, latrines, or even a stockade or guards. (MOLLUS-Mass Civil War Photograph Collection, United States Army Heritage and Education Center, Carlisle, PA)

Thursday, October 6, 1864. At an early hour we were got on the march for Columbia, guarded heavily. The citizens showed signs of sorrow at our departure. We past up Bofain [Beaufain], King & Ann Streets to the Deport [Depot]. Saw, all along, the marks of shells, having perforated houses by dozens. The principal St. "King" seem almost vacated and grass growing in the centers. Surely this is the "doomed" city. Got on the cars, but the engine ran off the track and had to get another. We left Charleston certain of having spent a few months very happily for "Prisoners." Ran slowly all day, passing Branchville, Orangeburg, being the second trip on the rout[e] and got to Col. [Columbia] at 11 o'clock P.M. We were guarded strictly at night but the guard was very kind, being of the 32nd Ga. Feel well.

    Friday, October 7. Staid in the cars all night, some sleeping others sitting up for want of room to lie town. Got out at daylight and Bivouacked in the Depot Yard. The rest of the Officers were confined in a lot nearby so that all or nearly so, of the officers in the Confederacy, are now in Columbia. At noon they took [us] 1½ miles to the South west of the city to a broad open highland, where they put us in camp "among the pines." They wanted us to take the parole and they would furnish us tents and more ground, but they say if we do not take a parole, we shall not fare very well. Still the majority say no parole unless they give us something worth it. A company of Cadetts guarded us from the city & acted so meanly in driving up the rear with the point of the Bayonet that they shall be remembered for it. Some 10 or 15 escaped off our train, 50 or 60 from the others.

Saturday, October 8. Last night was very cold. The high winds blew fiercely through the "pines" making the same melancholy sound as formerly, when ensconced in our tents in the Regt. Some say there was <u>frost</u> last night. The camp is three or 4 acres in size. No water inside. The guard and a crowd stand continually for their turn to pass out with guard, 12 going at a time. The sink arrangements are worse, 10 going at once. No tents, but they promise we shall have some. They wanted us to take the parole but it shall hardly be excepted. The Sanitary Stores were distributed. I got pair drawers, towel, and handkerchief. There were some shirts and bed quilts. Many feel quite discouraged at the prospects of the coming winter, and that exchange is played out. But should another winter be ours, I feel as strong now as a year ago and perhaps better inured to prison life. Health good but very cold.

Sunday, October 9. Last night was very cold, a heavy frost fell, a high wind blew, and we nearly froze. We have a hard place of it & nothing but cornmeal, a little flour, salt, & rice, & molasses to eat. No cooking, baking, utensils, and have to eat mush and rice alternately. Lt. Wilson, 6 U.S. C, is said to be killed trying to escape off the train.[4] None have been brought in, but I suppose they are put in the Jail in Columbia. Rumors of exchange that Grant is going to exchange all captured since the first day of May '64. The papers tell of a meeting among us, when the Artillery opened, killing seven, wounding seven, but <u>we</u> know <u>nothing of it</u>. Sutlering is carried on, but prices higher than at Charleston. 'Tis said we are going back there as soon as the Y. F.[5] dies away.

Monday, October 10. Weather getting warmer but the nights continue very cold with frost. Still get no meat rations. Some comes in at $2½ per lb., small loaves of bread 1/5 lb. costs 75 cts. Potatoes $24 per bu. They are clearing off a cam[p]ing ground west of this, having water &c. Carry our wood from the adjoining woods, ten going at a time. Built a house of pine boughs to keep the due [dew] off, as well as the wind. A few are sick. A few having, 'tis said, the Yellow Fever, but such weather as we have had of late will soon knock "Yellow Jack." Some are being brought back who had escaped, as usual hunted by hounds and citizens, so that all vow that when released their first aim will be to kill all dogs in their way. We have near 1400 officers, some being left behind sick. Health is good and am getting along very well, having got used to <u>any</u> treatment. The guards have dress parade, and a great show of <u>ignorance</u> they display.

Tuesday, October 11. Today was warm, and comfortable, but the morning and evening wet with cold dew. Affairs about the camp remain in "Status Quo," giving us nothing to eat but meal, but allowing the Suttler to sell plenty of beef & bread, at enormous prices. Nearly a thousand lbs. of meat was sold at from $2½ to $4 per lb. We had a shank bone having 2 mouthfuls of meat at $3, but we had a large pot full of rice soup from the bone. News are of very little import. Sherman is still in Atlanta with Hood in the rear tearing up the R.R. occupying Resacca & Marietta but the Rebs fear he shall move onward to Savannah & Charleston.[6] Col. Harris, Beauregard's Chief of Staff, died of Yellow Fever at Charleston a few days ago.[7] Tonight one year ago I was made captive. Who dreamed of me passing an anniversary of that day in the hands of the Rebs. But such is the fact with no hope for immediate relief.

Wednesday, October 12. The weather continues fine with no changes in our situation. News rather bad from Ga., as the Rebs say they have torn up the R.R. in Sherman's rear filling up the track or <u>cuts</u>. But the latter remains at Atlanta apparently careless abt. [about] Hood's movement. Hope he may be equal to the occasion. Some are escaping nightly, only to be brought back in a few days. Some having Rebel uniform got a good way, but the entire South is so strictly guarded that the chances of getting away to that of recapture don't invite escape. Wrote letter to mother. Got rations of meal and "grits." Sutlers have plenty of meat to issue to sell, many think they sell our rations. Happy for us, we have money to buy a few things. Have good health, and passing the time as comfortably as expected.

Thursday, October 13. Colder today than yesterday, but are favored with dry weather. Capt. Wenrick, 19th Pa. Cav., died in Camp Hospital of the Yellow Fever. Another case, Lt. Spofford, said to be amongst us.[8] Two or three officers died in Columbia of the same disease. Don't hear of any new cases; all thought to be contracted at Charleston. News are of none account. Hood is still on Sherman's line of communications but the east is becoming gloomy for the Rebs. Grant is closing around Lee and his army with deadly certainty. Papers say 600 officers & 7000 men have left Libby & Belle I [Isle] for the south, perhaps for this place, as they are enlarging the grounds. Maj. Charles P. Mattock of Maine was taken away today by special exchange.[9] Wrote to Hilton Head for box of clothing. Health good. Plenty of Sorghum issued. No meat.

Friday, October 14. The day passes slowly and night and morning seems each in their turn a relief from the monotony of this kind of life. Clouds begin to darken the sky, and we portend a rainstorm, fearing it. News of little import, since they know nothing of Sherman's situation, or Hood['s] probabilities of capturing or routing the former. The papers speak of putting our Negro Soldiers, prisoners of war, to work upon the fortifications at Danville, Va., when they mutinied and made their escape with 25 muskets. Good for Cuffie. May they escape, and publish to the world the fact of making prisoners of war work on fortifications. Lt. Spofford is said to have died of Yellow Fever. All things seem to be prosperous in the North. Gold 195. Sheridan is destroying all mills and provisions in the Valley of S. [Shenandoah]. Have good health. Meat is 2.50 for beef, $7.00 for Bacon. Can get a pair of worn shoes for $6.5.

Saturday, October 15. Today was very pleasant, warm and dry. No news in the papers but quotations from the north. Sherman seems all contented. Had a fight with the enemy at Altoona, whipping them badly.[10] New York Paper states that Lt. Col. Brinton, 18th Pa. Cav., was wounded on the 19th ult. [ultimo] while leading the Regt. upon the breastworks of the enemy at Winchester.[11] The regt. seems to have done its duty nobly, but should we loose our Lt. Col. no one could fill his place. Got a pair of boots, those of Capt. Wenrick, coming in good time, being barefooted for many months. The idea of wearing a dead man's boots disappears as I look at my bare feet. An election for President & V.P. is to be held in Camp on Monday with voting at the quarters of the Senior officer of his state. Some twenty-five state[s] are represented. Had a dinner off [illegible] worth of beef. Health good.

Sunday, October 16. Very pretty day, qui[e]t and lonely. Spent the day reading a portion of the bible. Sleeping a while & talking over exchange rumors, which ran riot through the camp. Altho Sabbath, electioneering ran high on account of the coming election tomorrow, and many discussions grew out of the different conversations. 'Tis said Pa., Ohio & Ind. have gone Rep. or Union by large majorities and Lincoln is sure of election.[12] The Reb papers all beginning to find it out and are trying to persuade the people that it is better for them that Lincoln is elected. The Health of the officers is good. Have had no rain, which we dread, as our brush houses would be poor protection from the storm. Suttlers shops are open, officers are playing cards & chess, and but little respect paid the sabbath. Preaching in the evening. Health good. Went to bed reflecting.

Monday, October 17. Sleep well. Cold enough to keep the mosquitoes quiet and make us wrap up in our blankets. The day was fine and the Election made it lively. Lincoln ran high considering our situation, since many blame the present Administration with our non-exchange. Still withall the most thought fit to support Lincoln and renounce "milk and water" McClellan. Twenty-six states were represented as follows:[13]

	Lincoln	McClellan		Lincoln	McClellan		Lincoln	McClellan
ME	25	0	NH	7	0	VT	29	1
MA	42	5	RI	13	0	CT	34	3
NY	171	29	NJ	25	6	PA	187	35
DE	2	0	MD	21	2	[W]V	19	1
OH	142	15	IN	72	11	IL	79	8
MO	10	0	KY	13	16	TN	26	0
AL	1	0	WI	19	0	MI	40	10
KS	1	0	CA	1	0	FL	1	0
IA	36	0	MN	[8]	0			

Making 1024 for Lincoln and 143 for McClellan. Johnson ran higher than L. Pendleton less than McC. Some 204 did not vote. Even giving McClellan all that did not vote Lincoln had a huge majority.[14] The news from Sherman is quiet, and it is rumored that Forrest has been defeated, but the Rebs remain quiet. From the Shen. Valley all seems prosperous, and our Cavalry are winning bright victories. Custer is said to be in Command of 3rd Div.[15] The Rebels are trying to bring the people over to the idea of arming the slave, and the papers say next Congress will pass the bill. Oh, what a change in the affairs of men and of nations. Slavery is falling of its own weight and should they (the Rebs) arm the slave, slavery will be no more.[16] Rations the same. Health do. [ditto] Rumor quiet. Exchange dead.

Tuesday, October 18. The morning betokened rain and we prepared for the worst, but it passed by. A change of Commandant is to take place in a few days, to the satisfaction of all prisoners & guard as all declare Capt. [E. A.] Semple little short of "<u>simple</u>." It appears that Butler has put the prisoners to work on fortifications in retaliation for them putting negro soldiers at like work. Sheridan is carrying out Grant's order to burn all provisions in the Valley of the S. [Shenandoah]. He has burned 2000 barns full of grain & 70 mills full of flour being the only way to stop the guerrillas. Confed. loans have fallen 6½% in England from the news of the assurance of President Lincoln's reelection. Gold in the north in the ascendency quoted up 212. Health good, a slight hope of exchange remaining since the rebs talk of putting the negros in the field.

Wednesday, October 19. Some 30 prisoners came back from Macon, part of those sent there for exchange, but failed for some reason. 'Tis said that no enlisted men were exchanged at all. Some were sent from Columbia for exchange. Specials are going on continually to the dissatisfaction of all and from the move of things we expect to stay here all winter. The Rebs had a large mass meeting to condemn the conduct of their Congressman W. W. Boyce, who had written to Davis advising him to make overtures to the Peace Party [in the] north in which he spoke many despondings, which offended. He seems to be a sharp Reb but is not understood by his brethren.[17] Election news is contradictory but 'tis pretty certain that Pa. has gone Republican.[18] The papers say gaining 5 Representatives for the Union Party. Continued good health with dinner of rice soup.

Thursday, October 20. Last night four officers ran the guard and escaped. Four guns were fired at them but missed. The Rebs were dreadfully scared and the Artillerymen were summoned to their guns, while the officers were hallooing "fall in Co. G." "Fall in Co. B." "Double quick." The only danger was of their opening the Artillery when we would be compelled to capture them. Lt. Col. Stark Mean took command of us.[19] He moved the Artillery to an adjoining hill. He seems a good kind of Reb belonging to the Reb Invalid Corps, formerly to the 17th S.C. It seems that Hood and Forrest are not doing such grand exploits.

All quiet at Richmond. Moseby captured two U.S. P.M. [Pay Masters] with 180 thousand dollars on the B & O R.R.[20] Had a dinner of $7 worth of beef. Wrote a letter to Sister Amanda. Weather cool. Rumors of going to Charleston as soon as the frost kills Y.F.

Friday, October 21. Today is my twenty fifth birthday. One year ago I little dreamed of this day finding me in the confederacy. But 'tis so, with but little hope of getting free again this day one year. Oh length of weary days; how slowly it passes by! Is there no releaf for us? Been here for two weeks, and yet no tents, no cooking utensils, and with the greatest difficulty can get out for wood to cook a little mush. Such treatment was never given the vilest criminals. Lt. Young, 4th Pa. Cav., was accidentally killed by the gun of a guard who was in the act of "cap-ping."[21] Another victim to the carelessness of the guard. Cold frosts fall at night and high winds go sighing through our houses of pine boughs. Some money came for prisoners from Richmond. Health good.

Saturday, October 22. Very cold last night. Frosts fall heavily. Wind cold and shrill. Stood two hours in line to get out for wood and finally got an armful of limbs or brush to cook our little grub. Truly this is the worst treatment we have ever received, and beneath the horror or dignity of even a robber. News of a great victory in the Valley over Erley, the Rebs loosing twenty three cannon in the nett, capturing eight before they broke.[22] Gold in the north 212, rather variable. Election in the North is creating considerable excitement but Lincoln, 'tis said, will have a good show. Rumors of exchange of 10000 enlisted men at Savannah but no hope of general exchange for time to come. Plenty of meal and sorgum to eat, nothing else. Health good.

Sunday, October 23. Very pretty warm day. Heavy frosts. Had a search at Roll Call for several quarters of beef that disappeared from the Sutler's tent last night. The Sutler carries on such embezzling that little sympathy is with him, being a United States officer. The meat was not found. Sold half bushel of meal, the surpluss over what we used since we came here, having bought a good deal of bread for a mess of beef. Getting 24 cts. per pound. A broker is in camp buying Pay Rolls giving two confed. for one. I don't sell, since the authorities give $7 for [a] GreenBack, $24 for Gold. One case of small pox out side of camp in a shelter tent. Lt. Young's funeral sermon was preached in the evening. Preaching at noon, by an officer. Tried to get up an exchange rumor. Capt. [Stephen] Mobley went to Genl [William] Hardee abt. [about] 4th [Regiment]. Expect to do same for 18th.

Monday, October 24. Very pretty day. Wonderful how dry it keeps to our comfort. Got out today for wood and brush, having to carry it for half a mile. Guarded on all sides. Issues of cornmeal as course as grits continues, with more sorgum than we desire. The Broker who intended to buy Pay Rolls was prevented by the Rebs from making the transaction for some unknown reason. News from

Sheridan continues good, and had not night intervened the destruction of Earley's Army would have undoubtedly been the result. Am reading Campbell's Poems.[23] Admire a few but not many of his effusions. Health continues good, and but little sickness among the officers. Still expect to go back to Charleston. Oh, that we may. This is a hard lot, a severe trial.

Tuesday, October 25. Began building a new and better shelter out of pine boughs, being one among 500 others of every shape, so that the camp presents a novel appearance. Had a big job going after more brush. In the evening they deployed a guard around the timber and let us cut. 'Twas a fine sight to see so many blue coats ascending the hill with such eagerness. Five axes and 14 shovels were issued today, the first utensils they have issued since we came here. Those who sent after money got the envelope but no money. No explanation, but 'tis thought they will get weekly allowances. Yesterday a unfortunate pig wandered in our camp, when immediately a hundred men were after him, killing and skinning him in a trice. The others wished for more. Having a large days work felt tired, but had a taffy pulling after dark. Get an amount of sorgum.

Wednesday, October 26. Weather continues good, but threatens rain soon. All busy in fixing up their tents or shelters, some building log huts. The uncertainty of staying here prevents us from doing the same. The officers that were on Morris Island have gone to Fort Pulasky[24] so that hopes are still left of those six hundred being exchanged. Sheridan gives good account of the fight 19th inst. [instant]. We had the worst at first, loosing 20 guns, but victory hind [hied?] and we captured over 50 leaving us over thirty nett. Gen'l Bidwell was killed and three other Gen'ls, Ricketts, Wright, [blank space in MS] were wounded on our side. The Rebs lost Gen. Ramseur, mortally wounded & captured, since died, and 3 other Gen'ls wounded.[25] The blockade runner "Flora" was captured at Charleston a few days ago.[26] Foster has refused from Sanitary consideration to hold Flag of Truce communications with Charleston.[27] No mail yet, strange to say, since we came from Charleston.

Thursday, October 27. Three or four officers ran [the] guard last night, five shots being fired at them. The only casualty was the killing of a Reb in their own camp. A few recaptures come in but some must get through to our lines. But there is little inducement to attempt the escape. Made additional improvements to our tent by thatching with a coat of brush. Soon the rain began to fall and continued all the remainder of the day falling thick and fast. Spreading a blanket on the top of our tent we were kept dry. Most in camp were thoroughly drenched looking like drownded rats. I had to cook dinner about the worst time; got wet but was thankful for a dry place to crawl into and a change of dry under clothing. Gen'l Birney has died in Phila. some time this month of Fever. Judge Taney of U.S.C. about the same time. Talk of <u>Chase</u> taking his position.[28] Another Blockade runner with 600 Bales of cotton was captured.

Friday, October 28. Last night was rough and wet many having no shelter from the winds that blew cool after the rain stopped. Some ran [the] guard, several shots being fired, no casualties. Our hut was warm and dry. News today of heavy fighting both at Petersburg and Richmond with advantage to our side. On yesterday at Charleston a 200 Parrot shell exploded in a building killing Lts. Mays and Darden, wounded Lt. Willis, and frightened Capt. Mobley of 32nd Ga.[29] Butler has succeeded in seducing the Rebs to take our negro soldiers off the fortifications by retalliating in like manner, putting Reb prisoners on Dutch Gap.[30] A party of Guerrillas invaded St. Albans, Vt., robbing & killing, most are recognized or confessed to be Rebs. The Leader is caught, will likely hang.[31] Nothing from Sherman but lattest he was all right. Was busy fix[ing] up our Hut, putting door in it & thatching. Health good. Had 5 days rations issued, living on mush.

Saturday, October 29. Pretty weather again, the [sun] shines brightly but not very warm. Heavy frosts fall at night making the ground white. News from the fighting around Petersburg by the Rebs reports all against us driving us back from the gained position, Jerusalem Plank Road.[32] Papers say Butler & Ould have made arrangements for each Party to feed their own prisoners, at which we all rejoice providing satisfactory plan can be adopted to prevent the Rebels from stealing the most of our rations, as heretofore. Col. Moseby has captured Brig. Gen. Duffield at Bunker Hill on 25 ins.[33] All are busy in camp, getting huts put up and preparing for the coming winter; but still none expect to stay here especially under present circumstances. A good many are in hospital tents and are very sick. They are parolled. My health remaining good. Busy on our hut.

Sunday, October 30. Fine weather. Pretty day, quiet and peaceful. Nothing new to get up excitement. The "Carolinian" is published today. It says that our forces were driven from the Boydton P.R. with heavy loss.[34] We had hoped that this last move would be the victorious one. They say that Hood is on the backward track, not caring to go into Tennessee. How calm is the Sabbath. Often my thoughts break away from this emprisoned body, and soars away to more congenial scenes. This cruel war has taught me to appreciate <u>peace</u>, a home, and liberty. By reflecting on the future I grow dissatisfied with all and deep horrors[35] seize me but breaking the monotony I try to be myself again. Glad to have good health and even enough to eat.

Monday, October 31. Threatening rain. Nothing new today in the papers. Getting a new sutler as the Authorities have grown dissatisfied with Mr. King, since he smuggled out orders to draw pay in the north, against the order of the officials. Got a letter from home, and disappointed in getting no more since this one was written 9 Sept. The old fish are making out a list of all officers captured prior to May 1st 1864, in order to insure ourselves favor in position in case an order for the first captured comes to be exchanged. Capt. Sprig of Mich. died at

Charleston 14th inst. of Diarrhea.[36] Many <u>now</u> explain the delay of exchange by the idea that the Gov. [Government] does not want to throw itself open to the charge of exchanging only for electioneering purposes.

Tuesday, November 1. Several shots were fired last night and some eight or ten escaped taking camp kettles and grub along. This is the most daring attempt yet. One officer was shot in the leg, a flesh wound but the rest got off. Frank Krepps [Kreps] escaped in the day bribing the guard while after wood for $10 confed. 'Tis certain, than, more than a hundred have escaped, and only a few recaptured. Those who are brought back say 'tis by mere accident they are captured. They all say the field negros are loyal to us. Occasionally one will betray. Still after all, the way is so long, the road so rough having to wade swamps and swim rivers, that my heart almost fails me, fearing recapture. Why the Rebs don't move us, escaping so freely, is a matter of surprise. The day fine, finished our hut, receiving a thousand branches from our neighbors &c.

Wednesday, November 2. At midnight the rain began to fall, and with a cold east wind making all things disagreeable and giving an opportunity of trying our hut. It leaks only a little, but putting on a blanket we were kept dry. Continued to rain all day, was very cold, and disagreeable, and now promises to be a dark night, and many preparing to skedaddle. Capt. Holderman[37] came in, being out 15 days, getting within 40 miles of Atlanta. He says the negros are all loyal giving them all the information and food they could. One gave them some coffee, saved before the war, showing that they will make any sacrifice to assist us. No news of any description in the papers. Jeff Davis calls for a day of fasting & prayer on the 16th inst. All are eagerly waiting till after election for a turn in the affairs of state. Had nothing but rains today and am glad to have good health.

Thursday, November 3. Rain fell in spells all night and the most of today making it cold and disagreeable. Some officers were let out on parole not to escape to get wood or logs for tents. A few shots were fired last night. Don't know how many escaped, having no roll-call for two days. News from the west good. Rosecrantz has whipped Price, capturing Gen'ls Marmaduke and Caball.[38] Sheridan's report says he has captured in the [Shenandoah] valley 8600 prisoners, 80 cannon, 12100 small arms, 25 caissons, & 260 wagons. The Reb. Ram Albemarle at Plymouth has been sunk by a Torpedo. Unfortunately all the party but the Capt. commanding were afterward captured.[39] Penn. has gone 12000 [for the] union.[40] Papers say Torbert, Custer, and Merritt have been promoted Major Gen'ls.[41] A Flag of Truce to be held today on Savannah River between Elba & Long Islands.[42] Hope fine day weather soon.

Friday, November 4. Rained most of the night. Some ran [the] guard, others stepped over the guard line, while those paroled were carrying in wood. Today was clear, with very high wind. Was cook and had hard work to get the fires to burn.

Papers say the Flag of Truce at Savannah was held and 10 thousand sick are there for exchange. Hopes all had for some officers to go also. Plymouth was recaptured on 31st ult., by our forces after 3 days fighting.[43] The parolling was continued, and escaping increased. 'Tis thought 200 officers have left camp in these two last days. Wilson & I had got ready to go also but the Rebs found out the trick and the parolling ceased. A tunnel was dug from a brush tent to a tent of the hospital, but unfortunately fell in, preventing a good thing in that direction. Some six or eight were recaptured. The most are making for east lines. Health good, meal issued.

Saturday, November 5. Very pretty day. The sun shines brightly, and air is pleasant. The roll-call was made, and many officers to deceive the Rebs as to the number that got out yesterday, when counted on the right of the line fell in on the left keeping the count nearly the same. The parolling was stopped and we went out under guard as usual for wood. The officer of the day says no one broke their parole, but others took advantage of their own carelessness. Rumors of exchange as Lt. Cooper (unreliable Reb) says "400 or 800 officers will undoubtedly be exchanged next week." Wrote a letter to sister Jennie, having to put on a Confed. stamp, as all our letters came back a few days ago, when Col. Huey paid $20 express and sent them to Charleston. No papers today, consequently no news. Health good. Mush to eat.

Sunday, November 6. Last night was very cold and this morning the ground was white with frost, the heaviest this fall. We had a strict roll-call, being kept in line until they got through, when they found they had only 1147 men, instead of about 1400 they should have had. A few recaptured are coming in but very few, only two today that I am aware of, so that good fortune seems to be theirs. Capt. Lodge[44] got a pair of English shoes, cowskin, paying eighty ($80) dollars for them. The rations, 5 days, were issued giving us this time meal, flour, rice, salt, sorghum, and soap. The day was warm and pleasant, and having good health with a good dinner of rice soup made from a bone of beef bought by selling meal. I felt happy especially as the hope of exchange is getting better. (Held religious exercises, Catholic one).

Monday, November 7. Not so cold last night as formerly. Pretty day, warm and comfortable. 13 recaptured officers were brought in, having built a fire and were discovered. 'Tis said the authorities are giving $100 Confed. for all captured Yanks. Col. Means is sick. Capt. Martin is in command.[45] No money, of all the officers have got, is yet delivered and no likelihood of it being soon, as they would buy shoes and clothing to escape. Hence the Rebs leave all [to] starve for want of it. Read "The Tale of our Ancestors" a good newsletter.[46] Played Cribbage & solitaire the rest of the day. Tomorrow is the Election, which shall decide the fate of this Confederacy. Our Government will be established anew or the Confederacy will be a success. Have good health.

Tuesday, November 8. Had glorious news late last night as Capt. Hatch[47] came to camp and told Col. Huey that he "was on his way to Savannah, that he had succeeded in exchanging 10,000 prisoners, a large proportion of whom would be officers, and all from this camp. He would send for the list as soon as he would arrive at S[avannah]. That he would try to exchange all." &c. He also said the arrangements had been made for each gov. [government] to feed its own prisoners, and at the present, supplies were coming to Savannah! A strange idea is that the Rebs are to get provisions and clothing from Europe, by the permission of our Authorities. This coming so straight even the "old incredulous fish" took stock in exchange and confidently expect 6 or 8 hundred exchanged. The only alloy in our prospects is the fear that money will buy out leaving old captures to remain as last spring. Five recaptures last night, seventeen today came in. Fine day, warm & clear. Good health and buoyant spirits.

Reb congress met yesterday. The President's address was introduced. Speaking of arming the Negros he says, better detail them for pioneer corps and other menial duty rather than arming them.[48] The papers speak of Forrest making great captures in Tennessee of steamboats, barges, transports, &c.[49] The citizens of Columbia protests again the stockade prison the Authorities are erecting near the city, having petitioned the Gov. Bonham to have it removed.[50] See the account of the trial of a monster gun at Pittsburg being 6 ft. across the breech with 20-inch muzzle throwing a solid shot weighing 1080 lbs., taking 100 to 125 lbs. of powder for a charge.[51] Again this time 'tis pretty certain that Abraham Lincoln is reelected President of the U.S. Oh what destinies hang upon this day's actions. A Lt. came in recaptured bitten in many places by dogs, having them set on him by their Master after he has surrendered. This is the worst specimen of southern chivalry I have heard of yet.

Wednesday, November 9. Very pretty last night and pleasant day. The sun shines warmly again, so the [that] we seek the shade. Exchange remains the same, but still some prefer to escape as six left last night. The authorities say all recaptures will be held to the last for exchange. About twenty recaptures came in today; McKay of our Regt[52] along, having got 50 miles. About seventy-five in all of the last general escapes have been brought back leaving about 130 out yet. The papers still discuss the speech of Hon. Boyce. The Army is beginning to speak, sustaining Boyce and lashing those who stay at home at a fearful rate. Gold at N.Y. was 245. $2,000,000 had gone to Europe. This may have caused the rise.

Thursday, November 10. Have no need of fires at night as the moon serves for light, and the cold is not annoying. 'Tis said that several escaped last night. Some 15 were recaptured and brought to camp making about 90. Papers give exchange news. Col. Hatch (late Capt.) being at Savannah having succeeded in exchanging the 10,000 to be delivered at the rate of 1000 per day. He seems to have succeeded Judge Ould, as a Mr. O'Bryan, is appointed his assistant. Rumor says the sick will leave last of this week. The "Carolinian" came out in double sheet but nothing in it worthy of note. The Arming of the negro is being discussed warmly. Hear nothing from Congress (Reb), not a Telegram today. Lt. Fairfield died in Camp Hospital on last Tuesday.[53] A good many unwell. Weather continues pleasant. Hoping in exchange.

Friday, November 11. Night colder. Day pleasant yet cool. The Exchange lingers as Maj. Mulford[54] has not got to Savannah. Expect him there again Tuesday next. Some are getting discouraged and even doubt the <u>probabilities</u> of any extensive exchange taking place. Election news from North beginning to come in, unanimously for Lincoln. No news from Grant. The Macon papers say that 8 thousand troops have come to Atlanta, and threaten a raid on Macon. Had rations, mostly rice, got cheated out of most of ours, as the Squ[a]d 14 was disbanded and put with the others. A good deal of corn meal has been traded for meat and bread, and the Rebs will doubtless cut our rations down. Had mush & bone for grub, with good health and <u>vigorous</u> appetite.

Saturday, November 12. Cold last night. Heavy frost this morning. Fifteen officers were brought in yesterday of the recaptures. Lt. Wilson who was reported killed trying to escape between Charleston and this place was among the no. having got as far as Wilmington. Twelve more came in this morning, some out for twenty & thirty days. Four large loads of boxes came for the officers from the north. They had been examined, and the Rebs issued them as fast as they could find the owners, but still they are not done (at sunset), and Harry[55] is there waiting for his name to be called, expecting one. Had a little corn meal issued today with sorghum. Wind High & day cold. The papers had but little or no news. The President's Message was printed, a prototype of all his as well as other nbs [numbers of] productions, determined to fight to the bitter end.

Sunday, November 13. Ground white with frost this morning. The day cold. No news of importance, except the affirmation of the capture of the Privateer <u>Florida</u> off in the port of Bahammah.[56] Letters, which <u>had</u> contained money, but now empty were delivered. The money is promised to be delivered in a few day[s] converted to Confederate, at the rate of <u>seven</u> for one greenback. New suits came out this morning all over the camp, and occasionally a white collar, so that some could hardly [be] recognized as old prisoners & acquaintances. Such a change good clothes make compared to rags. Had meat for dinner <u>buying</u> it, as no meat has been issued since we left Charleston. Hard lot for those who have no money. Fortunately Guy B[57] got $70 in hand placed today in letter.

Monday, November 14. Very cold last night and all day. The meteoric shower expected last night or tonight caused some talk, but as yet it has not appeared yet. Expect it tonight. Papers speak of 2000 Rebs being exchanged at Savannah yesterday, 1200 expected today. No officers yet left, but rumors of some going to-morrow. Northern news say Lincoln is elected. Have no official report yet. Have to drag our wood for nearly a mile, and having no axes to cut it we have to gather brush. Oh, what a horrid life and what despicable treatment toward prisoners of war. Had the pleasure of reading northern papers, finding many little scraps of news. We are getting behind sadly in the news of the day. Rumors of Sherman reinforcing Atlanta, Burning it, & moving on Charleston with 4 Corps leaving Thomas to take care of Hood.[58]

Tuesday, November 15. The night passed and the meteoric display failed to make its appearance. Election news is good. Lincoln has got all the states but Ky., New Jersey & Delaware, making only 21 electors. Pa. goes 20 or 30 thousand for Lincoln. In Nashville, Lincoln got 20,000 to 27 for McClellan. Papers say McClellan had resigned his commission in the Army. That Lincoln has called for a draft of 1,000,000 men. Few believe it, altho' many hope it is correct. The Money held by the Rebs is to be sent to Richmond for Conversion. It seems they are trying to keep it from the officers in order to steal it, when they are exchanged. 'Tis shameful to, thus, use starving men living on mush & sorghum. Capt. Zarracher[59] was noti-fied of his being specially exchanged. Does not know how soon he shall start for the north. Made arrangements with him to draft $500 of my pay, send me a box of clothing & one of eatables, sending the remainder to my father.[60]

Exchange is played out again as we have it from good authority that we will soon be moved to the Stockade on the other side of the City. Thus again gloom settles over us. Once more deceived, and duped doubtless by the Rebs to prevent us from escaping. But although the future looks dark yet I shall not dispair. Maj. Griswool is in command.[61] Lt. Col. Means being put in Command of the post Columbia with a radius of six miles. Capt. Holderman, Ill. Regt., who escaped and was recaptured, died in Hosp. of Typhoid Fever contracted while out.[62] 12 came in recaptured, Hayes among the number. Got pair drawers & shirt from Capt. Daily.

Wednesday, November 16.[63] Day splendid and warm, 12 more officers came in with one Col., a Georgian, [John H.] Ashworth of the 1st Ga. Fed. Cavalry. He was stripped of all his clothing and gray Rebel clothing given in its place. Bricker, Hines, Meany, Mundy were among the officers brought back.[64] Exchange is bet-ter today, as letters have been received by some in camp promising exchange. Papers are qui[e]t except stating the weather too rough to land prisoners. The sick are to be exchanged at City Point, our sick at Savannah. Today is devoted by the Rebels to "prayer and supplication," for the good of their cause. "The prayer of the unrighteous is an abomination in the sight of the Lord."[65] Capt. Lodge got $45 making a fine addition to our mess fund. Capt. Zarracher has not gone nor knows when going.

Thursday, November 17. Had no papers today and no news of any importance, so the day passed slowly. Not even a credible rumor broke the monotony of the arduous day. Col. Ashworth, 1st Ga. Cav., was taken out by the rebels, doubtless to be put in solitary confinement. He says they charge him with being a deserter, but that he never belonged to the Army. He also says that eleven of his men were shot when captured. Emprovements are still going on in camp, erecting houses, mud ovens, building chimneys, &c., while a doubt of our moving soon or being exchanged pervades all. The weather is delightful, and warm. Hopes of Exchange inspires us to endure all these privations & sufferings. But how long the time appears. Thankful for good health, and even mush to eat.

Friday, November 18. Still pretty weather, warm & dry. Had a mail, but none for me. Also some money letters, but the gold and greenbacks will go the way of all the rest. I was so disappointed in getting no letter that I wrote one to mother, did not scold. The papers say 1100 Rebs were landed at Savannah; 4 Cols., 2 Lt. Cols., 3 Majors, 13 Captains, 38 Lieutenants. Total 60. Also of 1800 more on the road. The exchange hangs so long that we get out of heart but hope we may soon be among the blessed. Our treatment grows ridiculous to the extreme, leaving only a few out for wood, who have to cut it from the stump and carry it a mile [and] all this with only seven axes to the 1400 men. Thankful for health such as I have. Have soup & mush.

Saturday, November 19. Last night was very pretty and warm, so warm that we kept the door of our tent open all night. A few drops of rain fell, and promised to make a wet night & day. This morning was pleasant, rained a few slight showers today and blew up cold toward evening. Eight recaptures were brought in yesterday, some getting up to North Carolina, among the mountains. But as they say "a mere accident" captured them. But "mere accidents" seem very numerous, so that escape is being played out with some twenty-two recaptures came in this morning, but seventeen escaped last night, leaving the rebs a gain of five. Escaping is a small matter as the guard are easily bribed, some saying they can get out for "two brass buttons." If not for <u>that</u>, it is certain a few Confed. dollars secure the desideratum. But getting <u>out</u> is not all, scarcely a beginning. Were it so I should not be here, but having no hope of success I prefer not to undergo the dangers & privations of such an exception.

No news today of exchange. The papers say Sherman has burned Atlanta, Marriatta & Rome, and is marching by two columns, at the head of five corps upon Augusta & Macon, having got as far as Griffin, 60 miles from the latter.[66] South Carolina has ordered out all the militia comprising all between the ages of 16 & 17 years with farmers &c. They are to furnish four days rations for themselves, and clothing requisite. The <u>Cadetts</u> are to hold themselves in readiness to move in a moment's notice, &c, showing the dreadful scare. This will give an incentive to escape, as the country will be cleared of all likely to recapture the escaping. The following order was sent to Col. Means, and by him sent to us:

> Head Quarters Dept. S.C., Ga. & Florida, Charleston S.C. November 17, 1864. The Lt. Genl. (Hardee)[67] directs that you report to these Hd. Qrs. the names of every officer and man who escapes from your custody. Also that you notify the Federal Officers that they <u>must</u> give a parol not to attempt to escape, or else they will [be] confined in a <u>pen</u> in the same manner that the privates now are. Very Respy, your Ob't Sev't (Sgd) R. G. Gilchrist, A.A.A.G.[68]

This is the most <u>insolent</u> act in the part of the Rebs we have experienced yett. So dictatorial, and after making us drag & carry wood & brush nearly a mile to build huts to keep off the dew. Now compelling us to take a parol not to escape, or go again in a place where we shall have no shelter, nor anything that right demands. Still, the general feeling of the officers is not to except the preferred <u>boon</u> but let them do their worst, and may Heaven repay the indignity. The wind blows cold. Men are discussing the parol warmly and no good feeling pervades the camp. We wait for the result.

Sunday, November 20. Several shots were fired last night, one hitting Lt. Hinckley, 10th Wisconsin, in the elbow, shattering it so that it had to be amputated.[69] A good many escaped. News from Sherman is encouraging, as his [army] is closing on Macon, being within a few miles of Forsythe, 40 miles of Macon. Distance from Atlanta to Augusta 171 miles, to Macon 101; from Atlanta to Savannah 290. Rained a good share of the day and we fear a wet spell will set in to impede Sherman. A good deal of talk about the parol, but nothing new. The most adverse to accepting any parole just now. One thing is certain. Exchange is played [out], since the communications will soon be cut off. Promises to be a good night for escaping and many are getting ready. Was cook today. Had no religious service of any kind. Religion has fallen to a low ebb. Good health.

Monday, November 21. Rained last night and most of the day. Our tent leaked a little, but we put a blanket on the roof, after which it did very well. Several shots were fired last night at the escapers, none hit. A good many escaped. Sherman is still advancing getting near Macon. All are confident of his success but lament the wet weather, fearing it will interrupt his progress. Nothing of news from any other quarter. The Banker, Potter, is about paying out money for "Powers of Attorney," but the Rebs are so afraid of us getting a little something, even Confed. rags, to live upon that he has a hard time to please them. Going to Charleston to see Gen'l Hardee about it now. Nothing more of the Parol. As the evening was wet and cold I went to bed early with the setting of the sun. Glad to be in good health.

Tuesday, November 22. Last night was very cold, the rain ceasing, and the high winds blew fiercely over our Sylvan bowers. Slept tolerably well, and tolerably warm, altho this morning, ice was found on all the puddles to the thickness of a wafer, the first ice I have noticed. The day was very cold, the high winds continuing all day, freezing ice over a pan in front of our tent at midday. This truly is seldom seen in the sunny South at this time of the year. We were disagreeably cold all day. Had a load of boxes issued via Charleston. None for me or any of the mess. Harry [Wilson] got $50 from the Bro. of Maj. Mitchell, who writes that he has also sent a box of provisions. In consequence we had dinner of beefsteaks, sweet potatoes and wheat bread, a meal God sent to Prisoners like us. The sun is going down clear, threatening a cold night, but fortunately dry.

Wednesday, November 23. Capt. Flamsburg died yesterday of [blank in MS].[70] Very cold last night. None even desiring to escape. Some three or four escaped yesterday while after wood. Froze ice to the thickness of an inch last night, the high winds prevailing. Got out by special guard to cut and carry wood to fix our house and build a chimney. Carried all forenoon until my shoulder got very tired and sore. What a way of living. But we even think it a favor to get the chance of toting poles ½ mile. Began propping and covering rest [of] hut. Had a soup off of a $7 piece of mutton. Had a good dinner. Papers are quiet about Sherman, only giving news of last Sabbath. Then our forces held Milledgeville, and had struck the Central R.R. at Griswoldsville, 10 miles east of Macon. So Sherman is not going to stop at that place, probably it is fortified.[71] Two escapers came back.

Thursday, November 24. Nights cold with heavy frosts. Day pretty and sunshiny, just cold when at work. We were busy all day at the house, building the chimney, getting it pretty well done, and covering the house. Had a fire at night burning nicely in our new chimney, making it more pleasant, and comfortable. Could not get the papers as something was in them that we were [not] allowed to hear, but 'tis said that our forces burned the capital of Ga. posting up in various places the word, "Chambersburg."[72] Also Gordon with a large supply of R.R. stock. The bridge over Oconee was destroyed with its large tressel work.[73] All Columbia is excited. 200 pieces of Artillery were taken away; the guard was increased by a company. A good many escaped to the number of 30 or 40.

Friday, November 25. Escape has been the order of the day, bribing, running [the] guard, eluding the guard while after wood, and passing to the hospital on forged passes. The officers think <u>any</u> means of getting away from the horrid place legitimate and honorable. The day was very fine, even warm, altho the ground froze the depth of some inches. Continued at our house completing the chimney but as the frame of the house was to weak to hold the clay we had to shovel it off again. Our fire burns finely and altho failed in the covering of the house, we are happy for the improvement. No news today of any kind, since the papers could not be brought in. But we trust Sherman will travel on to Augusta and send the Cavalry raid to release us. They gave out some of the money, $100 to each of those sending to the north, which has been in the hands of Capt. Martin for a long time. Potter[74] paid some draft giving $50 at a time. Guy got hold of his.[75]

Saturday, November 26. Last night was very cold, the white frost falling in copious showers. In consequence of our failure in building our house, we were idle today not having come to any decission as to how we should next build. When we were let out for wood such abundant chances of escape presented themselves that two hundred or more took their leave. Capt. Lodge & Lt. Wilson of our mess left us. Leslie, Fortescue & Davis of Pennypacker's [mess] making us lonely.[76] Two or three have been brought in already. Strange to say the guard don't seem to care how many escapes, and the fear of punishment is the only thing that deters them of our leaving us all go. No papers alowed, but rumors say Sherman is approaching Augusta. C.C. Cooper has got back and 'twas under his administration so many escaped. Had good dinner, good health. Am getting $180 from Guy for $30.

Sunday, November 27. Lt. Aikins, 3rd N.J. Infantry, was shot dead and Lt. Pierce, Connecticut Vols., was wounded while trying to run the guard and escape.[77] It seems <u>so</u> strange they would run the risk of being shot, when such good chances of escape, as yesterday, are of <u>so</u> frequent occurrence. This make 7 dead since we came here, two killed, two of yellow fever, one Diarrhea, two of typhoid fever. This morning had a strict roll-call in <u>four</u> ranks, having 1189 including those in hospital, some 70 being in the hospital. Had our squad broken up, being put in Sq. 8. Got rations due on 25th. Wrote two letters to mother and Bro. Jno. The day seemed quiet and lonely but being cook it passed of fastly. Had some apples paying $1 for three small ones. No news. No papers. Some few escapes brought in having got into North Carolina.

Monday, November 28. Very warm all last night. A cow got into camp, all tried to catch her, but she broke out. The sentinels shot five or six times, either thinking it some officer running guard, or wanting to kill her for beef. The bullets came nearly hitting some of us so that the fun turned into a more serious matter. Capt. Pennypacker escaped leaving only four of our Regt. in camp. Capts. Davis and McHugh & Lt. Heffner were captured and brought in.[78] Had got 10 miles away to Lexington. Rumor says that Saturday's paper reports Sherman in Augusta. He's right making for Savannah. Wrote a letter to Coz Bell. Had a dinner of steak & wheat bread costing $7 for us two without the extras. The day fine, but my spirits are very low. The time hangs heavily.

Tuesday, November 29. Very warm and pretty day. Was out all day on parol cutting and carrying poles for a hut, wanting to build a stronger [one]. With Guy [Bryan] cut and carried 20 for nearly ½ mile, feeling very tired. The most of them growing in the swamps. What places the S.C. Swamps are. A great many escaped, by pretending to carry away the ploles [poles] as they were brought in, when getting a good chance they would slip the guard. Col. Butler[79] left, and somewhere in the neighborhood of 100. Some few were caught. The Rebs surgeons were examining the halt, sick & diseased, they say preparatory to exchange. Nearly 200 were examined. No news of Sher[man].

Wednesday, November 30. Got up early feeling sore and tired from yesterday's work. Began tearing down the old one and digging out the new. Spent all day and got the timbers up ready to roof (pine Boughs with clay 1 foot thick on top). It was a heavy job. Got a mail, getting four of last July & Aug sent to Macon, Ga. One from mother, from Kitty having her and Mr. Smeltzer's photographs,[80] one from Bro. Jno., and one from J. C. Lightcap. Nothing of note occurred. Very few escapes were brought back and more eager to go. No parolling today nor wood party. Roll call showed only 985 men.

Thursday, December 1. Having no house, slept last night with Herrington & Airey.[81] Fine day, warm and sunshiny, with indications of dry weather. Was busy at the house working hard getting the roof pretty well on. Carried six blanket fulls of pine boughs from the woods. Lt. Torfain 66th N.Y. was shot by a guard having gone near the "dead line" while going for wood.[82] Our party had only passed a few minutes before when he threatened to shoot us. A house stands nearly on the "dead line" and no good road to get around without passing outside. So this cool blooded <u>villain</u> took advantage of the circumstances and murdered an unarmed prisoner not even beyond the "dead line." The authorities came in, but did not seem to care much about it, seeming inclined to take the sentinel's word in preference to Yankey's. The verdict pronounced by all, was to kill the perpetrator should he ever be caught in camp alone. The ball passed through the Lt's. chest, he dying instantly. The Reb was a S.C. militia but lately on duty here. One more murder added to the many that proceeded, which demand vengeance, and duly shall it one day be meted out.

The money question took an advance today as Potter is said to be in the city and has his Agents in camp but no money has come to hand yet. He gives $2 for greenbacks and $6 for gold. I am getting $30 in gold. This is sacrifice since the <u>Rebs</u> give $25 for gold. Felt unwell in the morning, had headache. Have got poisoned on the forehead while out in the woods. Nothing definite from Sherman. Ten escapees came in.

Friday, December 2. What fine weather! Warm and pleasant. The rain delays wonderfully, but it looks like rain in a short time. Continued busy at the house getting the roof on. The Rebs brought a lot of negros to camp to cut our wood, so that we shall not get out of camp, and have no chances of escape. The worst is we can get no wood to finish our house. The guard that murdered Lt. Trofain was on duty today when he came in camp he had a heavy guard around him doubtless afraid of some of the officers killing him. Ten officers came in captured. One "fresh fish" from Sherman. He reports Sherman having 100,000 men and marching directly to Savannah. The Sixth Corps has landed at Pocatalligo and fighting was going on at the Bridge.[83]

Saturday, December 3. No rain today but threatens. Finished the house all except the rear gable and bunk having no timber. One man who had extra timber asked $5 per pole, six inches through and 10 ft. long, but we had not the spare change to buy. Got wood issued, a ration, four ft. long by two inches square, not enough to boil one pot of mush. This state of things cannot last long surely. Twenty-eight men came in recaptured, some having got to Atlanta, but found it occupied by rebels. None of our party came in. The rumor of the Rebels going to parol us to go home and not to enter the field until exchanged, but altho all would willingly take such parol none scarcely hope for such good news. No papers yet & the news is scarce. Weather pretty. Health good. Eating do. [ditto].

Sunday, December 4. Today was delightful. Scarcely a cloud overcast the bright sky and the air was calm and warm enough to make [one] fall in love with the sunny south. But tonight the air grows chill and the breezes grow tempestuous. Nothing but rumors, that our forces had been repulsed between Pocateligo & Savannah. Gen'l Winder visited camp a few days ago. He is in command of all prisoners.[84] 'Tis said he spoke of parolling all to go home and not to go in the field until exchanged. This would doubtless be the best thing the rebels could do with us, as this would set them right before the world in regard to the treatment of prisoners, and our Gov. [Government] would likely send them an equal number in a short time in order to put us in the field by exchange. The report is, "that Reb Congress had decided to arm 50,000 niggers immediately and put them in the field." If this be so, it will relieve our Government of a great embarrassment in regard to the negro, as will as divide their own people since many, if not a large majority, are opposed to arming their negros.

Wrote four letters today, to Mother, sister Kate, Bro. Jno., and J. C. Lightcap, having to put a C.S. [Confederate States] Postage Stamp on each. This is a difficulty to get, as the sutler says they cannot be got in Columbia. But many think they don't want us to write so much, or try to incommode us. It is pretty certain that many of our officers, when recaptured, get handled very roughly, robbed of all blankets and overcoats, especially all passing the officials at Augusta, and it is to be feared many are killed by guerillas in the mountains, which is asserted by negros. Nothing religious passing today and the day seemed long. Feel well. Had good eating today.

Monday, December 5. Heavy frost this morning, Day pretty and warm. Seeing no prospects of getting timber to complete our house, we tore up the bunk and filled the gable. Slept in it at night, having a fire, and although two feet underground we slept warm and dry. Have a good substantial house, and altho the objectional mining, yet under circumstances it is better than cold.

Ten officers came in recaptured. Capt. Eagan, 5th R.I. Art.,[85] tells his experience which shows how demoralized the negros and even white people are getting by having so many escaped officers running among them. He was recaptured the first time by a young man with hounds & gun, who took him to his mother's house. While eating the Capt. engaged the sympathies of the old lady by praising the eatables & telling how long it had been since he had heard from home. She at once grew interested and when the young man was asleep she said she would hold the hounds if they wanted to get away. She did it, and Capt. with his chain was again free, but only for two nights longer. A Dr. told him the Confederacy had better send all prisoners across the lines, than to have them escaping and mixing among the negros and white people, as all the negros talked about now is "freedom" "the war" &c., feeling [and] appreciating the struggle on hand for their Emancipation. They are pronounced by all who have had any conversation with them, fully up to the expectations of the most sanguine, and ahead of the most of the poor whites, in intelligence, shrewdness, and business tact generally. It seems there is an underground R.R. for getting yankees away but the lines are guarded so closely nearly all who went by Augusta is or will be recaptured.

Saw today's "Guardian." It says Sherman is at Millen grinding corn, enrout[e] for Savannah or destruction. But from what they say the former is his evident destination.[86] Hood got a good whipping in Tenn. by Schofield loosing 6000 men killed & wounded, and 1 Brig Gen'l and 1000 men prisoners. Our loss said to be only 500.[87] So this is "the movement that would astonish the world" of Gen'l Hood. Surely he must now feel very small, and out-generaled completely as Sherman is playing in the former's territory. The State Legislature has passed a resolution advising their Senators to vote for the measure of sending our enlisted men home on parol. Gov. Bonhome recommends the Lunatic Asylum to be made into a Military Prison for us officers. Rumors are that we shall be moved down to it shortly, on parrol they say. Health good. Eating mush & sorghum.

Tuesday, December 6. Cold last night, with frost. Pretty sun-shiny day. At roll call noticed the following parody stuck up at the letterbox by anonymous individual. Thinking it good I coppied it.

A Psalm of Prison-Life[88]

What the heart of the "old fish" said to Uncle Sam

Tell me not in empty numbers
Prison life is but a dream;
'Tis but little that one slumbers
Swarms of lice in every seam.

As 'tis real deadly earnest
And Exchange is not its goal
Tho not exchanged & home returned
Scarce is spoken of a soul.

Captured on the field of battle
Robbed of everything but life
We've been treated more like cattle
Than like heros of the strife.

Ah! No longer, time seems fleeting
Patient though our hearts be brave
While Commissioners are treating
We are dropping in the grave.

Inward gripings still remind us
Meal and sorghum ain't sublime
While we're leaving stools behind us
Thinner, broader every time.

Stools that some "Fresh Fish" or other
Hurrying to the sink again
Some poor griped & starving brother
Seeing looses heart again.

Uncle Sam! be up & doing
Free us from the awful fate
Soon good regimen pursuing
We'll regain our fiting weight

Full of wrath or something stronger
Where the vollied thunder tolls
Rebel foes will feel our anger
And will quickly hunt their holes.

Got out for wood again as the niger arrangement played out, having got no wood since Saturday. Had the pleasure of receiving $300 on an order to pay $50 in gold on [blank in MS], Capt. Zarracher's friend. They [The] money came in good time being out. Gen'l Winder has stopped the buying of drafts, &c, but it is got in by underground Rail Road. The Rebel guard came nearly mutinying, as Capt. Martin had a stock built and put three Rebs in it. A Company started armed to release them, but their hearts failed, when another went up and after a slight talk they went to their quarters, and the men were released. Ten recaptured came in this morning. Still none of our party in yet. So many officers have escaped, and been recaptured & robbed of clothing that the camp presents a mixture of Rebs and Yankees. Got rations today but instead of the usual pint of flour we got a pint of "shorts."[89] Some say the next will bee "oat straw and bran." Are getting a new Sutler in place of big-bellied Staunton. Living on mush and slapjacks but shall have a change tomorrow.

Wednesday, December 7. Rained this morning but not much. Our house did not leak. Had breakfast of mush. Dinner of steak $5 worth and Slap Jacks made of cold mush and "bran." Had good meal. It was a difficulty getting meat of the sutler, as all were eager to buy. Over a thousand pounds must have been sold today. Apples at 3 for a dollar, 2 turnips for two dollars, Ten, "nine penny" nails for [a] dollar, a handful of sweet potatoes for [a] dollar. Nothing except Peanuts sold for less than one dollar. They are 50 cts. per pt. Plenty of money current now and prices going up. The sutler Bowen is a Baltimorean (one of the party who fired on the Union troops in Baltimore in beginning of the war).[90] The exchange to continue at Charleston Harbor, but no indications of any officers going. Good health.

Thursday, December 8. Four guards deserted their posts last night, taking along their guns. This morning an old Planter brought his dogs to hunt them. Two hounds got into camp and in a trice they were killed and buried. The guard came in and found them. The Planter was very angry and says he shall kill 4 Yankeys in retalliation. The mutiny yesterday resulted in the marching of 25 or 30 men to the Columbia Jail. $50,000 were distributed by Col. Huey on the Drafts given some time ago. This gives the sutlering an increased patronage.

Exchange is again on the topics. Names were called and paroled. Two Colonels, Frazier and Miller, One Lt. Col. Cunningham, Three Majors, English, & Marshal both absent, & Major [blank in MS], 25 Captains, and 44 Lieutenants.[91] H. C. Potter's name was called and he being among the escapers, I went out & answered to his name. Others did the same. One hundred sick are to go also, sometime tomorrow and all the camp is in an excitement. The most seem to be specials sent for by one government and taking a good many "fresh fish." A good deal of complaining was heard among the "old fish."[92] But, as I have a fine thing of it, I shall not complain. Still although I have many arrangements for going home, and accepted messages to convey north, still I am not over elated at the prospects, since "many a slip there is, between the cup and the lip." Rumors of the exchange going to be general, but hoot at the idea, since they have been disappointed so often. Happy am I tonight and the sky looks more beautiful. Oh! Shall this be the auspicious time!

Friday, December 9. Sat up late last evening preparing for tomorrow &c. Slept rather poorly. Woke this morning and in a few moments who should come into Camp but Lt. Potter, who we thought had got into our lines. This put the veto to my going home as he took his own place. I felt badly, but not having built up very buoyantly on the matter I did not take it to heart. Wrote a letter to my mother sending it by the hand of Lt. Potter. Had to have someone to represent us at any rate. The Paroling of sick officers continued today with a good many not sick, as Col. Huey was added to the number. Capts. Daily & Ricket, Rollins, Baldwin, Christopher, Lts. Bricker, and many others was among the number exchanged.[93] About 200 in all left at 3 P.M. and rumors of 300 men going tomorrow. Oh how elated we grew, seeing so many leaving for <u>God's</u> country! Twelve recaptures came in at noon. Capt. Lodge, Lts. Wilson, Leslie and Fortescue came with the number, having been captured nearly a week. They were at Florence. Saw our Enlisted men. They are being exchanged 1000 per day. Say they look better than at Charleston. They were captured near Augusta and fell in with a fine old gentleman Gregg, owner of a large factory, who treated them well, and when they left gave them $100 a piece.[94] They represent it almost impossible to get to Sherman.

Had a large mail; got letters from Mother, Kitty, Jenny, Bro. Jno. & Ed McChesney. They tell me of Eph. Brunner's capture by Moseby's guerrillas, [an] inglorious fate.[95] The last tell me of Lizzie of L. [Latrobe] going to be married to Mr. Bowen. Doubtless is now <u>Mrs.</u> <u>Bowen</u>. Better likely altho once such news would have shocked me. The day was very cold, and blew hard with a little rain. Have good steak for dinner.

Saturday, December 10. Rained last night. Was cold and disagreeable. Cold & wet all day. Got out for wood carrying or dragging 3 loads ½ mile. Having no ax, had to gather limbs and brush. What a picture this would present north. A thousand officers hauling on their back enough wood to keep them from suffering for fully ½ mile. Felt badly all day, thinking so often how happy I would be had I got away! But another's luck was my misfortune. Major [Elias] Griswold says we will have a mail tomorrow. $30,000 came for the officers. He thinks we shall all be exchange[d] before this shall stop. Nothing new; no papers. Sutlering advancing in prices. Butter $14 per lb., shoes $100, nails 10 for dollar, steak from $3 to $4 per lb., apples 2 for dollar, &c., &c. Living pretty well but costs a great deal. Good health, and hope for exchange.

Sunday, December 11. Cold last night. Today the same the winds blowing fiercely. The day passed quietly, mostly being buried in our hut, which was warm. Capt. Martin says we move tomorrow to the city in Barracks in the Insane Asylum yard. This shall be worse than here, as we shall likely have no fires. Capt. Z.[96] things [thinks] he has made a good thing for us for exchange if any more go soon. Hope he may succeed. Only our Col. Shedd left in camp.[97] The field officers will soon be all gone again for the third time since I was captured. The day passed without any marks of a "day of rest." Nothing is observed by soldiers it seems.

Eight

"Sitting Outside My Tent Penning
These Lines"

Camp Asylum, Columbia, South Carolina,
December 12, 1864–February 13, 1865

Aware of Camp Sorghum's poor security and local government officials' opposition to housing hundreds of inmates in Columbia, Gen. John H. Winder, who had been recently appointed general superintendent of all Confederate prisons east of the Mississippi River, decided to relocate the prison away from the city. Until a new facility was ready, he secured permission in early December to use the grounds of the South Carolina State Hospital, then known as the South Carolina Lunatic Asylum, designed by noted architect Robert Mills in the 1820s. After burning Camp Sorghum on the morning of December 12, 1864, the authorities marched about a thousand officers, under heavy guard, three miles to their new quarters, a three-and-a-half-acre compound surrounded by the asylum's brick walls and topped with sentry boxes and a deadline marked five feet inside the enclosure. The site had city water but unfinished wood-framed shelters. Soon "the hammer & saw were heard through the camp and shelters are going up as if by magic," Weaver recorded, "so that the Rebs are surprised at the tact of the Yankees." Each timber-planked building was to be twenty-four feet square with two fireplaces to house thirty-six men each, which constituted a mess. The prisoners suffered from an unusually cold, rainy winter that delayed finishing the thirty-two buildings all arrayed in rows. Camp Asylum—so named by the prisoners from the "frequent shouts" of the hospital inmates—appeared like a winter military encampment.[1]

As Weaver settled into his sixth prison, he devoted more time to his diary as he sat outside his shelter on a homemade, three-legged table. He also read sentimental fiction; poetry; religious pamphlets from the American Tract Society, a publisher of Christian literature founded in 1821; William Shakespeare's plays; and the Bible. A string band gave concerts and provided music for dances held at a show tent. "Sherman's March to the Sea," a song written and composed in Camp Asylum, was a particular favorite. Not surprisingly, however, the inmates' physical exposure, interminable idleness, and limited mail lowered their morale. Weaver recorded several satirical verses—one excoriated "hospital bummers" who pretended to be sick—and increasingly vented his anger at the Union government's "no exchange" policy. "Why should we remain idle here dying and dropping in the grave for the sake of policy?" he lamented in December, "I cannot contemplate the subject in good humor." But Weaver's sharpest critiques were against his fellow messmates whose pranks threatened retaliation by the authorities and whose morals "have become degraded in virtue, religion and even decency" with frequent drunkenness, profanity, obscene stories, blasphemy, card playing, and gambling.[2]

By February, his mood brightened as he joined like-minded men in daily Bible classes, twice-weekly prayer meetings, and a newly formed patriotic organization. Continued reports of Sherman's advance from Savannah toward Columbia, the capture of Wilmington, North Carolina, and the Confederacy's dwindling fortunes raised morale even more. "From all accounts the Rebels are playing out faster than for a long time," Weaver recorded on January 21, "and we now begin to look to the end of the war as the day of our release." The waiting game played out soon: on February 14 the prisoners were hastily taken from Camp Asylum for "parts unknown" just three days before Columbia surrendered to Union forces.[3]

Monday, December 12, 1864. Last night was a stinger, freezing a tin full of water to the bottom, bursting the bottom of the tin. The day fine and sun shining, but still cool. Prepared to move. The most of the camp was burned, some of the brush houses making lofty fires, and smoke in abundance. Got in line about noon having a piece of Artillery in front and six or eight hundred guards. We numbered 950 so that nearly as many guards as Yankeys. Passed through the central Portion of Columbia passing State House, Town Clock, Jail, getting to Insane Asylum in the northeastern part of the city. We found a stockade, the brick wall that surrounds part of the Insane Asylum yard, being about 140 yds. by 120 yds. inside of "deadline," the latter 5 yds. from the wall. About 30 guards surmount the walls in sentry boxes. Have no shelter, but they have begun sheds wanting us to finish them. 36 to be in each shed, having two fireplaces. If builded properly they will be warm. Good water trough, having a spigit attached from the water works of town. The sink arrangements are the most modest and accommodating of any we have had yet. The asylum is not far away and frequent shouts proclaim that it is not wanting of inmates. The Rebs seem accommodating today, telling us they shall give us all the wood and timber that we want. Say we shall have all our money and letters. The citizens seemed very quiet and one lady shook her kerchief to <u>us</u>. 120 officers came from the Jail yard. Didn't know any of them. Some

Fig. 19. Camp Asylum, South Carolina Lunatic Asylum, Columbia. Prisoners lived in huts they constructed inside the walled asylum yard. Weaver was here from December 1864 to February 1865. (MOLLUS-Mass Civil War Photograph Collection, United States Army Heritage and Education Center, Carlisle, PA)

were captured as long as 18 months ago. Col. Crook[4] & 3 others were exchanged in the last party. Have a tent to sleep in tonight but many will have to sleep out.

Tuesday, December 13. Last night was bitter cold, many sleeping out in the open air. Water freezing in the tent. Nine of us slept in a wall tent, but I still slept cold. The night was clear and bright the moon shining brightly. Morning came, the Confederacy having been cursed repeatedly, and justly too, for turning us out in the open field, during this inclement air. Especially did they meanly trap the officers in the Jail as they brought them out just at dark, turning them loose without any shelter. Scumy trick was that.

All day the hammer & saw were heard through the camp and shelters are going up as if by magic, so that the Rebs are surprised at the tact of the Yankees. Our party are in Shed 11th. Worked some getting up the lower part of the frame. Could not get tools nor timber, but the citizens, 'tis said, turned out in the afternoon, volunteering to haul our lumber, and the rattling of waggons and cracking of [whips] goes on outside, so that we expect to have more tomorrow. 30 sheds are going to be built now. The draft of camp comprise 90, making quarters for 3240 men. Pretty thick for 3½ acres. The day was dry, and warmer than yesterday. Drew rations but no sorghum. The sutlers are doing heavy business. A list of money in hands of Quarter Master was posted & the Rebs give evidence of going to act decently, but it may be show. Rumor of Sherman fighting at Savannah, and capturing the place.[5] It is likely premature. Rumors of exchange but nothing definite. Good health. Good grub (by paying for it) & we will soon have good quarters.

Wednesday, December 14. Threatened rain, but cleared away. Was working on the huts. Nearly all the frames were got up, but the boards do not come in as fast as we would desire. The Rebs are very particular how the buildings are put up as No. 10 & 21 have to pull down their frames and put them up in line. Ten or twelve recaptures came in at night, some getting as far as Greenville,[6] caught in a snowstorm discovering their tracks. The[y] still speak of the negros feeding them well and some wanted to and did kiss the officers for joy. Selling chestnuts at $4 per qt., vinegar $4 per pt., coffee $8 per ½ lb. The day was warm but hope the weather may continue dry until we get in huts. Have good health.

Thursday, December 15. Day pleasant, slightly cold but not severe. Some recaptures came in this morning, Adams & Osbourn among the number.[7] Some had been out for 4 or 5 weeks. Cooper got back from Charleston.[8] He says the officers got off on last Saturday. That the exchange continues. Papers say the Pulaski Officers[9] are to be exchanged soon, so there may be a chance for some of us yet. The buildings are at a stand still for want of lumber. Nothing new from Sherman, but the rumor prevails that he has made a junction with Foster and is surrounding Savannah [and] that the Rebs are throwing open the storehouses to the citizens.[10] This looks like surrender. The day passed lazily, having nothing to do or read. Wrote a letter to mother. Hope soon to be free, but how little I know of the future.

Friday, December 16. Pretty day. Sun even warm, continues dry. A few boards came in. A few sheds going up slowly. Wrote letter to my mother, Bro. Jno., Sister Jennie and Edward McChesney. Rumors of Savannah being captured again, but having no papers we are left the dupes of any who may feel disposed to make a rumor to deceive. From all the information we can get it seems the Exchange at Charleston has been closed, and nothing more will be done until after holidays. The spirits of the officers suffered a fall in proportion to their elevated state caused by recent hopes of Exchange. Why cannot we be set free? Why not exchange us since the Rebels are willing. I cannot contemplate the subject in good humor.

Saturday, December 17. The weather continues warmer. A mail was delivered but none for me. Several circulars came from Lt. Col. Bennet[11] commanding Flag of Truce at Hilton Head stating that the order had been revoked allowing boxes & moneys to be sent to prisoners. Bitter words were breathed against the authorities on both sides, especially when we heard of the Commissioners having adjourned till after Holidays. 'Tis as the poetry goes, "While commissioners are 'busting' we are dropping in the grave."[12] Wrote three letters to Senator Cowan, Hon. Jno. Covode & Mr. Lightcap on the subject of special exchange since Mulford has said nothing but specials will take place this winter.[13] Got postage stamps being a matter of difficulty. Felt badly on the subject of exchange but hope the state of affairs is not as bad as represented. Good health. Plenty to eat. Rebs only giving 3½ for greenbacks.

Sunday, December 18. How very fine the weather continues! Warm and pleasant. The alloy to our happiness is the hopelessness of exchange, while the most ridiculousness is the fact of the commissioners going home to spend Christmas. Wrote letters to G. W. Shryock, Major Phillips, Sergt. White, Miss Mollie of M[eadeville] and Sister Mattie. Capt. Hatch was in Camp.[14] Took some names for special exchanges. This seems to be the style; consequently, I am beginning to pull wins for the same object. Feel lonely and desolate, and the time passes slowly. How shall we spend the coming winter. Sabbath was observed very well today by the building parties. Still many spend the day in playing cards, even for gain, profaning God's name, and in obscene conversation. Capt. Whitesides preached at night.[15] How glad I am that the influence of pious instructions keeps me from such out breaking sins. Good health with good diet &c.

Monday, December 19. Nothing of interest passing and nothing definite as all is rumor. Wrote two letters to Prex Loomis and Aggie of S. The houses are going up slowly getting only a few boards at a time. The Gettysburg Prisoners had a meeting, at which the [they] determined to notify our Gov., that they are hear yet. A project is on hand for one senior officer to request the Rebs to Parol us to go home, as 'tis said, that Gen'l Winder thinks it would then be done. Lodge still in hospital.[16] Today [is] my cook day. Gave them a soup. Day warm and pleasant but threatens rain. Rumors of Hood and Thomas having some fighting in Tennessee. Sherman is besieging Savannah. Also a force making for Mobile.[17] Good health, good spirits.

Tuesday, December 20. Colder today, even uncomfortable. 'Tis said Hood got gloriously whipped by Thomas, loosing 19 pieces of artillery. And had to retreat 5 miles through the snow.[18] Spent most of the day reading "Victoria," in "The Heiress of Castle Cliffs" By May Carleton.[19] A good love affair, getting me deeply interested. Rations were issued by new messes, each building of 36 constituting a mess, 3 messes a squad. 32 building in camp. Get better issues of wood than at first, but small enough yet. Am not [now] sitting outside my tent penning these lines on a three legged table, put up by having 3 pins drove in the ground. Very cold, my hand refuses to act and my bones shake reminding me of cold winter months. None are escaping but there are indications of tunnels being dug. Small piles of fresh sand on the ground.

Wednesday, December 21. Rained a good share of last night, and today blew up cold, the winds growing fierce so that all go shivering around. Some hunting shelter from the storms and cold of tonight. The Bankers are now giving $33 for one in gold, $28 for one in silver & we are to ge[t] the same rates. Officers coming from Charleston say gold is $60, greenbacks 30, but we only get 3½. The sutler says they are going to give more. Several recaptured officers came in from the North Car. rout[e] saying it is impossible to get through that way, as the mountains are full of guerrillas, and a band of Cherokee Indians who pick up all.[20] Major Griswold[21] gave Col. Shedd to understand it was useless to petition authorities concerning our parol, so the matter drops. Very cold this evening, many having no shelter from the stormy blasts. Glad to have shelter, good health.

Thursday, December 22. Heard many officers last night out through the camp <u>double quicking</u> to keep themselves warm. What a situation! Having to spend the dull bitter cold hours of night in running with break neck speed to keep himself from freezing? A slight ice was formed, but high winds were bitter cold. Today continued the same the most of the day. At eve the wind lulled, and we shall likely have pretty weather again. Was cook having a cold job. Only four sheds are yet completed as but a few boards come in daily. Turning out as we feared. The Rebels don't seem to understand dispatch. Gen'l Winder was here inspecting Hospitals. These are in good condition, bunk with straw tick and one quilt. Read Bulwer's "Godolphin."[22] Find in it his same philosophising stile. Got many good ideas from him. The times creeps slowly on, but soon Christmas will be upon us again.

Friday, December 23. Last night was bitter cold, freezing ice to the thickness of several inches. Many slept, or rather passed the night uncomfortable. Bitter curses were pound out against the Rebels for thus throwing us into this open yard without protection from the storm. Good news today. Gen. Johnson has lost another Division as our forces captured him with his entire Division. 'Tis said that Gen'l Forest is killed, 1800 of his men captured.[23] A raid is being made against Mobile, &c. Hardee & Staff has got out of Savannah, arriving at Hardeeville.[24] Have no particulars about the fall of Savannah. The Rebs say it was evacuated last Tuesday. Lincoln has another call for 300,000 men, which shall doubtless end this Rebellion. Their prospects look dark. They [The] day continues cold, having to go to bed at dark to keep warm. Good health but sick of this treatment.

Saturday, December 24. Last night very cold, freezing hard. Today prettier than yesterday. Sun shone brilliantly. No news of any importance. Most preparing for Christmas; buy chickens & Turkeys at $30 a piece. Business took an advance and the sutler shop was thronged, buy steak or something for tomorrow's dinner. While all this is going on many, among whom is myself, feel badly reflecting the days and years go by without freeing us from this hell on earth. Oh why does not the Gov. relieve us. Why should we remain idle here dying and dropping in the grave for the sake of policy? Read Mrs. Grays "Old Dower House."[25] Not so good as Bulwer or Dickens. Good health, evening cold expecting to have a cold night.

Christmas Day 1864. Last evening Lt. Chandler with his band discoursed "dulcet strains" to the enraptured auditors.[26] But our ecstasies were short lived as the violin string snapped, the bridge broke and the party dispersed, a simile to the most of our late expectations. The day passed tardily having tried to satisfy our appetites by dining on a steak costing $12.50 beside lard enough to fry it. So the second Christmas is almost past, and having written 3 letters to Mother, Jennie and Bro. Jno., I spent the most of the day in somber reflections. Rained some in the evening, and we were confined to our tent.

A few strangers came in and the usual scene began. Although sabbath evening and Christmas, they spent all evening in telling obscene stories, blaspheming God's holy name, at each sentence, and seeming to delight in defying God & man, Virtue & religion. With feeling of deepest disgust I loathed their society, and had no[t] the pelting rain prevented, I should have gone forth from such vile mouthed society for relief. Nor did I lift my voice in reproof knowing it would be "casting perls before swine."[27] How strange that men who, at home, try to pass for gentlemen, when they get in the Army, seem to forget every tender sentiment and become the degraded sensualist and besotted blasphemers. The most of the officers have become degraded in virtue, religion and even decency, so that not a dozen officers can associate together without spending the time in degrading language and libellous sentences. May a kind Providence guide me, and protect me from taking a part in such debauchery of mind & soul. Felt lonely and tired, and without a hope of this imprisonment sooning [soon] ending, I would feel as guilty Cain's "Thy load is greater than I can bear."[28] But hope is the teacher of the soul.

Monday, December 26. Today was gloomy, but not cold. Six recaptures came in being nearly within our lines. Major Vickers came in; Major Wauser some few days ago.[29] They tell us that the Rebels are very disconsolate at the success of Sherman, while the Augusta Paper thinks now is the time for the people to sue for peace. Strange infatuation. Jeff Davis has bound them hand & foot and when he chooses, they will <u>sue</u>. Rumors of Kilpatrick[30] on a raid, and that we will be moved somewhere, but even fancy cannot picture a place less likely to raid than here. The building of the huts has been discontinued from reasons construed into removal.

The money crisis is upon the Rebels, their money is going down to nothing. Already they give us $33 for one in Gold while on the street, 'tis said, to be almost worthless. Still, through the chicanery of Gen'l Winder, who has got his agent, Mr. Brown, acting sutler, green backs are only bringing us $3½ and that only in orders to the sutler, we not being allowed to finger a dollar. In camp, greenbacks are selling for $10 while on the street they are nearly double. This is the way the <u>old hory</u> headed sinner is cheating us while he sells everything at fabulous prices. Bought a small piece of pork for $9, which I could have eated at one meal myself. Day after day money arrives here from the north for prisoners, but how we are fleeced! Aigan, Gamble, Durfee and Hinds left the tent for building No. 5 leaving Bryan, Wilson, Adams, Osborne (Lodge, in Hospital) and myself.[31] Had rations issued. Have roll call at 9 A.M. & 4 P.M. superintended by a sergeant for each square (3 buildings), 108 men. Good health, and hopeful against hope.

Tuesday, December 27. A pretty day, clear and pleasant. Warm enough to be comfortable. The news of removal has died away, and a few more boards for Building 7 came in. The rumor is that Wilmington is in our possession. Burnsides with his negros having captured it.[32] This is good news and many are inclined to believe it. All appeared on the "qui vive"?[33] in the evening, and the band was called out but the strings again broke and we dispersed. A dark cloud is rising in the west, and occasionally a flash of lightning lights up the western horizon, threatening a storm. Lt. Fortescue came into our tent making six of us.[34] Two more are coming in tomorrow. The time seems passing by swiftly and we long to see the moments accelerated. Good health and tolerably good spirits.

Wednesday, December 28. Day wet and disagreeable. Washed my clothing still, but could not dry them. Wrote three letters to McAfee, Cunningham & sister Amanda.[35] There was a proposition made for having a general dinner on New Year as many have no money. It will likely be entered into. The papers were slipped in telling of Hood['s] utter rout loosing 9000 prisoners & 64 pieces of artillery. Was on the retreat still. Stoneman had whipped Breckinridge at Saltville, Va., taking good deal of Artillery.[36] An attack had been made on Wilmington but it was abandoned. Sherman had sent a coppy of Hood's order to our forces, when he demanded the surrender of Dalton, to the Rebs at Savannah say[ing] that if he had to reduce the fort, he would show no quarter to the Rebs nor would be accountable for the acts of his men.[37] The Rebs are dying out fastly.

Thursday, December 29. Last night was very cold, as the winds blew hard and cold. The day was very disagreeable and we could not keep warm by any means. Read part of Shakespeare Vol. 7th but had to quit, too cold. Made me a pair of suspenders out of an old pair of connection cables. Had mush for breakfast and slap jacks for dinner. Money played out, and can have no meat. Wind continued high all day and expect night to be cold. From good authority it seems a note was thrown over the stockade last night with "Be of good heart in a few [days] all will be well." If true none can imagine what it means. The Hospitals are growing full, but most are playing. Both buildings are now full. A few boards for huts came in, but slowly they come.

Friday, December 30. The day was cold and disagreeable. Passing by slowly, spending from dark to eight in the evening in our blankets to try to keep warm. Oh what a life to live the main object being to try to pass the tardy hours! Read "Romeo & Juliet" spending the rest of the day in cooking and roaming about. News of Senator Foot bidding the Rebs "good by" in Congress telling them he had make his last speech, and was now going to the land where he would be regarded as a fugitive to Yankeedom.[38] The Rebels acknowledged the fall of Fort

Jackson at Wilmington & say that the people must not expect so large a fleet to retire until the place is captured, preparing their people for its fall.[39] Have good health, and try to be happy.

Saturday, December 31. Last night was comfortable. Today wet & cold. Felt unwell most of the day, having sick headache. Busy all through camp preparing for tomorrow. Sutler busy selling beef turkeys, chickens, geese, and many other edibles, his tent besieged all day. 'Tis said the Commissary has bartered extra Sorghum to am't of $5000 for beef & potatoes, to serve as a feast tomorrow. News outside of little interest. Sherman's official report says he captured at Savannah 33,000 bales cotton, over 150 cannon, 16 Locomotives, 7 steamboats, 800 prisoners. Guy [Bryan] got $10 greenback exchanged or converted into 70 Confed., but now they only allow $5 for one. His had been converted some time ago, before the price fell. Boards come in slowly, work at squad 9.

The old year wanes fastly, and looking back one year how many changes have taken place, and altho I am not where I expected to be, still I am thankful for as favorable position in the world as I am. But for the future I have my fears. I cannot but desire to penetrate the future to see what fate may be 12 months hence, but this is all in vain. Many promises are being made by my mess mates to quit chewing tobacco, to stop swearing & "turning over a new leaf" as they commonly say. All acknowledge the folly of profanity, but how many indulge in the sinful habit, bringing good to none but hurt to their own souls. Last year the papers saw fit to call the year "Armies miserabilis" but surely this New Year they may term it a more disastrous one than the last. They have lost territory on all hands. Sherman has gone where he saw fit, and now threatens to go north through South & North Carolinas. Officers are again growing hopeful that another 12 months will see the Confederacy a thing that was, which shall proclaim us once more free. Oh what a happy day. Hasten on old time and bring us this looked for relief. As I write these lines the old year is almost out. Silently it is passing by so silently as to make its cadences unperceivable. This seems to admonish me to be preparing for the future while I reach for the future to tread a better path. I thank my kind Preserver that he has protected me so sedulously in the past. Health good.

Sunday, January 1, 1865. Last night was very cold. The wind blew bitterly, freezing hard ice. Many thought it the coldest night this winter. Being damp doubtless made the weather colder. New Year was spent as all other days. Had steak & wheat bread for our holiday dinner. Cold all day, so that all were kept either in bead [bed] or running around camp double quick to keep warm. News or rumors of the most fabulous run through camp. 1st, Jeff Davis poisoned himself on hearing of Hood's defeat. 2nd, that we would be removed to Texas in a few days, &c &c. Read Hamlet having many items to ponder in that deep philosophic Tragedy. The "mortal coil." The "distant bourn," &c., brings to the mind subjects worthy of reflection.[40] Boards brought in, working all day in huts. Will get some but I did not work. Good health.

Monday, January 2. Cold moderated, having a good sleep last night. Today was pretty. The sun shone out gaily, making us feel happy. Worked some on house, got the weather boarding on, and bunks up. No timber for roof. The contemplated feast of meat and potatoes did not come to time, and have an idea the entire thing was a farce. No news of any importance, except the rumor of Lee being put in command of the entire Reb. Army, sending Hill's Corps from Va. to confront Sherman in his victorious march. Head Quarters (Col. Shedd's)[41] were removed from the building to give room for hospital. Making room for about 150 persons. Very few sick, but have plenty of surgeons who want to fill up the Hospitals to give them position. The band had a drunken revel last night. Playing and dancing in Surgeons qrs. [quarters] until midnight. Little they respect Sabbath.

Tuesday, January 3. Warm nights, and pretty days. Rained some today after noon, but was warmer than usually when wet. Got no more boards as they were all given to headquarter tent which is now building. Rumors of little import. 'Tis said that Major Mulford has arrived at City Point to argue upon a new Cartel, seeming to indicate exchange. Major Griswold was telegraphed for a few days ago, to go to Richmond with Rolls, &c., [and] has gone. These rumors are verified by the Reb. Surgeons so that they seem to give us a slight hope again. Was cook, having a hard time to get meat for dinner, as the crowd at the Sutler tent seemed more like a mob than a party of U.S. Officers. More than 1000 lbs. must have been sold. Read "Part Third of King Henry VI." Terrible characters that Queen Margaret & "Hunchback Dick," Duke of Gloster.[42] Good health. Hope Abiding.

Wednesday, January 4. Today was magnificent. The sun shone brightly and air feels warm. Feel rather happy in hope of exchange, as the papers say Major Mulford is to be at Richmond this week to form a new Cartel. All things conspire to make us hope against hope, altho. having been disappointed so often. Had our Christmas dinner issued, about 50 bushels sweet potatoes, 900 lbs. beef & some little pork in lieu of the extra sorghum, amounting to $4800. But what does all this money am't to at buying beef at $3 or $4 per lb., pork $5 or $6, potatoes $20 or $25. Read "King Richard Third." Admiring many of the characters but disgusted at the wickedness of the principle ones. The day passed pleasantly and should hope of exchange grow brighter we should be happy. Wrote a letter to S. S. Jack[43] for aid in procuring special exchange. Health good. [Hopes?] ditto.

Thursday, January 5. Last night was very cold & frosty having the ground covered with a white coat this morning. Some officers having plenty of money got whisky smuggled into camp and they were disregardful enough of themselves to get drunk. Ended in getting a pounding from someone whose tent they threw down. Plenty of money coming into camp by underground, getting 6 for one. This make some have a desire to dissipate. The day passed a[s] usual. Nothing in shape of news. Got rations, eight bowls sorghum. Had taffy made in the evening. Read "King Henry VIII" admired the characters of Wolsey and Queen Katharine. Altho Wolsey was an ambitious man, still when he says "Had I serve my God half so faithfully as my king, he would not now forsake me." I pity him.[44] Good heath &c.

Friday, January 6. Last night was very wet, the rain fell fast and the winds blew hard. Wet all day. Very disagreeable. Read "Troilus and Cressida," a pretty good thing but none of the best.[45] News from Savannah in papers say the soldiers a kept in strict subjection, not allowed to abuse citizens. A yankey store is opened, a paper edited. "The Daily Loyal Georgian."[46] From the papers we gather many items of interest. That the Rebs fear that <u>all</u> of Hood's army is lost. That Hood & Forrest were killed but not confirmed. A train of soldiers came to city this evening from direction of Charlotte. Some say a Brig [Brigade] (Shaw's) from Wilmington; others say Kershaw's from Longstreet's.[47] Had music by the band for the accommodation and amusement of the Reb surgeons. Rained in the evening. Day passes fastly. Health good. Soup of beef and collard (cabbage).

Saturday, January 7. Cold disagreeable day, passing with little of any interest. Papers speak of Mayor of Savannah, calling a meeting of its citizens, resolving themselves back into the union,[48] wishing the Gov. to devise some method to take the sense of the State in regard to returning to the Union, sending coppies of Resolutions to Mayors of Augusta, Columbus, Macon, & Atlanta. All this looks well. Sherman is advancing on Grahamville.[49] Troops passed through the city in the evening. Many think they are from Richmond. Wrote letter to Bro. Jno. Read Wilkie Collins "Stolen Mask, or the Mysterious Cashbox."[50] Also "Timon of Athens," being a good take off on the fickleness of friends, &c.[51] Cotton is now King, as it is running a rage, being bought (raw) for matresses at $1.60 per lb. Everything is getting dearer; a candle now $2.50, a few leaves of Collard $2.00, a turnip $1.00. Gave a draft for $100 in gold, expecting the money or rags in a few days.

Sunday, January 8. Last night was very cold forming ice. Day pleasant tolerably cold. Papers in camp, not of any importance. Still gassing about Hood, think he's not so badly off after all. The New York papers mostly blame Butler for the Wilmington failure. The Tribune throws it upon Porter having charge of the Navy. It is too bad such a large fleet, 59 gunboats & Ironsides, nearly 200 vessels in all, should thus be a failure.[52] Felt unwell all day, not physically but spiritually having the horrors.[53] Nothing in camp to wake the senses or give us heart for the future. The Reb Surgeons got very drunk one getting outside the Guard Line or dead line and came near being shot. Troops passing by, and it is pretty certain, Longstreet is reinforcing Hardee.[54] Health good.

Monday, January 9. Rained a little last night. Was not very cold. Day warm and pleasant. Nothing in the way of news. Troops still moving on the Rail Road. Spent the day gadding around, reading a little in "Arabian Knights," not caring much for Mr. La Sagis fun, and some of Bascuris Lectures.[55] The latter is worthy of attentive perusal. Autographs now rampant again. Album's being bought outside for $25 and $50. A few (5) fresh fish, recaptures came in today. Some have got a good distance, others only a few miles. It seems but few are getting thru. No chances of escape here. Again dependent on Confed. rations having got out of money, and 'tis difficult to get money in camp from outside. Have breakfast on "mush and sorghum" and supper & dinner on "pone & sorghum." Exchange grows dull. Nothing in the shape of rumor. Good health, and good appetites.

Tuesday, January 10. Rained hard nearly all last night and very warm, even to unpleasantness. Thundered & Lightinged. Some tents (pieces) were issued yesterday, said to be fifty in number. Fighting the Tiger[56] is the rage. Men spending and making money of games of <u>Faro</u> and <u>Sweat</u>.[57] <u>Some</u> loose money. <u>All</u> loose honor and characters as gentlemen in my opinion. This is a <u>hard</u> place. Scarcely a man to stand up in defense of religion, temperance or virtue, hooting at the first and boasting of repeated violation of the two latter. How sadly has my opinion of human beings fallen!

Five more recaptures came in. Major Griswold came back from Richmond. Don't know much of exchange. Lt. Sigmond, Count Brady of Austria is to be exchanged.[58] Brother died. He goes home, having resigned. Intends to marry a Yankee lady and take her home with him. Some few others expect to be specially exchanged. A list of $17,000 was put up from Quarter Master Richardson. He give $40 for $1 in Gold being about half what it is bringing outside. Rebel currency is at a very low ebb and the prices are rising proportionately. It makes large prices for us who have to give Drafts for gold getting $6 for $1. Read part of "Beulah" by Augusta J. Evans, who lives near Macon Ga., 'tis said.[59] It is a delightful work so far, and is a decided success for a <u>Lady</u> Novelist. Expect to have a mail in a few days, as one is outside. The day was rather wet, raining terribly in the forenoon, but was not very cold. Rations, corn meal and sorghum. No meat rations since we left Charleston (Oct 6th), and don't expect to get any more. Had musick by the Band after dark. Health good. Eating slim. Hope medium.

Wednesday, January 11. Cold night. Cold day. Was cook, having wet pinewood to cook by. A friend favored the mess with money to buy meat for dinner. Got mail, one letter from Bro. Jno., dated Oct. 24, 1863. He hopes exchange, condemns specials. Thinks something wrong in the exchange bureau, since date of capture is entirely ignored. No Exchange news. Many are getting discouraged again. Got a few more board[s] for the huts, but they come in slowly. Major Griswold roud [rowed] madly on finding the <u>dead line</u> burned. Expect the money to be confiscated or enough taken to pay for it. The day comes and goes, and shivering the evenings away we naturally curse the fate that keeps us here. Demoralization grows apace. Good health.

Thursday, January 12. Last night very cold, day sun-shiney and pretty, but cold. Finished reading "Beulah" being wrapped up by it more than by any work

Fig. 20. S. M. H. Byers and J. O. Rockwell, "Sherman's March to the Sea" (1864). A song composed by the prisoners in Camp Asylum celebrating Gen. William T. Sherman's campaign through the South. Weaver copied the lyrics to this and other songs in his diary. (Library of Congress, Music Division)

I have read for a long time. It shows the folly of females attempting to battle with masculine ambition, trying to win a <u>name</u>, rather than devoting their time to domestic pursuits. Also shows how many indels [infidels] are made by the inconsistencies of professing Christians. Mail today. I got none. Yesterday was feasted on the sight of a beautiful lady, said to be a Miss Banchers or Boosen. She was dressed in red, white & Blue, white hat, blue dress, and red bodice, so that we all say "she is union." She came upon the stockade in three different places, nor can I forget her appearance.

Friday, January 13. Weather pretty. Not cold. The sun shining brightly, bringing us out of our tents to seek the grateful sun. Wrote two letters to Mother and Bro. Jno. Taking autographs very high, as tables were set out all through camp calling all they saw to draw near and give their signatures. Read the correspondence between the Gov'ts in regard to sending supplies to prisoners. That was in Oct. and arrangements seems to have been completed. Still nothing has come for us yet. Can't understand it. Had music by the band. Also Major Izard sang the song composed by Adj't. Byers and music composed by Lt. Rockwell, entitled "Sherman's March to the Sea."[60] It is delightful in diction and the music in pathos, so that when it was finished cheer followed cheer until it was called for the second time. Health good.

Saturday, January 14. Last night was cold. The day pretty with high winds. Got rations. The flow was cut off for the tearing down of the source of the sink. Although we have not wood enough, still it is not becoming an officer to act in this manner. But what can be expected of drunkards & gamblers. Rumors of the Fleet reappearing off Wilmington. Gold said to be selling for $100 Confed. for one in Richmond. Read "Coriolanus" & "Julius Ceasar." How I love the writings of Shakespeare! Got boards enough to put a roof on our building. Will move in a short time. The days come and go, tardily sometimes, and rapidly at others. And altho more than 15 months have rolled their weary rounds since I come to the Confederacy, I look back as if it were a few days only. Forward I dare not look or anticipate. Glad for life and something to eat, even mush and sorghum.

Sunday, January 15. Cold nights but pretty days. The sun shining brightly. Had sermon by a Rebel minister, Rev. Dow a Presbyterian, who preached from last two words of 26 vr. of 5 chap. of Mark, "only believe."[61] Altho not powerful speaker, still I felt well under his sermon and thinking of other days I was happy. No news of any importance, rumors of exchange and parol run rampant, but no confidence placed in them. Had dinner of $10 steak, $12 pork and $3 lard, having a good meal. Got a copy of "Sherman's March to the Sea."[62]

Our camp fires shine bright on the mountains
That frowned on the river below,

While we stood by our guns in the morning
And eagerly watched for the foe.

When a rider came out from the darkness
That hung over mountain and tree,
And shouted "Up boys & be ready
For Sherman will march to the sea."

Then cheer upon cheer for bold Sherman
Went up from each valley and glen,
And the bugles reechoed the music
That came from the lips of the men.

For we knew that the stars in our banner
More bright in their splendor would be,
And that blessings from Northland would greet us
When Sherman marched down to the sea.

Then forward, boys, forward to battle
We marched on our wearisome way,
And stormed the wild hill of Resaca
God bless those that fell on that day.

Then Kenesaw dark in its glory,
Frowned down on the flag of the free;
But the East and the West bore our standards,
When Sherman marched down to the sea.

Still onward we pressed till our banners
Swept out from Atlanta's grim walls,
And the blood of the patriot dampened
The soil where the traitor's flag falls;

But we paused not to weep for the fallen
Who slept by each river and tree,
Yet we twined them a wreath for the fallen
As Sherman marched down to the sea.

Proud, proud was our army that morning
That stood by the cypress and pine,

When Sherman said, "Boys you are weary
This day fair Savannah is thine."

Then sang we a song for our chieftain
That echoed over river and lea,
And the stars in our banner shine brightly
When Sherman had marched to the sea.

Monday, January 16. Fair day. Got the House covered, table and stools made. Will move in a few days. Major Griswool [Griswold] says if our gov. does not except their propositions for exchange they will parol us. This creates no high expectations. The sutler puts up a notice that he will give twenty-five for one in coin checks. This is so much high [higher] than <u>six</u> that all are eager to make an investment. It seems the checks were put up to the highest bidder. He took the posist [posit?]. Read "Antony and Cleopatra." Night after night dissipation runs riot while the devotees of Bacchus make night hideous with their drunken orgies. Pity grows into contempt as I reflect on the position they hold in society. I feel my strong increase to live a sober and virtuous life. Had a fireplace built in the tent, making the cold evenings pass by more comfortably. Have good health. Wrote Kitty a letter. Am tolerably happy.

Tuesday, January 17. Rather pretty weather, clear and sunshiny. Nothing but rumors, one that our fleet has passed Fort Fisher, another that Sherman has got Augusta.[63] Only rumors I suppose. A few more tents came in, making shelter for all. Some were formerly our tents but were captured, mostly Sibleys.[64] Capt. Zarracher is in the hospital, on his back, with a large carbuncle. Lt. Gay with the fever.[65] It seems that sickness is increasing somewhat. Lt. Osbourn of our tent is sick also. Have no boards to make bunks. So we have to stay in the tent until we get them. Altho whiskey costs $50 a qt. yet plenty of officers buy it and spree all night. Health good. Living in hopes of getting free someday.

Wednesday, January 18. Day delightful, warm and comfortable, mild as June. To us it is a God send, as our thin worn clothing are poor protection from the cold winds and frosty nights. Bowman's money checks are not what was anticipated, as he gives $25 for only checks sent from the North. Wrote a letter to Mother using invisible ink. Have good news from Wilmington. Gen. Lee telegraphs that our forces captured Fort Fisher with all its garrison [and] one Gen'l.[66] Expect the city to follow soon. At any rate this will stop Blockade-running. Someone composed a Burlesque poem on the hospital Bummers,[67] putting it upon the Hospital. It gave Lt. Sinclair "hail Columbia."[68] The Reb surgeons got angry and tore it down. It gave us some amusement. Day ending gloriously promising good weather for some time.

Thursday, January 19. Continued beautiful weather but indications of rain, dropping some in the evening. Got boards and finished our bunks. Rumors of Kilpatrick fighting at Branchville some saying they heard the firing last night.[69] On this head many rumors were raised, even to sending us away. On the other hand they say the officers from Salisbury [Prison] are coming here. Nothing of Exchange. Winter is passing swiftly by, and it seems as if Spring is to find us in Rebeldom. Autographs took a rage. Read "Cymbeline." Was cook, having mush for breakfast, rice soup & slap-Jacks for dinner. Sickness is on the increase, but none very serious. Gay has got the Typhoid fever. Osbourn has the Fever and ague. I am very thankful for good health, as sickness in prison is a terrible life. Oh that exchange would soon be made general.

Friday, January 20. Weather fair. Enjoying prison life better than I had expected if enjoyment it may be called. Wrote a letter to Bro. John. Read "Titus Andronicus," considering it the bloodiest Tragedy of S. [Shakespeare]. Have a new Commandant. He got us in line with a good deal of noise and spirit, when he begins "Attention Shentlemens, I takes command dis day. Ise from Fort Delaware,[70] I was myself a prisoner. You taught me how to be a gentleman and how to take care of you. Break Ranks, March." Then, with a yell all broke for their tents. Lt. Smith, 149 N.Y., came in from Wilmington. He thinks Gen'l Butler failed ingloriously in his attack. An Artillery Capt. came in from Savannah. Rumors of Fort Caswell on Cape Fear River half between the city & Fort Fisher.[71] Ed. Everett is said to have died of apoplexy. Provisions on the road to the poor of Savannah. Altho they may be loyal, still it grinds the prisoners to see their neglecting us and aiding them.[72]

Saturday, January 21. Commenced raining at dark last night at dusk, raining incessantly till morning. Not very cold today usual with wet days. A great many rumors run through camp. Pocotaligo is said to be evacuated.[73] Tennessee coming back to the Union, and going to elect Parson Brownlow for Governor.[74] That the Tallahassee ran into Cape Fear river, anchoring under Fort Fisher before they knew it belonged to us. She is said to be captured of course.[75] Read "Taming the Shrew," also Sept. number of U.S. Service Magazine.[76] The magazine is a good think for the army. Our dutch or French commandant is making a fool of himself. Came in drunk, ordering all around as Reb privates. He wasn't taken well. Rained all day. Got no wood and the night will be gloomy. From all accounts the Rebels are playing out faster than for a long time, and we now begin to look to the end of the war as the day of our release.

Sunday, January 22. Last night was wet and dank. Additional rumors of our forces within a few miles of Wilmington and no forces to oppose them. Gradually we are closing around them, and no seacoast cities left for them to run blockade. Our Frenchman and the Reb surgeons fell out, wanting to put a poster on the Hospital. This was sport for us. He has only one roll call at 11 A.M. by

Adj's (Prisoner) of Squad. The Sergeants dismissed. He orders policing and inspections, but he shall as signally fail as his predecessors. Wet most of the day but not very cold. Have but little wood. No religious exercises. Very few indeed miss these, and most seemingly mock at religion and all the finer qualities of the mind. Good health. Grub as usual. Hope for brighter days.

Monday, January 23. Rained most of last night. Kept on raining today, the mud getting deep in camp. Was cook today. Had a wet time. Our French Commandant is said to be relieved from command. His race was short. None liked him, not even his own people. A large money list came in today from Charleston, being converted there into Confed. at Rates of $7 of greenbacks $24 for gold. While here they give $57 for gold, $50 for silver. Guy [Bryan] got $350, coming in good time as the last meal of beef was eaten today, had we not got money. Selling checks is played out. Got rations today, small rations of wood, got no flour, taking it to pay for the boards of sink burned by the officers. Rumors afloat but not reliable. Subscribed for three of Fisher's "Southern Prisons."[77] Good health. Appearance of a wet spell on weather. Got the following copy, which raised so much ado around the Reb doctors and Hospital Bummers a short time ago.

> From this terrestrial Hell, O heavenly muse,
> An humble bard thy inspiration woos.
> Give him some "Attic salt"[78] that he may rail,
> At all the Bummers here full-fledged & hale.
>
> That to the Doctor with convulsions rush,
> To drain his Physic and to eat his mush.
> O shame! That men who spent the knightly spurs,
> Should so demean and of themselves make currs.
>
> Ye gods of war how must your temples glow,
> When from above you see these dogs below.
> Disgrace your glorious arms & cur-like wait,
> To clean a chair and shave a doctor's pate.
>
> See how they cringe and bow, this crowd of bums,
> Whenever Sir Galen[79] thro' the portals comes.
> O muse, relate whereof this Condescension,
> This bowing, scraping, this polite attention.
>
> Just list and hear two Bummers' conversation:

"Tell me," says one with rather rummy face,
"Can you perchance the latest rumor trace?"
"What rumor's that?" replied the other beat,
With gracious mien & accents soft & sweet.

"Why that the doctor told us here today
"That all the bums will shortly go away
"I tell you covey[80] we have played it well
"We've sold our fellows & the Rebs will sell.

"We must confess 'tis mean & looks ill bred,
"But then the Devil, don't we get a bed?"
Among these bums distinguished wide & far,
Is one by name St. Clovus or St. Clar.[81]

This gallant youth is not unknown to fear,
He drills the bums & cleans the Physics chair
There is a saying old, but quite uncivil,
That "Beggars mounted ride straight to the devil."

But here, quoth ye, this adage will not pass,
It says the "Beggar mounted" not an "Ass."
More apt the story of the ancient toad,
Who puffed & swelled & grew the more he blowed.

Not unlike him this modern toady blows,
And while he puffs in self-importance grows.
He lords it o'er the crowd of healthy Bums,
And on each croc that in his mansion comes.

He plies his tongue quick lets loose,
A tirade of illiterate abuse.
But late in all his majesty he stood,
To stop intruding evers not of his brood.

When look! Bold Magrew onward winds his way,
When up cur-like he starts & cries "hold stay."
"What business hast thou here, 'tis not for thee,"
"Oh such as thee, to tread my suasion free."

When (muse excuse me, out the truth must come),
He took the toady by the neck & bum.
And from the landing with a mighty thrust,
He sent him trailing in the mother dust.

Now all ye bummers from this, warning take,
Your tongues keep still lest you a lion wake.
And for your bumming got you just deserts,
A cuff, a blow, a kick beneath your skirts.

In charity I tell you no one comes,
To help these loafing convalescent Bums.

These lines having caused a great commotion among the Bummers and many threats made the following lines were added. The whole production, as well as the Parody of Longfellow's "Psalm of Life," is said to be the work of Lt. A. Wilson Norris, 107th Pa.[82]

At this my lay, O Muse, some Bums have sworn,
That from my brow the laurels shall be torn.
And not content to stop well-worded strife,
They curse my being, swear to take my life.

The shoe must fit and yet the blame is theirs,
The one who tries it on, the pinch he bears.
'Tis strange how many these curs lines awake,
They must be Bums, else why this umbrage take.

Then be it known where ere these lines pursue,
And for their anger therein find excuse.
I tell them here, none but the Bums find fault,
With this my song, this bit of "Attic" salt.

Read "Winter's Tale." Did not take much interest in it. Had Preaching by Rev. Palmer, formerly of New Orleans. He and Gen'l Butler had several contentions. He is a good speaker. Took for a text: "All things work together for good to those who love God."[83] The men were busy on the chimney, getting it up at dusk. Draws well and having four fireplaces the most can get warm. Good health. Good spirits, although all things seem against us. But my hope is in the future.

Tuesday, January 24. Pretty day but promises to be a very cold night. Got 10 lbs. of cotton for a mattress, which shall make us sleep more comfortably. Papers speak of 14 Peace Commissioners gone to meet a like number of our Government in order to negotiate for peace. But little hopes are had of their accomplishing anything.[84] The Prisoners to a man don't want our Government to back down one mite, but require the Rebs to lay down their arm[s], as a conquered people, since our army has got the advantage of the[m] badly now. Moved down to the Building. It contains 38 men, a good proportion Germans, and it is amusing to hear their honest gabblings. They are cleanly, though, and not the worst neighbors in the world. Some sit up very late while others go to bed early. The house is tolerably comfortable. A few "mess kettles" 20 or 30 were issued today. Good health.

Wednesday, January 25. Last night was very cold, but slept very well, having our cotton additional, making good mattress. Ice was formed in good quantities. Lt. John H. Henderson, 14 Ill. Infantry, died last night in Hospital of Typhus Fever, the first officer dying in this camp. Cold all day but we had good fires, and our hut was tolerably comfortable. Read "Comedy of Errors" and "Macbeth." Both good productions. Gen'l Hood has been relieved and Gen'l Johnston put in his place. Davis refuses to put Lee in command of <u>all</u> the armies. Secretary Seddon (Reb) has resigned his position.[85] Like the hut very well, dark but not so cold. Amused by the click of Dutch from morning to night. Get up later than usual till 9 or 10 o'clock. Good health.

Thursday, January 26. Last night was very cold freezing ice to the thickness of ½ inch. Today the cold winds blow hard and comfort is out of the question. A little wood came in, but some officers made a Raid on it, so that they brought no more in. This, altho just on the part of the Rebels, was severe on the innocent. Have roll call at 12 M. [meridian] by Reb Sergeants as usual. Capt. Stewart in command of interior of camp. Read "King John" admiring as usual the art of "Arthur."[86] Rumors of various kind but we cannot rely on anything. Prices getting higher. Pay $7 per pound. Gold outside $125 for $1 (so reported) while at N.Y. it is down to $1.80 for $1. All the things indicate the favorable change that has taken place North & South, for which we feel thankful. Good health. Good appetite.

Friday, January 27. Last night appeared to be the coldest one of the winter, freezing bitterly cold all day. Rumors of an Armistice having been agreed upon by the Governments for 90 days, but cannot get at the foundation of the story. Lt. Mosley had a watch (Gold), which he raffled off for $1500 (50 chances at $10 each). Capt. String, 11 Ky. Cav., & Capt. Campbell, 152 N.Y., tied on "42" when they decided to put it up again in partnership.[87] Strict orders concerning roll calling and tearing down buildings for wood were posted up by the Commandant of Camp, threatening to confiscate all the money in their hands. Discussion about the Armistice grow warm, some wanting peace on honorable terms others thinking the Rebs had not been whipped badly enough. Was cook having nothing but mush.

Saturday, January 28. Night cold. Day colder. Winds cold and high. But little fire, and not comfortable. Nothing definite concerning the reported armistice, but rumors more obscure increase. Read "King Richard II," and "1st Part of King Henry IV," admiring the fiery Hotspur, and the amusing Falstaff.[88] Thomas' official report is in the papers. Claims to have captured 500 wagons nearly all H. [Heavy] artillery and only needed a little cavalry to destroy Hood's army.[89] Money checks or Drafts are abundant, so many that the market is stagnated, and it is a difficult matter to sell a gold Draft to $6 for $1. Fortunately got a little money in the mess to get meat for dinner. This prison life goes from hand to mouth, and the greatest aim of our lives is to get something to eat.

Sunday, January 29. Very pretty day, warm and sun shining brightly, drawing us out like from our holes to bask in its warm and genial beams. Wrote two letters to Sister Mattie and Ed. McChesney. Rumors still afloat but cannot get anything reliable.

> Rumor is a pipe
> Blown by surmises, jealousies, conjectures
> And of so easy and so plain a stop
> That the blunt monster with unco[u]nted head
> The still-discordant wavering multitude,
> Can play upon it.[90]

No religious exercises. Lt. MKee of W. Vir. came into our house and sang the most of the evening away the number "Eighty years ago," "Her bright smiles haunt me still,"[91] and "Sherman's March to the Sea." I felt rather happy considering our situation. Oh how happy I would be were I at home tonight. Is it true that "Everything works together for good to them that love God?" It must be true but we cannot appreciate it.

Monday, January 30. Cold nights, but days getting much warmer, and as the case generally is, the warmer the more wood. Got ration. No flour as usual. Great rumors from outside. The Rebs think or pretend to think that the war is over, the last gun fired, & but strange to say they say also that gold has come down to $15 in Wilmington, and $20 in this place. But this must be all bosh. The closing up of the blockade will doubtless bring gold down, but such a fabulous fall as this appears ridiculous since every indication would insure the Rebs that if Peace be declared their money will be repudiated. Had mail, got no letter. Wrote to Bro. John. Read, "Second Part of King Henry IV," & "King Henry V." The day was fine. My health is good and a lingering hope of something transpiring to release us.

Tuesday, January 31. Very pretty day, warm as spring. Letters distributed. None for me. Yesterday's papers say Stevens, Hunter and Campbell have gone to Washington to make propositions of peace.[92] Frank Blair has been to Richmond twice. Many think there is a likelihood of obtaining an end to these wars. Sherman is still on the move. Left Savannah in 3 columns, marching on Augusta, Branchville, and Charleston.[93] Oh how I hope the latter place may fall into our hands before the war ends! Hood is stuck in the mud with a remnant of 7000 men. Badly was he beaten. Altho the Rebs say gold is falling, prices are steadily advancing, sheeting costs now $10 per yard, formerly $4.50. Tugged 2 hours in the crowd at Sutter tent to get a piece of beef.

Wednesday, February 1. Weather pretty. Warm as Spring so that we flatter ourselves that the worst of winter is over. Had an alphabetical Roll call, taking the most of the day. Papers give us a few items of news. Grant has entire control of exchange of prisoners. Some regard this a good cheer for us, others the reverse. The Rebels blow about Peace, but don't speak of anything but recognition as a Confederacy. They crowd their papers with such twaddle. Part of the Smithsonian Institute was burned a short time ago, losing some engravings &c.[94] Sherman still advancing on Branchville, being the "persuader" to induce them to sue for peace. Read First & Second Parts of "King Henry IV." Had music in the evening. A party of ladies came on the stockade to listen. They called for "Sherman's March to the Sea." Letters but none for me. Eat mush and had good health.

Thursday, February 2. Very Pretty Day, indications of rain. Rumors of various kinds, the most important to us is that Gen. Hays, Prisoner at Danville, has been appointed to distribute clothing to the prisoners.[95] We all stand in need of some badly. It seems strange that so many months pass before we received anything from the north, arrangements having been made last Oct. Lee is said to be whipped at Richmond, having made a sortie upon Grant. Had nothing to read and the [day] passed very slowly. Wrote a letter to Bro. John. Sherman is still advancing on Branchville and Augusta. Card playing, night & day, is carried on in our Hut. Good health. Back again on Confed. rations—<u>mush</u> & <u>sorghum</u>. Shall this last always.

Friday, February 3. Rained most of last night and today making camp muddy and the weather cold and disagreeable. Nothing sure in the way of rumors. Wrote three letters to Sisters Kitty and Amanda & to J. C. Lightcap. 'Tis said no mail has left here for more than a month. It seems that friend and foe conspire to crush us. Rations getting very small and the money hard to get. The purchasers get afraid of our Exchanges. Had a taffy pulling at Show Tent. Most for once have played out of sorghum. Finished our portion the second day. Thankful for life, even tho it be dependent entirely on mush.

Saturday, February 4. Although we expected cold weather after rain, yet the day was fine and warm. It seems spring is upon us. A tunnel was discovered on the east side of camp. It was eight feet underground and twenty ft. long, under the Brick wall. Deep was the chagrin, and intimations were given that one of our party betrayed us again. Major Griswold issued an order that if any more tunnels would be discovered that he would take out all tents and barracks, or if any injury was done [to] any fellow officer on suspicion of having betrayed the matter, force would [be] used for force and the guilty parties punished, showing that a traitor is amongst us. No rations today and meal all gone. No money and starvation stares us in the eyes. Good health, leave stomach.

Sunday, February 5. Partly warm day. No rations came until night, and most all without anything to eat. Papers have good news from Sherman, he being within six miles of Charleston, and also close to Branchville. They say they have no forces to meet him. Northern news say the Reb. Commissioners passed through the lines on their way to Washington both armies playing "Home sweet home."[96] Mr. Sumner offered a resolution in Congress tendering to the Prisoners of War a vote of thanks for their heroic endurance in Southern dungeons for the long time they have been prisoners.[97] Grant has appointed Com. Of Ex. [Exchange] who met the Reb. Com., and they say a special exchange has been procured or rather a partial one. They hope to have a <u>general</u> exchange.[98] Letters from Danville speak very favorably of Ex. Good health. Mush and no sorghum for many days.

Monday, February 6. Cold Blustery day. The Rebs took down all the frames of the unfinished sheds, the most of them being torn down heretofore by our officers for wood. Thirteen sheds have been completed. Spent good share of the day reviewing "Tates Natural Philosoph."[99] Rumors of good import, if true, that resolutions were put in Congress to retaliate on Reb. prisoners for our treatment, and that Senator Wilson said it was uncalled for as Secretary Stanton had informed him that a general exchange was about being made.[100] As yet got nothing but meal, the sorghum having played [out]. Fears are entertained least they are going to cut it off. We are all growing very fond of it. Sherman is making headway and soon Charleston [and] Augusta will be ours.[101] Then we must leave this. Where we shall go is a mystery. Good health.

Tuesday, February 7. Rained hard all night and the most of the day. Cold and disagreeable. Papers say the Peace Commissioners had returned from Washington having accomplished nothing. Pres. Lincoln and Congress notified them that unconditional surrender and immediate emancipation were the only terms of their returning to the Union. Spend the evenings singing songs around the "magic circle." The following song was sung, with good effect. Composed in Camp by Lieut Norris.

The Reb's Soliloquy

I've said it oft, I say it here,
Old Abram is an Ass.
But then 'tis strange, 'tis passing queer,[102]
That things go like such a pass.

That cities fall at old Abe's call,
And forts yield up their hosts.
And at his beck our Generals all,
Give o'er our strongest posts.

Chorus:
A very great Joker is old Abe,
A very great Joker he.
With all his jokes we must confess,
His greatest jokes he plays on us.
A serious old Joker he.

I've said it oft, I say it now,
The Yankees are all knaves.
And 'fore old Abram's footstool bow,
A cringing lot of slaves.

But then 'tis strange, 'tis strange I know,
That slaves bear arms so well.
And every time they deal a blow,
They deal them where they tell.

Of late we sent our gallant Hood,
To fix mad Sherman's fate.
When he and all his maniac brood,
Were thundering at our gate.

But now alas; grim fact here lies,
The madman's reached the sea.
And 'ore our proud Savannah flies,
His cursed emblem free.

Ev'n now we hear the cannons roar,
About Fort Fisher's wall.
And see our cherished bars gone o'er,
Before the Yankee balls.

And yet the knaves are not content,
But onward press their way.
And for our Wilmington are bent,
With such another fray.

That madman he old Sherman bold
Is onward pushing fast.
I'll tell you friends,—it must be told—
This blow will be his last.

If Charleston goes, Atlanta falls,
And then Columbia too.
I tell you friends, though me it galls,
That things look mighty blue.

Old Grant at Richmond thunders still,
And still keeps closing in,
But then I swear he never will,
O'er Lee a victory win.

But tho we can't, we must avow,
Withstand the wear and tear.
We must beneath the yoke soon bow,
And Abram's burthen then bear.

All things now look like success to us, and many are sanguine that we shall be exchanged. We need it badly. Rags cover our bodies and our stomachs grow lean. Good health. Longing for something to turn up.

Wednesday, February 8. Cool night. Clear day with high wind. But short rations of wood. Got sorghum, all glad to have it again. Dr. Martin has taken out $50,000 in checks without paying anything to the owners. He says he destroyed them. Griswold thinks he sold them, and notifies the officers if they write letters home forbidding the payment of them he will forward them. Sutler tells of Genl Winder dying of Appoplexy at Florence.[103] This gave us joy unconfined, as he has been so cruel to our prisoners as to merit our lasting hatred, and unforgiveness even in death. A court of inquiry was called at the request of Mr. Saber, who has been passing himself off as our officer. They find him only an enlisted man and generally unsound. He should not have made the request as it has gone against him. A meeting was held in No '9' to organize the "American Patriots legion."[104] Cold all day.

Thursday, February 9. Cold day and night. And the winter was not so nearly past as we had thought. Nothing definite from Sherman. Reb. Commissioners were met by Seward, who told them to go home and throw down their arms [before] sending representation to Washington. But the authorities would not receive them or recognize them as States of the Union.[105] A [vigil?] was held in our house. Capt. Foster had his pockets picked of $180 but when he went to searching, the money was dropped on the floor. The suspicion fell on Lieut. C_____r, 21 N.Y. C., who was searched but nothing found.[106] Too bad for one prisoner to steal from another. All these little items will be settled when we get out. Accident gave us a soup of meat & rice. Good health.

Friday, February 10. Cold night, freezing ice. The day was pretty and warm. Got rations, 3 qts. meal (of which ¼ is bran of the coursest kind), one ½ pt. rice, and a tablespoon full of salt, a piece of soap as long as my little finger. This is the ration for five days. Exchange good again, as the Rebs say Grant has notified them he intends to carry out a general exchange as soon as possible. Some are buoyant, others faithless. Washed clothing. Spent the day rather idly as reading grows laborious. Singing is the go at night. Keeping late hours, and sleeping late ("burning up three of four hours of daylight"). Good health. Have hopes of something good happening soon.

Saturday, February 11. Pretty day. Sun shining warm again. Rumors of Kilpatrick being near this place. Cattle are coming in from the country and the people have a general scare. Expect the Rebs will move us. Exchange is the same. Reb. Col. says Judge Ould says it will commence the 1st of March. Preaching by Rev. Palmer, Text Acts 17 ch., 31 vr.[107] The main idea being to prove that Christ in his human character should be our Judge on the Judgment day. This idea seemed good. No hope of <u>future</u> redemption would be left us since the Redeemer condemned us. Terrible thought! Had music. Many ladies came upon the Stockade to look upon us. Miss Bossier among the number. She is very pretty. Had a mail nothing for me. Chance of Selling Checks of Exchange. I gave one to Sutler. Eating mush. Good health.

Sunday, February 12. Today was pretty and warm, but blew up cold toward evening. Had preaching by Lieut. Grier in the morning. Went to bible class at 12 M. [meridian] and Prayer meeting at Night. These are held, the Bible class every day, Prayers on Sunday & Thursday evenings, consisting of from twenty to thirty officers. I felt happy in attending as it reminded me of other days, when I used to participate in similar exercises. Besides, I felt happy having formed a determination to try to be a better man for the future. Wrote a letter to my mother having got one from her dated Jan. 6th in answer to the one sent by Lt. Potter.[108] Got acquainted with some good men whose good fellowship I must cultivate. Good health and happy.

Monday, February 13. Very cold night, freezing ice ly [lay] freely. Day cold and windy, but sun shining brightly. Was at B. [Bible] Class, Reviewing "Romans." News of none import. Potter is trying to sell or buy "Powers of Attorney" at $2½ for one but none are investing. All preferring to give Gold checks at $10. Were notified that we should leave here in the morning, for parts unknown (to us), from which we concluded that Sherman is closing in upon us. Oh may he come quickly, but no hope of him capturing us. The first, six and 11th squads are ordered to be ready. Was weighed and find it 170 pounds. Very good weight on mush and sorghum. The first meeting of the "American Patriot Legion" is being held tonight. Good health.

Nine

"Altho All These Things Seemed as of Former Days, Yet I Could Not Realize That I Was Free"

Homeward Bound, February 14–April 1, 1865

By early 1865, as Federal advances in Virginia and the Carolinas diminished Confederate territory and destroyed more and more of the South's resources, Southern officials, well aware of the horrific conditions in their prisons, eagerly sought to renew the July 1862 exchange cartel. Issues that had led to its gradual collapse—Davis's refusal to accord African American soldiers prisoner-of-war status and Lincoln's calculation that he could replace Union captives with new recruits while his enemy could not—became less compelling as Northern victory seemed imminent. By November 1864, special exchanges of officers and of sick and wounded soldiers had increased, and by late January procedures were arranged to parole about a thousand prisoners daily starting in February. Sherman's unimpeded romp through the South Carolina upcountry, however, complicated moving thousands of Union prisoners on the South's increasingly dilapidated railroads to an agreed exchange point outside Wilmington, North Carolina.[1]

If Weaver's transition from soldier to prisoner was abrupt, his reverse journey from incarceration to freedom coursed over a month. The hastily evacuated troops left Columbia, South Carolina, on February 14, and arrived at Charlotte, North Carolina, at midnight. Hopes brightened four days later when the rumors of a general exchange proved true, and their new prison was dubbed "Camp Exchange." Weaver marked his liminal state, noting he "felt happy knowing I am on my way home and implicit confidence in it makes me plan for the future." The newly minted veterans of a soon-to-be-victorious Union collected photographs and autographs and organized a chapter of the Loyal League, dedicated to maintaining the Union and the Constitution, to "good fellowship among the survivors of the present war," and to render "aid to each other as far as our means will allow." Continuing their literary activities, they composed doggerel excoriating General John H. Winder, head of Confederate prisons, and another celebrating emancipation. The prisoners increasingly interpreted their guards' lax treatment and civilians' war weariness as evidence of latent Union loyalty. Leaving Charlotte on February 20, Weaver remained in Raleigh for five days before moving to Goldsboro, where he took the parole oath on February 27. Two days later he reached the exchange point at Long Bridge, nine miles north of Wilmington. Soldiers' cheers, rousing bands, and "as much coffee, hardtack and boiled beef as I could eat" greeted Weaver and the other newly released prisoners. The next day he boarded the USS *General Sedgwick,* a coastal transport, and marveled at the "moving city" of steamships filling the harbor. Traveling through an Atlantic gale, "a boiling abyss ready to devour our <u>little world</u>," a frightened Weaver recorded that he and many returnees suffered from seasickness until they reached the Chesapeake Bay's calm waters four days later.[2]

Weaver's arrival at Annapolis, Maryland, on March 7 marked the final phase of his return to civilian life. The next few days were a whirl of activity: reunions with comrades, news of the 18th Pennsylvania, bathing and acquiring new clothes, and attending religious services, concerts, and church festivals. After a week, he marveled that he was "losing my ravenous appetite." Only the enlisted prisoners' sufferings and visits to the large burial ground of the war dead tempered his buoyancy. Weaver secured a thirty-day leave of absence and left for Philadelphia on March 18, where he enjoyed three days walking around, visiting the sights, and attending theatrical productions. Returning home to Westmoreland County, Weaver recorded a whirlwind of visiting family members and friends, "talking of days past and gone," catching up on local news, and writing letters. The final entry finds the diarist at home with "nothing of any importance to do; I got tired and lonely." Still, Weaver's strong constitution (he weighed 170 pounds upon leaving Camp Asylum), his unshaken Methodist faith in Providence, and emotional equanimity left him optimistic about an undetermined future: "The day was fine and [I] felt happy," he concluded.[3]

Tuesday, February 14, 1865. Cool night. Day disagreeable. Was notified early to be ready to move. Got out by 3 P.M. but only 550 instead of 700. Commenced raining and rained all night, sleeting, also, and freezing, forming coats of mail upon the guards who rode upon the tops of the cars. Some of them came near freezing and lied to get down. In the car we were partly comfortable, but having sixty or seventy in each car we were so crowded that lying down was out of the question. Being so compact we warmed each other. So another move is upon us. Having got comfortable quarters, circumstances required a move, and we have a doleful prospect ahead of us, thrown out in an open field without shelter. Movements indicate that a fight will be made near Columbia. But the Rebs are getting out everything valuable.

Wednesday, February 15. Ran slowly all night stopping frequently to allow trains to pass. Lost two cars and had to go back for them. It was a dismal night, the most severe of any this winter, but still some escaped, as many as 12 out of one car. Got to Charlotte at 12 M. [meridian] and amid shoe-top mud, disembarked and marched to camp one mile north of town, having an old barn. So the most got shelter of some kind. I got on the floor. Have plenty of pinewood, being among the pines. A company of Salisbury Guards met us here and say the[y] expect to take us there tomorrow. They are good fellows, treating us splendidly, leaving us go out anywhere. 'Tis said they are mostly of Union proclivities forced into service. Still cold and expect to have a hard time of it. Got "hard tack" and pork. Prices tho are fully as high as at Columbia.

Thursday, February 16. Had a splendid sleep, warm and comfortable. The Salisbury guards left for home, and reports are that we shall follow in a few days for Richmond for exchange, as a general exchange has been agreed upon, some Rebs having arrived at Varina.[4] But for the most part all these rumors are thought to be started by the Rebs to prevent us from escaping. Still, many as [are] leaving, walking out of the guard line on all sides, so loosely are we guarded. This makes me take some stalk [stock] in the rumor and for the present shall not escape. Got two letters from Mother & Bro. John of Nov. last. Rumor of Columbia being captured by our forces, also Charleston.[5] The rest of our officers got in tonight, but were left in the cars. Our camp is small yet and so little discipline that we shall doubtless leave in a few days. Good health. Meal and beef for rations.

Friday, February 17. Had a good sleep again. The day was pleasant, but rained in the afternoon. The rest of our officers joined us. They say they were hurried out of Columbia, and that it is certain we captured the place. Some 70 or 80 officers hid in the loft of the hospital, and will likely get free. Capt. Evans in trying to escape had his leg shot through above the knee, shattering the bone. Will lose his leg.[6] Exchange rumors grow brighter, but still some are escaping, being disappointed so often they have no <u>faith</u>. But trusting that all these news may be partially true I find myself arranging my conduct for the future as if I would truly be exchanged. We are all getting to feel better. Had soup of the issued beef of yesterday, the first ration issued since leaving Charleston (Oct. 6th). Good health and hopeful for the future.

Saturday, February 18. Wet rough night. Pretty day, warm and pleasant. We were notified that we should leave this morning or tomorrow morning for Richmond or Wilmington for exchange but we did not get off. Expect to go in the morning. All are taking <u>stock</u> in Exchange now as we have had accumulative evidence that a General Exchange has been agreed upon. All are merry, and the fear of being deceived again is our only alloy. The "Loyal League" had a meeting, reading "Constitution & By Laws." The object of Legion is "to protect and perpetuate at all times and under all circumstances the Constitution of the United States of America; to preserve the Territory of the American Republic intact by all lawful means; to promote and preserve good fellowship among the survivors of the present war and to render when necessary aid to each other as far as our means will allow." This promises to be a prosperous fraternity. Got the following writing in camp.

Winder Among his Friends.

To traitor knaves and devils there below,
To this may lay a list'ning ear bestow.
From earth to Haydes, Winder wends his way,
To Hell's grim shades a pilgrimage to pay.

Then tremble imps, for by dread Orcus throne,
I swear to thee you all will be undone.
Off o'er the Styx this ghostly shade e'er cross,
H'll from his seat old Harry quickly toss.[7]

And visit little devils with that love,
He showed to Yankee prisoners here above.
Then warming take, especially you, old Nick
Prepare thy fiery tongs and forked stick.

That when thy gates upon this traitor turn,
You may pitch him where the hottest embers burn.
For craftier fiend than he there ne'er did dwell,
Of all the fiends that e'er did people Hell.

His sins, old Nickolas, you can easily track,
By loads of curses heaped upon his back.
And groans & tears, & murdered victim's cries,
The orphan's wail and mother's bursting sigh.

Yes, tears enough on Earth has this fiend shed,
To quench the flames that burn about his head.
Then hasten imps and pile on high the fire,
And whelm this scoundrel in the burning mire.

To devils we can charity extend,
When they their fire on such a fiend expend.

Sunday, February 19. Pretty day. Warm and sun shining brightly. Did not move today but they tell us 500 are going tomorrow. This keeps us on the "qui vive" but some are getting discouraged, especially as the Rebs brought two cannon and trained them on camp. The sutler came with a load of provisions but they did not last an hour. He says he will cash all outstanding orders but none have confidence in his promises. Over $1200 Confed. was raised by subscription to be left with Capt. Evans whose leg was amputated above the knee. He is said to be getting along well. Can be sent home in a few weeks the Dr. says. Autographs, Photographs, and "Loyal League" are the order of the day. The[y] with discussions about exchange put in the day. The camp has been christened "Camp Exchange." Good health. Living in hope.

Monday, February 20. Last evening we were notified that two hundred would leave for Wilmington. As the first out were to be taken, there was hurry and confusion to get out, some going without rations and even clothing. Today another party left, (200), remnants of first 3 squads, and the rest notified they would be paroled. And we were as soon as the rolls could be made out. Even after parole some thought it a catch, at which the Rebs got offended, as we doubted their words. Three hundred left in the evening in passenger cars, being a luxury, but we were crowded so tightly that comfort was but small. Felt happy knowing I am on my way home and implicit confidence in it makes me plan for the future. Oh, how I long to be free. Even with the freedom we have already I seem myself again. Feel well and hopeful.

Tuesday, February 21. Ran all night at tolerably brisk rate getting to Greensboro by daylight, passing both the other parties who started ahead of us, making them feel badly, as otherwise as hopes were had of being the first Exchanged. Passed Hillsboro getting to Raleigh at dusk. Had a good easy time; guard not having any command of us. But getting to R. [Raleigh] we found two companies of Home guards ready to guard us. Many thoughts flew through my mind, but at length they told us we would have to get out and go to Richmond, as the Commissioner would not exchange at Wilmington. The fact is our forces have captured Fort Anderson and have doubtless taken the city.[8] Columbia has gone, Charleston also, and now Wil. Are lying between Rail Roads, waiting for train to take us back to Greensboro. Expect rations. Cool evening. Hope after being carried around this confederacy thru a few times to be exchanged.

Wednesday, February 22. Not getting off. Officers were sent to town to cook rations. They had to run all over town to get wood enough to cook them. Got bread & meat. Nearly all our officers came of last night. One train had been as far as Goldsboro, and returned. They saw some of our men at that place from Florence.[9] They say the sight was terrible, the poor men so weak as to fall in the street and eight or ten died there, some clawing their stomachs and gnawing their fleshless hands. Oh when shall these barbarities cease! Two trains are here of men from Salisbury &

Florence. They look famished, gaunt, haggard, and dark with dirt. We gave them all the extra food & clothing we could spare, and raised a subscription in one party of $600 to buy bread for the sick. They felt much better with hope of getting home. Heard of the death of L. Titus, Bailey, Hoffman, and [blank in MSS] of our Regt.[10]

Got this song from Davy Garbet.[11]

Oh you niggers come along,
And I'll sing to you a song.
But I warn you dat you keep it mighty still.
For this darkey hear dem say,
His own self, dis very day,
Dat old Abe had went & gone & signed de bill.

Chorus.
Old Abe has gone and did it boys,
Glory hallelujah home.
Old Abe has gone and did it boys,
Oh! Glory.
Old Abe has gone and did it boys,
He's signed the confiscation laws.
Liberty and freedom's ours,
O Glory.

And dem dey thought the way,
Massa Fremont first did say,
In Missouri where de 'bellion was so strong,
Dat de nigger must be free.
But Abe didn't just agree,
So he modify and dat we tink was wrong.[12]

Massa Burnside take de view,
Dat the nigger am as true,
As de white folk or any other man,
So he never drive us back,
When de hounds was on our track,
And de Lord stand by him every time he plan.[13]

McClellan thought the way
Was to have the niggers stay,

Digging trenches for the Rebels in de snow,
While de Yankee soldiers worked
With de shovel in de dirt,
When day ought to use de sabre & de gun.[14]

Massa Hunter did contend,
Dat de government did depend,
On de nigger with his pick ax & his spade,
Dat de Yankee boys would fight,
But dey never tink it right,
To take up digging ditches as a trade.[15]

Bless de Lord forever more,
For we almost see de shore,
Oh de happy land of Canaan in sight,
And our eyes dat look in tears,
Thou de long and bitter years,
Catch de gleaming of de coming ob de light."

"The Vacant Chair."[16]

We shall meet, but we shall miss him,
There shall be one vacant chair.
We shall linger to caress him,
When we breathe our evening prayer.

Just one year ago we gathered.
Joy was in his mild blue eye,
But the golden cord is severed,
And our hopes in ruins lie.

Chorus: Repeat first four lines.

Near the fireside sad and lonely,
Often will the bosom swell,
On remembrance of the story,
How our gallant Willie fell.

How he strove to bear our banner,
Through the thickest of the fight,

And support our country's honor,
In the strength of manhood's might.

They may tell me wreaths of glory,
Evermore may deck his brow,
But it soothes the anguish only
Clinging 'round my heartstrings now.

Sleep alone thou early fallen,
In your low and grassy bed,
Whispers from the pine & cypress,
Mingle with the tears we shed.

Quite a number of recaptures are brought in, but very little if any escaping takes place. Potter came in offering to buy Powers of Attorney. A good many sold. The guard remains as lax as usual, leaving us mostly do as we choose. Jokes are common, telling the guards we will escape if they don't leave us go where we wish. We lay in camp all day, awaiting orders. Capt. Hatch[17] came up last night, went onward to Wilmington to try to have us delivered there, as he has orders from Gen. Grant to deliver us at any point. Wilmington is ours. The papers in this place speak out boldly calling Davis hard names & seem to be tired of the war. Citizens are union, speaking their sentiments openly, while the rebels look gloomily on the progress of affairs, fearing that Sherman will close in on Gen. Lee at Richmond, ending the struggle. Am growing discontented as I had hoped to be exchanged again this time, but will wait with patience for the issue. Still the fear will brew in my mind, least something come up to stop the exchange. Pretty day, sun shines brightly, birds sing sweetly and having many liberties I am happy still. Expectation strong.

Thursday, February 23. No word from Hatch yet. Papers say our forces have cut the road between Goldsboro & Wilmington, and are likely to attack the former place. If so, we shall hardly get to Wilmington. The Editor of the <u>Daily</u> <u>Progress</u> was in camp. O how he cursed Rebellion, Davis, and all secesh. He seems thoroughly a union man.[18] I was astonished to find so many union men in this place, many speaking openly in the streets, even those carrying guns. Starvation stares them in the face. Desperation has got its heel upon their necks and Sherman is their only hope, which they all allow. Moved out to Camp Holmes, a Conscript Camp.[19] Keeping us out of the City (some having got drunk and raised a disturbance), and it threatened rain. Moved in cars 2½ miles North on Gaston R.R.[20] Have good quarters, will keep us dry, got 6 days ration of meal & pork. We are growing very tired of waiting thus. Some beginning to doubt Exchange. No guard.

Friday, February 24. Rained terribly all night. Some coming up late last night could find no shelter and got wet to the skin. Rained most of the day. Got no rations today. Had a guard around us occasioned by the improprieties of officers who left camp and went to town, contrary to orders. Felt unhappy all day until the word came at fall of night that Hatch had telegraphed to send us on, as we should be received at Long Bridge nine miles North of Wilmington. Then all care flew away and I was happy in the hope of soon getting home. Still many doubts and fears harass the soul least we be disappointed finally, and be doomed to further imprisonment. Have trouble getting water enough to use. The days pass very slowly, and being cold and wet the horrors would be mine were it not for the good hope of getting home.

Saturday, February 25. Day was wet, cold and disagreeable, raining most of the day. Drew ration of meal and sorghum, about enough to make a good mush. They told us we would leave in the afternoon. We waited anxiously, and every train that came by made our anxious hearts palpitate for fear we would be left. Disappointment was ours and night came finding us here without any good hopes of immediate departure. The cause doubtless is the want of transportation, as they are using every car and locomotive to transport troops & munitions of war. Great feeling is exhibited on the part of the officers, feeling that we are imposed upon while many demand the track back again, intending to escape. If not moved soon a demand for the parol will be made "en masse." Good health. Partly discouraged.

Sunday, February 26. Today came in gloomily as no train had yet come for us, and most begun to think the Rebels were going to keep us until they could conveniently send us using at the present the trains for transporting soldiers and running off goods from Sherman. A big hubbub was caused and the Rebels notified that we would demand our Paroles if they did not forward us immediately. This had the desired effect. A col. [column] started to Ral. [Raleigh] and at 3½ P.M. a train of 5 cars (three flats, one box, and one passenger car) came out. Loaded Col. Shed's party (300) and adding 8 cars of enlisted men at Raleigh we ran at a brisk rate getting to Goldsboro at about 8 o'clock, a distance of 50 miles. Found a train of privates starting to Wilmington. What enquiring after Regiments? We went to Court House for the night expecting to go on to W. [Wilmington] again tomorrow night. Thus the day dawned sadly, ended gloriously.

Monday, February 27. Slept soundly in the courtroom being a commodious building for so small a town. Goldsboro is the County seat of Wayne Co. containing nearly, I should think, 1000 inhabitants, having a good deal more ingenuity displayed than most Southern towns. Capt. Stewart brought up the residue of Camp Charlotte with recaptured escaped officers about 120 in all. Capt. Harris, who was held in confinement in chains for over two years at Columbia, joined us on route for exchange.[21] Col. Ashworth was sent to Richmond.[22] Capt. H. was marched from Col. [Columbia] six miles with his shackles on.

Had Alphabetic Parol List made out reading thus: "We the undersigned prisoners of war do give on parol of honor that we will not take up arms again, nor serve as military police or constabular force in any fort, garrison, or field work; nor as guards of prisons, depots or stores; nor discharge any duty usually performed by soldiers, until exchanged under provisions of Cartel entered into July 22, 1862." When nearly through the Capt. got a telegram to annex to the rolls: "Nor give any information we may possess to our Genl's or others," as this arrangement had been entered into by both parties. Got rations. Have a guard as many ran up town as usual looking for grub & whiskey. Bowen, our Sutler, has come up and says he will cash all orders. If not, he would have a hard job collecting the "Bills of Exchange" now in his possession.

North Carolina must be getting union. Yesterday the ladies and old men cheered us by waving handkerchiefs and throwing kisses along the great share of the road. They seem sick of the war. Perhaps our success of late has brought these changes upon them. Have traveled by rail in the Confederacy about 1400 miles and going to Wilmington will complete the round 1500 miles all free of charge. Liberal these Rebels, altho it was done at the risk of life and limb, as the Rail Roads are in a dismal condition. Was disappointed again by having to remain here for another day and perhaps more, but they say we shall go tomorrow sure. Capt. Stewart is trying to supercede Capt. Bartlett, who refuses to give up the Rolls until he delivers us at North East Bridge to our Commissioner. The day was fine. Indications of rain. Talked of taking us out to Camp but the order was not given. The time passes slowly and not having more than half rations we have additional incentives for going home. Good health. Good spirits. May the day of delivery soon arrive. All the officers come up today.

Tuesday, February 28. Slept in C.H. [Court House] as before. Before dawn was awakened by the hollering and shouting of the others who had awoken, and lay joking and punning each other on all sides, to the dissatisfaction of sleepy heads. Rainy day. Expectations of leaving at 4 P.M. today. The time came, and sure enough they called for us, taking all the officers in other camp, with 180 of our party in first train; the rest of us and 400 enlisted men in second, making 1001 officers. O how happy we felt in anticipation of so soon getting free from the Rebels. A few guards went along, but they treated us well. But many of the enlisted men die on the road, and graves mark the place where they have been, even passing along the Rail Road. Raining, some on top of car, 75 in each car, and they so filthy we could scarcely breathe. Being for exchange we endured.

Wednesday, March 1. Ran slowly, getting to Rocky Pt. 4 miles of our lines again 2 A.M. Had to wait till 9. Col. Hatch came up in special train and with a white flag on his train conducted us to our lines. O, the feelings of Joy we felt on beholding our officers and men. They counted us through, when three rousing cheers went up for Joy. Col. [blank in MS] conducted us 1½ miles across the Pontoon Bridge over North East River through a large number of troops who cheered us lustily. Saw their shattered banners. Hurrad them. Heard the band play, and then partly realized I was free. Saw the negro soldiers in abundance, thinking well of them. Halted and had as much coffee, hardtack, and boiled beef as I could eat, having had nothing for nearly a day I did my duty. Altho all these things seemed as of former days, yet I could not realize that I was free.

Started for Wilmington, a distance of 9 miles, and having no transportation (Rolling stock) for we have had to walk. All the officers but the sick voted to walk leaving the Boat in the N.E. [River] for the men. We made the march having a Military escort of the 7 Conn. Inf. Made good time making 1 mile in 17 minutes getting to W. in good time and after marching in two ranks through most of the city, we were quartered in churches for the night. Allowed to go wherever we wished. Sanitary Commission treated all who wanted with a milk punch. Got supper at the Soldiers Relief,[23] setting places enough to accommodate 600 men at a time. Had cof. [coffee], meat, & Hard tack. Some officers went to theater, being gratis or free to Prisoners, where Major Isett sung, "Sherman's March to the Sea."[24] Was cheered lustily 'tis said. Feel sore but happy in the thought of so soon getting home.

Thursday, March 2. Had a pleasant sleep in the Colonial Methodist Church.[25] Got up with thankful heart that the "stars and stripes" protected me, favored by a divine Providence. Got breakfast at Soldier's Relief. One transport load, (500), left for the North. We got aboard the Gen'l Sedgewick, at 3 P.M. and ran out into the middle of the River and anchored for the night.[26] The enlisted men are almost crazy to get along. Poor fellows they want to go home. Will go shortly. Stood upon deck and counted 30 long steamers making the river look like a moving city. Prisoners allowed to go wherever they want. This gives all soldiers a good deal of liberty. They run around on all sides. A Paper is begun in W. called "Herald of the Union," a rather fine daily for so short a time.[27] Abundance of troops in city and still are moving. Fourth Corps coming now. How jubilant it makes us feel, hearing the bands play and the soldiers cheer. Gen'l Schofield in Command of department of N. C., Gen'l Terry of 24 Corps, Gen'l Cox 23rd.[28] Many of the officers, finding friends, have dressed up and they are not recognizable. But most with good clothes have managed to get state rooms, others having to stay on deck or the lowest hole, where horses have been transported from the North. Good treatment I vow for U.S. officers! Sanitary Com. doing good business in aiding sick soldiers, and Army Chaplains are getting to be worth something except bumming. Good health. Got 60 gals of Coffee on board of the boat.

Friday, March 3. Having spent the night in sleep upon hurricane deck[29] got up & prepared for the journey. Started at noon. Passed Fort Anderson on the Right, Fort Fisher on the left, beside many obstructions in the river, getting out to the inlet we cast anchor to wait for tomorrow's tide. Many officers went to shore to Smithville.[30] Wind grew boisterous. The rain began to fall and we had a disagreeable time. Troops in transports pass us on all sides going to the front. Sanitary Com. sent a barrel of punch along, which was issued to the men, mak-

ing all merry, but a dissatisfaction exhists in consequence of our delay, all eager
to go home. The River today was placid and presented a magnificent sight, and
being my first trip on board I felt delighted. Hope the most of our journey may
be so pleasant. Good health.

Saturday, March 4. Slept soundly in our elevated position, altho gusts of rain
blew over us in fitful gales. At length, 12 m. [meridian] arrived and all having come
on board we were on the wing. Instead of going out at lower inlet, we passed back
to Fort Fisher and went through "New Inlet."[31] The wind blew a heavy gale, and
to the uninitiated it was frightening. The dark blue ocean loomed up before us, its
dark watters looked threateningly, and as far as the eye could penetrate, nothing
but "water, water everywhere."[32] Our craft tossed upon the billows as a thing alive
and struck the bar various times in crossing making everything rattle. But fortunately we passed safely & were "out upon the ocean." Gunboats & schooners lay all
around. A transport loaded with enlisted men followed.

The sea was said to be a calm one, but to me it seemed a boiling abyss ready
to devour our <u>little</u> <u>world</u>. The waves lifted us as a feather until we seemed to fly
through the air, then sank down to the depths, bringing to my mind the forcible
passages of scripture. We mounted to h & e.[33] Having to run in the "trough of
the sea" parallel to the waves our vessel rolled terribly being high upon the water
and having nothing for ballast. Soon many began to "pay their vows" by casting
up, and the others delighted themselves in laughing at others. They in turn soon
got sick and when evening came but few felt well. I staid upon deck all day and
kept my mind and stomach quiet by gazing upon the distant horizon. But when
night came I made for quarters in the Cabin between decks and getting in, the
first thing I knew I was upon my head and rolled upon my back on several of my
brethren in tribulation. Crawled upon deck and "paid my vows" of all I possessed
in my stomach. No land in sight for many hours. Occasionally a ship is seen toil-
ing upon the wave. With a prayer for a safe voyage and a secret promise, if I ever
get to shore safe that I would not imperil my life again I rolled in my blankets
and tried to sleep. A boiling ocean, a heaving stomach, a rolling ship forbid me
sleep. And many hours of the night passed ere I could sleep. At Midnight the gale
increased and the ship plunged forlorn having to run against a head wind and the
waves dashed over our bulwarks, frightening those in the hole below. The hatches
were then fastened down, and on we rolled and pitched till the break of day. Sick
at heart we all hail the morn.

Sabbath, March 5. Was sick all day, remaining in my bed nearly all the time.
The gale appears to increase. Mountains of water appear to rise in our path and
strange with what power they toss us about. They say we passed stormy Cape
Hatteras in the morning, the dread of all, and said to be the worst coast in the
world. Laughable to see the men crawl about and tumble over. No eating of any
consequence. Some are still themselves, but very few courageous enough to go

on deck. I have read of the sea, "the masts raking heaven & the keel the depths of Hell," but I would have no idea of the sensation that I feel when I look upon the illimitable ocean. An image has been indellibly fixed in my mind, never to be forgotten. Still sicker and have repeated the dose of puking three times today. This shall doubtless end it.

Monday, March 6. Slept last night. The winds ceased and the high seas were becalmed a little. Still heavy rolling. At about 10 A.M. land came in sight and we knew then we were nearing Fortress Monroe.[34] The sun shone brightly, and altho cold still. As we progressed the decks began to fill and before we got in the bay nearly all were out some looking pale and wan. I had eaten nothing while on the sea. Felt happy as we passed into Ch. [Chesapeake] Bay, between Capes Henry and Charles.[35] Got to the Fortress at 4 P.M. Saw "Rip Raps,"[36] many crafts of various kinds, monitors, tugs, schooners, &c, and Hampton Hospital in the distance. Col. Thorp went on shore and got us soft bread. What a feast having got over our sickness. A sick man "Bradley" was taken to shore, sick with the Fever. We then started up the bay passing lighthouses by the quayside. Felt well and happy.

Tuesday, March 7. Slept most of the night got up with severe headache. Had cast anchor at 4 A.M. waiting for day. Had passed York, Potomac Rivers. Had another barrel of punch issued. Calm day, beautiful prospects, and all happy but eager to get to destination. Poked slowly up the bay too slow for our excited spirits, but at last got to Annapolis where we found the other party who had got here on Sunday. Saw Lt. Grier, who was on sick leave, told me many news. Col. Bryan, Lt. Col. Brinton, Major Darlington, Major Van Voorhis, Capt. Kingsland, Capt. Hamilton had resigned the service. Capt. Britton was major; also Capt. Page, Lts. Smith, Blough were made Capts.[37] But the prisoners were forgotten. Had good news from the Valley. Early with 4000 were captured.[38]

Found the officers all ready to receive us. Registered our names and went to clothing stores who were kind enough to trust us, only charging 200%. We all took baths and put on new suits feeling ourselves again. No stages of our advance seemed so rapid as this one. Expect two months pay. Applied for a leave of absence, having to send to Washington. Wilson and Leslie[39] had a great disappointment, not being recognized as officers, had to go with the enlisted men. Grier tell[s] me of Major Phillips[40] & Lt. Blough's captures. They have gone home on furlough, Potter[41] has gone home also, on furlough. Rumors of the Boat that was loaded with enlisted men was sunk, but hope 'tis all rumor. Got Blankets from Capt. Davis, Commandant of the Barracks (College Green), a fine man, who is trying to do all for us he can.[42] Felt happy now in prospect of Exchange soon getting home.

Wednesday, March 8. Had a good time in bumming round town, getting something edible to eat, which made us realize that we had got to God's Country. [My] Self in the Barracks getting blankets from Capt. Davis, the Commandant of College Green Barracks. Two loads of enlisted men got in today amounting to 700 or 800. Got two month's pay ($222.23) of Major [blank in MS]. Sent to Paymaster Gen'l trying to get the remnant. Wrote letters to Mother, Bro. Jno., Sister Kitty, Ed. McChesney & Mollie of M. [Meadville]. All Annapolis is gay with paroled officers in new uniforms living high and making up for past time. Harry & Leslie had to go to Enlisted men's camp. Feel sorry for them. Rained in the evening. Expect to sleep in Barracks again good health and long to go home.

Thursday, March 9. Rained last night. Slept in the Barracks. Changed Boarding to "McCullough Hotel" on State St., pay $2.50 per day.[43] Get good grub having abundance to eat. Ran around town most of the day. Visited <u>State House</u> with Lt. T. J. Grier and looked out from the observatory upon the city which presents a diversified appearance.[44] Officers are enjoying themselves in their various manners some drinking, frolicking, bumming. Some going to excess, which disgusts me to the soul. Enlisted men arriving from <u>Dixie</u>; others going home. Western men reporting to Camp Chase, and Camp Douglass.[45] Oysters and All are the [gr?]. Saloons on every corner and the streets filled with officers. Early not captured, but whipped, loosing [losing] 1500 prisoners. Capt. Bradford (Rebel) is in the city. Good health. Gay Spirits.

Friday, March 10. Day cold. Sleeting a little. The only snow or sleet I have seen this winter. Prisoners arriving. Good news from all sides. Sherman and Sheridan doing good service. Had cornbread for breakfast. Was diverted to see our officers eating of it since they had almost taken a solemn oath not to touch anything made of corn hereafter. Went to Pres. S.S. concert.[46] It was a good recreation. Paroled Officers patronized it well. How much better to spend an evening this way than in rioting. Had also a meeting of National League.[47] Wrote letters to Major Phillips, Major Britton & Mr. Lightcap.[48] Am waiting anxiously to go home. Harry & Leslie left today. Expect to leave first of the week. Good health.

Saturday, March 11. Very pretty day. Enjoying the time well, but should like to go home soon. Many are getting their leaves of absence and leaving for home. Potter came today. Had a great jubilee at City Hotel having Grier and Mackey[49] there. He gives us news of the Regt. Wrote to Jno. Crode and Major Darlington[50] concerning promotion. The day was fair. Good news from all the armies. More men, paroled prisoners, coming. Out of 800 brought in one load of 520 had to be carried off the ship. Such suffering is beyond description. Raising money to make Col. Thorpe a present for his exerting himself to attend &c.

Sunday, March 12. Today was delightful. The air pleasant and made me feel very happy. Attended Methodist Church morning and night.[51] Heard two good sermons. They have a good quire [choir] with melodeon. A very large attendance by the officers. They are keeping up the dignity of the service. While at services, a train of 60 dead men were haul'd past, taken out of the boat. A large burying ground containing thousands is near the city with its white head boards, painted, pointing out the barbarity of the Rebels. Visited Parol camp.[52] Saw six or eight of our men. They are looking well having been paroled in Dec. Felt happy in attending church today. Some men got leave.

Monday, March 13. Day very pleasant. Officers leaving as fast as the[y] get permission. Expect Col. Bryan here but came not. A good many officers are being mustered out having been dropped from the Rolls while prisoners. More men came from Richmond, five or six of our Regt., have as bad a time as all the others. Can hardly pass the day it goes so slowly. The ladies of the city are not as affraid of soldiers as usual, but the officers are behaving so well they have no need of fear. Wrote letter to Mother, one to City Point, relative to the box sent me last spring. Good health. Am losing my ravenous appetite.

Tuesday, March 14. Continued pretty weather. Got my leave of absence. Did not go home, waiting for my Pay-account. Herrington, Penny, and McKay left, the latter mustered out.[53] The city is nearly free from paroled officers. Good news from the armies. Sheridan still advancing up the valley. Bot Shakespeare and a ph. [photo] Album of Mr. Monroe, making his acquaintance. Attended a M.E.S.S Concert in Temperance Hall.[54] The crowd was so large not all could get in. I was among the fortunate. Had good performance, singing delightfully. To be repeated tomorrow night. Was happy to see so many happy children. Good health.

Wednesday, March 15. Guy [Bryan] got his Certificate of Pay and left for home. Col. [Timothy] Bryan came in morning and left for Washington. He was all honey and professed to due all, any favor for me I might desire. His address is 431 Market St., Philia., Pa. Not getting my Certificate I determined to wait for it. Went to a Methodist festival. They had a fine array of eatables, large cakes, which they sold by lot at $20 & $30. Albums in same way. I was fortunate to get an album, but gave them $15 or $20. So it was no paying operation, but being a laudable object, the fitting out of the parsonage, I considered it "lent to the Lord." Got acquainted with a number of fine ladies. Good health.

Thursday, March 16. Felt lonely today awaiting my papers, which came not. So the day was idly passed in running the streets. Went to the fair again. Not so brisk as last night, since the flush of the boy's money had run off. Was surprised to see the species of gambling they adopted, taking chances for Albums, cakes, books, selling these at 3 prices and the articles disposed of by drawing numbers out at the Rolet [Roulette]. I drew a cake, a handsome one, making it a present to Miss M. of this place. The Presbyterians are going to have a fair also. The Concert of the Second [charge?] is still going on. Good health but sick of this place.

Friday, March 17. Was disappointed badly in not getting my pay account as the Col. had assured me it would be here today. Getting more disgusted than ever at the Red Tape going on. News from the Army good. Saw a puff for the 18th in the Phila Inquirer.[55] The Regt. is at Torberts Hd. Qrs.[56] But few officers in the city and we are having a dull time. Went to both fairs tonight and got acquainted with more of the ladies of Annapolis. Men are dying fast of the number exchanged as paroled, and loads of corpses go through the street daily. Fine weather and with half treatment I would be happy. Felt unwell, having sick headache.

Saturday, March 18. Was disappointed again not getting my certificate of Pay. Got disgusted and left for Phila. Started at 2:35 and getting to Baltimore at 4. Ran around to six forty when we left for Phila. Ran slow by having to stop frequently. The Susquehanna was so high at Havre de Grace that the ferry could not take the cars over.[57] Changed cars. Crossed in the Ferry, being a tremendous raft. Got Phila. at 2 A.M. in morning, taking hack to the Continental.[58] Was put in no. 344 to sleep, on the 5 story. I thought I would never get up.

Sunday, March 19. Awoke after hard sleeping but fine room. Found Capt. Pennypacker. Guy [Bryan] had gone home. Went around the Hotel; what magnificence, everything so handy and neat as well as costly. Went to Church. Presbyterian on Bath and Arch Sts. [Streets].[59] Good services. Tried it at night, but going to Episcopal first, we could not get in, too full. Went to Presbyterian, it was too full also. Came away. Spent most of the day walking through the city. What magnificence, what display. Excelling anything I have seen or expected. Good health.

Monday, March 20. A very fine day. Slept so soundly last night as not get up till 10 this morning. Went down to the w[h]arf, having a long walk. Got measured for suit of clothes. Had chicken in style on Roast Turkey, Sc. [Scalloped] oysters, potatoes, tomatoes, turnips, peas, cakes, confectioneries, Italian Cream and Roman punch, beside these things too tedious to mention. Went to the Theater, Walnut St., to hear Mr. J. S. Clarke "Everybody's Friend" and "Toodles." He put on the comical to a high degree. Was pleased with part but disliked his making Toodle act the part of a silly Drunkard <u>all</u> the time. Mr. Herne was good. Mrs. Keach and Germin ditto.[60] Wrote to Mother, Jno., and Major Phillips.

Tuesday, March 21. Day fine. Capt. P. [Pennypacker] left for the country. Was to visit Independence Hall, seeing the painting of most of the Patriots of the Revolution, also went up in the tower looking out upon the city. What an extended prospect. What a beautiful city! After dinner visited Fairmount water works and Park. These are splendid places, but not being in verdure a good share of its beauty was lost. Went to theater (Arch) Saw Barney Williams and wife in their Irish character. Played "Ireland as it was," with good effect.[61] Had got suit of clothes of Stokes & Co.; pay $100. Was disappointed in not seeing Bryan. Telegraphed to Grier. Rained in the evening. Good health.

Wednesday, March 22. Got up early, getting breakfast. Took a stroll in city. Bot clothing. Saw Capt. Zarracher.[62] Told me of nothing coming to Annapolis

Fig. 21. Walnut Street Theater (1811), Philadelphia, 1865. Weaver attended a show here on March 20, 1865, to see *Everybody's Friend* and *Toodles*. (Library of Congress)

for me. Then I concluded to go home. Got my <u>negatives</u> taken for Photographs to be sent to Latrobe.[63] Almost missed the train. Hired a cab driving at break-neck speed for the P.R.R. Sta. [Pennsylvania Railroad Station]. Got there 5 minutes before time. Passed through a delightful valley (Chester), and all the way to Har. [Harrisburg]. Got acquainted with Miss Emma Pierce en route for Urbana, Ohio. Got to Latrobe at 1 A.M. and it looked so desolate and the scenes seem so changed there. I felt lonely. Stopped at Hotel (Loyalhanna) but a stranger kept it. Called for a bed and retired. Thoug[ht] of the many changes since my leave.

Thursday, March 23. Getting up, found a few of my acquaintances. But what changes. Most all gone, leaving only a few of my former acquaintances. Saw Geo. Keiht, who gave me a happy reception, as did all who saw me. Got a buggy and went to the Country. Snowing and raining all the day. Met my friends all will [well] with Bro. Jno. and Eph.[64] who had been in Dixie 4 months. He looks bad and had a bad siege of it. All congratulate me in looking so well. Spent the evening in talking of days past and gone, and the new house brought to my mind the scenes of other days. Feel well and happy, but the change is not as startling as I expected.

Friday, March 24. Left for Grapeville[65] with Mother, Bros. Jno. & Eph. John going to his station (Florence),[66] Eph. for his father's. Arrived at Sister Kate's having rode in a Farmer's wagon. She was glad to see us and we spent the day in talk

&c. Ed Smeltzer is quiet but by acquaintance gets social.[67] He seems an energetic, working man, making a good husband. The place was very quiet and I got lonely being used to so much company. Wrote to T. J. Grier and McKelvey. Felt very tired so the evening was short, and being sick with headache I was no company for men or women.

Saturday, March 25. Day stormy and snowing. But having spent most of the day at Grapeville, we left in a wagon for the station. Stopped at Miss Brown's, who made herself acquainted, and chatted loudly for a half hour, getting so well acquainted as to drop her affectedness. Train came. Saw Chaplin High, Wb., Pa.[68] We had a talk by necessity short. Saw none of my friends at Granger's Station.[69] Kept snowing and melting. Had a muddy walk home, getting there at dusk. The time is passing fastly, and as I think of the many places I wish to visit the time seems very short. Good health. Happy.

Sunday, March 26. Day fine, but wet underfoot. Had no preaching at Ross' as the minister Barbager had not got here yet.[70] Spent the day at home, reading news, talking and writing. Nothing new. All well and seem happy. The time of my leave of absence is going by very fastly. Good health, &c.

Monday, March 27. Started to Greensburg[71] with Sister Jennie, going on Accommodation. Saw Mr. Caldwell, Mr. Jno. Weaver, Isaac Hughes, besides a good many others. Stopped at McQuaids Hotel. Met Lt. Gageby, a former prisoner of war.[72] Was glad to meet him. Got introduced to some ladies getting them to play the <u>piano</u>. Saw Lt. Row getting up a Company at Greensburg. Left for Latrobe, leaving Jennie at George's Sta. Visited Mr. McChesney's having a great time in talking over the past, &c.[73] Got letters from Thos. J. Grier, Harry Wilson. Feel well &c.

Tuesday, March 28. Hired a buggy of Mr. Kirk and started for Ligonier.[74] Got there at noon. Saw Dr. Beam and lady. Mrs. Ashcon & daughters, welcomed heartily by all. Promising to call when going home, I drove on to Laughlinstown to Uncles. Found them all well. Liza teaching in the country. Lucinda the only one at home.[75] Had a pleasant time during the evening going among giving calls and getting acquainted &c. Saw Miss Miller, Miss Trauger, Misses Shafer, and Misses Naugle. Spending a happy evening, Cousin Lu and I went home.

Wednesday, March 29. Took Lucinda and drove up the valley to see cousin Lida teaching at Mr. Weavers School.[76] Had a rough time, rough road but pleasant. Saw Cousin L. with small school of eight. The day being fair they were all out making sugar, &c.[77] Had dinner at Mr. W. Weavers when we left for L. [Laughlintown] leaving Cousin L. at the School feeling lonely enough to see us leave. Got to town in good time. Visited some more. Spending the evening with Miss Miller and at Squire Luthers.[78] Day fine and feel happy.

Thursday, March 30. Started for home bringing Cousin Lucinda along. Stopped at Ligonier to bid good by with the folks. Had a <u>warm</u> reception and

Fig. 22. On March 22, 1865, shortly after his parole, Weaver visited F. S. Keeler's studio to have this portrait taken. He later sent copies to fifty prisoner friends. (Ronn Palm Museum of Civil War Images, Gettysburg, PA)

affectionate good by. Came through Youngstown,[79] getting home at 1 o'clock P.M. Rained the most of the day, making the roads muddy. Got dinner at home and left for Latrobe, but not until I saw Mr. Lightcap who called to see me. Staid all night at Richts. Got my photographs, sending some 50 to my prisoner friends. Getting along well. Saw Alex & Mr. Lightcap at L[atrobe].

Friday, March 31. Raining hard. Could not go to see Mr. Lightcap. Spent the forenoon writing letters to more than a score of my friends. Saw Revs. Wakefield[80] and Barbager. Got dinner of Mr. Devertens, chatting with the ladies. Walked home, being very muddy. Day passed finding me at home for the night, and spent it copying my diary. Good health. Good spirits.

Saturday, April 1. Remained at home most of the day. Having nothing of any importance to do, I got tired and lonely. The day was fine and felt happy.

Students Are "Co-Laborers with the Instructor in the Investigation of Specific Subjects"

Weaver's Postwar Career, 1865–1920

Weaver's military service and his Methodist and collegiate connections shaped his postwar career, but like many ambitious young men in Gilded Age America his immediate plans were unsettled. Weaver rarely ruminated about the future in his diary, but his pious Methodist upbringing initially led him to the ministry. He attended Methodist General Biblical Institute in Concord, New Hampshire, in 1865, and the following year completed theology studies at Garrett Biblical Institute in Evanston, Illinois, where he received a Bachelor of Sacred Theology degree. In 1866 Allegheny College awarded Weaver a Master of Arts degree in recognition of this additional coursework.[1]

Education, not preaching, however, became Weaver's calling. In 1866, he was the principal and a teacher at Dixon Seminary, Dixon, Illinois. The following year, the Rev. Alexander Martin, Weaver's Greek instructor at Allegheny College and president of the recently established West Virginia University, invited his former student to Morgantown to teach mathematics and serve as the Cadet Corps' first commandant for the required instruction in military training at the all-male institution. The school opened in September 1867 with six faculty members and 124 students; all but six were in the preparatory department. Breveted lieutenant colonel of volunteers "for faithful and meritorious service" in October 1867, Weaver drilled his student-soldiers in infantry, artillery, and cavalry tactics.[2]

Weaver's Methodist connections also contributed to a successful courtship of Anna Frances Simpson, the second daughter of Matthew Simpson, a prominent Methodist bishop, orator, and president of Garrett, who resided in Philadelphia. They met at a Fourth of July picnic in Evanston in 1867 and married on October 27, 1869, at the Spring Garden Street Methodist Episcopal Church, Philadelphia.

Fig. 23. The West Virginia University Corps of Cadets. Weaver, seen in the dark uniform in the back of the formation served as commandant from 1867 to 1869. (West Virginia and Regional History Center, West Virginia University Libraries)

The wedding was a society affair with live orange trees, exotic plants, caged songbirds, and fish tanks decorating the church. It was followed by a lavish reception and banquet (without music, dancing, or wine) at the Simpson home on Mt. Vernon Street, where the couple's many "elegant and costly presents" were on display. Attendees included Weaver's sister Katherine, cavalry comrades, church officials, the Philadelphia mayor, a senator, congressmen, members of Philadelphia and Mid-Atlantic society, and President Ulysses S. and Julia Grant. Weaver had just turned thirty; his bride was six years his junior.[3]

The marriage secured Weaver's future, as his father-in-law was one of the most popular and influential churchmen of his day. Simpson's fervent opposition to slavery and his enthusiastic support for the Union cause attracted President Abraham Lincoln's attention, and the two men became confidants. After the war Simpson moved in Radical Republican circles and used his political connections to secure government posts for Methodist laymen, including his future son-in-law. Several months before the wedding, Simpson had written President Grant soliciting a consulship for Weaver and even suggested Italy as a suitable post. He noted Weaver's military service and described him as a "young gentleman . . . of unblemished character, and of more than ordinary energy, but of little means." Living abroad would enlarge Weaver's horizons and prepare him for "the best literary [i.e., teaching] positions." Reportedly, Grant's nomination of Weaver for a consulship at Brindisi, Italy, was his "gift to the bride." Soon after the wedding, the newlyweds sailed for Europe on the *Pereire* accompanied by the bride's two sisters.[4]

For the next sixteen years the Weavers lived in and traveled throughout Europe. Consuls dealt with their home countries' commercial affairs and assisted US citizens traveling or living abroad. Brindisi, located on the Adriatic Sea in Italy's heel, was a minor port for US trade, and in March 1870, Weaver secured the consulate in Antwerp, Belgium, an important international hub on the North Sea with direct commercial and passenger service to Philadelphia and New York. For the next ten years Weaver earned high marks for compiling detailed statistical reports of traffic through Antwerp's harbor, adjudicating disputes between shipmasters and seamen, attending to the needs of US citizens, and assisting refugees from the Franco-Prussian War (1870–71) who sought asylum in the United States. The couple with their two daughters, Vernie Ellen, born 1870, and Ida Blanche, born 1871, opened their home weekly to international guests, American visitors, and the expatriate community. Anna Simpson, an accomplished musician, helped establish the Seamen's Bethel in Antwerp and played the organ for their worship services. Simpson continued lobbying on his favorite son-in-law's behalf, and in 1879 Weaver was rewarded with an appointment as consul general to Austria-Hungary in Vienna where, for a year, he also served as legation secretary and chargé d'affaires. On Sunday evenings, the Weavers hosted religious and social gatherings, which provided, a visitor recalled with fondness, "the picture of an American Christian home in a strange land" and friendship to Americans living in Vienna. Despite Anna's hospitality and James's professionalism, personal rectitude, and political contacts, Weaver lost his position after Democrats secured the presidency and control of the Senate in the 1884 election. The following spring he faced an uncertain future.[5]

In 1885, Weaver began his final and most influential career as a college educator, when the Rev. Alexander Martin, now president of DePauw University, a Methodist college in Greencastle, Indiana (Simpson had been the college's first president from 1839 to 1848), offered him a professorship of modern languages and literature. Although Weaver had not studied these subjects at Allegheny College, sixteen years of diplomatic service qualified him to teach German and French, and his theological training and Methodist connections matched DePauw's Protestant ethos. Weaver arrived at a critical juncture when the school was transitioning from a sectarian institution to a modern liberal arts college. With promised financial support from Washington C. DePauw, an Indiana industrialist and Methodist layman, the school had changed its name from Indiana Asbury to DePauw University in 1884. Still retaining close ties to the Methodist Church and an emphasis on evangelical piety and moral education, the institution envisioned becoming a national university with new schools of law, medicine,

Fig. 24. James Riley Weaver, ca.
1885, soon after arriving at DePauw
University. (DePauw University
Archives)

ministry, music, pedagogy, horticulture, art, and mechanical industries. Under
President John P. D. John, who succeeded Martin in 1889, the school embraced
the "new education": expanded course offerings on specialized subjects, greater
curricular choices with more elective classes, required majors and minors in academic disciplines, and pedagogies that emphasized lectures, laboratories, and student research over recitations. After 1890, most new faculty members arrived with
graduate training in their academic disciplines.[6]

Weaver enthusiastically embraced the new educational methods and introduced the modern social sciences to DePauw's curriculum. He drew on his diplomatic experiences, especially the interconnections between economics, politics,
and diplomacy and the value of empirical data, to broaden his teaching far beyond
language instruction. Within a year Weaver introduced a course on political philosophy, or the "philosophy of History and the evolution of political associations."
Other new courses included constitutional histories of the United States and of
England, political economy, international law, and history of civilization. In 1890
Weaver headed the Department of History and Political Science and offered ancient, medieval, and modern history; national histories of England, Germany, and
France; the "theory of the state"; and economics. Three years later, he expanded his
repertoire of courses to include principles and applications of sociology, history
and philosophy of socialism, and economic theory, and, after 1905, commerce and
business law, US government, and American economic history.[7]

Like other pioneering social scientists of his generation, Weaver believed that combining history, theory, data, ethics, and applications provided a unified, systematic way to examine society and contemporary social questions. Political science, he noted, was "the Science and Philosophy of the State or society *politically* organized," yet its study also "depends so essentially on organized society in general." Positivist faith underlay Weaver's belief in the science of sociology. "Were there no sequence in society legislation would be in vain," he noted, "but as there is manifest causation, the result is the effect of forces. Hence the necessity of discovering these forces, their law of operation and method of co-operation." All social theory and philosophy, moreover, "must be tested by historical data properly interpreted," and ethics must shape practical applications; the latter he considered the "art" of political science. "The Historical-Philosophic method," Weaver concluded, "is the only safeguard against Ideology on the one hand and Empiricism on the other."[8]

Although course content naturally reflected the intellectual currents of the Gilded Age, especially Social Darwinism and the biological origins of "abnormal man," Weaver's course structure would be familiar to students today. It began with theoretical questions about the definition and nature of the discipline (i.e., "Can there be any sociological science?"); methodology and data collection (statistics, observation, comparison, inductive and deductive methods, and objectivity); followed by specific topics that constituted the discipline's field; and concluded with applications to contemporary issues. A unit on "Practical Sociology," for example, examined education, religion, and industrial conflict. "Economics, Money and Banking" and "International Law" applied theory to current fiscal, monetary, and diplomatic policies. "Theory of the State" examined political thought and institutions, including the origins of the state; its essential prerequisites, historical development, and functions; and comparative politics. The course "Socialism and Reform," first developed with his students, was remarkable not only for including readings by theorists and supporters of communism and socialism but also for seeing social discontent as responses to the dislocations of the Industrial Revolution. Weaver explored various explanations for labor unrest, poverty, and trade unionism in Europe and in the United States and traced the development and appeal of communal societies and socialist movements. Social reform, he argued, was the "golden mean between individualism and socialism" and, if leavened with Christian ethics, provided better solutions to the problems of monopoly, labor conditions, concentrated wealth, and political corruption.[9]

Weaver inculcated in his students the empirical methods of social science, most notably in his *Seminarium,* a capstone course he introduced in 1890 that required the "investigation of original and unsettled problems" based on research in primary and secondary sources. This approach underlay his teaching philosophy, which sought to instill in his students "a scientific method of investigating, accumulating and utilizing historical data . . . to follow the growth and evolution of societies, governments and institutions, and especially to inspire . . . a love of independent investigation. . . . [and] to awake in the student an enthusiasm for personal individualized effort. To this end subjects rather than authors are studied. . . . since the student is thereby obliged to develop his individual powers of investigation." This "laboratory method" of using resources from a departmental library "containing the best literature on the subjects taught" rather than regurgitating facts from textbooks allowed students to be "co-laborers with the instructor in the investigation of specific subjects" and to "work out each topic for ourselves." He strove tirelessly to build the department's book collection, which included theorists (T. R. Malthus, Adam Smith, Auguste Comte, Charles Darwin, Karl Marx, and John Ruskin); public intellectuals (Booker T. Washington, Edward Bellamy, Herbert Spencer, Henry George, Charlotte Perkins Gilman, Washington Gladden, Josiah Strong, and John Dewey); academics (Richard L. Ely—a personal favorite—Woodrow Wilson, John Stuart Mackenzie, and Carroll D. Wright); government documents, periodicals, and academic journals.[10]

By 1899, Weaver required students in his introductory classes to give reports and write research papers based on library resources. Suggested topics in the sociology class, for example, spanned a range of subjects and divergent viewpoints, including sociology's interdisciplinary nature; important theorists; methodology (statistics and data collection); theoretical topics such as the "place of conflict in progress," the "organic character of society," or the "necessity of social inequality"; contemporary issues on labor unions and strikes, monopolies, educational reform, temperance, political reform, the "future of the American Negro," and women's rights; and investigations of local penal, child welfare, and educational institutions, including DePauw.[11]

Weaver mentored Charles Beard, the preeminent US historian, social scientist, and public intellectual of the first half of the twentieth century. Mary Ritter Beard attributed her husband's intellectual awakening to his favorite teacher. Minoring in political science, Charles took five of Weaver's courses, including "Sociology, Principles and Applications," "History and Philosophy of Socialism," "Law: Elements of Jurisprudence," and "International Law and Diplomacy." These classes exposed the small-town Hoosier to modern social theorists; an understanding of the material basis of industrial society; the importance of rigorous analysis based on critical examination of evidence, underlying assumptions, and possible bias; an openness to questioning accepted intellectual paradigms; and faith in human progress and the possibilities of social reform. Weaver's classes brought "knowledge of social realities to bear on life for its improvement," Mary Beard recalled. It was Weaver who likely encouraged Charles to spend the summer of 1896 in Chicago engaged in "practical sociology," where he met Hull House residents and social reformers and saw, firsthand, modern urban and industrial society's class divisions and widespread poverty. This experience, Mary Beard remembered, "made a deep and lasting imprint on his mind and influenced his future activities."[12]

On Weaver's recommendation, Charles went to Oxford, England, to study constitutional history after graduating from DePauw in 1898. Weaver's protégée became involved in trade unionism and workers' education and helped establish Ruskin Hall in 1899 to provide educational opportunities for working-class men. Beard's first book, *The Industrial Revolution* (1901), was a primer on the material origins of English workers' social and political condition with much of its conceptual framework, topics, and references borrowed from Weaver's courses. Beard absorbed his mentor's belief that every individual could "acquire for himself that knowledge which will give him the power to deal intelligently with the problems of the new century." Education, social science investigation, and reform were necessary, Beard argued, "to get a true perspective of the most marvelous century in all of the history of man"; but more important, this newly acquired knowledge must be utilized "to show us 'what ought to be,' and how we can build on 'what is' to attain it." Beard's intellectual curiosity, belief in impartial analysis, reformist zeal, and faith in the power of ideas to improve society were first learned in Weaver's classes, the highest tribute any teacher can receive.[13]

Weaver was an immensely popular teacher. DePauw's small size, three to five hundred college students with forty-five to seventy graduating each year, fostered close ties between teachers and students. Always addressing Weaver as "colonel," students remembered him as a "gentleman of the old school" whose "manly dignity . . . [,] courteous speech, . . . chivalrous manner, . . . intellectual and social hospitality, [and] . . . honesty of his convictions" earned wide respect. He was a demanding teacher who expected students to spend at least ten hours of "laboratory time" each week in preparation for the four hours of class meetings that were devoted to lectures, discussions, and reports. Students were drawn by his lack of dogmatism and his encouragement "to approach the subject with an open mind" beyond a narrow Protestant worldview. Teacher and students, he believed, could become "independent thinkers" as they "arrived at conclusions together." Weaver was among the first initiates of the newly established Phi Beta Kappa chapter at DePauw in 1889, and served as its president for twenty years. Students also prized Anna Weaver's hospitality at chapter initiations and frequent social gatherings in their home and the encouragement she offered to young women at the college.[14]

Weaver continued teaching political science, economics, and sociology until the latter two disciplines became separate departments in 1908 and 1912, respectively,

Fig. 25. (*Above*) Anna Simpson Weaver, ca. 1895. Weaver's first wife, Anna was the daughter of DePauw University's first president and Methodist bishop Matthew Simpson. Anna and James Riley Weaver were married from 1869 until her death in 1895. (Anna Simpson Weaver Printed Memoriam, Matthew Simpson Collection, Drew University Methodist Collection, Drew University, Madison, NJ)

Fig. 26. (*Above right*) Emma Matern Weaver, Weaver's second wife, was an art professor at DePauw University and an accomplished artist from Sandusky, Ohio, who had studied art in Germany. The two were married from 1897 until Weaver's death in 1920. (*The Mirage*, DePauw University, 1896)

Fig. 27. (*Right*) James Riley Weaver, ca. 1910, near the end of his time teaching at DePauw. (DePauw University Archives) and offered courses, part-time, until 1917. Two years after Anna Weaver's death on October 4, 1895, Weaver married Emma Matern, a member of the DePauw School of Art.[15]

Weaver joined the Greencastle chapter of the Grand Army of the Republic, a fraternal organization of Union veterans, and contributed to the 1909 history of his regiment. Ten years earlier, he published his only writing about his war experiences, a short essay in his fraternity magazine, "A Phi Psi's Christmas in Libby." Weaver's moving recollections, undimmed in their intensity thirty-six years later, "commingled emotions of joy and sadness," but without rancor. In vivid detail, Weaver traced prisoners' daily tribulations of physical and mental survival as "each one nerved himself to the demands of the hour or the dreaded future" while confined to living among "the general whirlpool of restless humanity." Yet, Weaver's story was one of human resiliency, leavened with humor, as the prisoners carefully prepared a Christmas celebration, jostled for space on the cook stoves, shared food with those who had none, shed tears in recalling Christmases past, danced joyously at an all-male Christmas ball, and participated in late-night ribbing.[16] Weaver received a pension as a Civil War veteran in 1905. He died of heart failure at his home in Greencastle on January 28, 1920, and was buried in Sandusky, Ohio, his widow's hometown.

Appendix

James Riley Weaver, "A Phi Psi's Christmas in Libby," *The Shield of Phi Kappa Psi* (1899)

Though a full generation has passed away since then, the events of that unique Christmas tide have lost none of their vividness, so deeply were they impressed upon memory's tablet. To live them over again brings commingled emotions of joy and sadness; sadness for the dead but joy for the living. The flight of years eases the pain, however, without diminishing the gratification of having participated in such misfortunes.

We had been gathered from all departments of the Union army, captured on many battle fields, or in many an otherwise novel and strange adventure. Colonel Streight and his raiders[1] had been among the first, Gettysburg and the subsequent vicissitudes of the pursuit of Lee south of the Rapidan, had recruited hundreds of officers from the army of the Potomac. Later Chickamauga had added as many more from the army of the Cumberland, and when to these three main divisions scores of unfortunates were gathered from every quarter, of every rank from brigadier to lieutenant, and of every branch of service, naval as well as land forces, the motley character of that crowd of over 1,000 prisoners, consisting exclusively of officers, may be faintly grasped.

Young men largely prevailed, and these were mostly of the line, as only rarely were general or regimental officers exposed to capture. Nearly all nationalities were represented, but the foreigners were principally Germans, Irish, French and Italians. All stations of life from city to hamlet had sent contingents, the cultured and refined, the boor and blackguard, the native patriot and the foreign mercenary. From their external appearance little of their inner life and character could be determined, for worn and faded uniforms by reason of hard actual service, or forced exchanges with the captor's gray, had transformed the enterogeneous [heterogeneous] mass into a most extraordinary motley crowd. We had been confined in the

236

upper two stories of Libby's tobacco warehouse, consisting of triple rooms measuring about 45 feet in width and 150 feet in length, but in addition to these six upper rooms all had access during the day to the middle ground floor, as a common kitchen, supplied with three cooking stoves of ordinary size. That they sufficed in any sense whatever for the demands of our inconveniently overgrown family can only be realized when the extreme paucity of our cuisine is considered.

The novelty of the situation, for most, had long since worn off. Days had multiplied into weeks, and weeks into months since the great majority had been admitted. Prospect of exchange so long deferred had made the heart sick; the chaplains had gone, 'tis true, then the doctors, nearly five score, filed out before our eager hungry eyes bound for God's country, as we, with childlike fervor, expressed it, leaving us still more lonely because of their fortunate parole. Day after day we talked of, waited and prayed for our release, but when the chill of fall turned into the shiver of winter, as the ice closed over the surface of the canal passing by our prison, all grew apprehensive and strangely silent. Every return of the flag of truce boat with supplies from the Christian commission and friends in the North, drove into our souls the iron logic of the necessity of our passing the winter and maybe the entire war in Libby, if not long before that time we should be mustered out of service into the bivouac of the cold and silent dead. Yet few, indeed, murmured or complained, for we knew that the great hearted Lincoln would not willingly or for trivial reasons consign us to such a dire fate; hence each one nerved himself to the demands of the hour or the dreaded future, unknown or unrevealed, for weal or woe, for life or death.

Happy indeed for the human mind that it can at times rise superior to its environments and lay the most adverse circumstances under contribution for its happiness. The nature of the soldier's life naturally prepares him for unfortunate and hard lines, often rendering him insensible to the most imminent danger, so that when the future looks the darkest he acts most recklessly, dances most desperately, and casts most fully his fears to the wind. So it was that Christmas in Libby. Great preparations had been made during all that week, the last confederate money received for the greenbacks taken from us on our arrival, exchanged seven for one, had been sent out for supplies. Chickens, turkeys and the most costly viands[2] in the city had been laid in store without regard to cost. The best of the boxes of good things sent by devoted friends from home had been sacredly preserved for that Christmas dinner, and he that had neither money nor friends grew bold upon that occasion and put comradeship to the hardest and truest test conceivable by borrowing, but really begging, part of his supplies. To this day a certain soldier's heart goes out in profound admiration to a comrade's generous act that day. The luscious ham, received from loved ones, had been carefully preserved and very sparingly partaken of. It may mean death in the future to share it, but when urged by an overpowering need, a comrade modestly begged a little slice for Christmas, the magnanimity with which it was granted made it actually painful to accept, but bound the suppliant to the donor ever afterwards with hooks of steel. The name of Lieutenant Ben Herrington was inscribed from that day above that of Abou Ben Ahdem, for Abou had only loved his fellow man, but never shared his ham in prison with a destitute companion.[3]

But Friday morning dawned at last. It was Christmas. With the first faint streakings of gray we awoke, not to receive our presents in our stockings, but in our noses in the form of smoke. Sleeping late was practically out of the question, not so much on account of the noise as from the impossibility of finding room for one's bed, even if it consisted only of a blanket for covering and a pair of shoes or a coat, if one possessed them, for a pillow. Washing in the common water trough in the corner of each room and letting evaporation take the place of a towel constituted our toilet, and then taking some cold corn bread and washing it down with water drawn from the James river, served as an early appetizer for a hearty dinner. Now followed the daily routine of occupation. Roll call came at 9 A.M., all being crowded into Chickamauga and then counted back into the army of the Potomac,[4] but if the count did not tally, as was frequently the case, the process was repeated until it did, or else we were called off by name, to the mutual disgust of both prisoners and prison officials, but with the happy result that it killed time. That Christmas day, one count sufficed, so we shortly resumed our daily task of walking the floor, playing cards, cribbage, chess or checkers; and such as had books sought a secluded spot near the iron barred windows and strove to concentrate their minds upon the subject. But the noise grew louder and the tobacco smoke grew denser, until the brain swam and the eyes refused to focus, so that the reader soon joined in the general whirlpool of restless humanity. This in the main continued until the hour for preparing dinner, which that day began early and absorbed the greatest attention.

It was late before the cook succeeded, by dint of close watching, to get his pot or pan upon the crowded stoves that day. Even high officers, growing more heated than their utensils, lost their temper and settled by fistic encounters several disputes as to their right of way to a choice hot spot on the stove; so inhuman does man became when subjected to the abnormal restraints of prison life. But to add to our chagrin, that day of all days, we were denied wood sufficient to cook our dinners. In a spell of recklessness stools, tables and whatever could be thus used, were confiscated and consecrated to furnish fuel. At last as the declining sun was sinking to rest our little family party of three and one guest gathered about an unusually rich repast, and with the aid of several confederate tallow dips purchased expressly for the occasion, we commemorated the event of the world's Redeemer, whose life work had been to open rather than to close the doors of prisons. We lingered much longer than usual at our dinner and postprandial[5] speeches, but as we sat there in the ghastly corridors so dimly lighted that every pillar and moving form seemed a weird phantom, we felt almost as if we were disembodied spirits playing at hospitality and good cheer, much as we would in dreams. When the conversation lulled, as it often did, and particularly at mention of exchange or home, it was easy to perceive that our spirits had gone in fancy and were in other climes communing with those we most fondly cherished. Visions of Christmas trees and childish glee, of happy days gone by, came to us again with redoubled intensity because of our present deprivation of them, and in the gravest and most unexpected moment we were startled with the sorrowful plaint of a home-sick child, uttered in deep distress, 'I want to go home.' Though intended for a joke, it was so truthful and earnest as to become too real for mirth, for who of us that Christmas evening was not only home-sick but also childlike and even childish by stress of our environments? Photographs, hidden deftly in old letters, or pocketbooks, were at times produced or furtively glanced at, and moistened eyes or tender voices were passed by, not unobserved, but without remark.

Before the minor chord of one mood could develop into deeper melancholy the sound of instruments,—violin, flute and bones,—came up from the kitchen below, and the shuffling of many feet called us to the ball. By mutual instinct we crowded down into the suffocating room where everything seemed as merry as a marriage ball, but with none of its attendant conventionalities. Our attires were in exact keeping with the surroundings, hatless, sockless and even shoeless, except for the moccasins made of the useless portions of once elegant military overcoats. Upon that floor, not waxed but greased, whirled hundreds of once dignified officers, and of all this motley crew only one form simulated the fair sex, and she was but the coarsest personification of a negress. While many soon grew tired of this coarse frolic, others prolonged it until a late hour.

"Lights out at 9 P.M." had long been the standing rule, but that night we had an extension of two hours time, so that when 11 o'clock told us that our candles must be extinguished, tired and sad we crept away to our contracted sleeping spots—but not yet to sleep. A unique custom had grown up in Libby, which that night was even further emphasized, for the catechism nightly was more in vogue than lullabys or lay-me-downs, and woe to him who had by indiscreet word or act put himself at the mercy of that torturing, merciless crowd of inquisitors. Questions called out publicly to be answered as openly by all conversant with the facts, such as "Who was captured while robbing a hen-roost?" "Who washes his clothes in the soup pot?" "Who has brigadier on the brain?" or scores of others even more personal were resorted to, in enforcing deference to public opinion. The concert of voices responding to the inquiry by giving specific names was a lash of scorpions that but few could disregard.

But the hour of midnight came at last, and the guard's shrill cry of "Twelve o'clock, post number one, and all's well," gradually rang out upon the chilly wintry air; then the unusual tintinnabulation of distant sleigh bells faintly jingling fell like a spell upon the palpitating crowd with such profound effect as to start many a heavy sigh, accompanied by an occasional hot tear. But it was only for a moment, for both were bravely choked down or brushed aside, and the now heavy hearts but recently so gay and frolicsome, found surcease from all their actual sorrows and anticipated woes in the encircling soothing arms of Morpheus.[6]

Thus passed our first and last Christmas in Libby. What a blessed providence that we could not foresee the future, since even the second Christmas found the most of us still prisoners of war in the hands of our captors.

But what a still more blessed providence it is that now, a generation later, so many of us captors and captives remain to see the old animosities forgotten, the fratricidal strife of the early sixties transformed into the grand Republic, united as never before, through a wider diffusion of knowledge of our integral elements, as well as by passing through a fresh baptism of blood in a foreign war, undertaken at the unanimous behest of a righteous and indignant people, to further the teachings of the Prince of Peace.[7]

Chronology

1839

October 21   Born in Youngstown, PA, to John Weaver (1812–86) and Eliza St. Clair Weaver (1810–85).

1850

August 30   James Weaver, 10, living in Unity Township, West-moreland County, PA, with parents, John, 37, and Eliza, 38; siblings Elizabeth, 16; Catherine, 14; John W., 13; Francis A., 8; Jane A., 6; Rebecca, 3; and Amanda, 8 mos.

1856   District schoolteacher, Westmoreland County, PA.

1860–62   Attends Allegheny College, Meadville, PA.

1862

October 21   Enlists as a private in the 18th Pennsylvania Cavalry, Company B, in Meadville, Crawford County, PA.

November 15   Mustered into service at Camp Simmons, Harris-burg, PA.

December 6   Promoted to regimental sergeant major by order of Lt. Col. James Gowen.

December 8   Leaves for Camp Hyatt, Montgomery County, MD.

December 31   18th Pennsylvania Cavalry mustered in as a regiment and assigned to Percy Wyndham's Cavalry Brigade, Defenses of Washington.

1863

January 8   Regiment stationed at Germantown, VA.

January 13–March 15   In winter camps with rotating picket, guard, and scout duties and continued drilling and training.

January 15–March 9   Periodic raids by John S. Mosby's Confederate cavalry.

February 2   Regiment assigned to Col. Richard Butler Pierce's Independent Cavalry Brigade, Department of Washington, 22nd Corps.

March 15–June 24   In camp near Fairfax Court House picketing and scouting.

April 21	Regiment transferred to Maj. Gen. Julius Stahel's Cavalry Division, 2nd Brigade, Department of Washington.
June 1	Begins second volume of his diary. With scouting party at Catlett's Station, VA, along the Orange and Alexandria Railroad.
June 11	Receives AB degree, Allegheny College, after examination by company officers.
June 18	Commissioned second lieutenant, Company C, 18th Pennsylvania Cavalry.
June 19	Stahel's cavalry coordinates movements under Maj. Gen. Joseph Hooker, Army of the Potomac.
June 25	18th Pennsylvania Cavalry crosses Potomac River at Edward's Ferry following General Robert E. Lee's invasion of Maryland and Pennsylvania.
June 28	18th Pennsylvania Cavalry transferred from the Department of Washington to the Army of the Potomac and assigned to 1st Brigade, 3rd Division, under Brig. Gen. H. Judson Kilpatrick.
June 30	Engagement with J. E. B. Stuart's cavalry at Hanover, PA.
July 2	Engagement with Confederate cavalry at Hunterstown, PA.
July 3	Advance on 1st Texas Infantry (General Law's Division) near Round Top, Gettysburg, on the extreme Confederate right.
July 4	Attack on General Richard Ewell's wagon train at Monterey Pass, MD.
July 6 & 12	Engage retreating Confederate soldiers at Hagerstown, MD.
July 8	Skirmish at Boonsboro, MD.
July 14	Capture enemy's rear guard at Falling Waters, MD.
July 17	Cross Shenandoah River at Harper's Ferry.
July 26–August 1	Encamped at Amissville and Warrenton Junction, VA.
August 2–12	Picketing and scouting along lower Rappahannock River in Stafford County, VA.
August 13–September	Return to camp at Warrenton Junction; picketing and scouting along the Rappahannock River in Culpeper and Fauquier Counties.

September 13	Skirmish at Culpeper, VA.
September 14–27	Picketing and occasional skirmishing along Rapidan and Rappahannock Rivers.
September 28–October 8	Camp on Robertson River, Madison County, VA.
October 10	Skirmish at James City, Madison County, VA.
October 11	Battle at Brandy Station; Weaver and thirty-one other men of the 18th Pennsylvania Cavalry captured by the 7th and 12th Virginia Infantry.
October 13	Weaver and other officers arrive at Libby Prison.
December 25	Christmas at Libby with singing, dinner, and a "grand ball."

1864

January 1	New Year's Day with singing and dancing.
February 10	Great Libby Prison escape with 109 fleeing in a tunnel; 48 are recaptured.
February 28–March 3	Kilpatrick-Dahlgren raid on Richmond to free Federal prisoners.
April 1	Promotion to 1st lieutenant, Company C, 18th Pennsylvania Cavalry.
May 7	Departs Libby en route to Danville, VA.
May 8–12	Officers' prison, Danville.
May 17	Arrives in Macon, GA, prison camp.
May 24	Becomes adjutant, 18th Pennsylvania Cavalry.
July 28	Departs Macon for Charleston, SC.
July 29	Arrives at the Charleston Prison.
August 16	Transferred to Marine Hospital, Charleston, on parole.
October 6	Departs for Columbia, SC.
October 7	Arrives in Columbia prison camp.
October 17	Mock election for president held at Columbia prison camp.
December 12	Transferred to Insane Asylum yard, Columbia.

1865

February 14	Leaves Columbia for Charlotte, NC.
February 20	Departs Charlotte toward Wilmington, NC.
February 21	Arrives in Raleigh, NC.
February 24	Learns all prisoners will be paroled at Long Bridge, north of Wilmington, NC.
February 26	Leaves Raleigh.
March 1	Paroled at Long Bridge, NC.
March 3	Departs for Camp Parole, Annapolis, MD, by ship.

	March 7	Arrives at Annapolis quartered in Naval Academy barracks.
	March 13–May 14	On leave of absence as prisoner on parole.
	March 18	Departs for Philadelphia, PA.
	March 22	Departs for Latrobe, PA.
	April 1	Diary ends.
	May 15	Mustered out of service by Special Order No. 189.
	Fall	Attends Methodist General Biblical Institute, Concord, NH.
1866		Attends Garrett Biblical Institute, Evanston, IL; receives a Bachelor of Sacred Theology degree. Awarded AM by Allegheny College, Meadville, PA.
1866–67		Principal, Dixon Seminary, Dixon, Ill.
1867		
	October 9	Breveted first lieutenant, captain, major, and lieutenant colonel of volunteers for "faithful and meritorious service" dating from March 13, 1865.
1867–69		Professor of mathematics and military tactics, commandant of the cadet corps, and part-time librarian, West Virginia University, Morgantown.
1869		
	October 27	Marries Anna Frances Simpson (b. 1846, Greencastle, IN), daughter of Bishop Matthew Simpson, in Philadelphia. President and Mrs. Ulysses S. Grant are among the guests.
	October 29	James and Anna, accompanied by Ellie Simpson and Libbie Simpson, depart for Europe.
	December 6	Appointed consul, Brindisi, Italy.
1870		
	March 4	Appointed consul, Antwerp, Belgium.
	October 11	Vernie Ellen born, London, England.
1871		
	November 15	Ida Blanche born, Antwerp, Belgium.
1879		Appointed consul-general, Vienna; served one year as secretary of the legation and chargé d'affaires.
1885		
	July 1	Returns to Philadelphia. President Alexander Martin, DePauw University, Greencastle, IN, offers position as professor of modern languages and literature.

1886		Appointed professor of modern languages and political philosophy.
1890		Appointed professor of history and political science.
1893		Appointed professor of political science.
1895		
	October 4	Anna Simpson dies in Greencastle, IN.
1897		
	August 30	Marries Emma Matern (b. 1862), member of art department, DePauw University, in Sandusky, OH.
1899		Publishes "A Phi Psi's Christmas at Libby."
1904		Applies for an invalid pension for Civil War veterans from "disability of age."
1912		Appointed professor emeritus and lecturer in political science.
1917		Retires from teaching.
1920		
	January 28	Dies, age 80, of heart failure, in his Greencastle home; buried in Sandusky, OH.
1932		
	March 29	Emma Matern dies in Sandusky, OH. Until her death, she received a Civil War widow's pension of forty dollars per month.

Notes

INTRODUCTION

1. This is the second volume of Weaver's war diary. The first volume covering his enlistment and early training and Weaver's wartime correspondence is lost. Except for going over some penciled entries with ink, Weaver made no alterations or additions to the original entries. The diary is in the James Riley Weaver Papers, Archives and Special Collections, DePauw University, Greencastle, IN.

2. Points first made by Hesseltine, *Civil War Prisons*, which includes a critical annotated bibliography of primary sources. Cloyd, *Haunted by Atrocity*, examines the polemical uses of prison narratives in shaping Civil War memory. For a recent assessment of the politics of imprisonment and prison narratives, see Springer and Robins, *Transforming Civil War Prisons*, 65–69, 80–94.

3. See, for example, Cavada, *Libby Life*, and Glazier, *Capture*.

4. Sanders, *While in the Hands*, blames leaders in both sections, while Hesseltine, *Civil War Prisons*, emphasizes civilians' wartime psychosis arising from hard war. Studies emphasizing the logistical challenges of maintaining wartime prison systems fault both sides; see Speer, *Portals to Hell*; Pickenpaugh, *Captives in Gray*; Pickenpaugh, *Captives in Blue*. For continuation of older debates on which side was more culpable, see Joslyn, *Immortal Captives*, and Gillispie, *Andersonvilles of the North*, who condemn and acquit Union officials, respectively. See Springer and Robins, *Transforming Civil War Prisons*, 117–24, for an excellent assessment of recent scholarship.

5. For Confederate prisons, see Marvel, *Andersonville*; Futch, *History of Andersonville Prison*; Bryant, *Cahaba Prison*; Derden, *World's Largest Prison*; and Cloyd, *Haunted by Atrocity*, which focuses on Andersonville. Even more extensive are studies of Union prisons, including Pickenpaugh, *Camp Chase*; Levy, *To Die in Chicago*; Gray, *Business of Captivity*; Fetzer and Mowday, *Unlikely Allies*; Pickenpaugh, *Johnson's Island*; Treibe, *Point Lookout*; Hall, *Den of Misery*; and McAdams, *Rebels at Rock Island*. All of these works trace prison administration, camp conditions, prisoners' activities, escape attempts, and the prison's closing and aftermath. Gray's study of Elmira is unusual for including the prison's impact on the town's economy and citizens.

6. Wheelan, *Libby Prison Breakout*; Schairer, *Lee's Bold Plan*; and Foote, *Yankee Plague*. Foote's pioneering study examines how escaping prisoners during the war's last year undermined the Confederacy.

7. The median age of enlisted Union soldiers was 23.5 and about one half came from farms. Pennsylvania sent the largest number of soldiers after New York. Weaver was also typical of the 10 percent of Union soldiers who became officers, as about half had white-collar occupations (McPherson, *For Cause and Comrades*, viii, 180, 182). Except for his college education, Weaver fit the profile of soldiers in the 18th PA Cav. Regt., with their median age of 24 and farming as the most common occupation. See Klingensmith, "Statistical Analysis."

8. James Riley Weaver diary, Jan. 12, 1864.

9. Weaver, "Phi Psi's Christmas in Libby."

10. Weaver was breveted lieutenant colonel for "faithful and meritorious service" on Oct. 9, 1867, effective May 13, 1865 (Weaver, Military Service and Pension Records).

1. Smith, *Allegheny,* 178–79, 183–84. Under the Militia Act of July 1862 states were authorized to draft men if they were unable to fill their quotas with volunteers. Recruits, almost all from Crawford Cty., joined Co. B between Sept. 15 and Nov. 26, 1862. Their median age was 24; almost 60 percent were farmers and another 26 percent were skilled workers; over 90 percent were born in the US. Klingensmith, "Statistical Analysis," 2.

2. US Bureau of the Census, *Population Schedules of the Seventh Census of the U.S., 1850, Pennsylvania,* Reel 838, Westmoreland Cty., Unity Twp. (American Library Association, Internet Archive, 1964), https://archive.org/stream/populationschedu0837unix#page/n1/mode/2up/search/unity (accessed Apr. 17, 2018); Boucher, *History of Westmoreland County,* 554–60. In 1860, John Weaver reported owning no real estate and had less than three hundred dollars in personal estate. Two siblings, both boys, joined the Weaver household in the 1850s.

3. Boucher, *Westmoreland County,* 554–60; "James Riley Weaver," *Annals,* 98; James Riley Weaver diary, June 14, 1864.

4. Smith, *Allegheny,* 153 (the reference is to President John Barker); Allegheny College, *Register of Alumni,* 4, 50–56; e-mail from Suzanne Williams, archives assistant, Wayne and Sally Merrick Historic Archives Center, Allegheny College, Meadville, PA, to Wesley Wilson, June, 10, 2015; Weaver, academic record, Allegheny College; Weaver diary, June 11, 1863. Only about one-fifth of the collegiate students graduated each year.

5. Smith, *Allegheny,* 159–65.

6. T. F. Rodenbough, "Historical Sketch," in PA Cav., 18th Regt., *History,* 13–14; Thomas J. Grier, "Itinerary of Service of the Eighteenth Regiment of Cavalry, Pennsylvania Volunteers," in PA Cav., 18th Regt., *History,* entry for Jan. 13, 1863, 35. Duck is heavy cotton fabric used for tenting.

7. Grier, "Itinerary of Service," entries for Jan. 15, 26, 27, 29 (quote) and Mar. 9, 1863, 35–37; Rodenbaugh, "Historical Sketch," 14–15.

8. Cox, *History,* 67; Dept. of Washington, 22nd Army Corps, *The Civil War in the East,* http://civilwarintheeast.com (accessed Mar. 24, 2016). Price's cavalry brigade included the 1st MI, the 5th NY, the 2nd PA, the 1st VT, and the 1st WV Regts. Maj. Gen. Samuel P. Heintzelman commanded the department, which included the counties in VA and MD surrounding Washington, DC.

1. "THE ARTS AND SCENES OF ACTIVE WARFARE"

1. Second lieutenants were platoon leaders who served under the company commander, the first lieutenant. Co. C had been raised in Greene Cty., PA, in Nov. 1862.

2. Theophilus Rodenbaugh, "Historical Sketch," in PA Cav., *History,* 15–16; Thomas J. Grier, "Itinerary of Service of the Eighteenth Regiment," in PA Cav., 18th Regt., *History,* 37–39; Lt. Col. John W. Phillips, "Hanover, Gettysburg, and Hagerstown, in PA Cav., 18th Regt., *History,* 77–79; Capt. H. C. Potter, "The Battle of Hanover," in PA Cav., 18th Regt., *History,* 87–89; James Riley Weaver Diary, June 26, 30, 1863; Klingensmith, "Cavalry Regiment's First Campaign." Excellent studies of the Union cavalry during the Gettysburg Campaign include Starr, *Union Cavalry,* chap. 15–17, and Longacre, *Cavalry at Gettysburg,* chaps. 9, 10, 13–14.

3. Rodenbaugh, "Historical Sketch," 16–17; Grier, "Itinerary," 39–41; Weaver Diary, July 2, 1863. See also Phillips, "Hanover, Gettysburg, and Hagerstown," 79–81; Klingensmith, "Cavalry Regiment's First Campaign," 59–68; Wert, *Gettysburg, Day Three,* 272–80.

4. Weaver Diary, July 4, 1863; Rodenbaugh, "Historical Sketch," 17–18; Grier, "Itinerary," 41–42. See also Phillips, "Hanover, Gettysburg, and Hagerstown," 85–86; Priv. Samuel St. Clair, "The Fight at Hagerstown," in PA Cav., *History,* 94–98; Klingensmith, "Cavalry Regiment's First

Campaign," 68–70. Casualties at Hagerstown were considerably higher than on July 3: eight killed, twenty-one wounded, and fifty-nine missing or captured.

5. Weaver Diary, July 10 and 7, 1863.

6. A station and supply depot in Fauquier Cty., VA, on the Orange and Alexandria Railroad. The only north-south line in central Virginia, the railroad was an essential supply line for both armies. The many encampments and skirmishes near its stations testify to its strategic importance.

7. Francis ("Frank") Asbury Weaver, b. 1842, Weaver's brother; Frank Asbury Arter, Phi Beta Kappa, AM, Allegheny College, 1864. Weaver apparently referred to his brother both by his first and his middle name.

8. Andrew Gregg Curtin, Republican governor of PA, 1861–67.

9. Lt. Samuel Montgomery, Co. C. The outcome of his court-martial is unknown, but he resigned from the service Oct. 23, 1863.

10. Domesticated.

11. Confederate currency.

12. Contraband included any property used by the Confederates—including enslaved workers who supported the war effort—and thus were subject to military seizure.

13. Photograph.

14. Elisha or Ebenezer H. McCall attended Allegheny College in 1863 and 1867.

15. Agnes W. Jack, family friend.

16. Presumably to aid Brig. Gen. Joseph E. Johnston, commander, Dept. of the West, by increasing his available forces to attack Gen. Ulysses S. Grant, who had laid siege to Vicksburg, May 18, 1863, and to relieve Gen. John C. Pemberton's Army of Mississippi holed up in the city. Lee's Army of Northern Virginia was moving west from its camps near Fredericksburg, VA, initiating a second Northern invasion.

17. Eleven soldiers from the 18th PA Cav. died from disease in this camp during June 1863.

18. Col. John S. Mosby, 1st VA Cav., also known as Mosby's Rangers, commanded partisans who operated in northern VA independently of James Ewell Brown (J. E. B.) Stuart's cavalry of the Army of Northern Virginia. Mosby's men were feared by the Federals for their lightning raids into Union-controlled territory and ability to melt into the civilian population. Weaver often misspells Mosby as "Mosbey."

19. Gen. Joseph E. Johnston's forces were in Jackson, MS.

20. Jane ("Jennie") A. Weaver, b. 1844, a sister; John Wesley Weaver, b. 1837, a Methodist minister and a brother.

21. Vicksburg did not fall into Union hands until July 4, 1863.

22. A rural area in western Fairfax Cty., VA.

23. Pvt. Milton Keeler, Co. M, 18th PA Cav., died of disease, Fairfax Hospital, June 5, 1863.

24. On Mar. 3, 1863, Congress authorized conscription when congressional districts failed to fill their military quotas with volunteers. All men aged 20–45 were required to register for the draft.

25. Located at Fairfax Court House.

26. Elizabeth ("Lizzie") St. Clair Weaver, b. 1833, and wife of Ephraim Bruner Jr.

27. Brig. Gen. Robert Ogden Tyler, Art. Reserve, Army of the Potomac.

28. Isabel St. Clair, b. 1840, lived in Laughlintown, Westmoreland Cty., PA. Her father, William St. Clair, was Weaver's mother's brother.

29. Capt. Louis N. Beaudry.

30. Adjt. George W. Nieman's wounding was not recorded in the unit roster. He was replaced by Lt. Guy Bryan Jr., June 12, 1863, who remained with Co. E to the end of the war.

31. Martha ("Mattie") Rebecca Weaver, b. 1847; Amanda ("Carrie") Weaver, b. 1850, sisters.

32. Col. Timothy M. Bryan Jr., US Military Academy, 1853, was appointed colonel, 18th PA Cav., Dec. 24, 1862. Lt. Col. William P. Brinton, 18th PA Cav.

33. On July 21, 1861, and Aug. 28–30, 1862, Confederates routed Union forces near Bull Run Creek, Prince William Cty., VA. Warrenton Junction on the Orange and Alexandria Railroad was a spur line to Warrenton, seat of Fauquier Cty., VA, and south of Catlett Station.

34. Maj. Gen. George Stoneman had been relieved as cavalry commander, Army of the Potomac, after his raid, Apr. 13–May 10, 1863, during the Chancellorsville Campaign. He was in Washington, DC, on medical leave.

35. In Mar. 1863, Hungarian-born Maj. Gen. Julius Stahel was appointed commander, 3rd Div. of Cav., Dept. of Washington (XXII Corps); Col. Richard B. Price, 2nd PA Cav.; Col. Charles H. Town, 1st MI Cav.

36. Bristoe Station, Prince William Cty., VA.

37. Lt. John S. Beazell, commissary/subsistence officer, 18th PA Cav.

38. At the Battle of Brandy Station, Culpeper Cty., VA, June 9, 1863, Maj. Gen. Alfred Pleasonton crossed the Rappahannock River and surprised J. E. B. Stuart's forces protecting Lee's Army of Northern Virginia encamped at Culpepper, VA. This was the largest cavalry battle of the war. Although Stuart held the field and the Federals failed to determine Lee's location, this was the first time the Union cavalry matched the Confederates in fighting ability.

39. Capt. John W. Phillips, Co. B, 18th PA Cav.

40. A bugle call ordering cavalry men to mount their horses and take their place in line.

41. The Rev. William Hunter, professor of Hebrew and biblical literature, Allegheny College, 1857–70. Weaver had arranged to complete the requirements for the AB degree by examination.

42. Dana L. Hubbard attended Allegheny College, 1865.

43. On June 10, 1863, Mosby raided the Union camps at Poolesville, MD, protecting the shallow fords of the Potomac, and routed a company of the 6th MI Cav.

44. On June 8, 1863, President Lincoln created the Dept. of the Susquehanna and the District of the Monongahela, commanded by Maj. Gen. Darius N. Couch and Maj. Gen. William T. H. Brooks, respectively, to defend PA from Lee's army. Couch's hastily trained militiamen slowed Lee's advance, while Brooks defended Pittsburgh and eastern Ohio.

45. Lt. David T. McKay, Co. B, 18th PA Cav., never received the discharge. He was captured, Culpeper, VA, Sept. 13, 1863, and remained a prisoner until Mar. 1, 1865.

46. The *Greensburg* [PA] *Herald,* published by D. W. Shryock, 1859–72.

47. Original text reads: "And while his comrades discharge their felt well shot over his rough mound, I cannot but regret a lot <u>so</u> unfortunate but borne."

48. Sgt. John L. Keys, Co. M, 18th PA Cav., was promoted to regimental sergeant major, June 19, 1863. Corp. Robert B. Fry, Co. F, 18th PA Cav.

49. Adjt. Lt. Guy Bryan Jr., Col. Timothy Bryan's nephew. Lieutenant Bryan was discharged from the 5th NJ Vol. Inf. to accept the adjutant's position in the 18th PA Cav.

50. Maj. Gen. Joseph Hooker, commander, Army of the Potomac, belatedly realizing Lee's intention to invade PA, started moving his forces away from the Rappahannock River. Lee, however, was already near the Potomac River as the Union cavalry had failed to track the movements of Lt. Gen. Richard S. Ewell's II Corps down the Shenandoah Valley.

51. Chantilly, a town in Fairfax Cty., VA.

52. Lt. James W. Smith and Lt. Thomas J. Grier, Co. B, 18th PA Cav., both Allegheny College graduates.

53. To prepare for the coming campaign, the regiment rotated sending men to the sprawling Giesboro Cavalry Depot near Washington, DC, to receive fresh mounts.

54. Maj. Gen. Henry W. Slocum's XII Corps was chasing Lee into Maryland, as Ewell's II Corps had already crossed the Potomac River.

55. Maj. Gen. Winfield S. Hancock replaced Darius Couch as commander, II Corps, after Chancellorsville. Maj. Gen. John Sedgwick commanded the VI Corps.

56. A novice.

57. These cavalry regiments were part of Maj. Gen. David M. Gregg's 2nd Div. The 1st Brigade with Col. John B. McIntosh, commander, included the 1st and the 3rd PA Regt., and the 3rd Brigade with Col. John Irvin Gregg, commander, the 4th and the 16th PA Regt.

58. Allegheny's commencement exercises were canceled because of Lee's invasion of PA. After graduating in 1863 with an AM degree, James H. Thomas entered the military and achieved the rank of captain.

59. Seeking to learn the location of Lee's army, Brig. Gen. Judson Kilpatrick's cavalry encountered Col. Thomas T. Munford's VA cavalry regiments near Aldie, Loudoun Cty., VA. After several charges by each side, Munford withdrew as Federal reinforcements arrived but he had protected the location of Lee's infantry, which was moving toward MD.

60. Edwin S. McChesney, Phi Beta Kappa, AM, Allegheny College, 1865, became a Methodist minister.

61. Quartermaster.

62. Crabbed; irritable or ill-tempered.

63. Catherine S. ("Kate" or "Kitty") Weaver, b. 1835, and wife of Edward Smeltzer.

64. Large officers' tents made of canvas or heavy cotton about 10 x 14 x 8 feet high.

65. Co. C initially fielded 95 men and added two more recruits in early 1863 for a total strength of 97 officers and men. Weaver's total excludes the sick and wounded as well as those without serviceable mounts. The 18th faced similar challenges: only 599 men out of a total strength of 1,224 men participated in the Gettysburg campaign.

66. Merrill carbines, invented by James H. Merrill in 1858, were single-shot, breech-loading weapons firing .54 caliber Minié balls. They were replaced by the superior Burnside carbines, designed by Gen. Ambrose Burnside in 1855, and widely adopted by the Union cavalry. Its special brass cartridge sealed the barrel from overheating.

67. Centerville, Fairfax Cty.; Gainesville and Groveton, Prince William Cty., VA.

68. On June 19, Maj. Gen. Samuel P. Heintzelman, commander, Dept. of Washington, loaned Stahel's cavalry to the Army of the Potomac, which soon became permanent.

69. Enslaved men who successfully fled to Union lines were emancipated. The Union army employed many of them as teamsters, laborers, cooks, and orderlies.

70. Hardtack, a food staple of the Union Army, was a very hard cracker three inches square and up to one half inch thick made of flour and water. Nicknamed "sheet iron crackers" or "teeth dullers," soldiers soaked them in water or fried them in grease to soften them enough to eat.

71. New Baltimore, Fauquier Cty., VA.

72. Archaic for "excepting."

73. Paper currency issued by the Federal government. Southerners accepted them in preference to inflated Confederate currency notes.

74. Waterloo, a village in Fauquier Cty., VA, on the Rappahannock River.

75. Bilious, ill-tempered or wrathful.

76. Determined to learn the location of Lee's infantry, on June 21, 1863, Maj. Gen. Alfred Pleasonton, Cav. Corps, Army of the Potomac, advanced toward J. E. B. Stuart at Upperville, VA, and along on the Ashby's Gap Turnpike. The dismounted Confederate cavalrymen delayed the Union advance and retreated to the gap as most of Lee's army had already crossed the Potomac.

77. Herndon's Station, Orange and Alexandria Railroad; Dranesville, Fairfax Cty., VA.

78. Lt. Ed Gay, 11th PA Inf.

79. Potomac River crossing in Loudoun Cty., VA, about twenty miles east of Harper's Ferry. Because of recent rains, some of the horses had to swim partway across the swollen river and were drowned, but boats rescued all the riders.

80. Villages in western Montgomery Cty., MD.

81. Sugarloaf Mountain (1,282 ft.) near Barnsville was a prominent local landmark.

82. A town in Frederick Cty., MD.

83. Learning that Lee's army had crossed the Potomac, on June 25, Hooker ordered the Army of the Potomac to cross into MD and concentrate at Middleton and at Frederick.

84. Lt. James Wilson Smith, Co. B, 18th PA Cav.

85. Confederate guerillas.

86. Forward-mounted scouts.

87. Stahel's Cav. Div., Dept. of Washington, was transferred to the Army of the Potomac, Maj. Gen. Alfred Pleasonton, Cav. Corps commander. They became the 3rd Div. under Brig. Gen. Hugh Judson Kilpatrick. The 18th PA, 5th NY, 1st VT, and 1st WV Regt. made up the 1st Brigade, commanded by Brig. Gen. Elon J. Farnsworth. Brig. Gen. George Armstrong Custer commanded the 2nd Brigade, composed of the 1st, 5th, 6th, and 7th MI Regts.

88. On June 28, 1863, Maj. Gen. George G. Meade replaced Maj. Gen. Joseph Hooker as commander, Army of the Potomac.

89. Weaver is likely commenting on the 5th NY Cav.'s behavior during Mosby's raid on Fairfax Court House in the early hours of Mar. 9, 1863. Sgt. James F. Ames, a deserter from the 5th NY Cav., guided Mosby's men past the Union picket posts and identified the locations of Union officers. Although the Confederates failed to capture Col. Percy Wyndham, their main target, they seized Brig. Gen. Edwin H. Stoughton, over thirty men, including four soldiers from the 18th PA Cav., and almost sixty horses. Lt. Col. Robert Johnson, commander, 5th NY Cav., fled "in a nude state," hid in an outhouse, and avoided capture.

90. A town in Carroll Cty., MD.

91. A borough in Adams Cty., PA.

92. Portions of the 18th PA Cav., led by Capt. Henry C. Potter, Co. L and M, and Capt. Thaddeus Freeland, Co. E, had been protecting the flanks and rear of Kilpatrick's column and had skirmished with Confederate cavalry prior to the column entering Hanover.

93. The 18th PA Cav. suffered seventy-one casualties at Hanover: five killed, thirty-two wounded, six missing, and twenty-eight captured.

94. On July 1, there was a brief skirmish between Stuart's cavalry and Union cavalry under Maj. Gen. William F. "Baldy" Smith. Confederates set fire to the Carlisle barracks but the engagement delayed Stuart's arrival at Gettysburg. Abbottstown and East Berlin are boroughs in Adams Cty., PA.

95. A borough in Chester Cty., PA.

96. Another false rumor. Although popular with the rank-and-file, Gen. George McClellan's failure to execute coordinated attacks against Robert E. Lee's army at Antietam and his desultory pursuit of Lee as he withdrew to Virginia resulted in Lincoln removing him from command of the Army of the Potomac, Nov. 5, 1862.

97. Co. C and Co. I comprised the 3rd Squad., 2nd Batt., 18th PA Cav. Weaver is describing the Battle of Hunterstown, PA, July 2, 1863.

98. The 18th PA Cav. suffered six casualties in this charge with one killed, four wounded, and one captured.

99. Headed by newly minted Gen. Wesley Merritt, the Regular Brigade consisted of the 6th PA Cav. and the 1st, 2nd, 5th, and 6th US Cav. regiments.

100. Emmitsburg, Frederick Cty., MD, just below the state border with PA. Monterey Pass, an eight-hundred-foot gap through South Mountain in Franklin Cty., PA.

101. A town in Washington Cty., MD.

102. Cavetown and Boonsboro are in Washington Cty., MD. Hagerstown is the county seat.

103. Capt. Samuel Sherer Elder, Batt. E, 4th US Art., US Horse Art. Brigade.

104. Probably Lt. William W. Williams, 5th US Art., killed near Smithburg, MD, July 5, 1863. Weaver provides the only account of his death.

105. A town in Washington Cty., MD.

106. Comprised of the 1st Squad., Co. A and G, and the 2nd Squad. Co. B and H.

107. Capt. William C. Lindsey, Co. A, was cut down by a Rebel trooper. Weaver was probably referring to a local physician's daughter, who, from a window, shot Sgt. Joseph Brown, Co. B, 18th PA Cav., who died four days later. Capt. Enos J. Pennypacker, Co. M, captured and escaped to the regiment; Lt. Henry C. Potter, Co. M, captured, imprisoned, and released Dec. 12, 1864; Lt. William L. Laws, Co. L, captured and died in Richmond prison, Jan. 24, 1864.

108. Brig. Gen. John Buford, commander, 1st Div., Cav. Corps, sought to reach Williamsport before Lee's infantry could cross the Potomac into Virginia, but retreated after Stuart's cavalry recaptured Hagerstown.

109. The 18th PA Cav. suffered fifty-nine casualties at Hagerstown, with seven killed, twenty-four wounded, and twenty-eight captured.

110. Military maneuvers.

111. Battle of Boonsboro, July 8, 1863.

112. A legendary story about seven Christian youths who refused to worship idols and hid in a cave near Ephesus to escape Roman persecution from Emperor Decius. They awoke 180 years later after Christianity had become the established religion of the Roman Empire.

113. After a forty-eight-day siege, Lt. Gen. Joseph E. Pemberton surrendered the city to Maj. Gen. Ulysses S. Grant, July 4, 1863.

114. At the Battle of Funkstown near Hagerstown, July 10, 1863, Buford's cavalry again tried to dislodge the Confederates and prevent Lee's army from crossing the Potomac at Williamsport. After fighting dismounted, the Federals ran low on ammunition by midafternoon and retreated toward Boonsboro.

115. Brig. Gen. Elon J. Farnsworth.

116. Second Battle of Hagerstown.

117. The peace faction of the Northern Democratic Party that opposed Lincoln's war policies, especially conscription and emancipation, and called for negotiating peace with the Confederacy. Republicans accused them of treason.

118. Militia units called to defend PA from invasion were assigned to Gen. Darius Couch's Dept. of the Susquehanna and supported Meade's pursuit of Lee after Gettysburg.

119. These were men in Lee's rearguard, Maj. Gen. Henry Heath's division, who were crossing the pontoon bridge at Falling Waters, Berkeley Cty., WV. Taken by surprise, Union forces captured two thousand prisoners.

120. At a war council, July 12, 1863, only two of Meade's seven senior officers recommended attacking the next day. After personally scouting the Confederate defenses on July 13, Meade ordered a general attack the next morning. By then, most of Lee's army had already crossed the Potomac River.

121. Berlin, now Brunswick, a station on the Baltimore and Ohio Railroad in Frederick Cty., MD.

122. Lt. John S. Coulter, 53rd PA Inf. Vol.

123. On July 8, 1863, Maj. Gen. Nathaniel Banks captured Port Hudson, MS, after a forty-eight-day siege. This gave the Union full control of the Mississippi River. Gen. Joseph E. Johnston, Dept. of the West, failed to attack Grant and lift the siege of Vicksburg. After Maj. Gen. William Rosecrans drove Gen. Braxton Bragg's Army of Tennessee from middle TN, the Confederates retreated across the Tennessee River to Chattanooga.

124. The Union's worst civil disturbance during the war occurred July 13–16, 1863, in New York City and resulted in almost 150 deaths. It started as an antidraft riot by working-class Irish residents with the encouragement of local Democratic politicians. The mob initially targeted the conscription office and homes of wealthy Republicans but soon attacked the city's black community. Troops from the Gettysburg battlefield finally suppressed the four days of violence.

125. Rohrersville, a rural community in Washington Cty., MD; Burkittsville, a town in Frederick Cty., MD.

126. Confederate cavalry occupied the fords at Shepherdstown to block Union forces from

crossing the Potomac River and attacked David Gregg's approaching cavalry, who withdrew at nightfall. Charles Town is the county seat of Jefferson Cty., WV, where John Brown was tried and executed, Dec. 2, 1859.

127. A tree native to the eastern US that produces a yellow-green to brown fruit.

128. A town in Loudoun Cty., VA.

129. A town in Loudoun Cty., VA.

2. "SLEPT TO DREAM OF WAR BUT WOKE TO FIND ALL QUIET"

1. James Riley Weaver Diary, Aug. 25, 8, 1863.

2. Thomas J. Grier, "Itinerary of Service of the Eighteenth Regiment," in PA Cav., *History*, 42–44; Henderson, *Road to Bristoe Station*, 36–41. In Aug., Gen. Henry E. Davis Jr., took command of the 1st Brigade, replacing Brig. Gen. Elon J. Farnsworth, who was killed at Gettysburg on July 3. The 2nd NY replaced the 1st VT in the 1st Brigade.

3. Weaver Diary, Oct. 11, 1863; Grier, "Itinerary," 43–44; Glazier, *Capture*, 30–32; Brig. Gen. Henry E. Davis Jr. to Capt. L. G. Estes, Oct. 21, 1863, in US War Dept., *War of the Rebellion*, ser. 1, vol. 29, pt. 1, chap. 41, 384–86; Henderson, *Road to Bristoe Station*, 78–81, 90–102.

4. T. F. Rodenbaugh, "Historical Sketch," in PA Cav., *History*, 19–30; Grier, "Itinerary," 44–71; Klingensmith, "Cavalry Regiment's First Campaign," 74n172. Klingensmith tallies 302 men in the 18th who died with 44 percent of the deaths in Southern prisons. The 18th's greatest humiliation occurred at Germanna Ford, Nov. 18, 1863, when most of the regiment was out on scout and the Confederate cavalry attacked, overran the camp, seized fifty prisoners, and carried off equipment including the regimental flag. The latter turned up in the Virginia capital in Apr. 1865 and was eventually returned and displayed in the museum of the Military Service Institution, Governor's Island, NY.

5. A 1,056-foot gap between Loudoun and Clarke Ctys., VA, with a turnpike connecting the northern VA Piedmont with the Shenandoah Valley.

6. 2nd Lt. Samuel H. Thresonthick, Co. E, 18th PA Cav.

7. Priv. Charles M. Keller, Co. I, 18th PA Cav. This is the first account of Keller's death.

8. Upperville, a village in Loudoun Cty., VA, now Bluemont, located at the base of Snicker's Gap.

9. A village in Fauquier Cty.; Ashby Gap is on the border of Clarke, Loudoun, and Fauquier Ctys., VA.

10. Manassas Gap is the lowest pass (887 feet) through the Blue Ridge Mountains between Fauquier and Warren Ctys., VA.

11. Piedmont Station, now Delaplane, Fauquier Cty., on the Manassas Gap Railroad that ran from Manassas Junction on the Orange and Alexandria Railroad to Mt. Jackson in the Shenandoah Valley. Orleans is in Fauquier Cty.; Amissville, in Rappahannock Cty., VA.

12. The 2nd Brigade comprised the 3rd Squad., Co. C and I, and the 4th Squad., Co. D and K.

13. Gen. George A. Custer's MI Brigade attacked General Longstreet's and Gen. A. P. Hill's corps as they traveled through Chester Gap toward Culpeper Court House. Vastly outnumbered, the Federals soon withdrew.

14. Col. Othniel DeForest, 5th NY Cav.

15. The 18th PA Cav. received only 105 new recruits in 1863 and remained severely understrength until 1864 when they added 567 men. The roster lists no draftees in 1863 and only 14 in 1864, and 42 in 1865.

16. Weaver was likely suffering from poison ivy while picking blueberries.

17. A US Army bugle call signaling "lights out" and cease loud talking in fifteen minutes when "Taps" is then played.

18. Men paid by draftees to serve in their place.

19. QM Sgt. William H. McGlumphey; Corp. Francis Clutter, Co. C; both 18th PA Cav.

20. The cavalry under Gen. Samuel Peter Heintzelman, commander, Dept. of Washington, XXII Corps, had been transferred to the Army of the Potomac on June 28, 1863, just before the Battle of Gettysburg. The department's headquarters was in Fairfax, VA.

21. A soldier's first battle.

22. Brig. Gen. David M. Gregg, commander, 2nd Div., Cav. Corps.

23. David L. McCullough, b. 1819, d. July 15, 1863. He served as chief burgess, Latrobe Borough, Westmoreland Cty., PA, and enlisted in 135th PA Inf. from Aug. 14, 1862, to May 24, 1863.

24. Warrenton was the headquarters of the Army of the Potomac. Maj. Gen. John Sedgwick commanded the VI Corps.

25. Capt. Andrew Cunningham, Co. D, 18th PA Cav.

26. The county seat of Stafford Cty., VA, about ten miles north of Fredericksburg.

27. A town in Stafford Cty. on the north back of the Rappahannock River across from Fredericksburg.

28. The Army of the Potomac had occupied this area in Nov. and Dec. 1862 during the Fredericksburg Campaign.

29. Rappahannock Station, now Remington, Fauquier Cty., VA, on the Orange and Alexandria Railroad. Aquia Creek, a tributary of the Potomac River; Aquia Creek Landing, Stafford Cty., VA, was the Army of the Potomac's supply line.

30. Part of the Potomac River Flotilla patrolling the Rappahannock River for Confederate smugglers and supporting Federal forces.

31. A struggle between two opposing forces.

32. Aquia Episcopal Church, Stafford Cty., VA, a brick structure built in the 1750s.

33. Maj. William B. Darlington joined the 18th PA Cav. on Jan. 7, 1863. He was wounded, lost a leg, and captured, Mine Run, VA, May 5, 1864.

34. Catherine S. Weaver; Francis A. Weaver.

35. A tidal creek in King George and Stafford Ctys., VA, entering the Potomac at Marlboro Point.

36. Capt. David K. Hamilton, Co. K, 18th PA Cav.

37. Tension or irritation.

38. Lt. Samuel Montgomery, Co. C, 18th PA Cav.

39. Capt. John W. Phillips, Co. B, 18th PA Cav. Wounded at Gettysburg, Phillips did not receive his promotion until Apr. 8, 1864. He was captured near Cedar Creek, VA, Nov. 12, 1864, and confined in Libby prison.

40. Located in southwestern PA bordering Ohio to the west and WV to the south.

41. Lt. James C. Golden, QM, 18th PA Cav.

42. The *Greensburg* [PA] *Herald.*

43. Drafted men could pay a three-hundred-dollar commutation fee to hire a substitute and avoid the draft. Andrew Gregg Curtin, Republican, won a second term as governor of PA that fall.

44. Hartwood Presbyterian Church (1856–58), Stafford Cty., VA, a brick Greek Revival–style structure.

45. On Aug. 12, 1863, the 2nd NY Vol. Cav. replaced the 1st VT in the 1st Brigade, 3rd Div. The brigade also included the 5th NY and the 1st WV, in addition to the 18th PA. Weaver was unaware that the 1st VT was being replaced.

46. Located in southwestern PA bordering Ohio to the west.

47. Reveille, a morning bugle call generally at sunrise.

48. Lt. Benjamin F. Austin, Co. H; Lt. Col. William P. Brinton; Capt. Peter Wise, Co. I, 18th PA Cav. Brinton was promoted to Lt. Col., 18th PA Cav. on Mar. 1, 1863. Wise received a medical discharge on Aug. 27, 1863.

49. Extreme depression.

50. Corp. Reuben Saunders, Co. C, 18th PA Cav.

51. Hemorrhoids.

52. Priv. Thomas Poland, Co. C, 18th PA Cav. On July 5, there was a skirmish between the 18th and Confederate cavalry at Smithsburg, MD. Poland was presumed captured and died while imprisoned in Richmond, VA, probably in 1863.

53. Malaria or other illness involving fever and chills.

54. A station on the Orange and Alexandria Railroad in Fauquier Cty., VA.

55. 1st Lt. David T. McKay, Co. B; Lt. James C. Golden, regimental QM, both 18th PA. Cav. The charges against Golden were apparently dropped as he remained with the regiment until his muster out on July 21, 1865.

56. Col. Henry E. Davies, 2nd NY Vol. Cav. Regt., was promoted to Brig. Gen., 1st Brigade, 3rd Cav. Div.

57. Charles E. Hall, AM, Allegheny College, 1864; S. J. Hayes, principal and professor of mathematics and natural sciences, Ligonier Academy and Normal School.

58. The throne of God.

59. Union soldiers' affectionate name for Abraham Lincoln.

60. Ecclesiastes 11:1.

61. S. M. Grannis (music) and Caroline A. Masion (lyrics), "Do They Miss Me at Home?" (Boston: Oliver Ditson, 1852).

62. Sgt. Maj. John L. Keys was wounded by a shot through the right knee and leg fracture when his horse fell on him.

63. Capt. Abram H. Krom, 5th NY Cav.

64. Bonuses paid by the federal, state, and local governments to encourage volunteering and avoid conscripting unwilling men into military service.

65. Popular outdoor religious gatherings that lasted several days with participants camping nearby.

66. Capt. A. J. Cohn, assistant adjutant general, Maj. Gen. Alfred Pleasonton's staff.

67. Maj. Harvey B. Van Voorhis, 18th PA Cav.

68. Capt. Marshall S. Kingsland, Co. G, 18th PA Cav.

69. A rural community in Westmoreland Cty., PA.

70. Fort Sumter in Charleston harbor and Fort Wagner, a beachhead fortification on Morris Island. On Aug. 26, 1863, the 24th MA Inf. captured Wagner's advance rifle pits and the Confederates abandoned the fort, Sept. 6, 1863. Two days later the Federals, firing from Fort Wagner, reduced Fort Sumter to rubble but failed to capture it.

71. 1st Lt. Thomas P. Shields, Co. G, 18th PA Cav.

72. Sgt. Martin V. Supler, Co. C, 18th PA Cav., received a gunshot to the left arm, Aug. 31, 1863, while on picket at Porcher's Dam, VA. He survived the war and died in 1908.

73. Privs. Jonas M. Ross, Oliver W. Beatty, John Ferguson, Co. K, 23rd PA Inf.

74. King George Cty., VA, located between the Rappahannock and Potomac Rivers.

75. Gen. Quincy Adams Gillmore, commander, Dept. of the South, and noted artillerist, attacked Charleston in July 1863 with two failed assaults against Fort Wagner, Morris Island.

76. On Aug. 28, 1863, Brig. Gen. Hugh Judson Kilpatrick led a cavalry force, which included the 18th PA Cav. and two artillery batteries, to destroy two Union gunboats, the USS *Satellite* and the USS *Reliance*, captured by Lt. John Taylor Wood's forces, Aug. 12, 1863. The Confederates had taken their prizes to Port Conway, VA, on the Rappahannock River to dismantle the machinery and engines where the Federals found and destroyed them.

77. Mollie Reads/Reids/Reeds, Meadville, PA, home to Allegheny College.

78. Ballad's or Ballard's dam, Spotsylvania and Stafford Ctys., VA.

79. A shallow river in northeastern Italy that marked Italy's boundary in the Roman Republic. Julius Caesar's crossing the river with his legion in 49 BCE challenged the authority of

appointed governors and the Roman Senate. "Crossing the Rubicon" means committing to a risky course of action, or the "point of no return."

80. Fort Sumter, Charleston, SC.

81. Possibly Samuel Gilson Lightcap, farmer, stockman, and justice of the peace, Unity Twp., Westmoreland Cty.

82. Probably Alexandre Dumas, *The Conscript: A Tale of the Empire* (1855), or John Ripon, *The Conscript, a Serio-Comic Romance* (1807).

83. Agnes W. Jack, a friend.

84. Priv. Philip Gump, Co. C, 18th PA Cav., continued to serve in the regiment and received a medical discharge on May 22, 1865, for a wound at Cedar Creek, VA, Oct. 19, 1864.

85. Sutlers were civilian merchants licensed by military commanders to sell food, drink, and supplies to soldiers from tents or wagons.

86. After devastating shelling by Gillmore's artillery, the Confederates abandoned batteries Gregg and Wagner, Sept. 6, 1863, but Charleston, defended by Gen. Pierre G. T. Beauregard, Dept. of SC, GA, and FL, did not surrender until Feb. 17, 1865.

87. Four days after Maj. Gen. William S. Rosecran's Army of the Cumberland crossed the Tennessee River, Sept. 4, 1863, Gen. Braxton Bragg abandoned Chattanooga.

88. A Rappahannock River crossing between Culpeper and Fauquier Ctys., VA.

89. After learning Gen. Lee had sent two divisions of Lt. Gen. James Longstreet's corps to reinforce Bragg's Army of Tennessee in early Sept. 1863, Maj. Gen. Alfred Pleasonton's Union cavalry left their camps near Warrenton, VA, crossed the Rappahannock River, and probed Lee's Army of Northern Virginia encamped along the Rapidan River.

90. Brig. Gen. John Buford commanded the 1st Div., Cav. Corps.

91. Union and Confederate cavalry forces skirmished at Culpeper Court House on Sept. 13, 1863. Gen. George Armstrong Custer's Michigan Brigade ousted J. E. B. Stuart's horsemen from the railroad depot as other columns occupied the town. By nightfall heavy skirmishing drove the Confederate cavalry south across the Rapidan River (Report of Brig. Gen. Henry E. Davis, Sept. 12, 1863, in US War Dept., *War of the Rebellion*, pt. 1, chap. 41, 120–23).

92. McKay remained a prisoner until Mar. 1, 1865.

93. Alternate name for Rapidan River.

94. The Confederate signal station on Clark Mountain south of the Rapidan River.

95. Maj. Gen. George B. Meade, commander, Army of the Potomac, planned to attack Lee's right flank south of Fredericksburg.

96. Capt. Augustus Barker, Co. M, 5th NY Cav.

97. On Sept. 9, 1863, Hood's and Johnson's provisional divisions from Longstreet's I Corps were sent to Bragg's Army of Tennessee. Gen. George Pickett commanded the Dept. of Southern VA and NC.

98. Maj. William Wells; Josiah Hall, 1st VT Cav.

99. An excerpt from "Knitting Socks," *Boston Evening Transcript*, Nov. 27, 1861.

100. Berea Baptist Church northwest of Falmouth, VA, founded 1852.

101. Chinquapins or chestnuts.

102. In two days of heavy fighting at the Battle of Chickamauga, Sept. 19–20, 1863, Bragg's reinforced Army of Tennessee soundly defeated Maj. Gen. William S. Rosecrans, commander, Army of the Cumberland, and forced his retreat back to Chattanooga, but Bragg missed an opportunity to smash the Union Army.

103. Vexing or disappointing.

104. On Sept. 22, Union cavalry advanced toward Madison Court House, VA, and were met by Confederate cavalry at Jack's Shop, now Rochelle. J. E. B Stuart's forces barely escaped capture.

105. Capt. John Britton, Co. F, 18th PA Cav.

106. A rural hamlet in Madison Cty., VA, now Leon, on the extreme Union right by the Robinson River.

107. Weaver had been promoted to 2nd Lt., Co. C, June 18, 1863, from rank of Sgt. Maj. The difference in pay was significant: a sergeant major earned $21 per month while a second lieutenant received $105.50.

108. Curtin was reelected to a second term Nov. 13, 1863, with a 15,000-vote Republican majority. The election was seen as a referendum on PA's support for the war.

109. On Sept. 24, 1863, three divisions from the XI and the XII Corps under Maj. Gen. Joseph E. Hooker were sent to TN to reinforce General Rosecrans's Army of the Cumberland.

110. Probably Lt. James Wilson Smith, Co. B, 18th PA Cav.

111. He resigned Oct. 23, 1863.

112. 2nd Lt. Samuel H. McCormick, Co. I, 18th PA Cav., was promoted from first sergeant on June 18, 1863.

113. Weaver needed to secure a discharge as sergeant major so he could accept a commission as second lieutenant. Enlisted men and officers entered military service under different contracted terms, as the former enlisted for a specified time, such as three years or the war's duration, while the latter could resign their commission at any time.

114. After learning Meade had sent three divisions to TN, Lee ordered Stuart's cavalry to probe the Union's right flank north of the Rapidan River.

115. Priv. Thomas Poland; see entry for Aug. 18, 1863.

116. Brig. Gen. Henry Prince's 2nd Div., Maj. Gen. William H. French, III Corps.

117. Corp. Dennis Murphy, Co. C, 18th PA Cav. was hospitalized from July to Dec. 1863 when he rejoined the regiment. Sgt. Martin V. Supler was wounded Aug. 31, 1863, and discharged Mar. 11, 1864.

118. A town in WV's eastern panhandle. Lee's army was moving toward Cedar Mountain, Culpeper Cty., VA, attempting to turn Meade's right flank.

119. Nickname for Confederate soldiers.

120. Hampton's Div., commanded by J. E. B. Stuart; Fitzhugh Lee's Div., commanded by Maj. Gen. Fitzhugh Lee.

121. Brig. Gen. George A. Custer's MI Brigade.

122. These units belonged to Hampton's Div.: The 1st NC, Gordon's brigade, and the 7th and the 12th VA, Jones's brigade, commanded by Cols. R. H. Dulaney and A. W. Harman, respectively.

123. Total casualties for the 18th PA Cav. at the Third Battle of Brandy Station included two killed, seven wounded, and twenty-seven captured.

3. "WHAT A LITTLE WORLD IN ITSELF HAVE WE IN LIBBY"

1. Hesseltine, *Civil War Prisons*, chaps. 5–6; Sanders, *While in the Hands*, chaps. 6–7; Pickenpaugh, *Captives in Blue*, chap. 5.

2. Speer, *Portals to Hell*, 89–92, 122–24; Zombek, "Libby Prison"; Parker, *Richmond's Civil War Prisons*, chap. 4.

3. Cloyd, *Haunted by Atrocity*, chap. 1; Glazier, *Capture*, chaps. 2, 3, and 18.

4. James Riley Weaver Diary, Oct. 15, Dec. 2, 1863; Bryne, "Libby Prison," 430–44; Kutzler, "Captive Audiences," 239–63.

5. Maj. Harvey B. Van Voorhis, 18th PA Cav., received a gunshot wound in his arm that required amputation.

6. Lt. Harry Wilson, Co. H, 18th PA Cav.

7. A railroad town in Orange Cty. at the junction of the Orange and Alexandria and the Virginia Central Railroads.

8. Brig. Gen. Hugh Judson Kilpatrick, 3rd Div., Cav. Corps, Army of the Potomac.

9. Lacking sufficient gold reserves and unwilling to impose heavy taxes, the Confederate

government paid for the war by printing paper money, which led to hyperinflation. Southern civilians preferred Union paper currency or greenbacks over their own rapidly depreciating currency.

10. Lts. David T. McKay, Co. B, captured, Culpeper Court House, Sept. 13, 1863; Henry C. Potter, Co. L, captured, Hagerstown, MD, July 6, 1863; Joseph L. Leslie, Co. D, captured near Stafford Court House, Aug. 3, 1863; William L. Laws, Co. L, captured, Hagerstown, July 6, 1863, 18th PA Cav.; Edward H. Gay, 11th PA Inf.

11. Prison currency exchanges were set below market rates. By fall 1863, it took about fifteen Confederate dollars to purchase one dollar in gold. See note 78 (page 261).

12. Lt. Samuel H. McCormick, Co. I, 18th PA Cav.

13. Body lice.

14. An open encampment for enlisted prisoners on Belle Island in the James River at Richmond.

15. Latrines.

16. Maj. Gen. George G. Meade responded to Gen. Robert E. Lee's northward movement on the Union's right flank by withdrawing along the Orange and Alexandria Railroad to Centreville, Fairfax Cty., VA.

17. Taught by Rev. Louis N. Beaudry, chaplain, 5th NY Cav.

18. Eight issues of the *Libby Chronicle,* edited by Beaudry, were produced starting in Aug. 1863 and were read aloud. A selection of poems, songs, essays, and jokes was published in Glazier, *Prison Life in the South,* 310–29, and in Beaudry, *Libby Chronicles.*

19. Minstrelsy, a popular form of entertainment, with white men in blackface performing humorous, satirical songs and jokes that caricaturized blacks. The Libby Minstrels performed the "Libby Ironical," a burlesque on the *Libby Chronicle,* and imitation roll calls.

20. The Confederate released eight chaplains Oct. 7, 1863, including Oliver Taylor, 5th MI Cav.; Louis N. Beaudry; Joseph T. Brown, 6th MD Inf.; George H. Hammer, 12th PA Cav.; Edward C. Ambler, 67th PA Inf.; David Eberhard, 87th PA Inf.; James Harvey, 110th Ohio Inf.; and Ebenezer W. Brady, 116th Ohio Inf. A ninth chaplain, Charles C. McCabe, 122nd Ohio Inf., was sick in the hospital and remained in captivity.

21. On Oct. 14, 1863, Maj. Gen. Gouverneur K. Warren's II Corps hiding behind the Orange and Alexandria Railroad embankment at Bristoe Station, Prince William Cty., VA, ambushed Gen. Ambrose Powell Hill's corps as the Confederates were attacking the rear Federal guard. This Union victory ended Lee's offensive campaign, although Meade continued retreating to Centreville. Brig. Gen. David M. Gregg's 2nd Div. participated in the battle.

22. Wounded during the first day at Gettysburg, Brig. Gen. Sullivan A. Meredith was the Union exchange agent stationed at Fortress Monroe, VA.

23. The Rev. John McGill, bishop of Richmond, 1850–72.

24. Dr. William P. Rucker, a Virginia Unionist, was held in VA on charges of murder and horse stealing. When the Confederates refused to release him, Union authorities held a Southern surgeon in retaliation. The matter was settled when Rucker escaped from prison Oct. 18, 1863.

25. Capt. Enos J. Pennypacker, Co. M, 18th PA Cav., captured Oct. 19, 1863, Buckland Mills, VA.

26. In fact, Maj. Gen. Nathaniel P. Banks, commander, Dept. of the Gulf, XIX Corps, had captured Port Hudson, LA, July 9, 1863, after a long siege.

27. A prison in Richmond holding Confederate deserters, Southern Unionists, Northern civilians, and political prisoners.

28. Andrew Curtin, Republican, and John Brough, War Democrat running under the Union label, governors of PA and OH, respectively, were strong supporters of the Lincoln administration.

29. Lee dispatched Brig. Gen. John D. Imboden to attack the Union garrison at Charlestown, WV. At dawn on Oct. 18, 1863, Imboden's cavalry surprised the outnumbered Federals

and seized the town and almost four hundred prisoners before withdrawing as Union reinforcements arrived.

30. The US Christian Commission, a private organization formed in 1861, sent volunteers to solders' camps and distributed Bibles and religious tracts.

31. After the decisive Confederate victory at Chickamauga in late Sept., Gen. Braxton Bragg's Army of Tennessee laid siege to Maj. Gen. William Rosecrans's Union forces in Chattanooga. On Oct. 23, General Grant, commander of the new Military Div. of the MS, arrived to take personal charge of the military operations there.

32. A minstrel show.

33. Lt. Charles P. Potts, Co. I, 151st PA Inf., captured, Gettysburg, July 1, 1863.

34. Wounded during an assault on Port Hudson, LA, then captured June 30, 1863, Brig. Gen. Neal Dow, commander, 1st Brigade, 2nd Div., XIX Corps, was the highest-ranking officer at Libby. He often gave temperance lectures to the inmates.

35. On Oct. 27, 1863, Maj. Gen. Joseph Hooker's reinforced Union forces opened up the "cracker line" to relieve Chattanooga then under Confederate siege. Gen. James Longstreet failed to dislodge the Federals in the Battle of Wauhatchie the following night.

36. Virginia's leading newspaper, the *Richmond Enquirer,* edited by O. Jennings Wise, was closely allied with the Democratic Party and strongly supported Confederate independence and the war effort.

37. The US Sanitary Commission, a private relief organization organized in 1861, provided food, clothing, medical supplies, and care for wounded, sick, and imprisoned Union soldiers.

38. Richard Baxter (1615–90), *The Saints' Everlasting Rest; or, A Treatise of the Blessed State of the Saints in their Enjoyment of God in Glory* (1650; repr., 1831). Baxter, a prominent Puritan minister and theologian, broke from strict Calvinism by arguing that Christ's death offered universal redemption to all who repented and had faith.

39. Samuel G. Lightcap, a friend; Ephraim Brunner Jr., Elizabeth Weaver's husband.

40. Union forces from the Army of the Cumberland at Chattanooga had united with Hooker's soldiers from Gen. Oliver O. Howard's XI Corps and Gen. John W. Geary's 2nd Div., XII Corps, who moved up the Tennessee River to secure the "cracker line" and break Bragg's siege of the city.

41. On Oct. 27, 1863, Union batteries on Morris Island under Maj. Gen. Quincy A. Gillmore, Dept. of the South, resumed shelling Fort Sumter in Charleston Harbor.

42. Relating to medicine; from Asclepius, the Greek god of medicine.

43. Asst. Surgeon Harvey Lindsley Pierce, 5th MD Inf., captured June 15, 1863, Winchester, VA, and killed by Libby prison guards Nov. 5, 1863.

44. Nickname for newly arriving prisoners.

45. Adjt. Lt. Guy Byran Jr., 18th PA Cav.

46. Lt. Col. William Irvine, 10th NY Cav.

47. Lee planned to make the Rappahannock River his defensive line, but at dusk on Nov. 7, 1863, Maj. Gen. John B. Sedgwick's infantry overran Brig. Gen. Harry T. Hay's La. Brigade and Col. Archibald C. Godwin's Hoke's Brigade, who were protecting the pontoon bridge at Rappahannock Station (modern Remington). Federals captured 1,600 prisoners, including Godwin. Maj. Gen. William H. French's forces secured Kelly's Ford five miles downstream.

48. Lincoln wrote Maj. Gen. Henry W. Halleck, "If Gen. Meade can now attack him [Lee] on a field no worse than equal for us, and will do so with all the skill and courage, which he, his officers and men possess, the honor will be his if he succeeds, and the blame may be mine if he fails" (Lincoln to Halleck, Oct. 16, 1863, Abraham Lincoln Papers, series 1: General Correspondence, 1833–1916, Library of Congress, https://www.loc.gov/item/mal2727000).

49. Attributed to Lord George Gordon Byron (1788–1824).

50. On Nov. 3, 1863, the Union ticket swept every election for state offices by 29,000 votes and secured overwhelming control of both houses of the NY state assembly.

51. Probably Lt. Willard W. Glazier, 2nd NY Cav., captured Oct. 18, 1863, at Buckland Mills, VA.

52. Brig. Gen. William W. Averell moved into southwestern VA to block traffic on the Virginia and Tennessee Railroad. He defeated Confederate forces under Brig. Gen. John Echols at the Battle of Droop Mountain on Nov. 6, 1863, and secured WV for the Union.

53. The Right Rev. John Johns, episcopal bishop of VA, frequently preached in Confederate camps and at Libby Prison.

54. At a minor skirmish in Greeneville, TN, on Nov. 6, 1863, Confederate forces dispersed and captured prisoners from the 7th Ohio Cav., Army of the Ohio, XXIII Corps, under Maj. Gen. Ambrose E. Burnside's command.

55. See chap. 5 introduction for background on the Danville prison.

56. Rev. George H. Hammer, chaplain, 12th PA Cav., "Union Prisoners in Richmond. Brutal Treatment by the Rebels. Our Men Are Starved to Death. Horrible Life in Libby Prison," *Philadelphia Inquirer,* Nov. 6, 1863. The article excoriated Confederate officials for their harsh treatment of Union prisoners, especially African American soldiers.

57. Lt. Samuel H. Tresonthick, Co. E, 18th PA Cav.

58. Mental depression.

59. Maj. Thomas P. Turner, Libby commandant.

60. Agnes Jack, a friend.

61. Adjt. Guy Bryan Jr., Asst. Surgeon Dr. George W. Withers, and Lt. Benjamin F. Herrington, Co. G, 18th PA Cav. The camp was overrun Nov. 18, 1863, near Germanna Ford on the Rapidan River. Fifty men, the regimental colors, and their equipment were captured while most of the regiment was out on scout (Report of Brig. Gen. Henry E. Davis Jr., Nov. 18, 1863, US War Dept., *War of the Rebellion,* part 1, 656–58).

62. Maj. William B. Darlington, 18th PA Cav. His leg was amputated at the hip while he was held captive for seven weeks. He was rescued by Gen. Philip Sheridan and discharged Oct. 3, 1864.

63. Probably Lt. William H. Jones, Co. M, 18th PA Cav., dismissed Jan. 4, 1864. Lt. Thomas P. Shields, Co. G, 18th PA Cav., captured, Hanover, PA, June 30, 1863, exchanged soon afterwards, and discharged Oct. 22, 1863, by surgeon's certificate.

64. Lt. Samuel Montgomery, Co. C, 18th PA Cav., resigned Oct. 23, 1863.

65. Lt. Roseberry Sellers, Co. A, killed; Capt. Marshall S. Kingsland, Co. G, 18th PA Cav., wounded, Germanna Ford, VA, Nov. 18, 1863.

66. "In the shade," marking their condition unimportant as compared to the 2nd NY.

67. Officers from the 18th included Lts. Samuel H. Tresonthick, Harry Wilson, Henry C. Potter, David T. McKay, Joseph L. Leslie, William L. Laws, James R. Weaver, Thomas P. Shields; Capts. Enos J. Pennypacker and Thaddeus S. Freeland; and Asst. Surgeon George W. Withers. Prisoners from the 2nd NY Cav. included Maj. Samuel McGuin; Capts. Henry H. Mason and Charles Hasty; and Lts. Henry Temple, Peter O. Jones, Butler Coles, Alexander Schaffer, Thomas Higgins, William H. Nyce, Willard W. Glazier, George C. Houston, and John A. Richardson.

68. Gen. James Longstreet, in fact, had failed to cut off Ambrose Burnside's retreat to Knoxville and settled into an unsuccessful siege of the city.

69. Col. Abel Streight, 51st IN Inf., led a Union raid into the Confederacy that aimed to destroy the Western and Atlantic Railroad supplying the Confederate Army of Tennessee. Leaving Nashville on Apr., 19, 1863, Streight and his 1,700-man force were captured May 3, 1863, near Cedar Bluff, AL, by Brig. Gen. Nathan Bedford Forrest. The Union officers were taken to Libby.

70. Acid indigestion.

71. An exchange point on the James River in Prince George Cty., VA.

72. Maj. Harry White, 67th PA Inf.

73. Confederate currency.

74. Attentive listening.

75. On Nov. 23, 24, and 25, 1863, Union forces successfully occupied Confederate positions at Orchard Knob, Missionary Ridge, and Lookout Mountain outside Chattanooga, forcing Bragg to withdraw across Chickamauga Creek into GA. Meanwhile, Longstreet failed to dislodge Burnside from Knoxville.

76. Pressured to attack Lee's Army of Northern Virginia, on Nov. 26, 1863, Meade's Army of the Potomac rapidly moved toward the Rapidan River, hoping to surprise Lee's right flank. This initiated the Mine Run Campaign.

77. On Nov. 11, 1863, Gen. Benjamin F. Butler replaced Brig. Gen. John G. Foster as commander, Dept. of VA and NC, headquartered at Fortress Monroe, Norfolk, VA.

78. Gold was priced in terms of paper currency; here, a $1 gold coin was worth $1.475 in greenbacks.

79. Union prisoners in Richmond hoped a raid by Gen. Judson Kilpatrick's cavalry would free them.

80. Maj. Gen. Robert C. Schenck, commander, VIII Corps, headquartered in Harper's Ferry, part of the Union defenses of Washington, DC. An Ohio politician, he resigned from the army in Dec. 1863 and was reelected to Congress.

81. On Nov. 30, 1863, Lt. Gen. William Hardee replaced Bragg, who had resigned as commander, Army of Tennessee.

82. Weaver accurately summarizes Lincoln's refusal to resume prisoner exchanges: the Confederate's exclusion of African American soldiers from parole, a belief that some paroled Confederates had returned to their units before exchange, and the calculus that the Union could more easily replace captures than the Confederates.

83. A renowned chess prodigy, Paul Morphy (1837–84) was considered by many to be the best player in the world until he retired from the game in 1859.

84. Maj. Gen. John G. Foster replaced Maj. Gen. Ambrose Burnside as commander, Dept. of the Ohio, Dec. 9, 1863.

85. After his capture by Union cavalry in eastern Ohio on July 26, Brig. Gen. John Hunt Morgan and his officers were held in solitary confinement at the state penitentiary in Columbus. On Nov. 27 he and six officers escaped to the Confederacy by tunneling their way to the prison yard and climbing over the wall.

86. Meade crossed the Rapidan on Nov. 27, 1863. After several fights along swampy Mine Run in eastern Orange Cty., VA, Meade decided Lee's entrenchments were too strong and on Dec. 1, 1863, withdrew to winter camp at Brandy Station, VA.

87. 1st Sgt. Jonathan Gregory and Priv. John D. Johnson, Co. C, 18th PA Cav., were prisoners at Belle Isle.

88. QM Sgt. William H. McGlumphey, Co. C, 18th PA Cav.

89. The surgeons paroled from Libby published an account, "The Horrors of Rebel Prisons," *New York Times*, Nov. 18, 1863, condemning Confederate officials for the poor conditions and the rising mortality in Southern prisons.

90. President Davis's message to the 4th Session, 1st Confederate Congress, was delivered Dec. 7, 1863. John Letcher, VA governor, 1860–64, generally supported the Davis administration. Weaver alludes to the Confederates' belief that their struggle for Southern independence against Northern tyranny was similar to the American revolutionaries' fight against British tyranny.

91. Henry S. Foote, Miss. Senator, 1847–52, moved to Nashville during the war and represented TN in the Confederate House. He was a vociferous critic of Davis's military and civil policies.

92. Mary Jane Johnson, 16th Maine Inf., aged 19, told authorities she had followed her lover, since killed, into the army. She was moved to Castle Thunder before being exchanged (*New York Times*, Dec. 19, 1863).

93. Probably Brig. Gen. George D. Wagner, commander, 2nd Brigade, 2nd Div., Army of the Cumberland, XXI Corps.

94. Lincoln's message to Congress delivered Dec. 6, 1863.

95. Capts. John F. Skelton, 17th Iowa Inf., and Marion T. Anderson, 51st IN Inf.

96. Averell continued his raids along the Virginia and Tennessee Railroad, Dec. 8–21, 1863, including an attack on Salem, VA, Dec. 16.

97. Col. Timothy M. Byran Jr. and the 18th PA Cav. were in winter quarters in Stevensburg, Culpeper Cty., VA, Dec. 7, 1863–Feb. 28, 1864.

98. The *London Times* sent war correspondents to cover the Civil War who were generally sympathetic toward the Confederacy.

99. Confederate authorities charged the white officers commanding black regiments with fomenting slave rebellions and threatened to execute them.

100. Col. Abel D. Streight; probably Capt. Edward M. Lee, 5th MI Cav. They remained in the dungeon until Jan. 8, 1864. Some accounts list Lt. Benjamin C. G. Reed, 3rd Ohio Inf., as the second escapee.

101. Edward Bulwer-Lytton (1803–73) and Sir Walter Scott (1771–1832), prolific British writers of historical fiction, plays, and poetry, were immensely popular in the US.

102. The James River and Kanawha Canal was visible from Libby. Begun in 1785, the canal reached Buchanan, VA, in the Shenandoah Valley in 1851.

103. Brig. Gen. John Buford, commander, 1st Div., Cav. Corps, Army of the Potomac, died Dec. 16, 1863.

104. On Dec. 19, 1863, Mary Caroline Allen was examined in Richmond for "carrying on treasonable correspondence with persons in the North" (*New York Times,* Dec. 25, 1863). Gen. John H. Winder, prison commandant, brought the charges against her.

105. Capts. Julius B. Litchfield, 4th Maine Inf.; Edward E. Chase, 1st RI Cav., and Charles S. Kendall, 1st MA Inf. The Confederate officers were held at Alton, IL. Salisbury prison, an old cotton factory, was established in 1861, initially for political prisoners and deserters.

106. Francis A. Weaver.

107. Maj. John E. Mulford, Union assistant exchange agent, commanded the truce boat.

108. "Rally 'Round the Flag," also known as "The Battle Cry of Freedom," composed in 1862 by George F. Root. Its strong themes of Union and abolition made the song popular among many Northern soldiers.

109. On Nov. 1, 1863, Brig. Gen. William W. Averell and Gen. Alfred N. Duffié, each leading separate forces, initiated a raid to destroy the Virginia and Tennessee Railroad bridge over New River. Encountering Confederate resistance, Averell's forces abandoned the raid.

110. Probably Lt. Col. Robert S. Northcott, 12th WV Inf. Autograph books were especially popular among college students in the mid-nineteenth century and often included personal messages and accounts of college life.

111. Judge Robert Ould, Confederate exchange commissioner, refused to recognize Gen. Benjamin Butler, whom Lincoln had appointed as the Union exchange commissioner, Dec. 17, 1863. Butler offered to exchange all prisoners, man for man, including African American soldiers and their officers, and parole the surplus.

112. Lt. Samuel H. Tresonthick, 18th PA Cav.

113. Cavada, *Libby Life.* Federico Fernández Cavada was in the 114th PA Inf. Weaver's name appears on p. 214 as one of the subscribers. Robert S. Northcutt's book was never published.

114. Moodiness arising from personal temperament or physical or mental condition.

115. Miserable year, the *Richmond Examiner,* edited by John M. Daniel. The paper was highly critical of Jefferson Davis's wartime leadership.

116. On Dec. 28, 1863, the Confederate Congress abolished the practice of hiring substitutes for drafted men and reduced the categories of men exempt from military service.

117. Usually a mild form of smallpox, but Laws died of the disease on Jan. 24, 1864.

118. Maj. Gen. William "Extra Billy" Smith, VA governor, 1864–65, had served in the Army of Northern Virginia, 1861–63.

119. Lt. Frank A. M. Kreps, 77th PA Inf.

120. Edward Bulwer-Lytton, *A Strange Story* (1862), an early novel about the supernatural.

121. The prisoners on Belle Isle had only tent shelters, tattered clothing, and few blankets and suffered greatly during the winter.

122. Brig. Gen. John Hunt Morgan; Lt. Gen. A. P. Hill.

123. Charles Dickens (1812–70), *Little Dorrit,* published serially between 1855 and 1857.

124. Prison officials appointed Lt. Col. James M. Sanderson, a captured Union commissary officer, to distribute clothes and provisions to the prisoners on Belle Island. Accused by some officers with dereliction of duty, after his exchange Sanders was arrested, found guilty by a military commission of "cruelty to Federal prisoners," and dismissed from the service.

125. Capt. Albert W. Metcalf, 14th NY Cav.; Henry H. Gregg, 13th PA Cav.; Maj. Harry White, 67th PA Inf.

126. Regina Maria Roche (1764?–1845), *The Children of the Abbey, A Tale,* 4 vols. (1798). Roche wrote popular sentimental gothic fiction.

4. "OUR HAPPINESS IS ALLOYED BY THE FEAR OF BEING DISAPPOINTED"

1. Byrne, "Libby Prison," 430–44.

2. Zombek, "Libby Prison"; James Riley Weaver Diary, Feb. 10, 1864. The mass escape is the narrative climax of many Libby Prison memoirs.

3. Luebke, "Kilpatrick-Dahlgren Raid."

4. Weaver Diary, Apr. 6, 30, Mar. 23, Apr. 24, 1864.

5. Sen. Henry Wilson, Republican, served in the US Senate, 1855–73. He raised and briefly commanded the 22nd MA Vol. Inf. and chaired the Committee on Military Affairs.

6. Elizabeth Weaver, Francis A. Weaver, Catherine S. Weaver, Jane A. Weaver.

7. In Regina Maria Roche's *Children of the Abbey,* a forged will deprives Amanda and Oscar Fitzalan of their rightful inheritance.

8. Col. Abel D. Streight, 51st IN Inf., squabbled with prison authorities over retaining possession of a thousand dollars in Confederate currency he had purchased when he was captured.

9. The committee was investigating conditions at Libby, especially prisoners' accusations of short rations.

10. Lt. William L. Laws, Co. L, was the only 18th PA Cav. officer to die in captivity.

11. A prisoner-of-war camp established in 1864 at the SC State Prison in Columbia, SC.

12. Lt. Charles P. Potts, 151st PA Inf.

13. Maj. Erastus N. Bates, 80th IL Inf., and Capt. Edward Porter, 154th NY Inf. Both were later recaptured.

14. On Sept. 26, 1863, Col. John S. Mosby and a hundred partisans, dressed in Federal overcoats, presented themselves as a squadron of the 18th PA Cav. and attacked a twenty-wagon Union supply train capturing the wagons, cargo, about twenty-five prisoners, and a large sum of cash.

15. The new law abolished the practice of hiring substitutes that allowed drafted men to escape military service.

16. The escapees included Capt. John F. Porter, 14th NY Cav.; Major Erastus Bates, 80th IL Inf.; Lts. Michael King, 3rd Ohio Inf.; James I. Carothers, 78th Ohio Inf.; and Morgan Kupp, 167th PA Inf. Porter was the only escapee who made it to Union lines.

17. Sgt. Erasmus Ross, Libby Prison clerk, conducted the roll calls and kept prison records.

18. Maj. Gen. Benjamin F. Butler, commander, Dept. of VA and NC, with headquarters in Norfolk, VA, and Union commissioner of exchange.

19. Lt. Morgan Kupp.

20. Probably from the Rev. H. F. Cary's 1814 translation of Dante's *Divine Comedy:* "All hope abandon ye who enter here," the alleged inscription at the entrance to hell.

21. USS *Smith-Briggs,* a Hudson River tugboat leased by the USN as a gunboat, was hit during the Battle of Smithfield, VA, Feb. 1, 1864, while attempting to rescue the 99th NY Inf. One hundred and ten Federals were captured and the boat looted and destroyed.

22. On Feb. 1, 1864, Maj. Gen. George Pickett hoped to recapture New Bern, NC, which the Federals had occupied since Mar. 1862. Finding the defensive fortifications too strong, Pickett withdrew on Feb. 1 but took about three hundred Union prisoners, who had gotten lost in the fog.

23. Judge Robert Ould, the Confederate exchange agent.

24. Capt. Isaac N. Johnston, 6th KY Inf. Unknown to Weaver and many of his fellow prisoners, Johnston was working on an escape tunnel under Libby and missed a roll call. He remained "missing" to avoid exposing the escape plan.

25. Capts. Robert O. Ives, 10th MA Inf., captured Sept. 1863, and Benjamin C. G. Reed, 3rd Ohio Inf., captured, Rome, GA, May 3, 1863. Salisbury Prison, an empty cotton factory, was established in 1861 to house political prisoners and deserters.

26. Some seven hundred of Gen. John Hunt Morgan's men were captured July 19, 1863, as they attempted to cross the Ohio River. They were held at Camp Douglas, a Union prisoner-of-war camp in Chicago, notorious for its high death rate.

27. A mule-led artillery wagon. Howitzers were short-barreled cannon firing projectiles at an elevated angle.

28. A reference to General "Beast" Butler, so called by Confederates for his alleged insult to the women of New Orleans when he was military governor of the city. See note for May 23, 1864.

29. On Feb. 6, 1863, the Federals probed Richmond's defenses northwest and east of the city. They crossed the Rapidan River at Morton's Ford, became pinned down by the entrenched Confederates, and withdrew. Meanwhile, General Butler's forces moved from Norfolk toward Yorktown and Richmond, hoping to release Federal prisoners in Richmond but retreated after skirmishes at Bottom's Bridge on the Chickahominy River and at Baltimore Store. Richmond's home guards were called out to meet the approaching Union forces. The Virginia Peninsula was the land between the York and the James Rivers.

30. A skirmish by Gen. George E. Pickett's Confederates against the Union Newport barracks near New Bern, NC.

31. Testing Lee's defenses, Brig. Gen. Alexander Hays, commander, 3rd Div., II Corps, Army of the Potomac, attempted to cross the Rapidan River at Morton's Ford on Feb. 6, 1864. Encountering strongly entrenched Confederates and heavy artillery fire, they withdrew that evening.

32. Col. Thomas L. Rosser, commander, 5th VA Cav., briefly occupied Romney, Hampshire Cty., WV, Feb. 3, 1864.

33. Henry B. Freeman, 18th US Inf., and Walter Clifford, 16th US Inf. Both men survived the war.

34. A community in New Kent Cty., VA, on the Chickahominy River.

35. In a surprise attack on Feb. 2, 1864, a Confederate boat crew seized the USS *Underwriter,* a steam gunboat, anchored in the Neuse River near New Bern, NC, and captured most of the officers and crew. Union artillery soon set the ship on fire.

36. Lt. Guy Bryan Jr., adjt., 18th PA Cav.

37. Lts. Freeman Gay, 11th PA Inf., and Frank Kreps, 77th PA Inf.; Capt. James F. Poole, 1st WV Cav.

38. Capt. Robert Pollock, 14th PA Cav., captured, White Sulfur Springs, VA, Aug. 26, 1863; Adjt. Albert Benton White, 4th PA Cav.; Lt. William A. Dailey, 8th PA Cav.; Maj. John R. Henry, 5th Ohio Cav.; Major Ivan N. Walker, 73rd IN Inf.; Col. John P. Spofford, 97th NY

Inf.; Henry B. Freeman, 18th US Inf.; Lt. Melville R. Small, 6th MD Inf.; and Col. William Grosvenor Ely, 18th CT Inf.

39. Embezzlement.

40. 1st Sgt. James Burns, Co. C, 18th PA Cav.

41. Probably Capt. William C. Rossman, 3rd Ohio Inf. This regiment was part of Col. Streight's command, which also included the 5th IN Inf., the 73rd IN Inf., and the 80th IL Inf. Col. Thomas E. Rose masterminded the tunneling and escape. He was later exchanged for a Confederate colonel, Apr. 30, 1864.

42. Forty-eight of the 109 escapees were recaptured.

43. On Feb. 3, 1864, guerillas from the 16th VA Cav. captured the USS *Levi* on the Kanawha River, including Brig. Gen. Eliakim P. Scammon, commander, Kanawha Div., IX Corps.

44. On Nov. 27, 1863, John Hunt Morgan and six officers tunneled out of the Ohio Penitentiary, took a train to Cincinnati, crossed into Kentucky, and returned to the Confederacy.

45. In Feb. 1864, companies C, D, I, L, and M, 18th Pa. Cav., were temporarily detailed to serve as guards for the V Corps Headquarters.

46. On Feb. 3, 1864, Maj. Gen. William T. Sherman and the Army of the Tennessee left Vicksburg for Meridian, MS, hoping to push on to Selma and Mobile. They occupied Meridian on Feb. 14, and over the next five days Sherman's men destroyed railroads and warehouses before returning to Vicksburg.

47. The unfinished prisoner-of-war camp for enlisted men at Andersonville, GA.

48. Spencer Deaton, a native of Knox Cty., TN, guided Unionists through the mountains of eastern TN into KY, where they could enlist in Union regiments. He was captured in Aug. 1863, imprisoned at Castle Thunder, Richmond, VA, tried as a spy, and hanged. While commander, Dept. of the Ohio, Maj. Gen. Ambrose Burnside had used military tribunals in 1863 to imprison or banish prominent Confederate sympathizers.

49. *Romeo and Juliet,* act 3, scene 5.

50. Gen. Neal Dow was exchanged for Gen. William Henry Fitzhugh ("Rooney") Lee, Robert E. Lee's son, Mar. 14, 1864. Capts. Henry W. Sawyer, 1st NJ Cav., and John M. Flinn, 51st IN Inf., had been selected for execution in retaliation for the execution of Confederate Capts. William F. Corbin and T. G. McGraw as spies by Major General Burnside, but the orders were never carried out.

51. Lt. Freeman Gay, 11th PA Inf., captured, Gettysburg, PA, July 1, 1863.

52. David S. Bartram, 17th CT Inf.

53. Maj. Nathan Goff, 4th WV Cav., was a hostage for a Confederate major held in close confinement at Fort Delaware.

54. *Harper's Weekly, A Journal of Civilization,* was published by Harper and Brothers, New York City, 1857–1916. Extensively illustrated, it was very popular during the Civil War for providing Northern audiences with thorough coverage of military affairs along with foreign news, essays, humor, and political cartoons.

55. The Judson Kilpatrick–Ulric Dahlgren raid on Richmond, Feb. 28–Mar. 3, 1864. The 18th PA Cav. rode with Kilpatrick's forces.

56. Castle Thunder.

57. Lt. Col. Allyne C. Litchfield, 7th MI Cav.; Asst. Surgeon Samuel F. Kingston, 2nd NY Cav.

58. Papers purported to be on Col. Ulric Dahlgren's body included orders to release the Union prisoners, assassinate President Davis, and burn Richmond. The *Richmond Examiner* published these papers and called for reprisals. General Lee sent a letter of inquiry to his counterpart, Gen. George G. Meade, who repudiated them as forgeries. Nevertheless, the Dahlgren papers hardened Confederate bitterness against the North and resulted in the mistreatment of the Union prisoners captured during the raid.

59. Lt. George T. Hammond, 22nd PA Cav., was at the latrine where a few boards had been removed for light. The guard saw him through the opening and took a deliberate shot, piercing his ear and hat.

60. Since the Union held more Confederate prisoners than the reverse, man-for-man exchanges would leave many Confederates in Northern prison camps.

61. Maj. Edwin F. Cooke, 2nd NY Cav.

62. Lts. Lewis R. Titus, 3rd US Inf.; James P. Brown, 15th US Inf.; and G. B. Coleman, 6th US Cav. The cell was a twelve-foot square on the ground floor with boarded-up windows to isolate Kilpatrick's men and the officers of African American regiments. Fellow prisoners pried loose a floorboard above the room to communicate and to pass provisions to them.

63. Capt. Harry Wilson, Co. H, 18th PA Cav.; Lt. Horatio G. Lombard, 4th MI Inf.

64. Belle Boyd (1843–1900), a Confederate spy, provided valuable intelligence on Union forces. Gen. Stonewall Jackson appointed her an honorary aide-de-camp for her assistance in the 1862 Shenandoah Valley Campaign.

65. Joseph E. Brown, governor of GA, 1857–65, sharply critical of Jefferson Davis's centralizing war policies.

66. Maj. John E. Mulford, Union assistant agent for exchange. The USS *New York* was a 995-ton steamer charted for carrying mail and exchanged prisoners of war between Fortress Monroe and Richmond.

67. Maj. Charles H. Beers, 16th IL Cav.

68. A short tributary of the James River near Suffolk, VA.

69. After the disastrous failure of the Kilpatrick-Dahlgren raid, Kilpatrick was transferred to command the 3rd Div., Cav. Corps, Army of the Cumberland, part of Gen. William T. Sherman's command. On Mar. 12, 1864, Lt. Gen. Ulysses S. Grant was appointed general-in-chief over all Union armies, replacing Maj. Gen. Henry W. Halleck, who became chief of staff responsible for army administration.

70. Col. James L. Davis, 10th VA Cav.

71. Col. Louis P. di Cesnola (often misspelled as De Cesnola), 4th NY Cav., wounded and captured, Battle of Aldie, June 17, 1863, and paroled from Libby in early 1864 for a personal friend of Jefferson Davis.

72. Edward S. McChesney, AM 1865, Allegheny College, reported on the awards at the college's commencement exercises: George W. Haskins, valedictorian, 1864; Charles E. Hall, Greek salutatorian, 1864; and David A. Pierce, Latin salutatorian, 1864. "Our society" was Psi Kappa Psi, Weaver's fraternity; Marion T. Bales, valedictorian, 1866; Dana L. Hubbard, 1865; William W. Painter, 1866; Capt. James H. Thomas, 1863; Lt. Carlo C. Mechem, 1866; Ebenezer H. McCall (nongraduate, 1867).

73. The Weavers apparently never owned land but rented farms.

74. Lt. Morgan Kupp, 167th PA Inf.

75. Brig. Gen. Eliakim Scammon, 3rd (Kanawha) Div., IX Corps, Army of the Potomac; Capt. John C. Whiteside, 94th NY Inf.

76. 1st Lt. Samuel H. Tresonthick, Co. E, 18th PA Cav.

77. A Union prisoner-of-war camp in Maryland at the confluence of the Potomac River and the Chesapeake Bay.

78. Hides.

79. Lt. Col. James M. Sanderson; Capt. Edward A. Forbes, assistant commissary of subsistence; and Lts. Robert C. Knaggs, aide-de-damp to Brig. Gen. Henry Baxter, and Peter Owen Jones, 2nd NY Cav. Sanderson faced enmity from some Union prisoners for allegedly imposing strict regulations when supervising the distribution of rations to the cooking messes and the clothing sent from the North, cruelty to the prisoners on Belle Isle, and exposing prisoners' escape plans. After Sanderson was paroled, Colonel Streight and General Dow had Sanderson arrested; although found innocent of the charges, he was dismissed from the military.

80. The *Richmond Whig* often criticized the Davis administration for Confederate reversals, especially on the battlefield.

81. That is, withdraw from the war rather than accept parole for eventual exchange and return to their military unit.

82. Napoleon I (1769–1821), *The Confidential Correspondence of Napoleon Bonaparte with His Brother Joseph: Selected and Translated, with Explanatory Notes, from the "Mémoires du roi Joseph,"* 2 vols. (New York: D. Appleton, 1856).

83. The privately owned Mammoth Cave Estate was a famous nineteenth-century natural landmark. Munfordville is in Hart Cty., KY; the Barren River flows into the Green River in Warren Cty., which, in turn, flows into Mammoth Cave.

84. Francis A. Weaver joined the 9th Ohio Cav. on Oct. 27, 1863, and served until he was mustered out, July 20, 1865. He previously served in the 11th PA Inf., a three-month regiment, Apr. 24–Aug. 1, 1861.

85. John W. Weaver, a Methodist minister, was attending the Pittsburgh Annual Conference of the Methodist Episcopal Church. Fayette Cty., PA, is south of Westmoreland Cty.

86. Maj. Gen. Franz Sigel commanded the newly created Dept. of WV; Maj. Gen. Julius Stahl commanded the 1st Cav. Div. in the department.

87. The Battle of Fort De Russy, Simsport, LA, Mar. 14, 1864, opened the Red River Campaign. A Union victory, the Confederates withdrew, leaving south and central Louisiana under Union control.

88. Truce boat from Fortress Monroe that sent supplies to prisoners and ferried parolees.

89. Issued by the War Dept. in 1841 with numerous reprintings during the Civil War. It consisted of three parts: school of the trooper, of the platoon, and of the squadron, dismounted; school of the trooper, of the platoon, and of the squadron, mounted; and evolutions [maneuvers] of a regiment.

90. Under the terms of the 1862 cartel, commanders could exchange enlisted prisoners (but not officers) in the field if they could not care for or guard them. By mid-July, 1863, Secretary of War Edwin Stanton banned general paroles, believing that the Confederates had sent parolees into the army before their formal exchanges. Special paroles at designated points, including Fortress Monroe, continued.

91. 1st Lt. Benjamin F. Campbell, Co. A, and Capt. Frederick Utter, Co. H, 18th PA Cav., were dismissed Feb. 10, 1864, by court-martial for absence without leave.

92. Before the spring offensive against Lee, Grant reorganized the Army of the Potomac, reducing the number of corps because of attrition.

93. Maj. Gen. Alfred Pleasonton's cavalry command was transferred from the Army of the Potomac to Maj. Gen. William S. Rosecrans, Dept. of the Missouri. After Maj. Gen. William H. French's III Corps was reorganized, he served on military boards for the remainder of the war.

94. Gen. Braxton Bragg was relieved of command of the Army of Tennessee in Dec. 1863, and on Feb. 24, 1864, became President Davis's chief of staff, supervising military supplies, hospitals, prisons, and conscription.

95. Hoaxes.

96. Owen Lovejoy (1811–Mar. 25, 1864), a Congregational minister, abolitionist, and IL Republican congressman, 1863–64. His brother, Elijah Lovejoy, was murdered in 1837 by proslavery men while defending the press of the Illinois Anti-Slavery Society.

97. "On the tapis": to be under consideration.

98. Lt. David McKay, Co. B, 18th PA Cav.

99. A white supremacist epithet mocking blacks' aspirations for equality in a white man's republic, and more broadly denigrating their very presence in the US. Prison officials detailed whites captured in the Kilpatrick-Dahlgren raid, probably the white officers of black regiments, to perform menial labor alongside African American prisoners or enslaved individuals hoping to inflame race hatred among the Union prisoners. Weaver predicted this retaliatory tactic would backfire.

100. On Mar. 25, 1864, Gen. Nathan Bedford Forrest attacked Paducah, KY, with some three thousand men. The outnumbered Federals retreated to Fort Anderson while naval gunboats shelled the Confederates. Although capturing supplies and horses, Forrest withdrew with a loss of fifty casualties.

101. On Mar. 28, 1864, a mob of Southern sympathizers attacked Union soldiers on furlough in Charleston, IL. Troops rushed to defend them; five men died and over twenty were wounded.

102. Robert Henry Newell (1836–1901), *The Orpheus C. Kerr Papers, Second Series* (New York: Blakeman and Mason, 1863). Newell was a popular humorist writing under the pseudonym Orpheus C. Kerr. These essays originally appeared in the *New York Sunday Mercury* and traced the inglorious exploits of the fictitious "mackerel brigade," among other topics.

103. Alain-René Lesage (1668–1747), *The Adventures of Gil Blas of Santillane* (1715–35). Lesage was a French novelist and playwright. *Gil Blas,* one of his most popular works, is a series of stories involving a picaresque hero. Weaver read the English translation by Tobias Smollett.

104. Thomas De Quincey (1785–1859), *Klosterheim: or, The Masque* (1832; repr., Boston: Whittemore, Niles and Hall, 1855), a romantic novel. De Quincey was a prolific English essayist, critic, and writer.

105. Lt. Aaron A. Scudder, 35th PA Inf.

106. Lt. Joseph D. Ayers previously served as 2nd Lt., Co. A, 1st Battalion, DE Cav. He joined the 18th PA Cav. on Apr. 11, 1864, replacing Capt. Peter Wise after his discharge. Ayers added 145 recruits to the company. The *Philadelphia Inquirer* was one of the most popular newspapers in the country and was noted for its extensive war coverage.

107. For the war's duration.

108. USS *New York* and USS *Express.*

109. Lt. Edward M. Timony, 15th US Inf.

110. John Bunyan (1628–88), *Holy War* (1682), like his best-known book, *Pilgrim's Progress* (1678), was an allegorical work of the Christian journey from sin to conversion and redemption.

111. 2nd Lt. Walter S. Stephens, 104th NY Inf., captured, Gettysburg, July 1, 1863; died, Libby prison, Apr. 10, 1864.

112. Lt. George D. Forsyth, 100th Ohio Inf., was standing near a front prison window when the gun went off, instantly killing him and slightly wounding Lt. Douglas O. Kelly of the same regiment.

113. The resolution is printed in Boaz, *Libby Prison and Beyond,* 132.

114. The spring run of shad up the tidal James River.

115. Brig. Gen. Alfred Torbert, 1st Div.; Gen. James H. Wilson, 2nd Div.; Maj. Gen. Philip Sheridan, commander, Cav. Corps, Army of the Potomac. Maj. Gen. Judson Kilpatrick, 3rd Div., Cavalry Corps, Army of the Cumberland.

116. Representatives Alexander Long, Democrat, Ohio, 1863–65; Benjamin G. Harris, Democrat, MD, 1863–67, and Fernando Wood, Democrat, NY, 1863–65. Wood was New York City mayor, 1860–62. All three strongly opposed the war, conscription, and emancipation.

117. Capts. Frederick B. Doten, 14th CT Inf., and Edward E. Chase, 1st RI Cav.

118. Capts. Benjamin C. G. Reed, 3rd Ohio Inf., and Julius B. Litchfield, 4th Maine Inf.

119. Phineas C. Headley, *The Life of Napoleon Bonaparte* (New York: Derby and Miller, 1856); Sir Walter Scott, *The Life of Napoleon Bonaparte, Emperor of the French* (1834); John S. C. Abbott, *A History of Napoleon Bonaparte* (New York: Harper and Brothers, 1855–56).

120. Likely Capt. Nathan H. Moony, 16th NY Cav., and Lt. Joseph R. Roger, 157th PA Inf., captured Apr. 16, 1864.

121. Salmon P. Chase, treasury secretary.

122. On Apr. 12, 1864, Maj. Gen. Nathan Bedford Forrest attacked Fort Pillow, TN, on the Mississippi River. The Union garrison had 557 troops, including 262 black soldiers. The Confederates massacred many of the Union soldiers, especially African American troops, as they were surrendering, resulting in at least 180 casualties. Confederate war policy treated black solders as insurrectionary slaves, a capital offense. Forrest also sent some of his cavalry back to Paducah, KY, to retrieve the Union horses hidden during his earlier raid on the city.

123. Varying.

124. Col. Richard R. Turner, Libby Prison commandant.

125. On Apr. 16, 1864, Kilpatrick gave a farewell address to the brigade before leaving for the West.

126. On Apr. 17, 1864, Brig. Gen. Robert F. Hoke and the CSS *Albemarle,* an ironclad ram, attacked the Union garrison at Plymouth, NC, under Brig. Gen. Henry Walton Wessells's command. Three days later Wessells surrendered. He was taken to Libby prison and subsequently moved to Danville, VA; Macon, GA; and Charleston, SC. On Aug. 3, 1864, he was exchanged and became commissary of prisoners, Nov. 11, which he held until the war's close.

127. In his Apr. 8, 1864, speech, Long condemned the war as an effort to subjugate the sovereign states and called for recognition of the Confederacy. The House censured him the following day for his "treasonable utterances."

128. Brig. Gen. William W. Averell, 4th Separate Brigade, VIII Corps, survived the war.

129. Col. Timothy M. Bryan Jr., commander, 18th PA Cav. The 2nd NY, 2nd Ohio, and 1st CT composed the 1st Brigade, 3rd Div., under the command of Col. John B. McIntosh.

130. Dr. Lugo, a Union spy working for the USN and traveling under a Prussian passport, arrived in Richmond in early 1864 and was arrested in Tappahannock, VA, Apr. 16, 1864, for espionage. A specialist on torpedoes, he collected information on Confederate coastal defenses in VA, Wilmington, and Charleston. Lugo was tried, convicted, and expelled from the Confederacy. Sterling King was a Confederate double agent arrested in Abingdon, VA, Apr. 20, 1864. To gain the confidence of the Confederates, he had participated in a plot to spring John Hunt Morgan from prison in Columbus, Ohio (*New York Times,* May 1, 1864).

131. By early Apr. 1864, Confederate forces had stopped Gen. Nathaniel Banks's advance up the Red River in LA, forcing Union forces to retreat back to New Orleans.

132. A tobacco warehouse in Richmond.

133. Capt. Enos J. Pennypacker, Co. M, 18th PA Cav.; Capt. John Craig, 1st. WV Inf.

134. A two hundred Parrot is a muzzle-loading rifled army cannon developed by Robert P. Parrott that fired 200-pound shells. On Apr. 19, 1864, the CSS *Albemarle* rammed and sunk the USS *Southfield* and damaged the USS *Miami* during a Confederate attack on Plymouth, NC.

135. Charles Dixon, 16th CT Inf.

136. A community in New Kent Cty., VA, on the south bank of the York River, formerly Doncastle.

137. Piracy, or a ruthless war giving no quarter and taking no prisoners.

138. Cols. Thomas E. Rose, 77th PA Inf., and Francis Beach, 16th CT. Inf.; Maj. John Henry, 5th Ohio Cav.

139. Dr. Mary Edwards Walker (1831–1919), the first woman surgeon employed by the Union Army, was captured by Confederate forces, Apr. 10, 1864, after crossing enemy lines to assist with an amputation. She was arrested as a spy, held at Castle Thunder Prison in Richmond, and exchanged Aug. 12, 1864, for a Confederate surgeon.

140. Probably the CSS *Virginia II,* built in Richmond, VA, and launched in June 1864.

141. Andersonville prison camp.

142. John Adams Gilmer, represented NC in the Second Confederate Congress.

143. Maj. Nathan Goff Jr., 4th WV Cav.; Capt. Emil Frey, 82nd IL Inf.; Lt. William C. Manning, 2nd MA Cav.

144. Gen. John C. Frémont had left military service in June 1862.

145. William R. W. Cobb, an opponent of secession and a strong Unionist, was elected in AL to the Second Confederate Congress. On May 3, 1864, a house committee investigated his credentials. Cobb died from an accidental gunshot wound, Nov. 1, 1864.

146. James Thomas Leach represented NC in the Second Confederate Congress, 1864–65.

147. Lts. Lawrence N. Duchesney, 1st MA Cav., and Leopold Markbreit, 28th Ohio Inf. Markbreit was captured at Craig's Creek, VA, Dec. 18, 1863, and exchanged Jan. 5, 1865. Johnson's Island was a Union prisoner-of-war camp in Lake Erie, Ohio.

148. A borough in Westmoreland Cty., PA.

149. Gen. Giuseppe Garibaldi, military leader of Italian unification, was immensely popular in England and the US. He received a hero's welcome in London and met with Prime Minister Viscount Palmerston.

150. At the Battle of Dybbøl (Apr. 7–18, 1864), during the Second Schleswig War, the Danes suffered a major defeat against the Prussians, resulting in the transfer of the duchies of Schleswig and Holstein to Prussian-Austrian rule.

151. Fort Darling was a Confederate fortification on Drewry's Bluff overlooking the James River and protecting Richmond. On May 5, 1864, 30,000 Union troops landed at Bermuda Hundred under Maj. Gen. Quincy A. Gillmore, who had been recently transferred to the Army of the James. Confederate reinforcements drove the Union forces away three days later.

152. At the Battle of the Wilderness, VA, May 5, 1864, Brig. Gen. John Marshall Jones, Stonewall Brigade, was killed in action and Gen. Leroy Stafford, 2nd LA Brigade, Stonewall Div., mortally wounded. This was the beginning of the Overland Campaign.

5. "THINK OF HOME AND WONDER WHEN THE SPACE THAT NOW
SEPARATES US WILL BE TRAVERSED"

1. Robertson, "Houses of Horror," 329–45; Speer, *Portals to Hell,* 126–28, 207–9; Pickenpaugh, *Captives in Blue,* 103–9; James Riley Weaver Diary, May 8, 1864.

2. Iobst, *Civil War Macon,* 131–44; McInvale, "That Thing of Infamy," 279–91; Speer, *Portals to Hell,* 266–68; Hesseltine, *Civil War Prisons,* 158–62; Pickenpaugh, *Captives in Blue,* 167–74; Sanders, *While in the Hands,* 209–10.

3. Aitkin's Landing, formerly known as Varina, in eastern Henrico Cty. on the James River.

4. Chester Station, Chesterfield Cty., on the Richmond and Petersburg Railway.

5. Brig. Gen. James S. Wadsworth, V Corps, mortally wounded, the Wilderness, May 6, 1864, died two days later. Brig. Gen. Alexander Hays, III Corps, killed in action, the Wilderness. Carr was probably Gen. Samuel Sprigg Carroll, II Corps, wounded, the Wilderness and Spotsylvania.

6. Brig. Gen. Truman Seymour, VI Corps, captured, the Wilderness, May 6, and exchanged Aug. 9, 1864. Brig. Gen. Alexander Shaler, VI Corps, was captured the same day when Brig. Gen. John Brown Gordon's troops outflanked his brigade.

7. The Virginia Central Railroad, Richmond's main supply line westward.

8. Maj. Gen. Philip Sheridan's cavalry raid toward Richmond, May 9–24, 1864, was designed to draw Stuart's Confederate cavalry away from Meade's Army of the Potomac and destroy supplies and communications lines to Lee's Army of Northern Virginia.

9. The Piedmont Railroad, built and operated by the Richmond and Danville Railroad and funded by the Confederate government, connected Danville and Greensboro, NC. The poorly constructed line was not completed until May 21, 1864.

10. "Greens" written above "Goldsboro."

11. By Oct. 1864 the Salisbury prison held 5,000 inmates in a facility designed for 2,500 men, and a month later the population had doubled to 10,000. At least 3,700 men died, second only to Andersonville.

12. Pee Dee River.

13. Millen Junction, the crossing of the Augusta and Savannah Railroad and the Central of Georgia Railway.

14. See notes for Apr. 26, 1864.

15. Brig. Gen. Henry W. Wessells, captured, Battle of Plymouth, NC, Apr. 20, 1864. Brig. Gen. Eliakim P. Scammon, Kanawha Div., IX Corp, Army of the Potomac, captured Feb. 3, 1864, by partisans from the 16th VA Cav.

16. Maj. Gen. J. E. B. Stuart, Lee's cavalry commander, was mortally wounded at the Battle of Yellow Tavern, May 12, 1864.

17. Capt. George M. Van Buren, 6th NY Cav., captured, Williamsport, MD, July 6, 1863.

18. Capt. Henry H. Mason, 2nd NY Cav., captured, US Ford, Sept. 16, 1863.

19. Since May 7, 1864, Maj. Gen. William T. Sherman, Military Div. of the Mississippi, had been marching slowly toward Atlanta in a series of flanking maneuvers against Brig. Gen. Joseph E. Johnston, Army of Tennessee. Sherman sent Brig. Gen. Jefferson C. Davis, XIV Corps, to seize the ironworks at Rome, GA, on May 17.

20. Failing to capture Shreveport, LA, in the ill-fated Red River Campaign, Mar. 18–May 22, 1864, Maj. Gen. Nathaniel Banks, commander, Dept. of the Gulf, was retreating toward Alexandria, where Confederate forces had failed to capture the Union gunboats trapped above the falls at Alexandria.

21. Capt. W. Kemper Tabb of MD assumed command of the Macon prison on May 18, 1864, and soon gained a reputation among the prisoners for his cruelty.

22. That is, four or five Confederate dollars for one greenback.

23. Gov. Joseph E. Brown (1821–94), Democrat and ardent secessionist, was first elected governor in 1857. Popular among the yeomanry he resisted expanding Jefferson Davis's war powers and sought to retain control of the GA militia from Confederate authorities.

24. Liver disorder.

25. Out of the fight.

26. Charles Mattocks, 17th Maine Inf., recounts another version of this story in Racine, *"Unspoiled Heart,"* 159–60.

27. As military governor of New Orleans, Gen. Benjamin F. Butler issued General Order No. 28, May 15, 1862, which stated than any woman insulting or disrespecting a Federal officer was to be treated as a common prostitute. Outraged by this perceived insult to Southern women, Confederates labeled him the "Beast of New Orleans" and refused to recognize him as the Union exchange commissioner.

28. Lt. Jackson Woods, 82nd IN Inf.

29. Capt. Frederick Zarracher joined Co. C, 18th PA Cav., Apr. 23, 1864. After just two weeks' service, he was severely wounded in the left leg, pinned under his horse, and captured, Mine Run, VA, May 5, 1864.

30. Maj. William B. Darlington lost a leg and was captured, Mine Run, VA, May 5, 1864. Maj. John Phillips was wounded, Gettysburg, July 3, 1863, and Hanover Court House, VA, May 31, 1864; captured, Cedar Creek, VA, Nov. 12, 1864; and sent to Libby Prison. Lt. Samuel H. McCormick, promoted 1st Lt., Co. L, killed, St. Mary's Church, VA, June 15, 1864. Capt. George W. Nieman, Co. E, survived the war, remained with the regiment, and mustered out Oct. 31, 1865. Weaver had been commissioned 1st Lt., Co. C, Apr. 1, 1864.

31. Col. Timothy M. Bryan Jr. received command of the 18th PA Cav., Dec. 24, 1862. After engaging with the Confederates in the Overland Campaign at the Wilderness, Spotsylvania Court House, Yellow Tavern, and Malvern Hill, by mid-May the 18th was in bivouac along the James River.

32. The *Daily Confederate*, Raleigh, NC, published 1864–65.

33. Edward A. Pollard, associate editor of the *Richmond Enquirer* since 1861, also wrote popular histories of the Confederacy during the war. In 1864, he was captured running the Union blockade on his way to Europe on a book tour and confined in several Union prisons, including Fort Lafayette in the narrows of New York Harbor.

34. White House Landing, New Kent Cty., VA, on the Pamunkey River was an important Union supply base during the Overland Campaign.

35. Capt. George C. Gibbs, former commander of the 42nd NC Inf., was prison commandant, May 25–Oct. 1864, when he was transferred to Andersonville.

36. Capt. Francis Irsch, 45th NY Inf., owned the watch. "Bucked and gagged" was a punishment where the offender was placed in a sitting position, gagged, and wrists tied and placed over bent knees with a stick wedged beneath them and the forearms for an extended period.

37. Capt. Ralph Olmstead Ives, 10th MA Inf.; Capt. Charles Kendall, 1st MA Inf.; Maj. Harry White, 67th PA Inf.; Capt. Julius B. Litchfield, 4th Maine Inf.

38. June 3–5 entries have ink bleeding from the back side of the page.

39. Sen. Howell Cobb, a GA Democrat, rose to major general in the Confederate Army. Lee appointed him to negotiate prisoner exchanges, but under Davis's directive he refused to parole captured African American soldiers. Cobb had supervised construction of the Macon prison.

40. USS *Water Witch*, a wooden-hulled gunboat built in 1851, was serving in the South Atlantic Blockading Squad. in 1864. While patrolling the Savannah area, a Confederate marine boat force boarded the vessel on June 3, 1864, Ossabaw Sound, GA, and captured thirteen officers and forty-nine men.

41. Brig. Gen. Charles Heckman, commander, 1st Brigade, 2nd Div., Army of the James, Maj. Gen. Benjamin Butler, commander. He was captured, Battle of Procter's Creek, May 12–16, 1864, in the Bermuda Hundred Campaign, which failed to take Richmond from the east.

42. Establishing a Union Party for the 1864 presidential election, Republicans replaced Hannibal Hamlin, a Maine Republican, as Lincoln's running mate with Andrew Johnson, a Southern Democrat and governor of the loyal TN government, in an effort to attract War Democrats and border-state Unionists. George McClellan was the Democratic presidential candidate; John Frémont ran for president as a Republican in 1856.

43. Phonology is the study of the system of sounds in a language.

44. They were sent to Charleston as hostages for Union guns bombarding the city from Morris Island.

45. Brig. Gen. Charles A. Heckman, Dept. of NC and VA, wounded, Port Whitehall, VA, May 7, 1864; captured, Drewry's Bluff, VA, May 16, 1864.

46. Lt. Otto Gerson, 45th NY Inf., captured, Gettysburg, July 1, 1863. Priv. W. F. Belger claimed Gerson was escaping and had passed the deadline; however, Union witnesses said Gerson was sixteen feet away from the line.

47. African American soldiers were among the guards deployed at this Union prisoner-of-war camp that held up to 20,000 prisoners, including a few black soldiers' former owners.

48. Teachers' Institutes were annual weeklong gatherings usually held at county seats. In addition to the social aspects, teachers heard lectures on subject matter, pedagogy, and educational reforms. Lancaster Cty., PA, had its first institute in Jan. 1853 and often published its proceedings in the *Pennsylvania School Journal*.

49. Leonidas Polk (1806–64), called "the fighting bishop," was killed at Pine Mountain near Marietta, GA, June 14, 1864, by Federal artillery as he was scouting enemy positions with his staff. Appointed the Episcopal bishop of LA in 1841, Polk secured a military appointment in 1861 from Jefferson Davis, his fellow classmate at West Point.

50. On June 9, Gen. Sam Jones, commander at Charleston, requested fifty Union prisoners from Macon be sent to Charleston as hostages to pressure the Federals to end their shelling of the city. They were subsequently exchanged for Confederate prisoners held by Union artillery units on Morris Island. The original Mills House hotel opened in 1853.

51. Gen. John A. Dix (Union) and Gen. Howell Cobb (Confederate) had long been involved in exchange negotiations. Judge Robert Ould was the Confederate exchange agent.

52. Maj. Gen. David Hunter, commander, Dept. of WV, had invaded the Shenandoah Valley to deny supplies from reaching Lee's army. They defeated Confederate forces under Brig. Gen. William E. "Grumble" Jones at Piedmont, VA, June 5, 1864, where Jones was shot and killed leading a charge against the Federals. Hunter's forces occupied Staunton the next day.

53. All untrue: Sherman captured Atlanta on Sept. 2, 1864; Petersburg did not fall until Apr. 2, 1865; and Jubal A. Early repulsed Gen. David Hunter's attack on Lynchburg, June 18, 1864.

54. Lt. David McCully, Co. E, 75th Ohio Inf., captured, Cemetery Hill, Gettysburg, PA, July 2, 1863.

55. Gen. John D. Imboden survived the war and died in 1895.

56. The National Union National Convention, a coalition of Republicans and War Democrats, met June 7–8 in Baltimore and renominated Lincoln by 484 votes over 22 for Grant. On the first ballot for the vice-presidential spot, Johnson received 200 votes, Hamlin, 150, and Daniel S. Dickinson, a NY War Democrat and former senator, 108. Loyal governments from the Confederate states sent delegates to the convention.

57. Probably Lost Mountain, which along with Pine and Brushy Mountains northwest of Marietta, GA, formed Gen. Johnston's defensive line protecting Atlanta. The Confederates withdrew from Pine Mountain after Gen. Leonidas Polk was killed by Union artillery fire, June 14, 1864.

58. Battle of Brice's Crossroads, or Battle of Guntown or Tishomingo Creek, June 10, 1864. Concerned that Maj. Gen. Nathan Forrest might cut Union supply lines outside Nashville, Sherman ordered Brig. Gen. Samuel D. Sturgis and cavalry under Brig. Gen. Benjamin Grierson to advance from Memphis and attack Forrest in north MS. Forrest routed the Federals, capturing over 1,500 prisoners. The rumors that Sturgis was drunk on the battlefield were false.

59. On June 12, Grant began moving his army south of the James River hoping to surprise Lee with an attack on Petersburg, Richmond's southern backdoor.

60. This was the most notorious of the Confederate stockades built to hold 10,000 enlisted prisoners. Construction began in Jan. 1864 but it was unfinished when men began arriving in late Feb. By June there were over 22,000 captives and 29,000 the next month. Inadequate shelter, scant rations, overcrowding, and poor sanitation led to horrific suffering and over 13,000 deaths.

61. The Battle of Kennesaw Mountain, June 27, 1864. Sherman made a rare frontal assault against Johnston's heavily fortified position outside Marietta, GA, but was unable to dislodge them. While a tactical defeat for the Federals, this setback failed to stop Sherman's steady advance on Atlanta.

62. Maj. William T. Beatty, 2nd Ohio Inf., captured, Chickamauga, GA, Sept. 19, 1863; Maj. William S. Marshall, 5th Iowa Inf.; Maj. William N. Owens, 1st KY Cav.; Acting Master George H. Pendleton, USS *Montgomery,* captured Jan. 7, 1864, while attempting to rescue crewmen of the USS *Aries.*

63. Confederate authorities hoped that publicity about the worsening condition of Union prisoners because of the alleged "change of climate and the hopelessness of exchange" would pressure Lincoln to resume exchanges (Glazier, *Capture,* 123–24). Mattocks also recounts this incident in Racine, *"Unspoiled Heart,"* 160–61.

64. Brig. Gen. Philip H. Sheridan, cavalry commander, Army of the Potomac, with divisions under Gen. Alfred T. A. (Thomas Archimedes) Torbert and Gen. David M. Gregg, moved west to divert the Confederates as Grant crossed the James River to attack Petersburg and to destroy the Central Virginia Railroad, Richmond's supply line. At Trevilian Station, June 11–12, 1864, Confederate cavalry under Wade Hampton and Fitz Lee blocked the Federal advance and forced Sheridan to retreat.

65. Lt. Col. David B. McCreary and 111 other officers and men from the 145th PA Inf. were captured, Petersburg, VA, June 16, 1864.

66. During the Second Battle of Petersburg, June 15–17, men from Maj. Gen. George G. Meade's Army of the Potomac repeatedly charged the fortifications outside Petersburg, VA, which had been hastily erected by Gen. P. G. T. Beauregard's Confederates. Unable to break through the city's defenses, Grant initiated a ten-month siege.

67. Probably Capt. Joseph N. Hetzler and Lt. Frank H. Knapp, 9th Ohio Veteran Vol. Cav., captured Apr. 13, 1864, Florence, AL.

68. Lt. Col. Gustav Von Helmrich, 4th MO Cav.

69. In the book of Esther, Haman was a high official in the Persian court who plotted to kill all the Jews in the empire. Exposed by Queen Esther, Haman was seized and hanged.

70. Probably Capt. Joshua M. Dushane, Co. H, 142nd PA Inf.

71. Brig. Gen. David Hunter, X Corps, failed to capture Lynchburg, VA, June 16–18, 1864.

72. Lt. Herman Bader, 29th MO Inf., captured, Ringgold, GA, Nov. 27, 1863.

73. Capt. Julius B. Litchfield, Maj. Harry White, Capt. Benjamin C. G. Reed, Lt. George R. Barse.

74. 1st Sgt. John M. Ashbrook, Co. C, 18th PA Cav., captured May 5, 1864, Mine Run, VA, held at Andersonville, and died in prison, Florence, SC, Nov. 18, 1864.

75. Lt. Col. Thomas Thorpe, 1st NY Dragoons. The flag, 4 by 6 inches, was displayed by Capt. Henry H. Todd, 8th NJ Inf.

76. Maj. Gen. James B. McPherson, commander, Army of the Tennessee, was making flanking attacks against Johnston's Confederate forces defending Atlanta.

77. Lt. Robert P. Wilson, 5th US Cav.

78. The Richmond and Danville and the South Side Railroads; the latter ran from City Point on the James River to Lynchburg, VA. Both were vital supply lines for Richmond and the Army of Northern Virginia.

79. The Central of Georgia Railway ran alongside Camp Oglethorpe.

80. Col. Henry M. Hoyt and Lt. Col. John B. Conyngham, 52nd PA Vol., and over a hundred men of the 52nd PA Inf. were captured during the assault on Fort Johnson, Charleston Harbor, in the early morning hours of July 4, 1864.

81. Lt. Edward P. Brooks, Co. F, 6th WI Inf., captured Nov. 4, 1863, Greenville, VA. In a personal letter, President Abraham Lincoln directed Gen. Benjamin Butler to arrange for his exchange, which occurred Mar. 23, 1864. Brooks was recaptured June 1864.

82. Lt. Samuel H. McCormick and Capt. Samuel H. Tresonthick, both 18th PA Cav. Tresonthick's left leg was amputated and he died from complications (gangrene), July 26, 1864.

83. Battle of Stony Creek Depot, or Battle of Sappony Church, VA, June 28, 1864. Federal cavalry commanded by Brig. Gens. James H. Wilson and August V. Kautz attempted to cut the Weldon Railroad, which supplied Lee's army from North Carolina. Already turned back by Confederate cavalry under Wade Hampton and Fitz Lee at the Battle of Staunton River Bridge, June 25, 1864, the Federals were attacked again three days later at Stony Creek Depot.

84. The USS *Satellite*, a steam-powered tugboat acquired by the USN in 1861. Under command of Capt. John F. D. Robinson, acting master, it was assigned to the Potomac River Flotilla. Confederates captured the vessel Aug. 22–23, 1863, in the Rappahannock River while it was patrolling rivers emptying into the Chesapeake Bay. See note for Sept. 3, 1863.

85. Lee ordered Lt. Gen. Jubal A. Early's Corps to sweep Union forces from the Shenandoah Valley and menace Washington. Early crossed the Potomac River into MD, July 5, 1864, and attacked Fort Stevens northwest of Washington, July 11–12, before being forced back by units under Maj. Gen. Horatio G. Wright.

86. Col. Pennock Huey, 8th PA Cav.; Col. John Fraser, 140th PA Vol.; Col. Homer R. Stoughton, 2nd US Sharp Shooters; Col. Francis T. Sherman, 88th IL Inf.; Maj. Jacob H. Dewees, 13th PA Cav.; Capt. Samuel S. Elder, 1st US Art.

87. Col. George H. Covode, 4th PA Cav.; Maj. Michael Kerwin, 13th PA Cav. Col. Frederick A. Bartleson lost an arm at Shiloh, Apr. 6–7, 1862. After recovering, he was elected colonel, 100th IL Inf., and captured, Chickamauga, GA, Sept. 18–20, 1863. After his release from Libby, he rejoined his regiment and was killed at Kennesaw Mountain, GA, June 23, 1864.

88. The CSS *Alabama* was built in England to raid Union commercial and naval vessels. Under Rear Adm. Raphael Semmes, commander, the ship made seven successful expeditionary raids before being sunk by the USS *Kearsarge*, Capt. John A Winslow, commander, Battle of Cherbourg, France, June 19, 1864.

89. At the Battle of Pace's Ferry, July 5, 1864, Union forces captured the damaged Chattahoochee River bridge and crossed the river three days later on Federal pontoons.

90. Sutlers were civilian merchants licensed by prison commandants to sell goods to the prisoners from tents or wagons. These purchases of fresh vegetables and meat supplemented their meager rations. Authorities required payment in Confederate dollars at official exchange rates for greenbacks or gold coins that were substantially below black market rates.

91. Founded by Arthur Tappan and Samuel Morse in 1827, the *Journal of Commerce* focused on trade but frequently took political positions. Opposed to Union war policies, Lincoln ordered it closed after the paper published a bogus story that the president was calling for 400,000 additional volunteers. Horatio Seymour, Democratic governor of New York and fierce critic of the administration, especially the draft, narrowly lost reelection on Nov. 8, 1864, to Republican Reuben E. Fenton.

92. The Northern Central Railroad connected Baltimore to Sunbury, PA, and the Susquehanna River. Confederate cavalry attacked this important supply line, July 10, 1864, and cut the telegraph. Maj. Gen. Darius Nash Couch, commander, Dept. of the Susquehanna; Brig. Gen David Hunter, commander, Dept. of WV.

93. "Flitting" is gear or baggage. See note for June 5, 1864.

94. Capt. Daniel B. Meaney and Lt. Edward O'Shea, both 13th PA Cav.

95. On July 17, 1864, Jefferson Davis relieved the cautious Gen. Joseph Johnston as commander, Army of Tennessee, and appointed Gen. John Bell Hood as his replacement, who promised a counteroffensive against Sherman to protect Atlanta from Federal occupation.

96. On July 10, 1864, Federal cavalry under Maj. Gen. Lovell H. Rousseau left Decatur, AL, to destroy the rail line between Columbus, GA, and Montgomery, AL.

97. The reported number of deaths was 1,200.

98. The Montgomery and West Point Railroad ran from Montgomery, AL, to West Point, GA, and was an important Confederate supply line. By July 17, 1864, Union cavalry under Maj. Gen. Rousseau had destroyed thirty miles of track and burned stations, supply depots, and warehouses.

99. Augusta and Atlanta Railroad.

100. Lt. Henry Appel, 1st MD Cav.

101. Lt. Col. Allyne C. Litchfield, 7th MI Cav.; Maj. Samuel J. Crooks, 22nd NY Cav.

102. Col. Samuel J. Crooks, 22nd NY Cav., was captured during the Wilson-Kautz Raid in late June 1864.

103. Col. Timothy M. Bryan Jr., 18th PA Cav.

104. Lt. Col. William P. Brinton, 18th PA Cav.

105. Capt. Joshua M. Dushane, 142nd PA Inf., captured, Gettysburg, PA, July 1, 1863.

106. Milledgeville, Georgia's capital, remained in Confederate hands until Nov. 22, 1864.

107. Emeric Szabad, *Modern War in Its Theory and Practice, Illustrated from Celebrated Campaigns and Battles* (New York: Harper and Row, 1863). A Hungarian, Szabad was involved in nationalist movements in Hungary and in Italy before moving to the US in 1861. He served on the staffs of Gens. John C. Frémont, Daniel W. Sickles, and Gouverneur K. Warren. His experiences in Libby Prison have been published in Beszedits, *Libby Prison Diary*.

108. Maj. Gen. James B. McPherson commanded the Army of the Tennessee and was killed, Battle of Atlanta, July 22, 1864.

109. Probably Lt. Samuel H. Byers, 5th Iowa Inf., captured, Missionary Ridge, TN, Nov. 24, 1863.

110. Pones: cornmeal cakes or flat bread.

111. The Central of Georgia Railway ran from Macon to Savannah. Sherman's army destroyed the line during their March to the Sea.

6. "THEY GO HIGH LIKE A SHOOTING METEOR AND FALL ABRUPTLY AS A STAR"

1. "Old Jail," and "Old Marine Hospital," in *Historic Charleston;* Hesseltine, *Civil War Prisons,* 154–56, 164–65; Speer, *Portals to Hell,* 213–15; Armstrong, "From Cahaba to Charleston," 223–24; Sanders, *While in the Hands,* 227; Peckenpaugh, *Captives in Blue,* 174–76, 178–79.

2. James Riley Weaver Diary, Aug. 2, Aug. 7, Sept. 2, and Sept. 10, 1864; Kutzler, "Captive Audiences," 250–51.

3. Weaver is counting down the mileposts alongside the railroad.

4. Maj. Gen. Quincy A. Gillmore, commander, Dept. of the South, X Corps, until May 1, 1864, was succeeded by Maj. Gen. John G. Foster, May 26.

5. Cols. Henry Hoyt, 52nd PA Inf.; Francis T. Sherman, 88th IL Inf.; Pennock Huey, 8th PA Cav.; Thomas J. Thorpe, 1st NY Dragoons.

6. Lt. Col. William P. Lasselle, 9th IN Inf.

7. On July 26, 1864, Gen. George Stoneman's cavalry raid cut the railroad south of Atlanta to choke off supplies to the Confederates. Gordon was a depot on the Central of Georgia Railway, Wilkinson Cty., GA.

8. General Stoneman and seven hundred of his soldiers were captured July 30, 1864, while attempting to raid Macon, GA, and release the prisoners at Andersonville.

9. Probably Lt. Frank A. M. Kreps, 77th PA Inf.

10. Maj. Gen. Edward Johnson, Army of Northern Virginia, captured, Spotsylvania Court House, May 12, 1865. Brig. Gen. M. Jeff Thompson, MO State Guard, captured Aug. 1863 in AR. Both were among the fifty Confederate officers held at Morris Island until their parole, Aug. 3, 1864.

11. Union prisons for Confederate officers on Johnson's Island, Ohio, in Sandusky Bay, Lake Erie, and at Point Lookout, a peninsula in Maryland where the Potomac River enters the Chesapeake Bay.

12. Parrott guns were rifled artillery widely used in the Civil War. Invented by Capt. Robert Parker Parrott and made at the West Point Foundry, they came in several sizes. The Union Army and Navy used thirty pounders with a range of 6,700 yards.

13. On Apr. 20, 1864, Maj. Gen. Sam Jones was appointed Confederate commander of the Dept. of SC, GA, and FL. "Calcutta" refers to inhumane prison conditions leading to premature death and named after the "Black Hole of Calcutta," a notorious dungeon at Fort William, Calcutta, now Mumbai. In 1756, the Bengali army captured the fort and held sixty-four prisoners in a 14-by-18-foot room. By the next morning, two-thirds of the men had died.

14. On July 30, 1864, Brig. Gen. John McCausland's men, under orders from Gen. Jubal Early, burned Chambersburg near the PA-MD line after the citizens refused to pay a ransom of $500,000 in cash or $100,000 in gold and also to retaliate for Union destruction of civilian property in the Shenandoah Valley.

15. On Aug. 5, 1864, Rear Adm. David Farragut ran four ironclads and fourteen other ships through mine-filled waters past Forts Morgan, Gaines, and Powell, which guarded the entrance to Mobile Bay. The Union lost the monitor USS *Tecumseh* to a Confederate torpedo mine, but forced the surrender of the CSS *Tennessee,* including its commander, Adm. Franklin Buchanan. In capturing lower Mobile Bay, the Union Navy completed the blockade of the Gulf of Mexico.

16. For almost a month, Union soldiers had worked on a tunnel under a Confederate battery and trenches, hoping a massive explosion would break up their defenses around Petersburg, VA. The explosion went off early in the morning of July 30, 1864, and created a massive crater, thirty feet deep, but Confederate artillery and infantry repulsed the uncoordinated Union assaults.

17. Deep depression.

18. The workhouse.

19. Col. Frances T. Sherman, 88th IL Inf.

20. Hilton Head was a Union-occupied island in the Carolina Lowcountry south of Charleston and the headquarters for the Federal Dept. of the South.

21. Capts. Henry C. Potter, 18th PA Cav., and Washington Airey, 15th PA Cav.

22. Port Royal Ferry linked this deep-water port with Hilton Head Island, SC.

23. Col. Henry Hoyt, 52nd PA Inf.; Lt. Cdr. Austin Pendergrast, USN; Capt. George Manning, 2nd MA Cav.

24. For the text of the parole, see Domschcke, *Twenty Months in Captivity,* 101–2; and Glazier, *Capture,* 159.

25. Capt. James Belger, 1st R.I. Art.

26. On Aug. 13, 1864, Lt. Col. John S. Mosby's partisan rangers resumed their raids in Union-held areas of northern VA, including Berryville, Clarke Cty., VA.

27. Located on the northern tip of Morris Island across Charleston Harbor from Fort Sumter.

28. Maj. Gen. Joseph Wheeler raided north GA and attacked the Union garrison in Dalton, Aug. 14–15, 1864, hoping to disrupt Sherman's supply lines. Meanwhile, on Aug. 18, 1864, Brig. Gen. Judson Kilpatrick cut railroad lines, burned depots, and destroyed Confederate supplies at Lovejoy Station.

29. Rear Adm. John A. Dahlgren, commander, South Atlantic Blockading Squad.

30. Probably Lt. Charles P. Potts, 151st PA Inf., or Lt. Joseph. H. Potts, 75th Ohio Inf.

31. The fire occurred Dec. 11, 1861. Driven by winds from a campfire of slave refugees from the seacoast, the fire destroyed almost six hundred buildings, which remained in ruins.

32. At the Battle of Atlanta, July 22, 1864, Hood attacked the Federal's left flank but failed to stop their advance toward the city. Confederate casualties numbered 5,500 (including over 1,000 killed), compared to total Federal losses of 3,400.

33. Inspector general.

34. After reaching Lovejoy's Station on the Western and Macon Railroad, Kilpatrick's cavalry was attacked by Confederate infantry from Patrick Cleburne's division and fled to avoid being surrounded.

35. Maximilian I of Mexico headed a puppet regime in 1864 supported by French troops who had invaded the country in 1861. Opposed by the US government and by Mexican republican forces, he was captured and executed in 1867.

36. Maj. Gen. Joseph Hooker, commander, Army of the Cumberland, XX Corps, asked to be relieved of command when Sherman appointed Maj. Gen. Oliver Otis Howard commander of the Army of the Tennessee. Hooker then took command of the Northern Dept., with headquarters in Cincinnati.

37. Gardiner Spring, *The Bible Not of Man, or, The Argument for the Divine Origin of the Sacred Scriptures, Drawn from the Scriptures Themselves* (New York: American Tract Society, 1847).

38. The *Charleston Daily Courier,* 1852–73, had opposed "northern aggression" and SC's secession in 1860.

39. At the Battle of Globe Tavern, Aug. 18–21, 1864, Union forces severed the Weldon Railroad, Lee's vital supply line into NC. Confederates counterattacked with heavy losses on both sides, including Brig. Gen. Johnson Hagood's Brigade.

40. Millard Fillmore, thirteenth president, 1850–53, an ex-Whig. Although a supporter of the war, he was very critical of the Lincoln administration, especially emancipation, and endorsed George McClellan, the Democratic Party nominee.

41. The *New York Herald,* one of the most popular papers in the country, supported the Democratic Party.

42. After defeating the Confederates defending Mobile Bay and securing Fort Gaines, Farragut turned his attention to Fort Morgan. Gen. Gordon Granger besieged the fort, forcing Gen. Richard L. Page to surrender unconditionally Aug. 23, 1864.

43. Clement Vallandigham of Ohio, leader of the Democratic Party's antiwar faction. Lincoln exiled him to the Confederacy for his opposition to the war but he returned to Ohio in June 1864 and attended the Democratic National Convention the following month.

44. Petersburg Railroad. Brig. Gen. Lysander Cutler was badly wounded by a shell fragment at the Battle of Globe Tavern and left the field of command.

45. On July 17, 1864, Rev. James F. Jaquess and James Roberts Gilmore, with President Lincoln's consent, interviewed President Jefferson Davis on his terms for ending the conflict. Edmund Kirke was Gilmore's literary pseudonym.

46. The Democratic Party.

47. Joseph A. Collier, *The Right Way; or, The Gospel Applied to the Intercourse of Individuals and Nations* (New York: American Tract Society, 1854).

48. CSS *Tallahassee*, a turn-screw steam cruiser built in London, was purchased by the Confederacy in 1864. Running the blockade from Wilmington, NC, Aug. 6, 1864, her crew destroyed twenty-six vessels and captured seven prizes in a nineteen-day raid along the Atlantic Coast.

49. On Aug. 24, 1864, the USS *Keystone State* and the USS *Gettysburg* captured the CSS *Lilian* off the coast of Wilmington, NC, as the blockade runner attempted to run a load of cotton to England.

50. The Democratic National Convention, held in Chicago, Aug. 29–31, nominated Maj. Gen. George B. McClellan, a War Democrat, for president and Rep. George H. Pendleton, a Peace Democrat, for vice-president. The convention adopted a peace platform that declared the Union war effort a failure and called for an immediate end to the conflict. Fernando Wood, New York City mayor, 1860–62, and congressman, 1863–65, was a Peace Democratic.

51. Pro-South sympathizers in the North.

52. Lt. Gen. Gen. William J. Hardee, commander, I Corps, Army of Tennessee, sought to prevent Union forces from cutting the Confederates' remaining supply lines to Atlanta. They failed to dislodge the Federals at the Battle of Jonesborough, Aug. 31–Sept. 1, and lost around two thousand men. That evening Gen. John Bell Hood began evacuating Atlanta and ordered the destruction of some eighty railcars with ammunition and supplies. Union forces occupied the city Sept. 2.

53. After a disastrous raid into KY in June 1864, Brig. Gen. John Hunt Morgan was appointed head of the Dept. of Western VA and East TN, Aug. 22, 1864, but was soon relieved of command under charges of banditry.

54. In fact, Brig. Gen. John H. Winder's duties expanded from supervising the Richmond prisons to command of the Andersonville prison, June 3, 1864, prisons in AL and GA, July 26, 1864, and commissary general of all Confederate prisons, Nov. 21, 1864.

55. Morgan was surprised by two Union cavalrymen in Greeneville, TN, and killed Sept. 4, 1864.

56. Sisters of our Lady of Mercy, an order of Catholic nuns who ministered to sick prisoners and soldiers of both armies.

57. On July 18, 1864, Lincoln ordered an additional 500,000 enlistments into Union forces. After fifty days (Sept. 5, 1864) men would be drafted if volunteers had not already filled each congressional district's quota. On Sept. 6, 1864, Lincoln reduced the quota to 300,000 to avoid triggering unpopular conscription.

58. The CSS *Georgia*, a steam cruiser constructed in England in 1862, entered Confederate service Apr. 9, 1863, to harass US merchant ships. She was captured by the USS *Niagara* off Lisbon, Portugal, Aug. 15, 1864.

59. A gang at Andersonville preyed on weaker prisoners, demanding food, shelter, clothes, money, etc. As Maj. Henry Wirtz was unable to suppress the raiders, Winder authorized a jury trial for the twenty-four arrested men. Twelve fellow prisoners heard evidence and pronounced six guilty. They were hanged July 11, 1864. The remaining eighteen ran the gauntlet of prisoners armed with clubs; three died from the beatings. Their graves were set apart, isolated from the graves of the other prisoners.

60. On Sept. 8, 1864, Sherman issued Special Order No. 67 requiring the evaluation of all residents. Those taking a loyalty oath could move north; otherwise, civilians were under Hood's protection. The evacuation of Atlanta was carried out Sept. 10–12, 1864.

61. The Washington Race Course, a one-mile track at Hampton Park, became an outdoor prison for enlisted men, including African American soldiers, where several hundred captives died. In Apr. 1865, the freed people of Charleston constructed a fence around the burial ground with "Martyrs of the Race Course" emblazoned over an archway. On May 1, 1865, a procession to the cemetery marked America's first Memorial Day commemoration.

62. Capt. David W. D. Freeman, 101st PA Inf., captured Apr. 20, 1864, Plymouth, NC, escaped from Camp Asylum, Columbia, SC, Nov. 29, 1864, with Maj. Henry L. Pasco, 16th CT Inf., and Capt. Henry B. Freeman, 18th US Inf. They were recaptured near Midway, SC.

63. Lt. Morris C. Foot, 92nd NY Inf., was eating dinner when the shell entered his room.

64. Brevet Maj. Gen. James H. Wilson commanded a division of cavalry under Maj. Gen. Philip Sheridan and participated in the Overland and the Valley Campaigns of 1864.

65. The CSS *A. D. Vance,* a sidewheel steamer built in Scotland in 1862, was purchased by North Carolina as a blockade-runner. After more than twenty successful runs she was captured by the USS *Santiago de Cuba,* Sept. 10, 1864, off Wilmington, NC. The USN purchased the *Vance,* recommissioned as the USS *Advance,* and the ship joined the North Atlantic Blockading Squad. off Wilmington, Nov. 14, 1864.

66. US currency, or "greenbacks."

67. At the Third Battle of Winchester or Battle of Opequon, Sept. 19, 1864, Confederate Maj. Gen. Robert E. Rodes and Brig. Gen. Archibald Godwin were killed and Maj. Gen. Fitzhugh Lee and Brig. Gen. William Terry were wounded.

68. Brig. Gen. John B. McIntosh was wounded and lost a leg, and Brig. Gen. David A. Russell was killed at Opequon. The Union victory over Maj. Gen. Jubal A. Early was a turning point in the Shenandoah Valley Campaign.

69. Joseph M. Brown, governor of Georgia, 1857–65, a fierce critic of the Davis administration.

70. At the Battle of Fisher's Hill, Sept. 21–22, 1864, near Strasburg, VA, Sheridan's forces routed Early's men and inflicted heavy casualties. With the lower Shenandoah Valley cleared of Confederate forces, Sheridan destroyed crops, barns, mills, and stores as he slowly withdrew.

71. A reference to Napoleon's invasion of Russia in 1812. After capturing Moscow, Napoleon was forced to retreat a month later, as his supply lines were stretched too thin and the Russians refused to capitulate. During the disastrous Great Retreat his army melted away from the harsh Russian winter and from attacks by Russian irregular forces.

72. Possibly Lt. Andrew Stoll, 6th US Cav., who died Sept. 28, 1864.

73. Harry White, 67th PA Vol.

74. Capt. Enos Pennypacker, Co. M, 18th PA Cav.

75. Possibly Nathaniel Parker Willis (1806–67), a popular writer of sentimental prose, poems, travel writings, and magazine articles.

76. Capt. Frederick Zarracher, Co. C, 18th PA Cav., captured, Mine Run, VA, May 5, 1864.

77. At the Battle of Peeble's Farm, or Poplar Springs Church, Dinwiddie Cty., VA, Sept. 30–Oct. 2, 1864, Union forces captured two Confederate works on Lee's western flank, extending the Union siege line against Petersburg and Richmond.

78. On Sept. 28, 1864, President Davis relieved Lt. Gen. William J. Hardee, Army of Tennessee, and appointed him to command the Dept. of SC, GA, and FL.

79. On Oct. 2, 1864, men from John Bell Hood's Army of Tennessee temporarily cut the Western and Atlantic Railroad, Sherman's supply and communication line from Chattanooga, in an effort to force the Federals to withdraw from Atlanta.

80. Supplies sent by the US Sanitary Commission, a private relief organization providing food, clothing, and medical supplies to Union soldiers.

7. "escape has been the order of the day"

1. Marvel, *Biographical Sketch,* 184; Lord, "Camp Sorghum"; Hesseltine, *Civil War Prisons,* 165–67; Speer, *Portals to Hell,* 270–73; Peckenpaugh, *Captives in Blue,* 180–83. The other men were Lt. Henry C. Potter, Co. M., 18th PA Cav.; Capt. Enos J. Pennypacker, Co. M., 18th PA Cav.; Capt. Washington Airey, 15th PA Cav.; and Lt. Louis R. Fortescue, 29th PA Inf.

2. James Riley Weaver Diary, Nov. 25, Dec. 9, 1864.

3. Weaver Diary, Oct. 21, Nov. 7, Dec. 6 and 5, 1864.

4. Lt. Robert P. Wilson, 5th US Cav., survived the war and remained in the army.

5. Yellow fever.

6. Gen. William T. Sherman remained in Atlanta until Nov. 15 destroying anything of value to the Confederacy. Meanwhile, Gen. John Bell Hood moved north toward Tennessee cutting Sherman's supply and communication lines, including the Western and Atlantic Railroad, hoping to draw Sherman away from Atlanta. Sherman refused the bait. In 1871, Resacca adopted its current spelling, Resaca.

7. Col. David B. Harris, Pierre G. T. Beauregard's chief of staff. A Confederate engineer, Harris planned Charleston's defenses and died of yellow fever at Summerville, SC, Oct. 10, 1864.

8. Capt. James E. Wenrick, 19th PA Cav., captured, Cypress Swamp, TN, Apr. 1864; Lt. Ara C. Spafford, 21st Ohio Inf.

9. Maj. Charles P. Mattocks, 17th Maine Inf. and 1st US Sharpshooters. The exchange did not go through. His diary is published in Racine, *"Unspoiled Heart."*

10. Allatoona, GA, was a mountain pass along the Western and Atlantic Railroad and an important Federal supply depot. On Oct. 5, 1864, Confederate forces under Maj. Gen. Samuel G. French attacked the Union garrison not realizing that it had just received reinforcements led by Brig. Gen. John M. Corse, 4th Div., XIV Corps. In heavy fighting the Confederates failed to dislodge the fortified Federals.

11. Lt. Col. William P. Brinton, 18th PA Cav., wounded and captured, Third Battle of Winchester or Opequon Creek, Sept. 19, 1864, but escaped as the Confederates retreated.

12. Each state set its own election calendar, and results in early state contests predicted the Nov. presidential election's outcome.

13. The votes are converted into a table for clarity. This is the first published state tally of this camp election.

14. This was a straw poll, as only seven states (CA, KS, KY, ME, MI, RI, and WI) allowed soldiers to vote in camp. Johnson received 1,031 votes and George H. Pendleton, McClellan's running mate, 112 (Domschcke, *Twenty Months in Captivity,* 112). In the general election on Nov. 8, 1864, Lincoln swept the Electoral College 212 to 21 and secured 55 percent of the popular vote, as McClellan won only NJ, DE, and KY. As in the camp vote, soldiers overwhelmingly supported Lincoln with 75 percent of their votes, and only KY soldiers gave McClellan a majority. The prisoners included soldiers from every state participating in the national election except NV and OR. Elections were held in Union-occupied areas of TN and LA, but Congress did not accept these returns.

15. George A. Custer took command of the 3rd Cav. Div. Oct. 2, 1864, which included Weaver's regiment, the 18th PA Cav.

16. As prospects for Confederate victory dimmed, Maj. Gen Patrick Cleburne, Army of Tennessee, circulated a proposal among the officers in Jan. 1864 proposing to arm slaves who volunteered to serve in the army and, eventually, free their families. President Davis initially suppressed the proposal, but by fall 1864 it was being debated in Southern newspapers. Davis suggested the possibility of raising a voluntary black regiment in his annual address on Nov. 7, 1864. Only after General Lee wrote Davis the following Feb. arguing that arming slaves was "not only expedient but necessary" did the Confederate Congress on Mar. 13, 1865, authorize raising black companies, just weeks before Lee's surrender to Grant.

17. William Waters Boyce (1818–90) represented SC in the US House, 1853–60, and the Provisional, First, and Second Confederate Congresses, 1861–65. He urged President Davis to call a convention to discuss peace terms and support Northern Democrats in electing George McClellan president.

18. Lincoln carried PA with 51.6 percent of the popular vote.

19. Lt. Col. Robert Stark Means, commandant, Camp Sorghum.

20. Col. John S. Mosby's Greenback raid on the Baltimore and Ohio Railroad west of Harper's Ferry, WV, Oct. 13, 1864.

21. Lt. Alvin Young, 4th PA Cav. Apparently the shot went off when the guard was adjusting the primer cap of his musket.

22. Lt. Gen. Jubal A. Early's surprise attack on Maj. Gen. Philip Sheridan's camp on the morning of Oct. 19, 1864, broke through Union lines and secured many prisoners, cannon, and supplies. As the hungry, exhausted Confederate soldiers halted, Sheridan counterattacked in the afternoon, routing Early's army. The Battle of Cedar Creek or Belle Grove secured Union control of the Shenandoah Valley, the economic lifeline for Lee's troops in besieged Petersburg.

23. Probably Thomas Campbell (1777–1844), a Scottish poet of sentimental poetry often on themes of politics, war, and patriotism.

24. Fort Pulaski, Cockspur Island, GA, captured by Union forces, Apr. 10–11, 1862, effectively closed the port of Savannah. After its capture, Fort Pulaski housed Confederate prisoners of war.

25. Brig. Gens. Daniel D. Bidwell, US Vol.; Charles. R. Lowell Jr., 1st Div., Cav. Corps; and Maj. Gen. Stephen D. Ramseur were all killed. Union Brig. Gens. James B. Ricketts and Curvier Grover, 2nd Div., XIX Corps, were wounded. Maj. Gen. Horatio Gouverneur Wright commanded the Union forces until Sheridan arrived in the afternoon.

26. The CSS *Flora,* an iron steamer, left Nassau, Bahamas, Oct. 23, 1864, on her inaugural run to Charleston. Pursued by the naval blockade squadron, she ran aground on the shoals outside Charleston harbor where Union guns destroyed her.

27. Maj. Gen. John G. Foster, Union commander on Morris Island, was undoubtedly concerned by persistence of yellow fever in Charleston.

28. Maj. Gen. David B. Birney became ill during the Siege of Petersburg and died Oct. 18, 1864; Roger B. Taney, chief justice of the Supreme Court, died Oct. 12, 1864. Lincoln nominated Salmon P. Chase, his former secretary of the treasury, to the court Dec. 6, 1864, and he was confirmed that day.

29. Lts. Louis P. Mays, W. J. Darden, David Ellison Willis, and Capt. Stephen D. Mobley, 32nd GA.

30. Gen. Benjamin Butler deployed Confederate soldiers and hired freed African American laborers to construct a canal at Dutch Gap on the James River below Richmond so Union naval vessels could approach Richmond safe from Confederate batteries.

31. On Oct. 19, 1864, twenty-one escaped Confederate prisoners led by Lt. Bennett H. Young robbed the town's three banks and fled to Canada. Authorities arrested the men, returned the recovered money, but refused to extradite them to the US.

32. Likely a reference to an engagement at the Boydton Plank Road, Oct. 27, 1864.

33. Col. John S. Mosby captured Brig. Gen. Alfred N. Duffié, 1st Cav. Div., Dept. of WV, Bunker Hill, WV, Oct. 20, 1864.

34. The Battle of Burgess's Mill or Boydton Plank Road, Oct. 27–28, 1864, was the Union's final effort to sever Lee's supply line to Petersburg by seizing the Boydton Plank Road and cutting the South Side Railroad. Failing to achieve either objective, the Union army withdrew and both sides settled into winter camp. The *Tri-Weekly South Carolinian* was published in Columbia, 1849–65.

35. Mental depression.

36. Lt. Asa W. Sprague, 24th MI Inf., captured at Gettysburg PA, July 1, 1863 died on Oct. 14, 1864.

37. Capt. John Halderman, 129th IL Inf.

38. In late Sept. 1864, Maj. Gen. Sterling Price led a cavalry invasion of MO hoping to rally popular support for the Confederacy and prevent Lincoln's reelection. Augmented with Confederate guerillas, Price was met by MO militia, infantry, and cavalry from Maj. Gen. William S. Rosencran's Dept. of the MO. Maj. Gen. John S. Marmaduke and Brig. Gen. William Lewis Cabell were captured in Marais des Cygnes, KS, Oct. 25, 1864. Price's forces wreaked havoc as they swept across the state, but by late Oct. they were driven into AR.

39. The CSS *Albemarle,* a steam ironclad constructed in 1863–64 to clear the Roanoke River of US naval vessels. During the night of Oct. 27–28, 1864, Lt. William B. Cushing and fifteen men stole up the Roanoke River on a steam launch to Plymouth, NC, where the *Albemarle* was docked, and rammed her with a spar torpedo attached to a pole. The *Albemarle* sank immediately but the torpedo explosion threw Cushing and the crew overboard. He and one crewman escaped, two drowned, and the rest were captured by the Confederates.

40. Lincoln carried PA by about 18,800 votes.

41. Alfred T. A. Torbert, commander, Cav. Corps, Army of the Shenandoah, was breveted major general, Sept. 9, 1864. George Armstrong Custer was promoted brevet major general, US Vol., Oct. 19, 1864, after the Third Battle of Winchester, Sept. 19, 1864, and Fisher's Hill, Sept. 21–22, 1864. Wesley Merritt was breveted major general following his routing of Confederate forces at the Third Battle of Winchester.

42. Small islands in the lower Savannah River below Savannah.

43. Union forces under Cdr. William H. Macomb, North Atlantic Blockading Squad., retook Plymouth, NC, Oct. 31, 1864, after three days of heavy bombardment.

44. Capt. George R. Lodge, 53rd IL Inf.

45. Capt. J. C. Martin, commander of the guards, Camp Sorghum.

46. Likely Judith Page Walker Rives (1802–82), *Tales and Souvenirs of a Residence in Europe by a Lady of Virginia* (Philadelphia, 1844). The first section, "A Tale of Our Ancestors," is a romantic novel set in England and PA that traces the fortunes of Percy Medwyn.

47. Capt. William H. Hatch, assistant to Robert Ould, Confederate exchange agent. This agreement would exchange five thousand sick and wounded prisoners at Ft. Pulaski.

48. President Davis proposed replacing the policy of impressing slaves from their owners with government purchases of slaves as military laborers who would be freed at the end of the war.

49. On Nov. 1, 1864, Maj. Gen. Nathan Bedford Forrest with two captured gunboats and artillery moved up the Tennessee River to Johnsonville, TN, an important Union supply center. Three days later the Confederates claimed they inflicted $6.7 million dollars in damages to Federal stores and transports and disrupted Maj. Gen. George H. Thomas's supply line.

50. Milledge Luke Bonham, SC governor, 1862–64.

51. This monster cast iron Rodman Gun, designed by Thomas Jackson Rodman, was one of two made at the Fort Pitt Foundry, Pittsburgh, PA. It weighed 116,497 pounds and could fire 1,080-pound, twenty-inch solid shots or 750-pound spherical shells about four and a half miles. One was positioned at Fort Hamilton, NY, but never used in combat.

52. Lt. David T. McKay, Co. B., 18th PA Cav.

53. Lt. Otho P. Fairfield, 89th Ohio Inf., captured Sept. 20, 1863, Chickamauga, GA.

54. Maj. John E. Mulford, assistant Union exchange agent.

55. Lt. Harry Wilson, Co. H, 18th PA Cav.

56. Built in Liverpool in 1862 as the *Oreto,* the CSS *Florida* destroyed several Federal ships before being captured Oct. 7, 1864, off the coast of Bahia, Brazil.

57. Lt. Guy Bryan Jr., adjutant, 18th PA Cav.

58. On Nov. 11, 1864, Sherman ordered Atlanta to be burned, sparing only churches and hospitals. Maj. Gen. George H. Thomas went after Gen. John Bell Hood, who had moved into northwestern GA and TN, attempting to draw Sherman away from Atlanta.

59. Capt. Frederick Zarracher, Co. C, 18th PA Cav., captured, Mine Run, VA, May 5, 1864, and remained a prisoner with Weaver until they were exchanged Mar. 1, 1865.

60. Prisoners continued to receive their military pay while incarcerated, which they used to send for care packages from the North.

61. Maj. Elias Griswold.

62. Capt. John Halderman, 129th IL Inf.

63. Weaver misdated this entry as Wednesday, Nov. 17.

64. Lt. William H. Bricker, 3rd PA Cav.; Lt. Henry H. Hinds, 57th PA Inf.; Capt. Daniel B. Meaney, 13th PA Cav., Lt. John W. Munday, 73rd IL Inf.

65. A reworking of Proverbs 15:8: "The sacrifice of the wicked is an abomination to the Lord, but the prayer of the upright is his delight" (KJV).

66. Sherman left Atlanta Nov. 16, 1864, dividing his forces into columns led by Maj. Gen. Oliver O. Howard's Army of the Tennessee on the right and Maj. Gen. Frank W. Slocum's Army of Georgia on the left. Maj. Gen. Hugh Judson Kilpatrick's cavalry burned Marietta. Union forces occupied Rome, GA, Nov. 11, 1864, and destroyed forts, ironworks, and the railroad.

67. Lt. Gen. William J. Hardee, commander, Dept. of SC, GA, and FL, provided the primary, if meager, opposition to Sherman's march to the sea.

68. Acting assistant adjutant general.

69. Lt. Lucius Dwight Hinckley, 10th WI Inf., captured Sept. 20, 1863, Chickamauga, GA.

70. Capt. David Flamsburg or Flansburg, 4th IN Batt.

71. Confederates resisted Sherman's advancing forces at Griswoldville on the Central of Georgia Railway on Nov. 22, but were unable to slow the Union march. Macon was not taken until Apr. 22, 1865.

72. Slocum's forces occupied Milledgeville, Nov. 22, 1864, but spared the city. The Confederates had burned Chambersburg, PA, July 30, 1864.

73. Gordon was a depot on the Central of Georgia Railway on the Oconee River.

74. Potter was the camp sutler who advanced funds drawing on prisoners' pay; see entry for Nov. 21, 1864.

75. Lt. Guy Bryan Jr.

76. Lt. Joseph Leslie, Co. D., 18th PA Cav.; Louis R. Fortescue, 29th PA Inf.; Capt. Enos J. Pennypacker, Co. M, 18th PA Cav.

77. Lt. Thomas K. Ekings, 3rd NJ Inf.; Lt. Henry H. Pierce, 7th CT Inf. Vols., captured, Bermuda Hundred, VA, June 4, 1864, survived his wound and successfully escaped.

78. Capt. John W. McHugh, 69th PA Inf.; Lt. William Heffner, 67th PA Inf.

79. Col. Thomas H. Butler, 5th IN Cav.

80. Edward Smeltzer, husband of Catherine S. Weaver.

81. Lt. Benjamin F. Herrington, Co. G, 18th PA Cav.; Capt. Washington Airey, 15th PA Cav.

82. Lt. George Turbayne, 66th NY Inf., captured, Petersburg, VA, June 17, 1864.

83. Maj. Gen. John P. Hatch left Hilton Head, SC, Nov. 28, 1864, intending to cut the Charleston and Savannah Railroad near Pocotaligo, SC. Encountering the Confederates two days later at Honey Hill, Hatch was unable to dislodge the entrenched troops and withdrew.

84. On Nov. 21, 1864, Brig. Gen. John H. Winder was appointed commissary general for all Confederate prisons.

85. Capt. John Aigan, 5th RI Art., captured May 5, 1864, Croatan, NC, and escaped again, Feb. 19, 1865.

86. Kilpatrick's objective was to liberate the Union prisoners at Camp Lawton, Millen, GA, but they already had been evacuated when the Federals arrived. The *Weekly Southern Guardian* was published in Columbia, 1857–65.

87. At the Battle of Franklin, Nov. 30, 1864, Lt. Gen. John Bell Hood's Army of Tennessee made several frontal assaults against Maj. Gen. John M. Schofield's entrenched forces. Heavy Confederate losses of 6,252 men, including six generals (Patrick Cleburne, John C. Carter,

John Adams, Hiram B. Granbury, States Rights Gist, and Otho F. Strahl), shattered Hood's army. Union losses totaled 2,326.

88. A parody of Henry Wadsworth Longfellow's "A Psalm of Life" (1838), an immensely popular poem that urged overcoming adversity through an active life.

89. A mixture of bran and coarse meal left over from milling.

90. On Apr. 19, 1861, a mob of antiwar Democrats and Southern sympathizers had assaulted the men of the 6th MA Vol. Regt. as they were passing through Baltimore on their way to Washington.

91. Cols. John Fraser, 140th PA Inf., and Francis C. Miller, 147th NY Inf.; Lt. Col. John B. Conyngham, 52nd PA Inf.; Maj. Duvall English, 11th KY Cav., and Maj. William S. Marshall, 5th Iowa Inf. Marshall was captured, Chattanooga, TN, Nov. 25, 1863, escaped from Camp Sorghum Nov. 28, 1864, and reached Union lines, Sweetwater, TN, Jan. 1, 1865.

92. "Old fish" were prisoners incarcerated for a long time.

93. Capts. William A. Daily, 8th PA Cav., and John Christopher, 16th US Inf.

94. William Gregg (1800–67) owned the Graniteville Manufacturing Co., one of the largest textile mills in the South that employed white wage laborers. An advocate for Southern industrialization before the war, Gregg became a secessionist in 1861 but was critical of Davis's industrial policies.

95. Ephraim Brunner Jr., husband of Elizabeth S. Weaver.

96. Capt. Frederick Zarracher, 18th PA Cav.

97. Col. Warren Shedd, 30th IL Inf., captured, Atlanta, GA, July 22, 1864.

8. "SITTING OUTSIDE MY TENT PENNING THESE LINES"

1. James Riley Weaver Diary, Dec. 13, 12, 1865; Hesseltine, *Civil War Prisons,* 168; Speer, *Portals to Hell,* 272; Peckenpaugh, *Captives in Blue,* 183–84.

2. Weaver Diary, Jan. 23, 11, 1865; Dec. 24, 16, 25, 1864.

3. Weaver Diary, Jan. 21, Feb. 13, 1865.

4. Col. Samuel J. Crooks, 22nd NY Cav.

5. Sherman's forces reached the outskirts of Savannah on Dec. 10, 1864, but did not occupy the city until Dec. 21.

6. Greenville, SC, is about one hundred miles northwest of Columbia in the foothills of the Blue Ridge Mountains.

7. Lts. John G. B. Adams and Frank Osborne, 19th Maine Inf.

8. Capt. Alonzo Cooper, 12th NY Cav.

9. See entry for Oct. 26, 1864. Fort Pulaski, GA, was an officer's prison holding 520 of the 600 Confederate officers who were used as human shields on Morris Island in retaliation for Union prisoners held in Charleston. These Confederate officers were moved to Pulaski after a yellow fever epidemic forced removal of the Federal prisoners in Charleston. The exchange rumor proved untrue; 13 of these officers died in captivity and the rest were transferred to Fort Delaware.

10. Brig. Gen. John G. Foster, commander, Dept. of the South, was supporting Sherman's advance toward Savannah with African American troops stationed at Hilton Head and at Morris Island, SC.

11. Lt. Col. W. True Bennett, acting Confederate agent of exchange.

12. See entry for Dec. 6, 1864.

13. Prominent Republicans from Westmoreland Cty., PA: Sen. Edgar Cowan, US senator, 1861–67; John Covode, a fellow Methodist, House of Representatives, 1855–63; and Samuel Lightcap, a family friend. Maj. John E. Mulford, Union exchange agent, was in Savannah and Charleston to exchange the sick and wounded prisoners.

14. Maj. John Wilson Phillips, 18th PA Cav.; Capt. William H. Hatch, assistant Confederate commissioner of exchange.

15. Capt. John C. Whiteside, 94th NY Inf.

16. Capt. George R. Lodge, 53rd IL Inf.

17. At the Battle of Nashville, Dec. 15–16, 1864, Maj. Gen. George H. Thomas's Army of the Cumberland struck a decisive blow against Lt. Gen. John Bell Hood's Army of Tennessee. On Dec. 17, 1864, Sherman demanded that Lt. Gen. William J. Hardee, commander, I Corps, Army of Tennessee, surrender Savannah. Three days later the Confederates evacuated the city. Despite the loss of Mobile Bay in Aug. 1864, Confederates retained control of the city.

18. Following their rout at Nashville, Hood's Army of Tennessee retreated into MS but their days as an effective fighting force were finished.

19. May Agnes Fleming (1840–80) (pseud. Cousin May Carleton), a Canadian writer of popular fiction, published *Victoria; or The Heiress of Castle Cliffs* in 1862.

20. These Cherokees had avoided removal in the 1830s to Indian Territory, now OK, and today are the Eastern Band of Cherokee Indians. The NC government courted their loyalty and assistance in capturing escaped Union prisoners.

21. Maj. Elias Griswold, commandant, Camp Asylum.

22. Edward Bulwer-Lytton (1803–73), a politician and popular novelist, poet, and playwright, wrote *Godolphin* in 1833, a satirical novel about the everyday lives of British elite families.

23. Gen. Nathan Bedford Forrest's cavalry were harassing Union supply lines in West TN. He survived the war and died in 1877.

24. Hardee evacuated Savannah Dec. 20, 1864.

25. Elizabeth Caroline Grey (1798–1869), *Old Dower House: A Tale of Bygone Days* (1844). Gray was a popular writer of romance and of Gothic novels.

26. Lt. George W. Chandler, 1st WV Cav., captured, Gettysburg, July 2, 1863. The band included Chandler, first violin; Lt. John S. Manning, 116th Ohio Inf., second violin; Lt. Justus O. Rockwell, 97th NY Inf., flute; and Maj. John Edward Pratt, 4th VT Inf., bass violin.

27. Matthew 7:6, "Give not that which is holy unto the dogs, neither cast ye your pearls before swine, lest they trample them under their feet, and turn again and rend you" (KJV).

28. Genesis 4:13, "And Cain said unto the Lord, My punishment is greater than I can bear" (KJV). After Cain, Adam and Eve's first-born son, killed his brother Abel, he lamented God's curse on him for his crime.

29. Maj. David Vickers, 4th NJ Inf.; Maj. George G. Wanzer, 24th NY Cav.

30. Maj. Gen. Hugh Judson Kilpatrick, commander, 3rd Div. Cav., Army of the Ohio, XXIII Corps, accompanied Sherman on his march through GA and the Carolinas.

31. Capt. John Aigan, 5th RI Heavy Art.; William H. Durfee, 5th RI Inf.; Lt. Guy Bryan Jr., 18th PA Cav.; Lt. Harry Wilson, 18th PA Cav.; Capt. George R. Lodge, 53rd IL Inf.

32. At the First Battle of Fort Fisher, Dec. 23–27, 1864, Rear Adm. David Dixon Porter's forces bombarded the fort guarding Wilmington. After two days the fort's guns were silenced, and naval vessels landed Union infantry led by Maj. Gen. Benjamin F. Butler's Expeditionary Corps, Army of the James, who besieged the fort. Maj. Gen. Robert Hoke's Confederates met the Federals on the beach, and on Dec. 27 Butler withdrew, leaving Wilmington in Confederate hands.

33. On the alert.

34. Lt. Louis R. Fortescue, 29th PA Inf.

35. Capt. Andrew Cunningham, Co. D, 18th PA Cav.

36. At the Second Battle of Saltville, Dec. 20–21, 1864, Maj. Gen. George Stoneman sent forces to capture and destroy the important salt works in this southwestern VA town.

37. Weaver is describing General Hood's demand to Col. Clark R. Weaver, commander of the Union brigade in Resaca, GA, Oct. 12, 1864, that he surrender to the Confederates. After Colonel Weaver refused, Hood threatened to take no prisoners. On Dec. 13, 1864, Federal

forces captured Fort McAllister on the Ogeechee River south of Savannah, establishing contact with the Union fleet and dooming Confederate control of the city.

38. Congressman Henry S. Foote, ex-senator and governor of MS, represented TN in the Confederate Congress where he became Jefferson Davis's most vociferous critic and an advocate for ending the conflict. In Jan. 1865, Confederate authorities arrested him as he attempted to cross Union lines to Washington, DC.

39. Probably Fort Johnston, which guarded the west bank of the Lower Cape Fear River.

40. In his soliloquy in act 3, scene 1, Prince Hamlet contemplates committing suicide to escape the trials and tribulations of mortal life ("For in that sleep of death what dreams may come / When we have shuffled off this mortal coil, Must give us pause.... But that the dread of something after death, / The undiscovered country from whose bourn / No traveler returns, puzzles the will / And makes us rather bear those ills we have / Than fly to others that we know not of.").

41. Col. Warren Shedd, 13th IL Inf.

42. *Henry VI, Part 3* (1591) examines the horrors of the War of the Roses. Queen Margaret of Anjou led the Lancastrian faction and by excluding Richard of York from the Great Council of 1455 precipitated the war. "Hunchback Dick," Duke of Gloucester and King Richard III (1483–85), was the subject of Shakespeare's *Richard III* (ca. 1592). Richard's defeat at the Battle of Bosworth Field ended the War of the Roses and established the Tudor dynasty. In exaggerating Richard's idiopathic scoliosis, Shakespeare associated physical deformity with moral callousness.

43. Samuel S. Jack was the superintendent for Westmoreland Cty.

44. *Henry VIII* (1513), act 3, scene 2. Cardinal Thomas Wolsey, archbishop of York and lord chancellor, was Henry's intimate advisor and confidant but fell from favor after he failed to secure an annulment of Henry's marriage to Catherine of Aragon.

45. *Troilus and Cressida* (1602) is set in the later years of the Trojan War and tells of a tragic love affair and the death of Hector, son of Priam, King of Troy. Many critics and theatergoers echo Weaver's judgment of the play.

46. The *Savannah Daily Loyal Georgian,* edited by M. Summers, began publication in Dec. 1864, and merged with an established paper, the *Savannah Republican,* later that month.

47. Maj. Gen. Joseph B. Kershaw, McLaws's Div., Army of Northern Virginia.

48. Realizing he could no longer defend Savannah, General Hardee withdrew his forces on Dec. 20, 1864. The next morning, a delegation including Mayor Richard D. Arnold, city aldermen, and prominent women, met with Brig. Gen. John W. Geary and offered to surrender the city if civilians and their property were protected. Federal forces occupied the city later that day.

49. A town on the Charleston and Savannah Railroad. Maj. Gen. John P. Hatch, Coastal Div., Dept. of the South, failed to cut the railroad at the Battle of Honey Hill, Nov. 30, 1864.

50. Wilkie Collins (1824–89), *The Stolen Mask, or The Mysterious Cash-box, a Story for a Christmas Fireside* (Columbia, SC: F. G. De Fontaine, 1864). Collins was a popular British writer of suspense and detective fiction and social commentary.

51. *Timon of Athens* (1605–6) traces how Timon's false friends take advantage of his generosity, eventually bankrupting him.

52. Butler's failure to capture Fort Fisher caused political fallout in Washington. On Jan. 7, 1865, Lincoln removed Butler's command of the Dept. of VA and NC, later Army of the James, and replaced him with Maj. Gen. Edward O. C. Ord. Rear Adm. David D. Porter commanded the Union fleet during the attack on Fort Fisher.

53. Deep depression.

54. Lt. Gen. William J. Hardee commanded the Dept. SC, GA, and FL, resisting Sherman's advance.

55. The first English edition of *One Thousand and One Nights,* a collection of Middle Eastern and South Asian folk tales, appeared in 1706 as *The Arabian Knights' Entertainment.*

56. Gaming.

57. Faro is a card game; players bet against the dealer on the order in which the cards appear from the top of the deck. Sweat is a gambling game using three dice.

58. Lt. Sigesmund Braieda, 2nd NJ Cav.

59. Augusta Jane Evans Wilson (1835–1909), *Beulah* (1859). The semiautobiographical *Beulah* traces a young woman's intellectual journey from religious skepticism to Methodist orthodoxy. A Confederate nationalist, Wilson was a popular writer of sentimental domestic novels with religious themes.

60. Maj. John H. Isett, 8th Iowa Cav.; Lt. Samuel H. M. Byers, 5th Iowa Inf.; Lt. Justus O. Rockwell, 97th NY Inf. See Jan. 15, 1865, for song text.

61. Mark 5:36b, "Be not afraid, only believe" (KJV).

62. Published in New York in 1865 by Wm. Hall & Son.

63. Union forces prevailed at the Second Battle of Fort Fisher, Jan. 13–15, 1865, and Wilmington was occupied a month later. Augusta, GA, remained under Confederate control until the end of the war.

64. Invented by Henry Hopkins Sibley in 1856, Sibley tents were constructed like tepees, stood twelve feet high and eighteen feet in diameter, and housed about a dozen men.

65. Capt. Frederick Zarracher, Co. C, 18th PA Cav.; Lt. Freeman C. Gay, 11th PA Inf.

66. The Federals secured Fort Fisher, NC, Jan. 15, 1865, and captured 1,400 men including Maj. Gen. William H. C. Whiting, commander, Dist. of Cape Fear.

67. Men pretending to be sick in hopes of securing better quarters or early parole. See Jan. 23, 1865, for poem text.

68. Lt. Robert B. Sinclair, 2nd MA Heavy Art. "Hail Columbia," a patriotic song composed by Philip Phile (1789), lyrics by Joseph Hopkinson (1798), that celebrated the heroes of the American Revolution, "who fought and bled in freedom's cause." It was an unofficial national anthem until the adoption of "The Star Spangled Banner" in 1931.

69. A small railroad community in Orangeburg Cty., SC.

70. A Union prisoner-of-war camp on Pea Patch Island in the Delaware River. By early Jan. 1865 it held over 12,000 Confederate prisoners.

71. After capturing Fort Fisher, Union forces destroyed Fort Caswell guarding Old Inlet on the Lower Cape Fear River, Jan. 17, 1865. Wilmington, however, held out until Feb. 23, 1865.

72. Edward Everett (1794–1865), statesman, educator, and popular orator, died Jan. 15, 1865, a few days after delivering an address in Boston to raise funds to relieve Savannah's suffering citizens. He is best remembered for giving a two-hour speech prior to Lincoln's Gettysburg Address.

73. Pocotaligo, SC, was an important railroad depot near Port Royal Island and targeted by Union troops in order to disrupt rail service between Charleston and Savannah.

74. William G. "Parson" Brownlow (1805–77), Methodist minister, newspaper editor, and opponent of secession fled TN during the war until Union forces occupied East TN in 1863. Nominated for governor in Jan. 1865 under the Union ticket, two months later he was elected almost unanimously as most Confederates were disfranchised.

75. The CSS *Tallahassee*, a steam blockade-runner and raider based in Wilmington, made a successful raid along the Atlantic coast in fall 1864. Renamed CSS *Chameleon*, she escaped Wilmington on Dec. 24, 1864, during the Union bombardment of Fort Fisher, and made her way to Bermuda and Liverpool, where British authorities seized her on Apr. 9, 1865.

76. *U.S. Service Magazine*, edited by Henry Coopée, published in New York, 1864–66. The Sept. 1864 issue included essays on the militia, naval hospitals, and the history of invalid soldiers' care in France; biographies of Sherman and Brig. Gen. Alexander Hays; patriotic fiction and poetry; literary reviews; and military appointments and dismissals.

77. Fisher, *Officers of the United States*. This broadside included twelve images of prison life, including Camps Sorghum and Asylum.

78. Elegantly witty.

79. A surgeon, named after Galen of Pergamon, a prominent Greek physician, surgeon, and philosopher in the Roman Empire.

80. A small group of people.

81. Probably a reference to Lt. Robert Sinclair; see entry for Jan. 18, 1864.

82. Lt. Alexander Wilson Norris, Co. D, 107th PA Inf.

83. Romans 8:28, "And we know that all things work together for good to them that love God, to them who are the called according to his purpose" (KJV).

84. With Lincoln's approval, Maj. Gen. Francis Preston Blair Sr. met unofficially with Davis, a personal friend, in Richmond, Jan. 12, 1865, to suggest that each side appoint commissioners to secure peace. Lincoln rejected Davis's insistence on recognizing the Confederacy, but negotiations continued and resulted in the Hampton Roads peace conference Feb. 3, 1865.

85. On Jan. 13, 1865, Hood resigned as commander, Army of Tennessee, and Lt. Gen. Richard Taylor was named his successor. James Seddon, Confederate secretary of war, did not resign until Feb. 1, 1865.

86. Shakespeare's *King John*, written in the mid-1590s, traces the dynastic struggles for political legitimacy and succession to the English throne. The claims of Arthur, nephew of King John (ruler, 1199–1216), was supported by King Philip of France. Arthur mysteriously disappeared in 1203, presumably at the hands of John's supporters.

87. Lt. Henry H. Mosley, 25th Ohio Inf.; Capt. Thomas Burke String, 11th KY Cav.; Capt. Lewis A. Campbell, 152nd NY Inf. Campbell was captured, Petersburg, VA, June 23, 1864.

88. Characters from Shakespeare's *King Henry IV, Part 1* (ca. 1597). Sir Henry Percy, known as Sir Harry Hotspur, initially supported Henry's struggle to seize the English throne, but led a rebellion against Henry in 1403 and died in battle. The fictional Sir John Falstaff, one of Shakespeare's most popular comic characters, was a vain, boastful companion to Prince Hal, the future king of England, but spent most of his time drinking at the Boar's Head Inn in London.

89. Remnants of Hood's Army of Tennessee escaped across the Tennessee River, but pursuing Federal Cavalry captured their supply train.

90. *Henry IV, Part 2*, "Prologue."

91. Lt. Thomas H. McKee, 1st WV Inf. Charles Sprague and J. F. Petri, "Eighty Years Ago" (New York: Wm. Hall & Son, 1856), a patriotic song praising the founding fathers' heroic sacrifices. J. E. Carpenter and W. T. Wrighton, "Her Bright Smile Haunt Me Still" (Macon, GA: John C. Shreiner and Son, 186?), a sentimental love song.

92. On Jan. 28, 1865, President Davis instructed Confederate Vice President Alexander H. Stephens, Confederate Senate President Pro Tem Robert M. T. Hunter, and Confederate Asst. Secretary of War John A. Campbell to meet with Lincoln to discuss peace terms.

93. On Jan. 19, 1865, Sherman began moving his forces from Savannah north toward the Carolina upcountry. He faced only token opposition from Joseph Johnston's Confederates. Branchville, Orangeburg, SC, was an important railroad junction.

94. The Great Fire of 1865 destroyed the south tower, two north towers, the second floor, and the roof of the central section of the Smithsonian Institution Building, popularly known as "the Castle." Losses included manuscripts, paintings, and book collections.

95. Brig. Gen. Joseph Hayes, wounded at the Weldon Railroad during the Petersburg Campaign, was assigned commissioner to oversee treatment of Union prisoners.

96. John Howard Payne and Henry Bishop, "Home! Sweet Home!" (1823).

97. Sen. Charles Sumner, abolitionist Republican from MA, spoke Jan. 24, 1865. While acknowledging Confederate authorities' cruel treatment of Union prisoners, he opposed the original motion from the Committee on Military Affairs, which called for reprisals against Confederates held in Union prisons. Seeking vengeance in retaliation for Confederate atrocities, he argued, would "degrade the national character," as "we cannot be cruel, or barbarous,

or savage, because the Rebels we now meet in warfare are cruel, barbarous, and savage" (Sumner, *Works*, 9:208–9).

98. On Jan. 24, 1865, Grant finally agreed to the Confederates' offer to negotiate a general exchange of all prisoners, as he was confident the Confederacy was close to military collapse.

99. Thomas Tate (1807–88), *An Elementary Course of Natural and Experimental Philosophy* (Boston: Hickling, Swan and Brown, 1856). Tate, a British mathematician and educator, wrote popular treatises on science, mathematics, engineering, and pedagogy with an emphasis on inductive reasoning.

100. Sen. Henry Wilson, abolitionist Republican from MA; Edwin M. Stanton, Union secretary of war.

101. By Feb. 1, 1865, Sherman's Carolina Campaign was in full operation and his forces were moving toward Columbia.

102. Weaver wrote "strange" after "queer."

103. Brig. Gen. John H. Winder died of a heart attack, Florence, SC, Feb. 7, 1865.

104. Likely a Union or Loyal League chapter, a men's organization established during the Civil War to support the Union, the Republican Party, and the Lincoln administration.

105. On Feb. 3, 1865, Lincoln and Secretary of State William H. Seward met the Confederate commissioners Stephens, Campbell, and Hunter at Hampton Roads, VA. Discussions quickly ended when Lincoln insisted that the Confederates disband their armies and accept Federal authority.

106. Capt. Eli F. Foster, 30th IN Inf.; Lt. Charles P. Cramer, 21st NY Cav., captured July 17, 1864, near Hillsboro, VA.

107. "Because he hath appointed a day, in the which he will judge the world in righteousness by that man whom he hath ordained; whereof he hath given assurance unto all men, in that he hath raised him from the dead" (KJV).

108. Capt. Henry C. Potter, 18th PA Cav., paroled Dec. 12, 1864. See entry for Dec. 9, 1864.

9. "ALTHO ALL THESE THINGS SEEMED AS OF FORMER DAYS, YET I COULD NOT REALIZE THAT I WAS FREE"

1. Hesseltine, *Civil War Prisons*, 227–32; Sanders, *While in the Hands*, 272–75; Peckenpaugh, *Captives in Blue*, 188–84.

2. James Riley Weaver Diary, Feb. 19, 20, 18; Mar. 1, 2, 4, 1865.

3. Weaver Diary, Mar. 13, 23, Apr. 1, 1865. Weaver extended his leave for another thirty days to allow processing an honorable discharge from service to the United States effective on May 15, 1865.

4. Varina or Aitken's Landing, Henrico Cty., VA, on the James River was a prisoner exchange point.

5. The Federals occupied and burned Columbia on Feb. 17, 1865, but Charleston was not occupied until the end of the war.

6. Capt. Bryon W. Evans, 4th Ohio Inf., captured, the Wilderness, May 6, 1864. He attempted to escape by cutting a hole through the bottom of the boxcar and was shot by a guard. A surgeon amputated his leg, but Evans died Feb. 21, 1865, Salisbury, NC.

7. Orcus was a god of the underworld who punished evildoers in the afterlife. The dead crossed the River Styx to enter the underworld, or Hades. Old Harry and Old Nick are nicknames for the devil.

8. After capturing Fort Fisher on Jan. 15, 1865, the Federals slowly moved up the Cape Fear River toward Wilmington, some thirty miles north. Fort Anderson's earthen batteries were the city's last defense line. On Feb. 11, Union forces attacked the fort by sea and by land; after three days, the Confederates abandoned the position and Wilmington surrendered on Feb. 22.

9. Hastily established in 1864 after Sherman threatened the Andersonville prison, the prison camp in Florence, SC, was a barren twenty-three-acre stockade. By Oct. 1864, over 12,000 enlisted men were held there under horrific conditions that rivaled the suffering at Andersonville.

10. Priv. Lowry Daniel Titus, Co. B; Priv. James F. Bailey, Co. K; and likely QM Sgt. Samuel P. Huff, Co. H; all 18th PA Cav.

11. Lt. David Garbet, 77th PA Inf. Set to a minstrel tune, the song traces Lincoln's gradual embrace of wartime emancipation.

12. Fearing the loss of the border states (MO, KY, MD, and DE) and seeking Democratic support for the war, Lincoln promptly overruled Maj. Gen. John C. Frémont's Aug. 14, 1861, declaration of martial law in MO that emancipated enslaved individuals of Confederate owners.

13. Likely a reference to Maj. Gen. Benjamin F. Butler, who, as commander at Fortress Monroe, VA, refused to return slaves of disloyal masters, declaring them "contrabands of war," or enemy property subject to seizure by the Federals. He employed them as army laborers.

14. Gen. George C. McClellan, a Democrat and advocate of limited war, strongly opposed emancipation or returning fugitives, including enslaved men impressed by Confederate authorities to work on fortifications.

15. On May 9, 1862, abolitionist Maj. Gen. David Hunter unilaterally emancipated all slaves in GA, SC, and FL. Lincoln promptly overruled the order.

16. Henry S. Washburne (lyrics) and George Frederick Root (music), "The Vacant Chair (New York, 1861) was based on the death of John William Grant, an eighteen-year-old MA soldier killed at the Battle of Balls Bluff, Oct. 21, 1861. The song was popular in both the North and the South.

17. Capt. William H. Hatch, Confederate asst. commissioner of exchange.

18. *Daily Progress*, Raleigh, NC, published by J. L. Pennington, 1862–67.

19. After passing the Conscription Act in Apr. 1862, Confederate Secretary of War George W. Randolph ordered each state to establish two training or conscript camps. Camp Holmes was located just outside Raleigh.

20. The Raleigh and Gaston Railroad opened in 1840.

21. Capt. Shadrack Harris, 3rd TN Cav., a conscript in the Confederate Army. After his capture he was tried for desertion and ordered to be shot. His sentence was commuted, but he spent over two years in irons in Columbia, SC. He was exchanged by special arrangements for Capt. J. P. Shaffey, 8th VA Cav.

22. Col. John H. Ashworth, 1st GA Inf. (Union).

23. Weaver may be referring either to the US Sanitary Commission or to the US Christian Commission.

24. See entry for Jan. 15, 1865. Maj. John H. Isett, 8th Iowa Cav., died of disease on Apr. 6, 1865, as he was returning home.

25. Grace United Methodist Church, founded in 1797, the oldest Methodist church in Wilmington.

26. The USS *General Sedgwick*, a side-wheeled paddle steamer built in NJ in 1862 as a transport ship. The ship's earlier name was the USS *General Hunter*, which was sunk on Apr. 16, 1864, in the St. John's River, FL. It was raised and renamed the *General Sedgwick*.

27. *Herald of the Union*, a pro-Union paper, began publishing Feb. 28, 1865.

28. Gens. John McAllister Schofield, Alfred H. Terry, and Jacob Dolson Cox.

29. A covered deck providing protection from the sun.

30. Located near the mouth of the Cape Fear River, Smithville became Southport in 1887.

31. In 1769, a hurricane cut a new inlet to the Cape Fear River to the north of Bald Head Island about six miles north of the Old Inlet. Fort Fisher guarded New Inlet.

32. From Samuel Taylor Coleridge, "The Rime of the Ancient Mariner" (1798). In retaliation for killing an albatross, who had led the ship out of an ice field, the crew later became becalmed near the equator, with "Water, water, everywhere / Nary a drop to drink."

33. Heaven and earth.

34. Fort Monroe, located on Old Point Comfort, guarded Hampton Roads and the Chesapeake Bay. The fort remained under Union control throughout the war.

35. Capes Henry and Charles marked the southern and northern entrances to the Chesapeake Bay, respectively.

36. Rip Raps, a small fifteen-acre artificial island at the mouth of Hampton Roads located midway between Fortress Monroe and Willoughby's Point.

37. Lt. Thomas J. Grier, Co. B; Col. Timothy M. Bryan Jr.; Lt. Col. William P. Brinton; Maj. William Baldwin Darlington; Maj. Harvey B. Van Voorhis; Capt. Marshall S. Kingsland; Capt. David K. Hamilton, Co. K; Maj. John Britton, Co. F; Capt. William H. Page, Co. L; James Wilson Smith, Co. B; and Henry J. Blough, Co. K—all 18th PA Cav.

38. At the Battle of Waynesboro, VA, Mar. 2, 1865, Brig. Gen. George A. Custer's forces destroyed Lt. Gen. Jubal Early's Army of the Valley. Federals captured about 1,500 prisoners, 11–14 cannon, and 150–200 wagons; only Early and his staff escaped.

39. Capt. Harry Wilson, Co. H, and Lt. Joseph Leslie, Co. D, 18th PA Cav.

40. Maj. John Wilson Phillips, 18th PA Cav.

41. Lt. Henry Clay Potter, Co. M, 18th PA Cav.

42. Capt. Charles W. Davis. Officers bivouacked at the Naval Academy.

43. McCullough's Hotel, also known as the Maryland Hotel, was built in the late eighteenth century and located on Church Circle, Annapolis.

44. Maryland State House (1772–97) constructed in the Georgian style and designed by Joseph Horatio Anderson.

45. Training, parole, and prison camps in Columbus, Ohio, and Chicago, respectively, named for Salmon P. Chase, treasury secretary, and Sen. Stephen A. Douglas, IL, Democrat.

46. First Presbyterian Church of Annapolis Sunday School. The church was established in 1846 and purchased the Haliam Theater, built in 1828, for its sanctuary.

47. Probably the Union or Loyal League.

48. Maj. John Wilson Phillips and Maj. John Britton, 18th PA Cav.; Samuel G. Lightcap, family friend.

49. Capt. Bethuel R. Mackay, Co. D, 18th PA Cav.

50. Maj. William B. Darlington, 18th PA Cav.

51. Calvary Methodist Church, established in 1785. In 1859 the congregation erected a large sanctuary on State Circle with an organ, choir loft, and bell tower.

52. Camp Parole was established west of Annapolis to house paroled Union prisoners of war until their exchange. Men who died in the camp or in hospitals were buried in Annapolis National Cemetery.

53. Lt. Benjamin F. Herrington, Co. G; Capt. Enos J. Pennypacker, Co. M; and Lt. David T. McKay, Co. B; all 18th PA Cav.

54. The Methodist Episcopal Sunday School rented Temperance Hall on State Circle, Annapolis, a two-story brick building constructed in 1853.

55. "The Shenandoah, Mr. D. Murdock's Letter," *Philadelphia Inquirer,* Mar. 17, 1865. Murdock describes the action at Rondes Hill, where the 18th repulsed an attack to release Confederate prisoners. "The Eighteenth," he concluded, "is ever ready and willing to go wherever duty calls."

56. After the Battle of Waynesboro, the 18th encamped in Kernstown, VA. Maj. Gen. Alfred T. A. Torbert commanded the cavalry of the Army of the Shenandoah.

57. There was no rail bridge over the Susquehanna River at Havre de Grace until 1866.

58. A luxury hotel built in 1860 located on the corner of Ninth and Chestnut Streets.

59. Arch Street Presbyterian Church, founded in 1724. Weaver worshipped in the neoclassical building built in 1855.

60. The Walnut Street Theater (1811), the oldest theater in the United States. John Steeper Clarke, a popular comic actor and husband of Asia Booth, John Wilkes Booth's sister, managed the theater. Clarke's favorite roles included Timothy Toodle in R. J. Rymond, *The Toodles: A Domestic Drama* (1854), and *Everybody's Friend* (1859), a British comic farce by J. Stirling Coyne. Other actors included James A. Herne and Effie German.

61. Barney Williams, a popular Irish-American comic actor, often performed with his wife, Maria Prey. Among his best-known roles was Ragged Pat in J. H. Amherst, *Ireland as It Is* (1853). Weaver saw the two-act version, *Ireland as It Was*. The Arch Street Theater was built in 1828.

62. Capt. Frederick Zarracher, Co. C, 18th PA Cav.

63. The photographs were taken by F. S. Keeler. Latrobe, Unity Twp., Westmoreland Cty., was on the Pennsylvania Railroad.

64. John W. Weaver; Ephraim Brunner Jr., Elizabeth Weaver's husband.

65. A rural community in Hempfield Twp., Westmoreland Cty.

66. Probably New Florence, Westmoreland Cty., where John W. Weaver had an appointment at the Methodist church.

67. Ed Smeltzer, Catherine Weaver's husband.

68. John High, Methodist Episcopal minister. Webster was a rural community in Rostraver Twp., Westmoreland Cty.

69. A station on the Pennsylvania Railroad between Latrobe and Greensburg.

70. Ross Methodist Episcopal Chapel, Crabtree, Unity Twp., Westmoreland Cty.

71. The county seat of Westmoreland Cty.

72. Lt. James Harrison Gageby, 19th US Inf., captured Sept. 20, 1863, Chickamauga, GA.

73. Edward S. McChesney, a college friend.

74. A borough in Ligonier Twp., Westmoreland Cty., on the Philadelphia–Pittsburgh Turnpike.

75. Uncle William St. Clair, a tailor; his daughters were Isabelle (Bell), Lucinda (Lu), and Eliza (Lida/Liza). They lived in Laughlintown, a rural community in Ligonier Twp.

76. Probably John S. Weaver, a cousin.

77. Maple sugar.

78. Probably William Luther, a teacher and William Sinclair's neighbor.

79. A borough in Unity Twp., Westmoreland Cty.

80. Rev. John S. Wakefield, minister, Latrobe Methodist Episcopal Church, 1863–65.

EPILOGUE

1. Curti, "Great Teacher's Teacher," 56–57. The Methodist General Biblical Institute was located in Concord from 1847 to 1867, when it moved to Boston and became part of Boston University in 1871 (Boston University, School of Theology, "A People's History of the School of Theology," http://www.bu.edu/sth-history/graduates/concord-students). Founded in 1853, Garrett Biblical Institute, the first Methodist seminary in the Midwest, had a three-year curriculum that focused on biblical learning and classical languages (Garrett Evangelical Theological Seminary, "Our History," https://www.garrett.edu/about-us/our-history).

2. Dixon Seminary, founded by two Methodist ministers in 1863, was coeducational and nonsectarian and occupied a "five-story brick edifice." When Weaver was principal, there were six faculty members and 142 students (Illinois General Assembly, *Reports Made to the General Assembly at Its Twenty-Sixth Session Convened January 4, 1869,* vol. 2 [Springfield: Illinois Journal Printing Office, 1869], 2:818–19); West Virginia University, Morgantown, "His-

tory" and WV Army ROTC, Mountaineer Battalion, "Battalion History: A Proud History—A Bright Future" (https://www.wvu.edu); US Senate, *Index to the Journal of the Executive Proceedings of the Senate of the United States, December 2, 1867 to March 3, 1869*, vol. 16 (Washington, DC: Government Printing Office, 1869), 79 (promoted to 1st lieutenant), 81 (captain), 83 (major), 88 (lieutenant colonel), 135, 169. Chartered as the Agricultural College of West Virginia, the school became West Virginia University in 1868. Weaver's promotions dated from his leave of absence, Mar. 13, 1865.

3. *In Loving Memory of Anna Simpson Weaver*, 5–9; *New York Sun*, Oct. 29, 1869. Simpson was born in 1846, Greencastle, IN, when her father was president of Indiana Asbury College. She graduated as valedictorian from Pittsburg Female College. Bishop Simpson continued as president of Garret Biblical Institute after he moved his family to Philadelphia.

4. Ulysses S. Grant to Adolph E. Borie, Oct. 20, 1869, in *Papers of Ulysses S. Grant*, 19:268–69n2; Clark, *Life of Matthew Simpson*, 291–92; Curti, "Great Teacher's Teacher," 58–59. Weaver and Simpson's lives intersected at several Methodist schools, including Allegheny College (Simpson, teacher and vice president, 1837–39), Indiana Asbury College (Simpson, president, 1839–48), and Garrett (Simpson, president, 1859–72). Simpson delivered the main eulogy at Lincoln's funeral in Washington, DC, and at the graveside in Springfield, IL.

5. US Senate, *Index*, 253, 384, 398, 408; Clark, *Life of Matthew Simpson*, 265; Curti, "Great Teacher's Teacher," 59–60; "From 'Representatives Abroad,' 1874," *United States Diplomatic and Consular Service: Our Representatives Abroad*, ed. Augustus C. Rogers [1874], James Riley Weaver Papers, DePauw Univ.; John C. Brown to Weaver, May 22, 1882; Carrie Gailbraith to Anna Weaver, Apr. 13, 1885, Letterbook, Weaver Papers; "James Riley Weaver Dies at Home Here," *Greencastle Banner*, Jan. 28, 1920, Weaver Papers; *In Loving Memory*, 9–25. Simpson also offered his assistance in securing a military appointment in order to "secure a place for life" (Simpson to Weaver, Dec. 27, Mar. 23, 1882, Letterbook, Weaver Papers). Chargé d'affaires were consuls with diplomatic duties.

6. Manhart, *DePauw through the Years*, 1:60–61, 206. Weaver made inquiries about positions at Wesleyan and at Dickenson Colleges before "permanently adjusting" himself to DePauw (James M. Buckley to Weaver, July 8, 1886; see also John F. Hurst to Weaver, June 25, 1886; Clinton Fish to Weaver, June 14, July 7, 1886, in Letterbook, Weaver Papers). DePauw's bequest proved to be smaller than anticipated and, by 1900, the school emphasized undergraduate education.

7. "II. Political Philosophy," in *Forty-Ninth Year-Book of DePauw University* (Greencastle, IN: DePauw Univ., 1887), 38–39; "History and Political Science," *Fifty-Third Year-Book of DePauw University* (Greencastle, IN: DePauw Univ., 1891), 49; "Political Science," *Fifty-Sixth Year-Book of DePauw University* (Greencastle, IN: DePauw Univ., 1894), 39–40; "Political Science," *DePauw University Bulletin*, n.s. 3, no. 2 (May 1906): 67; "Political Science," *DePauw University Bulletin*, n.s. 6, no. 2 (May 1909): 67. Weaver undoubtedly learned the value of empirical data in compiling annual consular reports; see, for example, Weaver, "Antwerp," *Commercial Relations of the United States with Foreign Countries, House Executive Documents, 1875–76*, vol. 15 (Washington, DC: Government Printing Office, 1876), 163–87. The year after Alexander Stephenson's arrival in 1892 with a PhD in history from The Johns Hopkins University, Weaver became professor of political science.

8. Weaver, "Political Science," *Fifty-Sixth Year-Book*, 38–39; Weaver, *Syllabus of Course II, Dep't of Political Science, on Sociology and Its Applications* (Terre Haute, IN: Moore and Langen, 1894), 4.

9. Weaver, *Sociology and Its Applications*; Weaver, *Sociology, Syllabus, Second and Third Courses, Department of Political Science* (Terre Haute, IN: Moore and Langen, 1899); Weaver, *Syllabus of Course VI, Dep't of Political Science, on Economics, Money and Banking* (Terre Haute, IN: Moore and Langen, 1893); Weaver, *International Law, Syllabus of Course VI, Department of Political Science* (Terre Haute, IN: Moore and Langen, 1901); Weaver, *Theory of the State, Syllabus, Course 1, Department of Political Science* (Terre Haute, IN: Moore and Langen, 1899);

Weaver, *Syllabus of Course III, Dep't of Political Science, on Socialism and Reform* (Terre Haute, IN: Moore and Langen, 1896), 39. All syllabi are in the Weaver Papers. Weaver extended the elective principle to the department as students could choose any six courses for a major or any three for a minor.

10. Weaver, "History and Political Science," 48–49; Weaver, "Political Science," *Fifty-Sixth Year-Book,* 39; Weaver to Richard T. Ely, Jan. 1, 1891; "Register of Books Borrowed, 1902–3," Political Science Library; Weaver to Guy Morrison Walker, Jan. 26, Apr. 2, 1906, Nov. 26, 1903, Weaver Papers. Weaver published his syllabi as partial substitutes for textbooks and to reduce lecturing and note taking in order to focus on class discussions and student research reports.

11. Weaver, *Sociology, Syllabus, Second and Third Courses,* 3–4. For other titles of student research theses, see Weaver, *International Law,* 3; Weaver, *Syllabus of Course III on Socialism and Reform,* Dept. of Political Science (Terre Haute, IN: Moore and Langen, 1908), 32, Weaver Papers.

12. "Academic Record of Charles Austin Beard," Charles Austin Beard and Mary Ritter Beard Papers, DePauw Univ.; Mary Ritter Beard, *The Making of Charles A. Beard: An Interpretation* (New York: Exposition Press, 1955), 14–16. For assessments of Weaver's influence on Beard, see Curti, "Great Teacher's Teacher"; Phillips, "Indiana Education," 7; Hofstadter, *Progressive Historians,* 169–71; Braeman, "Charles A. Beard," 116–18; and Nore, *Charles A. Beard,* 11–12.

13. Weaver, undated letter of reference for Charles Beard, Beard Papers; Beard, *Industrial Revolution,* 85, 90. Beard majored in history under Stephenson, who likely influenced his decision to seek a PhD in history at Columbia, but most of Charles and Mary Beard's writings combined social science with historical analysis.

14. "Tribute to Departed," *Greencastle Banner,* Jan. 30, 1920 (citing eulogy of President George R. Gross); Francis Calvin Tilden, "James Riley Weaver, Teacher," *Western Christian Advocate,* Mar. 10, 1920; Weaver to Richard T. Ely, Jan. 1, 1891, Weaver Papers; Curti, "Great Teacher's Teacher," 61–66; Manhart, *DePauw through the Years,* 1:63, 66; *In Loving Memory,* 27–28.

15. Emma Matern (b. 1862), Sandusky, Ohio, received art instruction at Adelphi College, Brooklyn; the Art Students League, New York; the Cincinnati Art Academy; and in Germany. She joined DePauw University's School of Art in 1895, but resigned after marrying Weaver in 1897.

16. Weaver, "Phi Psi's Christmas," 11, 13, 14.

APPENDIX

1. Col. Abel D. Streight, 51st IN Inf. See entry for Nov. 23, 1863, and note.

2. Provisions.

3. Lt. Benjamin F. Herrington, Co. G, 18th PA Cav. "Abou Ben Adhem," a short poem by Leigh Hunt (1784–1859), a Romantic poet, essayist, literary critic, and journalist. After an angel told Abou that he was not listed as one "who love the Lord," he replied: "Write me as one that loves his fellow men." The angel reappeared the following night declaring that Abou was first among "the names whom love of God had blest."

4. Rooms housing prisoners were named after the military campaign or the army of their occupants.

5. Occurring after a meal.

6. God of dreams and sleep.

7. Many Americans of both sections viewed the War with Spain (1898) as an altruistic, divine intervention to liberate the Cuban people from Spanish tyranny and to secure their independence.

Select Bibliography

JAMES RILEY WEAVER

Allegheny College. *Register of Alumni and Non-Graduates, Centennial Edition, 1915.* Meadville, PA: Tribune Publishing, 1915.

Beard, Charles. *The Industrial Revolution.* London: S. Sonnenschein, 1901.

Charles and Mary Ritter Beard Papers. Archives and Special Collections, DePauw Univ., Greencastle, IN.

Beard, Mary Ritter. *The Making of Charles A. Beard: An Interpretation.* New York: Exposition Press, 1955.

Braeman, John. "Charles A. Beard: The Formative Years." *Indiana Magazine of History* 78 (1982): 93–127.

Boucher, John Newton. *History of Westmoreland County, Pennsylvania.* Vol. 1. New York: Lewis Publishing, 1906.

Clark, Robert D. *The Life of Matthew Simpson.* New York: Macmillan, 1956.

Curti, Merle. "A Great Teacher's Teacher." In *Probing Our Past,* 56–66. New York: Harper and Brothers, 1955.

DePauw Univ.. *Bulletin,* n.s. 3, no. 2 (May 1906); vol. 6, no. 2 (May 1909).

———. *Year-Book.* Vol. 49–56. Greencastle, IN: DePauw Univ., 1887–94.

Hofstadter, Richard. *The Progressive Historians: Turner, Beard, and Parrington.* New York: Alfred A. Knopf, 1968.

In Loving Memory of Anna Simpson Weaver, Memoriam. Philadelphia, 1896. Matthew Simpson Collection, Drew University Methodist Collection, Drew Univ., Madison, NJ.

"James Riley Weaver." *Annals of the American Academy of Political and Social Sciences* 5 (1894): 98.

Manhart, George. *DePauw through the Years.* 2 vols. Greencastle, IN: DePauw Univ., 1966.

Nore, Ellen. *Charles A. Beard: An Intellectual Biography.* Carbondale: Southern Illinois Univ. Press, 1983.

Phillips, Clifton J. "The Indiana Education of Charles A. Beard." *Indiana Magazine of History* 55 (1959): 1–15.

Smith, Ernest Ashton. *Allegheny College—A Century of Education, 1815–1915.* Meadville, PA: Allegheny College History Company, 1915.

Weaver, James Riley. "A Phi Psi's Christmas in Libby." *Shield of Phi Kappa Psi* 20, no. 2 (Dec. 1, 1899): 11–16.

James Riley Weaver Papers. Archives and Special Collections, DePauw Univ., Greencastle, IN. MSD.0000.058.

James R. Weaver. Military Service and Pension Records. National Archives, Washington DC.

UNION ARMY

Backus, Bill, and Robert Orrison. *A Want of Vigilance: The Bristoe Station Campaign, October 9–19, 1863.* El Dorado Hills, CA: Savas Beatie, 2015.

Barney, William L. *The Oxford Encyclopedia of the Civil War*. New York: Oxford Univ. Press, 2011.

Bates, Samuel P. *History of the Pennsylvania Volunteers, 1861–3*. Harrisburg, PA: B. Singerly, 1869–71.

Boatner, Mark M., III. *The Civil War Dictionary*. Rev. ed. New York: Vintage Books, 1988.

Cox, Christopher. *History of Pennsylvania Civil War Regiments: Artillery, Cavalry, Volunteers, Reserve Corps, and United States Colored Troops*. Raleigh, NC: Lulu Publishing, 2013.

Grant, Ulysses. *The Papers of Ulysses S. Grant* Ed. John Y. Simon. Carbondale: Southern Illinois Univ. Press, 1995.

Henderson, W. D. *The Road to Bristoe Station: Campaigning with Lee and Meade, August 1– October 20, 1863*. Lynchburg, VA: H. E. Howard, 1987.

Klingensmith, Harold A. "A Cavalry Regiment's First Campaign: The 18th Pennsylvania at Gettysburg." *Gettysburg Magazine* 20 (Jan. 1999): 51–74.

———. "A Most Unlikely Plan: Judson Kilpatrick's Gunboat Expedition." *America's Civil War* 17, no. 4 (Sept. 4, 2004): 22–28.

———. "Statistical Analysis of the 18th Pennsylvania Cavalry." Unpublished essay, n.d.

Long, E. B., with Barbara Long. *The Civil War Day by Day: An Almanac, 1861–1865*. 1971. Reprint, New York: Da Capo, 1985.

Longacre, Edward G., *The Cavalry at Gettysburg: A Tactical Study of Mounted Operations during the Civil War's Pivotal Campaign, 9 June–14 July, 1863*. Lincoln: Univ. of Nebraska Press, 1975.

Luebke, Peter. "Kilpatrick-Dahlgren Raid." *Encyclopedia Virginia*, Jan. 30, 2009. http://www.EncyclopediaVirginia.org/Kilpatrick-Dahlgren_Raid.

McPherson, James. *For Cause and Comrades: Why Men Fought in the Civil War*. New York: Oxford Univ. Press, 1997.

Pennsylvania Cavalry, 18th Regiment. 1862–65. *History of the Eighteenth Regiment of Cavalry, Pennsylvania Volunteers (163d Regiment of the Line), 1862–1865*. Comp. and ed. Publication Committee of the Regimental Association, Theophilus Rodenbough et al. New York: Wynkoop Hallenbeck, 1909.

Starr, Stephen Z. *The Union Cavalry in the Civil War*. Vol. 1, *From Fort Sumter to Gettysburg, 1861–63*. Baton Rouge: Louisiana State Univ. Press, 2007.

Tighe, Adrian G. *The Bristoe Campaign: General Lee's Last Strategic Offensive with the Army of Northern Virginia, October 1863*. Philadelphia: Xlibris, 2011.

U.S. War Dept. *The War of the Rebellion: A Compilation of the Official Records of the Union and Confederate Armies*. 70 vols. Ser. 1, vol. 29. Washington, DC: Government Printing Office, 1880–1901.

Wert, Jeffrey D. *Gettysburg, Day Three*. New York: Simon and Schuster, 2001.

Wittenberg, Eric J., and J. David Petruzzi. *Plenty of Blame to Go Around: Jeb Stuart's Controversial Ride to Gettysburg*. New York, Savas Beatie, 2006.

Wittenberg, Eric J., J. David Petruzzi, and Michael F. Nugent. *One Continuous Fight: The Retreat from Gettysburg and the Pursuit of Lee's Army of Northern Virginia, July 4–14, 1863*. New York: Savas Beatie, 2008.

CIVIL WAR PRISONS: SECONDARY

Armstrong, William M. "From Cahaba to Charleston: The Prison Odyssey of Lt. Edmund E. Ryan." *Civil War History* 8 (1962): 218–27.

Bryant, William O. *Cahaba Prison and the Sultana Disaster*. Tuscaloosa: Univ. of Alabama Press, 2007.

Byrne, Frank L. "Libby Prison: A Study in Emotions." *Journal of Southern History* 24 (1958): 430–44.

Cloyd, Benjamin. *Haunted by Atrocity: Civil War Prisons in American Memory.* Baton Rouge: Louisiana State Univ. Press, 2010.

Denny, Robert E. *Civil War Prisons and Escapes: A Day-by-Day Chronicle.* New York: Sterling, 1993.

Derden, John K. *The World's Largest Prison: The Story of Camp Lawton.* Macon, GA: Mercer Univ. Press, 2012.

Fetzer, Dale, and Bruce Mowday. *Unlikely Allies: Fort Delaware's Prison Community in the Civil War.* Mechanicsburg, PA: Stackpole Books, 2000.

Foote, Lorien. *Yankee Plague: Escaped Union Prisoners and the Collapse of the Confederacy.* Chapel Hill: Univ. of North Carolina Press, 2017.

Fraser, Walter J., Jr. *Charleston! Charleston!: The History of a Southern City.* Columbia: Univ. of South Carolina Press, 1989.

Futch, Ovid L. *History of Andersonville Prison.* Rev. ed. Gainesville: Univ. Press of Florida, 2011.

Gillispie, James M. *Andersonvilles of the North: The Myths and Realities of Northern Treatment of Civil War Confederate Prisoners.* Denton: Univ. of North Texas Press, 2008.

Gray, Michael P. *The Business of Captivity: Elmira and Its Civil War Prison.* Kent, Ohio: Kent State Univ. Press, 2001.

Hall, James. *Den of Misery: Indiana's Civil War Prison.* Gretna, LA: Pelican, 2006.

Hesseltine, William B. *Civil War Prisons: A Study in War Psychology.* Columbus: Ohio State Univ. Press, 1930.

Hesseltine, William B., ed. *Civil War Prisons.* Kent, Ohio: Kent State Univ. Press, 1962.

Historic Charleston, Religious and Community Buildings. National Park Service, A National Register of Historic Places Travel Itinerary. https://www.nps.gov/nr/travel/charleston/index.htm.

Jobst, Richard W. *Civil War Macon.* Macon, GA: Mercer Univ. Press, 1999.

Joslyn, Mauriel. *Immortal Captives: The Story of 600 Confederate Officers and the United States Prisoner of War Policy.* Gretna, LA: Pelican, 2008.

Kutzler, Evan A. "Captive Audiences: Sound, Silence, and Listening in Civil War Prisons." *Journal of Social History* 48 (2014): 239–63.

Levy, George. *To Die in Chicago: Confederate Prisoners at Camp Douglas, 1862–65.* 2nd ed. Gretna, LA: Pelican, 2009.

Lord, Francis A. "Camp Sorghum." *Sandlapper: The Magazine of South Carolina* (Aug. 1975): 29–33.

Marvel, William. *Andersonville: The Last Depot.* Chapel Hill: Univ. of North Carolina Press, 1994.

———. *Biographical Sketch of the Contributors, Military Order of the Loyal Legion of the United States.* Wilmington, NC: Broadfoot, 1995.

McAdams, Benton. *Rebels at Rock Island: The Story of a Civil War Prison.* DeKalb: Northern Illinois Univ. Press, 2000.

McInvale, Morton R. "'That Thing of Infamy': Macon's Camp Oglethorpe during the Civil War." *Georgia Historical Quarterly* 63 (1979): 279–91.

Moore, John Hammond. *Columbia and Richland County, A South Carolina Community, 1740–1990.* Columbia: Univ. of South Carolina Press, 1993.

Parker, Sandra V. *Richmond's Civil War Prisons.* Lynchburg, VA: H. E. Howard, 1990.

Pickenpaugh, Roger. *Camp Chase and the Evolution of Union Prison Policy.* Tuscaloosa: Univ. of Alabama Press, 2007.

———. *Captives in Blue: The Civil War Prisons of the Confederacy.* Tuscaloosa: Univ. of Alabama Press, 2013.

———. *Captives in Grey: The Civil War Prisons of the Union.* Tuscaloosa: Univ. of Alabama Press, 2009.

———. *Johnson's Island: A Prison for Confederate Officers.* Kent, Ohio: Kent State Univ. Press, 2016.

Robertson, James I., Jr. "Houses of Horror: Danville's Civil War Prisons." *Virginia Magazine of History and Biography* 69 (1961): 329–45.

Sanders, Charles W., Jr. *While in the Hands of the Enemy: Military Prisons of the Civil War.* Baton Rouge: Louisiana State Univ. Press, 2005.

Schairer, Jack E. *Lee's Bold Plan for Point Lookout: The Rescue of Confederate Prisoners That Never Happened.* Jefferson, NC: McFarland, 2008.

Speer, Lonnie R. *Portals to Hell: Military Prisons of the Civil War.* Mechanicsburg, PA: Stackpole Books, 1997.

Springer, Paul J., and Glen Robins. *Transforming Civil War Prisons: Lincoln, Lieber, and the Politics of Captivity.* New York: Routledge, 2015.

Stuart, Meriwether. "Dr. Lugo: An Austrian-Venetian Adventurer in Union Espionage." *Virginia Magazine of History and Biography* 90 (1982): 339–58.

Treibe, Richard H. *Point Lookout Prison Camp and Hospital: The North's Largest Civil War Prison.* N.p.: Coastal Books, [2014].

Wheelan, Joseph. *Libby Prison Breakout: The Daring Escape from the Notorious Civil War Prison.* New York: Public Affairs, 2010.

Zombek, Angela M. "Libby Prison." *Encyclopedia Virginia*, Jan. 23, 2014. http://www.EncyclopediaVirginia.org/Libby_Prison.

CONFEDERATE PRISONS: MEMOIRES AND LETTERS

Abbott, A. O. *Prison Life in the South: At Richmond, Macon, Savannah, Charleston, Columbia, Charlotte, Raleigh, Goldsborough, and Andersonville during the Years 1864 and 1865.* New York: Harper and Brothers, 1865.

Armstrong, William M., ed. "Libby Prison: The Diary of Arthur G. Sedgwick." *Virginia Magazine of History and Biography* 71 (1963): 449–60.

Bartleson, Frederick A. *Letters from Libby Prison.* Ed. Margaret W. Peelle. New York: Greenwich Book, 1956.

Beaudry, Louis N. *The Libby Chronicles, Devoted to Fact and Fun.* Albany, NY: Louis N. Beaudry, 1889.

Beszedits, Stephen, ed. *The Libby Prison Diary of Colonel Emeric Szabad.* Toronto: B&L Information Services, 1999.

Boaz, Thomas M. *Libby Prison and Beyond: A Union Staff Officer in the East, 1862–1865.* Shippensburg, PA: Burd Street, 1999.

Boyer, Earl E., ed. *Civil War Diaries of Capt. Albert Heffley and Lt. Cyrus P. Heffley.* Apollo, PA: Clossen, 2000.

Byrne, Frank L. "A General behind Bars: Neal Dow in Libby Prison. *Civil War History* 8 (1962): 164–83.

Cavada, Frederick Fernández. *Libby Life: Experiences of a Prisoner of War in Richmond, Virginia, 1863–64.* Philadelphia: King and Baird, 1864.

Chamberlain, J. W., ed. "Scenes in Libby Prison." In *Sketches of War History, 1861–1865: Papers Read Before the Ohio Commandery of the Military Order of the Loyal Legion of the United States, 1886–1888.* Cincinnati: Robert Clarke, 1888. Vol. 2, 342–90.

Davidson, Henry M. *Fourteen Months in Southern Prisons, Being a Narrative of the Treatment of Federal Prisoners of War in the Rebel Military Prisons.* Milwaukee: Daily Wisconsin Printing House, 1865.

Domschcke, Bernard. *Twenty Months in Captivity: Memoirs of a Union Officer in Confederate Prisons.* 1865. Trans. Frederic Trautmann. Madison, WI: Farleigh Dickinson Univ. Press, 1987.

Fisher, Robert J. *Officers of the United States, Army and Navy: Prisoners of War, Libby Prison, Richmond, Virginia.* Cincinnati: Ehrgott, Forbriger, 1864.

Glazier, William Willard. *The Capture, the Prison Pen, and the Escape; Giving a Complete History of Prison Life in the South.* New York: United States Publishing Company, 1868.

Heaton, Lynda R. "War Experiences of Samuel Wheeler, Private in the First West Virginia Cavalry." *West Virginia History: A Journal of Regional Studies* 6 (2012): 45–69; 8 (2014): 65–88.

Heslin, James E., ed. "The Diary of a Union Soldier in Confederate Prisons [George W. Hegeman]." *New York Historical Quarterly* 41 (1957): 233–78.

Isham, Asa Brainerd, Henry M. Davidson, and H. B. Furness. *Prisoners of War and Military Prisons: Personal Narratives of Experience in the Prisons at Richmond, Danville, Macon, Andersonville, Savannah, Millen, Charleston, and Columbia, with a List of Officers Who Were Prisoners of War from January 1, 1864.* Cincinnati: Lyman and Cushing, 1890.

Jeffrey, William H. *Richmond Prisons, 1861–1862, Compiled from the Original Records Kept by the Confederate Government; Journals Kept by Union Prisoners of War, Together with the Name, Rank, Company, Regiment, and State of the Four Thousand Who Were Confined There.* St. Johnsbury, VT: Republican Press, 1895.

Jennings, Warren A., ed. "Prisoner of the Confederacy: Diary of a Union Artilleryman [Harlan Smith Howard]." *West Virginia History* 36 (July 1975): 309–23.

Johnston, I. N. *Four Months in Libby, and the Campaign against Atlanta.* Cincinnati: Methodist Book Concern, 1864.

Moran, Frank E. "Libby's Bright Side: A Silver Lining in the Dark Cloud of Prison Life." In *Camp-Fire Sketches and Battle-Field Echoes,* ed. W. C. King and W. P. Derby. Springfield, MA: W. C. King, 1887.

Peele, Margaret W., ed. *Letters from Libby Prison.* [Frederick A. Bartleson] New York: Greenwich Book, 1956.

Penfield, James A. *The 1863–1864 Diary of Captain James Penfield, 5th New York Volunteer Cavalry, Company H.* Ticonderoga, NY: Press of America, 1999.

Putnam, George H. "A Soldier's Narrative of Life at Libby and Danville Prisons." *Outlook* (Mar. 25, 1911): 695–704.

Racine, Philip N., ed. *"Unspoiled Heart": The Journal of Charles Mattocks of the 17th Maine.* Knoxville: Univ. of Tennessee Press, 1994.

Sabre, Gilbert E. *Nineteen Months a Prisoner of War.* New York: American News Company, 1865.

Sprague, Homer B. *Lights and Shadows in Confederate Prisons: A Personal Experience, 1864–65.* New York: G. C. Putnam's Son, 1915.

Sumner, Charles. *Works of Charles Sumner.* Vol. 9. Boston: Lee and Shepard, 1875.

Tusken, Roger, ed. "In the Bastile of the Rebels." [George R. Lodge] *Journal of the Illinois State Historical Society* 56 (Summer 1963): 316–39.

Index

Page references in italics refer to illustrations.